SACRAMENTO

Excursions into its history and natural world.

William M. Holden

Two Rivers Publishing Co.
P.O. Box 2384
Fair Oaks, CA 95628
(916) 967-7950

Cover illustration is courtesy of California Department of Parks and Recreation. Photos are by the author, except as otherwise credited.

ISBN 0-9619561-0-0

Library of Congress Catalog Number: 87-51538
Two Rivers Publishing Co.
Fair Oaks, CA 95628

Typography by Pacific Communications Group and
All Star Printing

Printed by American Litho
First Printing 1988
Second Printing 1991
Third Printing 1998

Cover transparencies by Color IV

Acknowledgments

The author is grateful for help from the following persons, listed alphabetically:

Charley Audet, an old salt, for nautical aid in re-enacting Sutter's arrival.

Ted Baggelmann, for new information on Captain Sutter's European roots, and for his fine drawing of the Fort in its high noon of historic splendor.

Maria Baker, for inside stories of zoo tenants.

Richard E. Brown, who has forgotten more about steamboats and steam trains than most people ever knew.

Ed Combatalade, for a camellia story.

Maxine Cornwell, for a tour of Indian country, and for valor beyond the call of duty, in rescuing Indian Stone Corral from impending disaster.

Werner Dillier, for his interest in and moral support of the author's project.

Carl DiStefano, for providing (in re-enactments) an authentic replica of the pinnace from which Sutter landed here.

Don Donaldson, for assistance at a river journey's end.

Don Dupres, for facts on gold mining and the geological puzzle.

Charles D. Fey Jr., rollicking companion for rafting, sailing and beverage quests.

Alan Fiers, the bird man of Sacramento, or at least one of them.

Sal Gianna, for skippering a voyage to Folsom Lake's mysterious island.

Sheryl Gonzalez, P.R. coordinator, Crocker Art Museum, for some fine-tuning.

Patty Gregory, for help with historical photos.

John Hardin, for piloting a voyage into the Twilight Zone to help re-trace the final leg of Sutter's arrival.

Bill Helms, for data on hell and high water.

Jim Henley, for various facets of history.

Laurie Hensley, for assists with the story of Old Sacramento as it is today.

Chris Hulbe, who told where a billion in gold remains unmined.

Victor Larson, in costume as Captain Sutter, for help in retracing by boat the final leg of Sutter's 1839 arrival and bringing a historic scandal to the mayor's attention.

John Morgan, because if there's anything about Folsom history he doesn't know, it may not be worth knowing.

Norman Olson of Levinson's Books, whose talk at a meeting of California Writers Club boosted the author's hope that his in-progress book would find a ready market.

Tony Peters, for more tales of zoo residents.

Mayor Anne Rudin, for being a sport when the ghost of Captain Sutter appeared, and for initiating steps to establish Sutter's Landing Park.

Meg Smart, for smartness in wildlife identifications.

Patricia Turse, for such fascinating information on the Stanford Mansion that it cried for a chapter of its own.

Mike Weber, for his vivid recollections of Effie Yeaw.

And Sacramento area Hawaiians, representing (in two re-enactments) the valiant islanders who landed here with Sutter and to whom he paid the supreme compliment when he wrote that he could not have settled the country without them. The local Hawaiians are: Darcy Haleamau, David Hanakeawe, Delbert Kaleikini, Alana Makekua, Kalaika Haudi Medeiros, and Albert Palapala. Also, Andy Ah Po, for gracious assistance.

Also, naturalists Rodi Fregien, Bob Holland, Mark Hooten, Harvest McCampbell, Darlene McGriff and Nancy Wymer, for intriguing lore.

Contents

1839 - 1989
And Counting

This book commemorates the 150th birthday of Sacramento, born with the epic landing on August 12, 1839, of Capt. John Sutter, one of the supreme adventurers of all time.

Five years earlier, Sutter had decamped from Switzerland as a fugitive, with no inkling he was launching himself on a 20,000-mile odyssey to the ends of the earth – to the grass shacks of Honolulu in the Sandwich Islands, to the frozen mountains of New Archangel (Russian Alaska), and to the drowsy pueblo of Yerba Buena on San Francisco Bay.

At last he ascended the unexplored Rio de Sacramento in the heart of the western wilderness and landed on the bank of the American near its junction with the Sacramento. Here he picked the site for his colony of New Helvetia, seed of Sacramento.

Sutter never could have surmised that the end of his long and incredible journey — on a wilderness river in California — would mark the spot where a splendid city would spring up, to become the capital of the greatest state of the greatest nation.

For Patricia
and
Candy, Kim, Kelly, Lori, Beverly and Chloe

Preamble

With Sacramento's skyline leaping to new heights, ditto sports fever, and suburban spaces mushrooming with chic subdivisions, it may be a bit difficult for the mind's eye to get a sharp focus on this area as a stage for historic dramas. Lacking the immediacy of current events, they somehow seem to have happened somewhere else. Not so.

Under the sophisticated veneer lie the authentic scenes where rough-and-ready performances became smash hits on history's stage — Captain Sutter's advent, gold stampede, pony mail, the telegraph's talking wires, transcontinental trains, steamboats swaggering 'round the bend, and more.

Yesteryear's actors have all made their exits — to plaudits, to boos, or unremarked — but the stage remains. This is the soil they trod. These are the rivers they drank and sailed on. This is the air that rang with their cries. Listen hard, and you can almost hear echoes of their hullabaloo. Can't hear 'em? Maybe you're not listening hard enough. Besides, I said *almost* hear.

This book also explores the natural world of Sacramento and environs — the rivers with their salmon and steelhead, beavers and otters; the riparian forests with their muledeer, jackrabbits, opossum and treefrogs; and the aerial dominions of the great blue herons and legions of other fine birds — Sacramentans all, are they not?

It's often observed that Sacramento lies midway between the coast and the mountains. Some people prize it as a place to live for that very reason — it's not too far from either lure. Others might observe that that's like saying Sacramento lies "in the middle of nowhere." Still others might say, Sacramento stands in a superb class by itself and has its own lures and distinctions. That's what this book is all about.

— *The Author*

Chapter 1
Genesis

Ages ago, foam-marbled waves of the open ocean rolled over the site where Sacramento reposes today, thundering onto its ancient shoreline as far east as the present Negro Bar State Park, 12 miles northeast of Sacramento.

Continents are, one might say, tremendous rafts of light rock, mostly granite, floating on the heavy black rock of the earth's hot mantle. Some 200 million years ago, Pacific Ocean-floor bedrock, traveling east at two inches a year like a giant conveyor belt from the mid-ocean ridge, began to jam under the North American continent.

It was almost like the irresistible force meeting the immovable object, for the energies involved are unimaginable. As the descending sea-floor slab sank into the earth's hot mantle below, it formed a deep trench, just as a dimple forms on water when a drain is opened. As the slab continued to stuff under, some of the accumulated sea-floor sediments were scraped off to form coastal ranges — the original Sierra Nevada. The inconceivable friction-heat generated as the sea-slab crowded under the continental slab fused the rock into molten magma. Some of this magma raged to the surface, spawning a chain of mountain-making volcanoes in the Sierra, a chain hundreds of miles long.

Meanwhile, other sea-floor sediments were dragged under the continent by the down-flowing sea-floor. For some reason, after

100 million years had gone by, the conveyor belt switched off. But — at a speed of two inches a year — if any humans had been alive then, who would have noticed?

Since the trench no longer had anything sucking it down, it floated upward — and its goulash of crumpled sediments rose and broke the surface to form the Coast Range. These mountains cut off and isolated part of the ocean, creating a vast inland sea between the ranges, an ancient sea that no human eyes would ever behold.

For millions of years, this great sea surged over what today is Sacramento. Its waters swarmed with primordial brutes, including long-necked marine reptiles called Plesiosaurs, up to 40 feet long. But the most savage predators in this sea were the Mosasaurs, terrible marine lizards up to 50 feet long, heads and jaws shaped not unlike those of the crocodile. Duck-billed dinosaurs (Prosaurolophus) lurked in the bordering swamps. Skies were ruled by giant flying reptiles known as Pteranodons — "dragons of the air." These long-beaked aviators glided over the sea, catching fish at the surface. Their wingspans of up to 27 feet made them the largest creatures that ever flew.

Geologists named this immense water the Ione Sea after the great Ione Formation of clays and sands running for 200 miles along the Sierra side of the Sacramento and San Joaquin Valleys. This formation was built up over millions of years by sediments deposited in the ancient sea. It was named after the town of Ione in our neighboring Amador County, where it visibly abounds in profusion, and where it was first described. The town, curiously, was named after the heroine in Edward Bulwer-Lytton's *Last Days of Pompeii*, a best-selling novel in the last half of the 19th century. Ione's citizens renamed their town because its former appellation of Bedbug —though perhaps historically apt — didn't conjure the proper image. If Bedbug's citizens *hadn't* changed the name to Ione, would that noble body of water have been called the Bedbug Sea? Bulwer-Lytton never could have dreamed that the heroine of his classic novel of the Vesuvius eruption would give her name to an inland sea on the far side of the globe — a sea so far back in time it dried up millions of years before he ever penned the name of the beautiful Ione.

As erosion endlessly abraded the Sierra, enormous layers of sediments piled up in the inland sea. Sediments piled on sediments to incredible depths. Deepest of all sediments in the Central Valley are those in the Rio Vista area, southwest of Sacramento, where

The terrible Pteranodon ruled Sacramento skies in the long ago. Its wings spanned up to 27 feet, nearly the height of a three-story building. This model was exhibited in Sacramento Science Center. Permission to publish this photo was granted by Dinamation International Corp., San Juan Capistrano.

they sink to an unbelievable 40,000 feet or more, according to Don Dupres, associate geologist with California Division of Mines and Geology, Sacramento. That's nearly eight miles deep. If you could bail out all those sediments (they're rock-hard today), you'd have a canyon eight times as deep as the Grand Canyon! The sediment-filled depression is so deep in that locus because the sea-slab created a downward buckle there as it shoved under the continental slab.

By degrees, the endless flow of sediments into the Ione Sea transformed it into floodplains, and no longer did Sacramento's future site lie submerged at the bottom of the sea. It emerged at last from its underwater eternity.

And it was about time.

Since 1875, entrepreneurs have exploited Ione Formation clays in Lincoln, Placer County, only 18 miles northeast of Sacramento. Here, one of the valley's oldest industries, Gladding McBean & Co., manufactures —from those clays laid down in the Ione Sea as long as 50 million years ago — sewer pipe, building block, floor tile, and terra-cotta, the decorative tile that adorns building facades of

Sacramento's Senator Hotel, State Library and Memorial Auditorium, and many others elsewhere in the nation.

Treasure of the Sierra Nevada: About 40 million years ago, volcanoes again erupted, and the now-eroded Sierra rose anew; mineral solutions in cooling lava deposited gold in veins and lodes. Meanwhile, the climate was warming. Rains fell in great profusion, fostering growth of such trees as conifers, ancestors of the redwoods, and broadleaf evergreens akin to today's magnolia trees. Falling water, with all the time in the world to do it, kept working away, gnawing relentlessly at the rock. When it reached gold-bearing veins, it freed the gold into the accumulating soil. Creeks and rivulets seized the gold and carried it downstream.

Roaring streams and rivers sluiced the gold ever farther down. hosing it into a million secret hiding places — in one of which James Marshall one day in 1848 would spy a golden shimmer in a green tailrace.

Near Sacramento, evidences of cataclysms when the world was young linger on the land. Some 20 million years ago, Sierra volcanoes erupted once more, and lava rivers raged down major stream valleys, sealing the gold-bearing gravels beneath, diverting the streams to new channels. The volcanoes spewed clouds of white volcanic ash over mountains and valleys. Avalanches of white-hot ash cascaded down the slopes, choking valleys and turning rivers into steam. Today you can see a layer of this volcanic *tuff* several feet thick, running for five miles through the American River bluffs between Hoffman Park and Negro Bar State Park on Lake Natoma. A good place to see it: From the south bank of the river near the old Fair Oaks Bridge, look for the whitish stratum on the high north bluff. Best time to see it is in winter, when bluff vegetation has shed its leaves. And the best kind of winter day to see it is a rainy one, because rain darkens the rest of the rock, improving the contrast. These 150-foot-high river bluffs are mainly flood-plain gravels deposited by the ancient American.

New streams in the Sierra eroded channels over the old abandoned channels, now mostly buried under volcanic debris. These new streams are today's rivers and streams, in which prospectors first found placer gold.

Rivers of mud: About 10 million years ago, still another chain of Sierra eruptions shook the earth's foundations. These eruptions triggered mudflows that choked river channels in the mountains and ground their way into the valley, at least as far as today's Sierra College Boulevard, 15 miles northeast of Sacramento. You can see this solidified mudflow today. You can even travel through it. From Douglas Boulevard, go north on Sierra College Boulevard about a mile, and you enter the stretch of highway that meanders over the hill in a northeasterly direction, slashing through the mudflow—visible on both sides of the road. It's boggling to see this hillcrest formation chock-full of water-rounded stones, like giant peanut-brittle, and try to imagine the cataclysmic forces that dispatched this great train of mud and its freight of round stones into the valley, until it ground to a halt at the end of the line.

In another area, 16 miles east of Sacramento, bones of ancient horses and other mammals overwhelmed by the mudflows came to light during road construction at Highway 50 near the Prairie City Road exit, but today there is nothing special in the gentle road-cuts to catch the casual driver's eye.

Five million years ago, long after the valley had filled to sea level with sediments, the later Tertiary geologic period was punctuated by eruptions that formed a large volcano on the valley floor, a few miles northwest of today's Yuba City. Its eroded remnants, 2,132 feet high, remain as an isolated clump of hills —the Sutter Buttes—looming above the valley floor. They've been called "the world's smallest mountain range." These Buttes figure in the Sacramento story, because they marked the northern boundary of one of Captain John Sutter's Mexican land grants.

Meanwhile, the climate was changing again. Three million years ago, it cooled rather suddenly, signaling the beginning of the last Ice Age. In the Sierra, ever-heavier snowpacks began to form ever-larger glaciers. The glaciers carved and scoured the mountains, dispatching tremendous loads of detritus down the American and Cosumnes Rivers, dumping them in the Sacramento region.

The ancient Sacramento River, draining the western Sierra, sculptured the Golden Gate channel through the Coast Range, chewing the route out as fast as the coastal mountains emerged. When the ocean rose as Ice Age glaciers retreated, it drowned the mouth of the Sacramento River, creating San Francisco Bay. In other words, the Bay is really the drowned mouth of the Sacramento, drowned when the sea rose 300 feet as the continental ice sheet melted in the Ice Age's finale 10,000 years ago. Since then, the Sacramento has been dumping sediments into the Bay, slowly filling it. Thousands of years from now, you'll be able to walk straight across on dry land.

Our fickle river: The American River apparently couldn't make up its mind where to flow, for it shifted course at least three times as it flowed through Sacramento County, relocating its bed northward each time. Three older channels have been discovered. The oldest and most southerly ran from Folsom southwest toward Elk Grove, where its bed lies 60 feet beneath the surface. The next oldest streamed from Folsom to Franklin, and its bed lies 40 feet deep today. The third lies 35 feet below the present channel, which dates from a mere thousand years ago. Much of Sacramento's gravel production has been mined from quarries that exploit the Franklin channel, where bones of horses, camels and even mammoths have been uncovered. You can see huge mammoth teeth and other bones in an exhibit in Mohr Hall, Sacramento City College, 3835 Freeport Blvd.

Two dozen bones — some from giant ground sloths measuring up to 12 feet tall, and bones of horses, camels and other beasts — were discovered in 1989 during excavations for Arco Arena in the Natomas area. These animals lived here 10,000 to 30,000 years ago, and their relics will be exhibited in an interpretive display at Arco.

Rivers meandering through floodplains often form their own natural levees, when over a long period of time high water keeps building up deposits of sediments in some stretches. Some prehistoric levees of an older channel of the American can be seen today in Sacramento. One is the little hill bounded roughly by 21st and 23rd Streets and S and V Streets. In Sacramento's early years, when floods battered the city time and again, thousands of flooded-out citizens huddled in misery on this high ground. Tents and shacks roosted there long after the floods were conquered, and the prominence became known as Poverty Ridge.

In later years, real estate developers recognized that the ridge offered ideal building sites, so they subdivided it and sold lots to affluent citizens. However, as a name on which to charm people into buying real estate, Poverty Ridge didn't hack it, so they renamed it Sutter's Terrace. Today, some of Sacramento's finest old houses stand on this natural levee that once had an unprepossessing name.

Southeast of Sacramento, you can see — exposed in road-cuts — remnants of the vast gravelly plain that once mantled much of the valley's east side. Follow Jackson Road eastward as it slices through low, rounded hills just west of Sloughhouse Road. Erosion ate away all but scattered remnants capping these hills. Farther east on Jackson Road, turn right onto Dillard Road, where for half a mile the route cuts through even larger remnants, called "haystack" hills, named for their shape. To see the largest haystack, turn back to Jackson Road and continue east. Just opposite the entrance to Rancho Murieta, the steep hill looms on the south side of the highway. Its sandstone cap was deposited probably as part of a large sandbar near a river mouth. The cut face north of the water tank yielded a fossil tree branch washed down from the mountains 12 million years ago.

The Sacramento story, as the story of people, is only the blink of an eye in the phantasmagoria of geologic time, but is the most interesting part of it — except perhaps to geologists and paleontologists.

Chapter 2
Of Time And the River

Just as a river rolls down to the eternal ocean, time's evanescent moments roll into the ocean of eternity, never to return.

Michael Lambeth

In the long ages during which the Ione Sea filled with sediments and became dry land, many rivers brawling down from the northern mountains combined to form the main stem, the Sacramento. The farther the shrinking sea ebbed, the more the trunk river, fed by ever more tributaries, grew in length and volume, draining the vast bowl rimmed by craggy blue mountains.

Unimaginable ages ticked by with geological slowness until the aboriginal Indians discovered the great valley. Ten thousand years later, the early fur trappers wandered in, questing for beaver and otter pelts. The trappers called the Sacramento the Buenaventura (Good Fortune), and believed it flowed out of Great Salt Lake or some other secret source in the Rockies, perhaps in the Wind River Range. They believed it because their maps showed it. But that great eastward reach of the Buenaventura was a mythical river, penned into the white space on the map by cartographers, like doodlers who couldn't leave a blank space alone. In all that unmapped space, there had to be a river somewhere. Where did it flow? Of course—into the great valley of California and out San

Francisco Bay to the Pacific!

Cotton-bale clouds fled across the azure one October morning in 1808 when Spanish sea captain Gabriel Moraga, 39, trekking up the big river in a horseback expedition, was struck by the lovely scene. Canopies of oaks and cottonwoods, many festooned with grapevines, overhung both sides of the blue current. Birds chittered in the trees and big fish darted through the pellucid depths. The air was like champagne, and the Spaniards drank deep of it, drank in the beauty around them. *"Es como el sagrado Sacramento!"* Moraga burbled. This is like the Holy Sacrament! So the river got its name, and likewise the lusty village that one day would hunker on its banks.

Moraga's expedition followed the Sacramento north and on October 9 camped on the lower Feather River — which Moraga called the Sacramento, thinking it was a continuation of the same river. He was understandably confused because, at the Sacramento-Feather junction, the wide Feather aligns with the Sacramento below the junction, while the narrower upper Sacramento angles in from the west at this point. So Moraga thought that was a *branch* of the Sacramento, and called it the Jesus Maria, a name that stuck for a time.

With 10 soldiers and 10 Indians rowing blunt-nose boats, Capt. Luis Arguello, bold commandante at the Presidio of Yerba Buena, in 1817 at age 33, journeyed upriver for seven days. From riverbank trees, masses of grapevines overhung the water. *"Es como un parque del rey!"* Arguello enthused. It's like a king's park! They glimpsed great herds of deer and elk and bands of grizzlies. Three years later, in October 1820, Arguello led another expedition up the Sacramento, continuing up the Feather. Marveling at the myriads of feathers floating on it during the migration of band-tail pigeons, he named it Rio de las Plumas. Plumas County later borrowed its name from the river. Often during Arguello's journey, Indians launched hails of arrows on the column, bloodying the horses. Supplies ran short. With Indians all around, hunting was nigh impossible, so they retreated in double-time.

In 1837, Capt. Edward Belcher of the British Navy explored the Sacramento in boats from *H.M.S. Sulphur*, and wrote: "Wild grapes in great abundance overhung the lower trees ... at times completely overpowering the trees on which they climbed, and producing beautiful varieties of fruit." He ordered his sailors to chop down several huge oaks and measure them. One had a trunk 27 feet around!

The Sacramento River two years later would enthrall Capt. John Sutter so much that, after his odyssey from Switzerland to the ends of the earth, he picked this milieu on which to lay the foundations of an empire.

Before pioneers trekked into the great valley, primeval forests spanned the Sacramento for miles on each side and up to five miles on each side of the American, creating a habitat for an assortment of wildlife unparalleled in California. Less than five percent of those riparian forests still stand. Stately oaks and tall cottonwoods grew not only in riparian areas but in other large valley stands where their roots could stretch down to find secret water even in the long dry days of summer.

The rivers once flowed as clear as glass and swarmed with fish. The air was alive with congregations of birds. Many were permanent residents, many others transients. With a great rustle of pinions, a billion waterfowl commuted over the valley on the Pacific Flyway, the birds' freeway, escaping the clutch of winter ice on the lakes of Canada and Alaska, or making the round trip in the great hemispherical warm-up of spring. Ducks and geese were so multitudinous their passing flights, great living tides, darkened the sun for days on end. In dwindled numbers today, the migrations continue. Some finish their long commute in valley wetlands, to winter here. Among them are the snow geese, pure white with black wing tips; a flock rising from the water sounds like a pack of yelping dogs. Others include the Canada geese; great wedges of them announce their arrival with a chorus of honkings high in the frosty air. For the many other waterfowl bound for southern climes, local wetlands offer a handy pit stop and fast-food restaurant. But the remaining wetlands are only 10 percent of the original.

Before early settlers reclaimed immense tracts of wetlands for farms, the Sacramento River and other valley streams wandered as they pleased. In flood season, high water flowed over oxbows, sloughs and swales, forming wide belts of tule swamps, or tulares, on both sides of the streams. Rich sediments nourished riparian belts of cottonwood, willow, sycamore and valley oak, often hung with grapes, while the ground was thicketed with blackberry, elderberry and wild rose.

Wood ducks abounded, nesting in tree cavities, plentiful then because trees were plentiful everywhere. Mallard, shoveler, cinnamon teal, pintail, redhead and ruddy ducks nested in the valley, as they do in sharply dwindled populations today. Antelope and tule elk once grazed our lowlands. Deer and grizzly haunted riparian woodlands. Fox, rabbit and coyote rambled on their appointed rounds. Streamsides offered secluded residences for beaver and otter. The beavers' corps of engineers built innumerable dams on many streams, creating ponds where waterfowl moved in as tenants to raise families, and never had to pay rent.

But the days of this Eden on the rivers were numbered. In the Gold Rush year of 1850 alone, nearly 100,000 fortune-seekers invaded the valley, which meant 100,000 ravenous appetites — every day. Busy market hunters blazed away at big game animals, and packed loads of provisions off to the mining camps. In the next two decades, most of the valley's deer, antelope, elk and grizzly would fall under the market guns.

Rivers were so thick with salmon, early settlers boasted they could catch them with pitchforks. They bragged they could shoot ducks and geese with their eyes closed, as a solid wall of spooked birds took off from the water. But the very prodigality of birds was becoming, by the late 1870s, a plague to farmers. Wheat dominated valley agriculture at this time, and by night flocks of geese glided into wheatfields, cleaning out acres and acres in mere hours. Farmers desperately sought ways to guard their grain. When poisoning and bright lights failed, they called in market hunters to slaughter the myriads of moochers. One Glenn County farmer hired up to 40 shooters a year and spent $13,000 annually on ammunition. Ducks and geese by the millions became cheap food for people in Sacramento, San Francisco and other towns as hunters peddled them for as little as 50 cents a dozen. In the 1910-11 season, an estimated 500,000 ducks were sold in the San Francisco market. Waterfowl seemed an inexhaustible resource.

But the great living tides were on the ebb. Unrestrained hunting was taking a dire toll, so in 1918 federal legislation banned market hunting. Reclamation of wetlands accelerated the decline.

Once a sea of wheat filled the valley, beyond compare in the world, so it is said. When the wind blew, the wheat rolled in golden billows, like the sea. For half a century, the valley's Wheat Kings grew prodigal harvests. But they robbed the soil by sowing it with only one crop, and in time the great wheat empire was succeeded by many other crops.

Many farmers today, with the same problem of the 19th-century wheat farmers, scare off waterfowl with explosions of Zahn guns, timer-equipped carbon dioxide cannon. Also today, four valley refuges offer winter stop-overs to millions of southbound waterfowl, refugees from the tyranny of Jack Frost. These wildlife areas are planted with grain and water plants to distract birds from nearby farmlands.

The Sacramento River is born as an icy stream gushing from glaciers over 11,000 feet high on 14,162-foot Mt. Shasta, the white-haired Old Man of the Mountains 200 miles north of Sacramento.

It took geographers and explorers 2,000 years to discover the source of the Nile — but you can discover the "official" source of the Sacramento in only a minute, once you enter the park on the north side of the City of Mt. Shasta, roosting on a flank of its namesake mountain.

You won't have any trouble discovering it because a sign identifies it as SAC. HEAD WATERS.

Melting glaciers drain through underground lava tubes, until the infant river burbles out of lava rocks into Big Spring, a pool impounded by a small rock dam. Over the dam it splashes, then gurgles downstream mile after mile, growing ever larger as it feeds on one tributary after another.

Does the infant river bear any family resemblance to the big, wide-shouldered Old Man River far down in the valley? Both are wet and sometimes wild.

South of Shasta, the juvenile river frolics through a canyon past Dunsmuir, then wanders past turreted mountains in the west, scene of the 1855 "Battle of Castle Crags." Starving Indians, incensed at miners killing countless fish with tons of silt discharged into the river, launched arrows. Bullets greeted them. Many were killed or wounded on both sides, but the Indians had to pull back to the craggy strongholds, as arrows were no match for bullets. This battle was one in a series that climaxed with the Modoc War.

Continuing south, the trunk river swells in volume, reinforced by more tributaries. The McCloud River is a brother of the Sacramento, as both are sired by Shasta glaciers, but it takes a roundabout way to rejoin the Sacramento in Shasta Lake. The Pit River also mixes with the Sacramento and McCloud in Shasta Lake, impounded by 602-foot-high Shasta Dam, which regulates the flow south. Water pouring over the dam's spillway falls more than three times the height of Niagara. Although the Trinity River rushes to the Pacific, some of its flow is diverted into the Sacramento via Lewiston Dam and Whiskeytown Reservoir, then to Keswick Dam, just south of Shasta Dam.

Some 10 miles south, the stripling river romps through a gulch that divides the City of Redding. Farther south it slips past Balls Ferry. For 30 miles beyond Balls Ferry, it snakes through rugged terrain, scampering through its wildest and most forlorn stretch, the gorge called Iron Canyon.

Many years ago the author, as a reporter for the Redding *Record-Searchlight*, shoved off in a rented rowboat at Balls Ferry, committed to the current, with no prior information on what hazards loomed for foolish boaters, save rumors of whirlpools and fearsome currents — alone because no one else in the newsroom would join him in his folly. Past rolling hills, the river flows. Past bluffs, tiny sandy beaches, groves of whispering cottonwoods. Past low-lying Bloody Island where in 1846 soldiers under Kit Carson and Capt. John C. Fremont massacred a band of Nozi Indians. Past mazes of willows and driftwood, and bayous where sleepy creeks join the main stream. A mud metropolis of swallows' nests was glued to a rocky bluff. In the north, Shasta's white cone gleamed in the sun. Sounds: call of a wild duck, lonely tinkle of a cowbell — and suddenly a muted roar, growing louder: white water ahead! Many stretches of turbulence seized the boat and whisked it along. The hiss and low roar of the riffles sang a haunting song. Foamy billows rollercoastered the boat to the next tranquil passage, where the oars went to work.

Now the Sacramento, bending to the east, rolls through desolate terrain strewn with dark-colored volcanic rubble, perhaps from an ancient eruption of Mt. Lassen, 35 miles east. The gorge closes in, throttling the river to 30 feet wide as it sweeps along at eight to 10 miles an hour. Soon it rolls through a steep canyon whose rock walls are softened here and there by patches of grass. The last riffles were run in darkness, and finally the lights of Red Bluff glistened. Good friend Don Donaldson awaited with car and trailer to help transport the boat back to Balls Ferry. Story and photos duly appeared in the Redding newspaper. Modesty almost forbids mentioning that the city editor gave it a five-column headline: "Intrepid Newsman Navigates River," Oct. 29, 1954.

Up into the 1880s, ox teams dragged thousands of logs to the Sacramento River, where they were fastened together with planks to make enormous rafts. Lumberjacks with pike poles in burly arms steered the rafts downriver, singing lustily as they shot rapids and braved the hazards of Iron Canyon. The rolling river carried them down to Marysville, Sacramento, and even San Francisco, where the rafts were sold to sawmills.

Today, to continue south of Red Bluff, or go north while coming upstream, boaters have to portage around Red Bluff Diversion Dam, which shunts some of the river into the Tehama-Colusa

This is where the Sacramento River begins. Two Rancho Cordova people happened to be on the scene — Bonnie Hutchins and Royce Tuter.

Canal and the Corning Canal, for irrigating crops. In years past, as irrigation systems began to water the land, farmers sowed many other crops besides wheat. Today, 200 different crops grow on seven million acres.

East of Corning, the Sacramento flows through Woodson Bridge State Recreation Area, a nearly unspoiled riverbottom forested with oaks, cottonwoods, willows and sycamores. In many other places also, riverbanks seem scarcely changed from what they probably were a hundred years ago. Deer browse on grassy banks and waterfowl wing over gleaming water. Here and there an iron bridge leaps the river. Now and then you can spy falling-down wharves of oldtime rivertowns.

In the Gold Rush epoch, debris washed downstream by hydraulic mining wrecked the flourishing passenger and freight business that cruised as far north as Red Bluff. In the foothills, cannon-like monitors shot implacable jets of water, washing away entire hillsides, choking streams and rivers, glutting ship channels.

At last a federal court decision prohibited dumping the detritus into ship channels, and large-scale placer mining hung up the "out of business" sign forever. But it was too late for many farmers, with thousands of rich acres buried under a shroud of clay and sand and gravel. And the shipping business went belly-up.

Decades ago, in a new wave of commercial traffic, tugs and barges lorded it over the river, shuttling big loads of sugar beets, petroleum and other cargoes to market. It had its heyday c. 1950-60, recalls Kenneth Hulme of San Rafael, grizzled tugboat captain who has herded barges for 32 years on valley rivers and lately on San Francisco Bay. Today all barges are gone from the rivers, save for an occasional scow hauling rocks for rip-rapping the banks.

The valley of the Sacramento is an immense level plain broken only by the 2,132-foot Sutter Buttes a few miles northwest of Yuba City. In the east, the Sierra Nevada is mantled with a snowpack covering up to 10,000 square miles, an enormous reservoir that rations its life-giving waters to the valley in rainless summers. In spring, as Sierra snowpack begins to melt, water dashes down many creeks and streams in the corrugation of steep ravines, paying tribute to the Sacramento. Tributaries also drain from the Coast Range in the west, but few compare with the big ones in the east. The Sacramento and all its tributaries, the American included, drain a basin of 23,000 square miles — over three times the size of New Jersey.

The greatest snowfall in North America descends on the Donner Pass area, and it was just the luck of the Donner Party to be trapped in such a place for the winter. If they hadn't had that bad luck, they wouldn't have had any luck at all. An average of 37 feet a year — nearly as high as a four-story building, though it packs down to a deal less — is dumped in the Donner Pass region. Much of its melt drains into the American. The upper American has three forks — North, Middle and South, all ramping down steep slopes, with plenty of white water for bold rafters, then flowing into the tranquil beauty of Folsom Lake. Gliding through Sacramento, the American surrenders some of its current to a treatment plant, to help supply the city with drinking water. The Sacramento River also gives the city drinking water. In fact, 13 million people — more than half of the state's population — depend on these two rivers for potable water.

Two-tone junction: The confluence of our two rivers is more or less sharply defined, as the blue-green American meets the cafe-au-lait Sacramento in a jagged line. You can see it from the Jibboom Street Bridge, or Discovery Park, or the Yolo County side. Best time to see it is in spring when the Sacramento, charged with sediment, is at its brownest. The American remains relatively blue because this hurrying river dumps most of its sediment when it shifts into low gear at Folsom Lake. But it carries no inordinate amount of sediment, because the granite rocks it courses through are tough cookies.

Indians surely were acquainted with awesome floods, for their legends speak of waters that "flowed from mountain to mountain," and of valley land disappearing. When that happened, they shifted their villages to high ground.

In recorded history, the most destructive floods in northern California have been spawned by unseasonably warm rainstorms tracking in from the Pacific, usually in December and January. Storms of this ilk in 1955 unleashed the flood that sundered the Yuba City levee, bringing on the valley's greatest flood disaster in this century, perhaps in all time. Rainfall started in November 1955. By December, rivers draining the Sierra were running full bore. When the swollen Feather breached the levee near Yuba City, 37 people died. The Red Cross also reported that 3,227 were injured, 467 homes were totally destroyed and 5,745 damaged.

Sacramento was spared from calamity apparently only because of newly-constructed Folsom Dam, which hadn't even been dedicated yet. The dam held back enough of the American to save the city. Sacramento's historic floods have always invaded by rupturing a levee on the overloaded American.

Floods also threaten when temperatures rise abruptly in a warm spring, accelerating Sierra snowmelt.

Coping with floods has been a perennial problem in the valley. Starting in 1910, federal, state and local agencies combined to beef up existing levees and build new ones. This flood control project today contains over 1,400 miles of levees, 1,100 of them lining the banks of the Sacramento River system, the rest in the San Joaquin system, plus nearly as many miles of private levees — all told, enough to run a levee from Sacramento to Chicago.

The clearinghouse for flood information in northern California is the state-federal Flood Operations Center in Sacramento. As flood conditions loom, staffers direct the combat via teletype and telephone. The center is ensconced on the 16th floor of the State Resources Building — lofty enough to keep the staff high and dry and sending out bulletins in the worst of all possible situations.

Completion of Shasta Dam in 1945, harnessing the upper Sacramento, reduced a big hazard. Two more big dams — Folsom on the American and Oroville on the Feather — threw two more big halters on rampaging rivers. Before Folsom Dam's completion, the lower American had flooded each year for many years. In olden days, it was navigable during high water. In 1882, the *Daisy* was the last big steamer to cruise up to the City of Folsom and return. Since then, sandbars from hydraulicking barricaded the way for all but shallow-draft motorboats. Today, Nimbus Dam bars the way.

Besides the big dams, a concatenation of reservoir dams sprinkles western Sierra slopes, setting up the first line of defense, short-stopping much of the immense outpouring from the mountains. Built by a mix of agencies, the dams also store water for irrigation, keep valley rivers running year long, and shunt torrents through turbines to generate kilowatts. Each year as flood season looms, reservoirs discharge water to make room for possible heavy runoff.

The great escape: Giant "safety valves" help tame the rivers. The Sacramento's levees are interrupted in five places by weirs designed to ease pressure on levees by letting workers spill some of the flood-stage river into escape channels called bypasses, as railroaders switch a high-balling train onto another track. Moulton, Colusa and Tisdale Weirs empty into Sutter Bypass, which drains into Yolo Bypass, while Fremont and Sacramento Weirs also flush into Yolo Bypass.

Three miles north of Sacramento the Sacramento Weir, with 48 gates, generally is the last to be opened. No gates here are opened until the river at the I Street Bridge "is 27.5 feet and rising," said Donald Meixner, chief of the Division of Flood Management, State Department of Water Resources, Sacramento. And workers open only enough gates to halt the rise. Opening them takes five minutes and three people — to control traffic on the road atop the weir, and trip the gates' levers. Water pressure forces them open. Closing them takes half an hour per gate, with a crew of 15 and a mobile crane to shut them against powerful water pressure. In some years, this weir idles unneeded throughout the rainy season. All 48 gates were opened only twice since completion of Shasta Dam in 1945 — in the 1964-65 and 1985-86 flood years.

Wrong way river: Strange as it seems, the Sacramento River just northwest of the city sometimes flows backward. This happens in some unusually heavy flood conditions when the American disgorges more water into the Sacramento than the latter's channel can handle. The extra water actually flows upstream three miles to Sacramento Weir, where it empties into Yolo Bypass. Tree trunks and other flotsam cruising upstream offer visible proof that the river is flowing backward, in flagrant violation of the natural law of rivers. Meixner says it's a rare event that happens only once in 12 to 15 years.

For five solid days, the river flowed backward during the February 1986 floods, reports Bill Helms, spokesman for the Flood

The Sacramento River today is a highway mainly for recreational and sport boats, as in Sacramento's annual water festival.

Center, Sacramento. On February 19, midpoint of the five days, Folsom Dam releases sent the American's flow surging to a record 130,000 cubic feet per second. Next day, a record 665,000 c.f.s. passed the city — through the Sacramento River and Yolo Bypass. The total *volume* for that one day was a record 1.3 million acre feet. To put that in perspective, it's enough to fill an empty Folsom Lake in only 19 hours.

In one year, the all-time record flow past Sacramento was 51.2 million acre-feet in the 1982-83 year. How much is 51.2 million acre-feet? A staggering volume. For the earth's 5 billion people, it computes to more than 9 gallons of fresh water for every person on the globe — every day for a year! In an average year, the annual flow is only 17.2 million acre-feet, but that still figures out to over 3 gallons for everyone on earth, every day, year after year. In other words, Sacramento's fresh water theoretically could slake the thirst of the world. In practice, there'd be a bit of a transportation problem. Of course, agriculture and industry use vastly more water than people drink, so maybe we better forget the whole thing.

The Sacramento River channel has a designed capacity of 110,000 c.f.s., including the American flow, past the city. The Yolo

Bypass capacity adds 490,000 c.f.s., nearly four and a half times that of the river channel.

And if that Bypass weren't there?

"We'd have to have a different design," Meixner said. "Downtown Sacramento, as we know it, would not exist —because the levees would have to be so far apart to carry a much wider river."

The Yolo Bypass is a 101-square-mile floodplain running from Fremont and Sacramento Weirs to the vicinity of Rio Vista, where it empties into the Sacramento River. When flooded, the Bypass is a body of water two miles wide, a sight familiar to drivers crossing the Yolo Causeway on Interstate 80.

We know about rights-of-way for roads and utilities and such, but this is surely one of the world's most bizarre rights-of-way: If you're one of the farmers in the Yolo Bypass, the State of California can open floodgates and turn the rampaging, flood-stage Sacramento River onto your property. Of course, flood staffers send out warnings so you have time to skedaddle for high ground before a wall of water comes down the chute. But if you haven't had time to harvest your crops, you can kiss them goodbye. Typical Bypass crops are rice, melons, corn and safflower. Those who farm the wild Bypass try to schedule crops for harvesting before the threat of high water materializes. Even so, sometimes farmers sow a late spring crop, gambling on a dry season ahead, then lose their gamble, which means a season's work literally down the drain.

Bev Brownell, manager for Liberty Farms on Liberty Island near the south end of the Bypass, remembers losing 600 acres of wheat — nearly one square mile — when floodwaters were switched through the Bypass. "It's always a gamble down here because of spring run-offs," he said. "Everybody can estimate and guess — and then you get a warm day and all the water comes at once." Formerly, as many as 18 families farmed Liberty Island, which had a school, post office and store. When Brownell came in 1973, the number had dwindled to 10. Today only one farming outfit remains — Liberty Farms. Brownell explains the decrease: "Same thing that is happening elsewhere — the big outfits are taking over."

In some stretches of the Sacramento River, notably from Chico Landing north to Red Bluff, high waters keep devouring riverbanks and farmlands. Some farmers have dumped junk car bodies onto the banks to fight erosion, but they merely retard the inevitable. Old Mȧn River eats junk food for breakfast. Fighting erosion, the Army Corps of Engineers has rip-rapped, or "rocked," the river at various points from the Delta northward for some 150 miles, nearly to Chico Landing.

With all the dams and weirs and bypasses in the Sacramento River system, one might imagine the valley is safer than ever from floods. Just the contrary, says Joe Countryman, chief of civil design for the Corps of Engineers' Sacramento office: "The flood threat is getting greater every year. We can't ignore it any longer." Why is it getting greater? Because, he said, sediment keeps raising levels of riverbeds and bypasses, reducing their water-carrying capacity.

On its final run to the Bay, the Sacramento mingles in the Delta with the north-flowing San Joaquin River, which carries only one-tenth of the Sacramento volume. The Delta also assembles the waters of the Cosumnes, Mokelumne and Calaveras into an immense marsh that early settlers turned into an archipelago of farm islands barricaded by high levees. Today, some of these islands lie as much as 20 feet below sea level.

Chapter 3
Indians: The First Sacramentans

It may be regarded as certain, that not a foot of land will ever be taken from the Indians without their own consent. The sacredness of their rights is felt by all thinking persons in America.

Thomas Jefferson

Indians once owned all of Sacramento — by right of first occupancy. They dwelled in the great valley at least 10,000 years before any other comers, weathering the hot sun and the chilling rain through the endless roll of the seasons. Until 5,000 years ago, they were wanderers, following the spoor of migrating game — horses, camels, bison and even mastodons. As the continent warmed up after the last Ice Age, for some reason the larger beasts became extinct, and the hunters concentrated on deer, elk and antelope. As centuries rolled by, the Indians gave up their nomad life and settled down and began to augment their diet with more plant foods.

On the floodplain where Sacramento stands, a population of perhaps thousands of the Nisenan, a southern branch of the Maidu, lived in villages of dome-shaped houses built of willow saplings thatched with tules, a tall sedge. Tule mats carpeted dirt floors. The men built small boats by lashing tule bundles together. Craft materials grew everywhere. The Nisenan wove baskets of willow and redbud — and poison oak, being largely immune to it from lifelong exposure. They built sweat-houses of willow and tules, and raised heads of steam by dashing water onto hot rocks. Scraping their skin with sticks, they plunged into a cold stream — even in winter, believing daily use of the sweat-house cleansed them both physically and spiritually.

Spiritual concerns dominated their lives. All natural objects had supernatural powers. "A tree could kill you if it wanted to," a Nisenan once explained. Sometimes they do, by falling on people. After the first rain in the fall, the Indians performed an Acorn Dance to thank the mountain spirits for rain, and to entreat the spirits of the oaks for an abundance of acorns. They worshipped a supreme being called the Earth Maker. They also believed in Coyote the Trickster, blaming him for bringing death and trouble into a beautiful world.

In torrid summers, the men wore breechclouts of deerskin or wire-grass, or wore nothing at all, while women garbed themselves in aprons of wire-grass or tules. Rabbit-fur or deerskin robes, with fur next to the body, kept the people warm in chilly weather. Men and women wore their hair long, trimming it with a knife or glowing ember, dressing it with porcupine quills or pine cones. They arrayed themselves in necklaces and bracelets crafted from animal bones, pretty stones, deer antlers, pine nuts, bear claws, bird beaks. Many Nisenan tattooed themselves by rubbing juices of mugwort or soap plant root into skin cuts.

Hunters and fishers: Their world was a cornucopia of fish and game and plant foods. Armed with willow bows, the men stalked deer, bear, jackrabbit and raccoon, killing them with arrows tipped with obsidian, a volcanic glass. Sometimes they dipped their arrows in venom obtained by teasing a rattlesnake to bite a deer-liver. At times they caught deer by digging pits, camouflaging them with grass and boughs. Or, one hunter might disguise himself with a deerskin cloak and antler headpiece, then creep upwind for a shot at a browsing deer. At other times, an individual hunter would simply run a deer to exhaustion, then shoot it. Sometimes many men would organize a *drive* or a *surround,* beating the bushes until they flushed a deer, then closing in until the champion marksman could launch an arrow. To capture quail, ducks and geese, they fashioned snares.

In winter, black bears curled up in snug lairs to hibernate. But sometimes their sleep was rudely interrupted by Indians, who threw flaming brands into the dens to drive out the sleepy, grouchy bears — into a hail of spears and arrows. Grizzlies once roamed the valley, but Indians dreaded them and tried to keep clear of the awesome giants.

Indian delicacies: Besides venison, bear meat and fish, the Nisenan consumed lashings of other protein-rich foods. Earthworms were favorite ingredients in soups. The Indians devoured lizards and frogs and ants and other insects. Grasshoppers were gourmet morsels. To catch them, they beat the grass, driving them into pits, and tossed in a bundle of burning grass to dispatch them. Sometimes they ignited a ring of fire in dry grass, to close in on the hoppers. They soaked them in water and baked them in an earth oven, then snacked on them whole or boiled them into mush.

In late summer, women gathered acorns, competing with pesky squirrels shopping for the same groceries. After shelling and cleaning the acorns, the women used round stones as pestles to pound the acorns into meal in the mortar holes of a grinding rock. They also pounded salmon in these holes, after it was dried. You can see grinding rocks with a few mortar holes in Negro Bar State Park, and dozens along the American River near the old Folsom Power House. With warm water, the Indians leached the tannic acid out of the acorn meal. With hot rocks in a watertight basket, they boiled it into porridge. In similar style, they cooked lupine seeds, grass seeds (timothy and wild oats) and roots such as wild carrot (Queen Anne's Lace). Today, black walnut trees grow on sites of some old Indian villages, indicating walnuts were a staple. Some grow by the Sacramento River near the aptly-named town of Walnut Grove, 20 miles south of Sacramento. Nisenan larders included numerous other nuts, berries, roots and seeds. They baked and ate the soap plant bulb, which also yielded cleansing suds. They munched on tender leaves of a plant later named miners' lettuce. They added buckeye seeds to soups and cakes — first cracking and boiling them to leach away the toxic stuff. They chomped on wild grapes — fresh, or dried as raisins for winter feeds. They ate half a dozen kinds of berries. They dried elderberries for use as a meat relish, cooking them first, as otherwise they are toxic. The blue elderberry juice was used in dyeing.

Few plants offer food for both body and soul, but the elderberry gets the laurel, so to speak. The Nisenan called it the Tree of Music, for it was easy to hollow out its stems to make flutes and whistles. Other Nisenan music instruments included rattles, clapper sticks, a foot-drum, and the "bull-roarer" — a slat tied to a thong. Whirled around the head, it makes a racket that explains its name.

Streams fairly wriggled with food. Nisenan dredged freshwater clams and mussels, speared salmon and sturgeon, and wove nets to catch other fish. They flung parts of certain plants into pools to stupefy fish, then caught them with bare hands. Such plants included soap plant root, buckeye seed pods, and turkey mullein, a.k.a. dove weed, so named because turkeys and doves go ape over them. Nisenan evidently preferred their chewing gum with a meaty flavor, for they manufactured it by heating milkweed juice, then blending it with deer or bear grease.

Medicines from nature: Nisenan people know how to doctor themselves with many plant medicines. For diarrhea, they drank a fusion from blackberry leaves. A laxative of fennel (anise) leaves, which smell like licorice, relieved constipation. So did the broad-leafed common plantain, which the Indians called White Man's Foot, because it seemed to grow wherever the early settlers stepped, around their homes and villages. It was introduced here accidentally, perhaps in cattle feed. Pine pitch also was used as a laxative, and dried and ground as a cure for sores and ulcers.

As a cold remedy, Nisenan brewed tea from roots of the wild rose, a plant chock-full of vitamin C. Health food stores today sell rose hips as a potent source of C, touted by some scientists, including Linus Pauling, as a cold-preventer. Another Indian cold remedy derived from leaves of the mugwort, a riparian plant. To banish a headache, an Indian plastered a mugwort leaf against his forehead. Mugwort also took the itch out of poison oak. Mugwort, incidentally, was the Indian symbol for peace, and they no doubt craved the peace it offered from headaches, stuffy noses and sore throats.

To cure an upset stomach, the Indians quaffed a brew from leaves of Mexican tea, or from bark of the toyon, an evergreen shrub also known today as the Christmas berry. Nisenan ate toyon berries, roasted or boiled to banish the bitter taste. Turkey mullein leaves, used to stun fish, apparently were deemed a cure-all, for they were prescribed for internal pains, asthma, fever and chills. Dutchman's pipevine also was a virtual cure-all. To soothe toothaches, the locals chewed Indian tobacco, the only plant known to be cultivated by Sacramento area Indians. As its name indicates, they also smoked it — in straight pipes while lying on their backs. They boiled goldenrod leaves to make a poultice for wounds. For perhaps thousands of years, the Indians were acquainted with aspirin as a painkiller. They extracted it by boiling leaves and bark of the willow, which contains salicylic acid, aspirin's main ingredient.

Rugged Indian dancer is depicted in this painting, "Toto at Bloomer Hill," by Frank Day. Toto means a dance that celebrates the joy of life. Bloomer Hill is in Butte County. Permission to publish photo was granted by Herb Puffer, Pacific Western Traders, Folsom.

As many as one-fourth of all medicines in the modern U.S. pharmacopoeia were originally derived from plants known to American Indians for curative powers. This means hundreds of

Indian-known medicines. And who can say how many more have been lost forever, because of the obliteration of Indian cultures?

War between tribes of central California Indians was not a frequent occurrence, it is said. When it did occur, it most likely followed a trespass on another tribe's hunting territory. When one tribe fought a battle with another, it was winner take all. Men prisoners were killed, while women prisoners were forced to join their captors' households. Some people might call that slavery.

Autumn of the Nisenan: For some ten millennia, the Nisenan lived in tune with their environment, until their world underwent an upheaval that was almost seismic. At the beginning of Spanish colonization in 1769, it is estimated that 150,000 or more Indians in 40 separate groups lived in California. Their long and in some ways idyllic life came to a shattering finale in the 19th century, with two calamitous events. In 1833, an epidemic of mosquito-borne malaria — first carried in by trappers — swept the valley, wiping out entire villages. Then during the 1849 gold stampede, prospectors carried in other diseases the Indians had no resistance to — cholera, smallpox, tuberculosis. Many whites persecuted the surviving remnants of Nisenan, driving them off their lands, wrecking their culture, killing many. Survivors fled towards the foothills, where some in time managed to find work in farming, logging, cattle ranching, and as domestic servants. By century's end, a mere 15,000 survivors remained, a pathetic tenth of the original population.

Ghost villages: A major Nisenan village named Kadema, with 200 to 300 people, once stood on the north bank of the American, perhaps approximately where today's Kadema Drive runs, south of American River Drive. Often the only trace of an Indian culture is a name on the land. Another Nisenan village hunkered on a terrace of the north bank of the American 15 miles upstream from its junction with the Sacramento. Originally this site had two mounds, but one was destroyed by early farming labors and later home construction. The remaining mound, 35 by 40 meters, is believed to contain undisturbed burials and perhaps artifacts 2,000 years old or more. It was partly excavated in 1937-38 by people from Sacramento Junior College (today's Sacramento City College), who found 112 burials. In 1973, test excavations by people from California Department of Parks and Recreation found five more burials, which were left in *situ.*

The most spectacular site of an Indian village in Sacramento County is the Indian Stone Corral, which deserves a chapter of its own.

Chapter 4
The Heroine of Indian Stone Corral

Granite outcrops like gargantuan teeth are the most eye-catching peculiarities of the rolling 64 acres of Indian Stone Corral, northeast of Cherry and Granite Avenues in Orangevale, and bounded on the north by the Placer County line. The county has designated it as a future park but the opening date is indefinite, said Gene Andal, director of the County Department of Parks and Recreation.

More than 100 mortar holes that pock the grinding rocks here are legacies of long occupancy by Nisenan Indians. Many are more than a foot deep. The terrain here also contains two sites of pitted-boulder petroglyphs up to 4,000 years old, of a type found nowhere else in Sacramento County. This type is not the more familiar, visually-striking petroglyph. At any rate, the evidence points to the area as a major Nisenan village and ceremonial site. The Corral setting also contains middens (refuse heaps), remains of a stone quarry and roadway and/or aqueduct, and a pond with a dam, some of these features being perhaps of Gold Rush vintage construction by Chinese miners.

High granite ledges here may have served bandits as lookout points. Legend says the Corral, a.k.a. Robbers Roost, was a lair for Gold Rush-era outlaws, who perhaps stationed lookouts on the ledges to spot approaching lawmen. Such miscreants as the Tom Bell Gang are said to have used the Corral as a hideaway and

Mortar holes a foot or more deep perforate granite slabs in Indian Stone Corral.

stronghold. Its granite monoliths created a natural fortress where outlaws could hole up, with water available from the creek for men and horses. (See chapter on Folsom for more on Bell and cohorts.)

Two small ravines formed by flanking outcrops created natural corrals. The robbers could barricade one end with piles of brush and rocks, and the other with their campsite.

The land here is garnished with oaks, cottonwoods, toyon and coffeeberry and populated with scrubjays, magpies, the bird known as a kite, and numerous other feathered fliers. Linda Creek, a year-round stream, gurgles through this little lost wilderness of trees and fields and granite upthrusts. In one scene, the creek chuckles through an enchanting mini-canyon choked with trees and jumbles of granite slabs tufted with emerald moss. A tributary creek murmurs through a sandstone ledge, where marine fossils have come to light, relics of the distant time when the central valley lay at the bottom of the Ione Sea. The creekbed is laced with water-rounded quartz pebbles washed downstream ages ago from the glaciating Sierra Nevada.

How Maxine Cornwell saved the Corral: The Corral most likely would have been destroyed forever — graded by bulldozers and studded with houses — except for Cornwell, who lives close by and has been guarding it for many years. She and her husband Bob in 1961 bought a house on land bordering the Corral, and soon learned from neighbors that the adjoining land once had been the site of an Indian settlement. They found numerous mortar holes in grinding rocks.

One Easter, Bob hid some decorated eggs in rocky terrain not far from the house. Maxine led the children out to look for the eggs — and discovered some pitted-boulder petroglyphs, a row of small depressions Indians had gouged out on the rim of a great slab of rock. Previously, an archeology class from Sierra College found some petroglyphs on the other side of the stream. These petroglyphs are small cupules, or cup-shaped holes, only an inch or so deep, gouged in granite boulders with sharp rocks. Dr. Gerald Johnson, anthropology professor at California State University, Sacramento, says they were carved by an unknown tribe that lived here long before the Nisenan. He said scientists don't know for certain what these petroglyphs signify, but know that similar markings by other Indian peoples were intended to entreat the spirits for fertility or rain.

Obviously the Corral was a vital, irreplaceable site, and had to be protected. In the absence of any official guardian, Maxine Cornwell appointed herself to fill the role, but *how* to protect it? At first, she hadn't a clue. By degrees it became clear the only sure way to save it was to establish it as a public park. She vowed to spend an hour on the phone every day, to find out how to achieve the goal.

This time was in addition to that required by her job as an adult education teacher and by her household duties as wife, mother and housekeeper. Year after year, she chipped away at the often baffling task of bringing Indian Stone Corral under the protection of county administration.

On occasion Cornwell had to shoo away vandals, mischievous kids and pot-hunters — collectors looking for Indian artifacts — and other intruders up to no good. One day she spied a landscape contractor astride a roaring bulldozer, prying out a huge boulder, no doubt intended to decorate some customer's front yard. Arms akimbo, the petite red-haired Cornwell confronted the burly despoiler. When he shut his engine off, she explained to him the desecration he was perpetrating. Explained the vital importance of preserving the Corral's primeval condition. Explained how hard she was working to have the county establish it as a park. All that was not enough to sway the rascal — he switched on his engine and recommenced. Only after she called him every scalawag name she could think of did he red-facedly abandon the boulder, leaving the red-headed Cornwell in control. Hell hath no fury like a woman with a righteous cause.

Cornwell found that Moss & Moss Realtors owned the property. Now and then a developer inspected its granite-studded rolling landscape with a gleam in his eye, envisioning a subdivision of luxury homes in an incomparable setting.

At last in 1978, seven years after she began her crusade, Cornwell won the battle: The County of Sacramento purchased the 64 acres from Moss & Moss and set it aside for a future park. The county paid $278,000, with Sunrise Recreation and Park District contributing $50,000 to the price. The Corral is now on the National Register of Historic Places. Incidentally, another neighbor who helps guard the Corral is a former mental patient with an itchy trigger finger.

Except for Maxine Cornwell, Indian Stone Corral, a priceless and irreplaceable heritage of the Nisenan culture, would have been lost forever, destroyed by subdivision bulldozers. The Corral is enclosed by a chain-link fence, and is *not* open to the public at this writing. Plans are to make it an interpretive park, with kiosks and guides to inform visitors about its ancient residents. Present lack of funds to provide minimum visitor facilities and security arrangements remains the only obstacle to a public opening. So this information is not an invitation to visit, but merely a preview of a coming attraction, come some wonderful year.

Chapter 5
State Indian Museum: Remembrances of a Lost World

Ishi was a Yahi
Yahi was his tribe
Tribe was in the wilderness
Wilderness was his home.

Scott Germond, 4th grade, Starr King School, Carmichael, in an exhibit at the Indian Museum.

This is a museum of a world that is lost and gone forever — the world of the Nisenan Indians of the Sacramento region, and of other tribes in northern California. The museum stands at 2618 K St., directly in back of Sutter's Fort, 27th and L Streets.

Look for the maps that depict Indian trade routes throughout California. Striking fact: The old Indian roads largely coincide with today's state and federal highways. You can examine a wide range of tools, weapons, cooking utensils, basketry, clothing and regalia. The centerpiece is an 18-foot dugout boat that Yurok Indians carved from a redwood log, by alternate burning and gouging, and sold to Hupa and Karuk people, who used it on the Klamath River. Yuroks made their boats only of fallen logs, a good conservation practice, whether or not intended. The boats were used to haul goods and persons along the river. Even an enemy expected, and received, a free ride — an ethical sophistication that may be difficult for many non-Indians to comprehend.

To the Indians, baskets were not only utilitarian, but a mode of artistic expression. Fine baskets are on view, with photos of basketmakers at work. A card informs: "California Indians made the finest baskets in the world. At the height of this art stand these treasure baskets produced by the Pomo people. Brilliant feathers from the woodpecker, jay and meadowlark are inserted in each stitch to form the design. Decorations of magnesite and clamshell disc beads and abalone pendants are added as a finishing touch."

"The Journey" exhibit displays baskets for carrying burdens, including infants. One learns here that most California Indians traveled a good deal — on short journeys to nearby hills, valleys, meadows and rivers to gather nature's sustenance.

Another display depicts the "Brush Dance" in photos and examples of bows, arrows, darts, and feather-adorned regalia. Medicine women organized these dances as a means of healing sick people. Odd fact: Among local Indians, medicine women were more numerous than medicine men, reports Elsie King-Gillespie, park interpretive specialist.

"The Hunt" exhibit contains skins of deer, rabbit, otter, bobcat and wolf, and the means of capturing the animals — bows, arrows, nets, sling, traps. But the Indians didn't rely only on these implements. To attract their quarry, they carried a charmstone made from soapstone. Fish and game didn't have a chance.

"The Gathering" offers glimpses of the plants that provided food and medicine, and harvesting tools.

"Preparing the Meals" pictures methods of cooking by: open fire, earth oven, stone boiling, and parching. Mortars and pestles for grinding acorns and other foods are on view. California Indians generally ate only two meals a day, morning and evening. But they were generous hosts: When visitors arrived, no matter what time, they promptly served them a meal.

"The Singers" illustrates the theme that music is "the heartbeat of the people." Without singers, there could be no dances. The singer's most important instrument is the clapstick — it provides the beat for the dance. Exhibited are clapsticks, flutes and a whistle, and the largest drumstick you ever saw — bigger than a baseball bat. It was used to drum on a seven-foot log that was partly buried horizontally in a trench. It is termed a foot drumstick not because the drummer operates it with his foot but because the drum is *at* his feet as he beats the tar out of it.

The "Water Bones" display shows strings of marine clamshell

disk beads, used for both money and adornment. The "European Beads" display offers lovely creations, including beaded bottles, that Indians fashioned from items obtained from other cultures.

Outside the museum, volunteers and staff are re-creating a full-scale Indian village, with round hand-game room 35 feet in diameter, a sweat-house, leaching pit, fire pit, bark house, tule hut and two acorn granaries. On some occasions, Indian volunteers demonstrate acorn processing, cooking, basket-weaving, and flaking arrowheads and spearheads from obsidian. The museum is open daily 10 a.m. to 5 p.m. except Thanksgiving, Christmas and New Year's. Call 324-0971 for information.

The story of Ishi: One of the museum's interior exhibits is described last in this chapter because it epitomizes, in the story of one man, the tragedy of California Indians and perhaps of all Native Americans. The dramatic photo exhibit recounts the ordeal of Ishi, who died in 1916, last survivor of the Yahi Indians of northern California. Ishi came to public attention in 1911 when he was found hiding — exhausted, starving and frightened — in a corral in Oroville, Butte County. Sheriff's deputies housed him in the county jail. Newspaper stories of "The Wild Man of Oroville" caught the eyes of Professors Alfred L. Kroeber and T.T. Waterman, University of California anthropologists, who hurried to the scene and "adopted" Ishi. By degrees they learned to talk with him, and learned he was born about 1862, making him about 49 when he came to public notice.

Ishi's tribe of Yahi was one of four in the Yana nation, which dwelled north of Oroville in a mountainous region of fast streams, steep gorges, lush meadows and thick stands of oak and pine. But the 1848 gold discovery drove the Yanas to the end of the trail. Prospectors carrying smallpox and tuberculosis decimated them. Deer and other game grew scarce. Hydraulicking's pollution killed the salmon. Worst, several massacres by whites wiped out all the Yana save 15 of the Yahi, who retreated into their heartland, their final stronghold. For 40 years, Ishi and a dozen kinsmen lived in dense brush deep in Deer Creek Canyon until at last old age, illness and violence left only Ishi alive — the last man of the Yana nation. He wandered to Oroville and collapsed in the corral.

In San Francisco, he was hired as an assistant janitor at $25 a month in the university museum, where quarters were equipped with living accommodations for him. He gave demonstrations on bow-stringing, making fire with a drill, and chipping arrowheads. After contracting tuberculosis, the plague that had struck down so

Tule hut near the State Indian Museum recreates a scene from bygone years.

many of his people, he died March 25, 1916, age about 54. He was cremated in a coffin containing a bow, arrows, basket of acorn meal, shell-bead money and tobacco. So ended the life of the man said to be the last wild Indian in North America.

In the Indian Museum, 17 photos depict Ishi in a variety of situations, some in his native environment, some wearing white man's clothes, one at the wheel of a vintage auto. Only two of the photos show this tragic man smiling — one as he enjoys a swim in a mountain stream.

Each year, the museum sponsors a contest among local elementary school children for the best poems, essays and drawings telling about Ishi. Winning entries appear with the exhibit for a year. One winning poem is that which appears at the head of this chapter.

The complete story is told in a book, *Ishi In Two Worlds*, by Theodora Kroeber, wife of one of the anthropologists who tried to help him find a happy place in his new world.

Chapter 6
The Adventurer

Something hidden. Go and find it.
Go and look behind the Ranges —
Something lost behind the Ranges.
Lost and waiting for you. Go.
The Explorer, by Rudyard Kipling

Sacramento founder Capt. John Sutter was one of the most astonishing adventurers of all time. Consider. He fled Switzerland in darkness, with the police at his heels. Five years later on the far side of the globe, he was the Lord of New Helvetia, carving out an enormous empire in the California wilderness.

He was a city boy who beat the country boys at their own game: In America, thousands of people in frontier states such as Missouri were born and bred in the wilderness. They cut their teeth on rifles, learned to ride horses while still in diapers, endured hardships and privations. They shot buffalo, fished the streams for salmon, raised cattle, grew crops, built houses, barns and corrals, hewed farms and towns out of raw wilderness, and at times engaged in life-and-death struggles with Indians, who didn't like this invasion of their territory one bit. Having company for a short visit was one thing, but this was ridiculous.

Meanwhile in Switzerland, Sutter was a creature of comfortable living in a long-established society. He was schooled in the civilized arts of bookbinding and merchandising groceries and drygoods.

Captain John Sutter sailed beyond the sunset to reach the land he dreamed of. Courtesy General Don Mattson, California National Guard.

He relished fancy clothes and high living. Who would have supposed this boulevard dandy, this cake-eater, could have survived the barbarisms of America's frontiers?

Yet he did survive — making two round-trips on the Santa Fe Trail, then a long trek on the Oregon Trail to Fort Vancouver, where he sailed for the faraway Sandwich Islands and New Archangel before he plunged into the wilderness of Mexico's Alta California.

He not only survived, he triumphed.

While Americans were slowly pushing the frontier westward from Missouri, he sneaked in the backdoor, as it were, and grabbed an immense empire in the heart of the western wilderness — beating the American frontiersmen at their own profession.

Consider that his puny expedition was no proper expedition lavishly-outfitted by the government or some huge commercial combine. Nor was he the mere figurehead of an expedition whose concept belonged to someone else. It was all *his* doing — conceived and executed by the incredible Captain. His was no expedition launched in full panoply with sound of trumpet. He hit the ground running — for the police were after him. His was a mere catch-as-catch-can affair of motley crew and meager supplies, recruited and bought on dubious credit in some of the most remote and isolated places on the globe — the Sandwich Islands, New Archangel, Yerba Buena — an expedition deficient in everything but the leader's magnificent audacity.

Consider that at journey's end — at the terminus of his five-year, 20,000-mile odyssey to the ends of the earth — the bold project he had hatched in his feverish imagination was not done — it was not even started! For he then went ahead and built his marvelous fort and conquered a whole wide wilderness, "with a sword in my fist," he boasted in flamboyant style.

Consider that, albeit a self-confessed poor businessman, he proved to be a splendid organizer and entrepreneur, for he put the bedazzled Indians to work, and everyone else he could recruit, tilling the soil, raising livestock, fishing and hunting, weaving cloth, blacksmithing, carpentering, toiling in numerous other crafts and new industries, building New Helvetia, building the fortress colony that would become the western anchor of America's Manifest Destiny, and the goal and haven for most of the sick, starved and exhausted overland travelers on the long, long trail to California.

He lived one of the most amazing adventures of the American West. In Europe, he would win renown as the Kaiser of Kalifornia.

The incredible Captain: From a flight in darkness to an empire in the sun — and only a tidal wave called the Gold Rush could sweep it away from him. But he knew how to choose prime real estate. From the wreckage of New Helvetia emerged the lusty rivertown that would become the capital of the Golden Empire that Sutter beleaguered in the wilderness had dared to dream of.

And now for his amazing odyssey.

Chapter 7
Captain Sutter's Odyssey to the Ends of the Earth

All experience is an arch wherethro'
Gleams that untravell'd world, whose margin fades
For ever and for ever when I move.
Ulysses, by Alfred, Lord Tennyson

He began his journey under inglorious circumstances. Johann Augustus Sutter was a fugitive from the law in 1834 at age 31 when he decamped from Switzerland and sailed for America, leaving in the lurch his wife and four children — and his creditors, who had gotten out a police warrant for his arrest. His family would rejoin him 16 years later in California, where he seemed to have the world by the tail. His creditors would not be paid until 28 years later, after his fame reached them, and they found out where to nail him.

But this is the story of his towering adventures in the years between.

Sutter lingered his first 15 years in Kandern, Baden, Germany, where he was born of Swiss parents. At age 16 he went to work in a Basel, Switzerland, printing house, but apparently showed no aptitude for the work and didn't seem to fit in. In Aarburg years later, clerking in a draper's shop, he met a customer named Annette Dubeld. They were married in the nick of time Oct. 24, 1826, for next day Annette gave birth to their son. After clerking in a

Burgdorf grocery, Sutter — bankrolled by Annette's widowed mother — opened a drygoods business.

Printer's devil, grocery clerk, drygoods merchant — an unlikely apprenticeship for a world-class adventurer. But wait. He also soldiered in Berne's infantry reserve, and here one glimpses the incipient man of action.

Sutter was of average height and build, but carried himself tall in a military way. Blondish hair, trimmed mustache, neat sidewhiskers and penchant for fancy uniforms made him a handsome dog — with roguish eyes ever on the alert for pretty ladies.

Four years after he launched his drygoods venture, bankruptcy loomed. He had been living beyond his means, and Mrs. Dubeld was adamant in her refusal to advance any more funds to her spendthrift son-in-law. Sutter skimmed cash from the ruins, said a painful farewell to Annette and the children and skipped town, vowing to repair his fortunes in America.

He joined 90 farmers from Baden and Bavaria for the trip to the New World. Sutter was one of 97 passengers on the sailing vessel *Andes* that departed Le Havre, France, and arrived in New York July 14, 1834. In New York, Sutter wrote Annette, promising to return when he could discharge his obligations. His family was reduced to living on charity from Annette's relatives. But they were among the most affluent burghers in Burgdorf, so perhaps her only hardship was humiliation over an errant husband. From New York, Sutter journeyed west with new friends, two Frenchmen and two Germans. They crossed New Jersey and Pennsylvania into Ohio, and parted. After lingering in Ohio two months, Sutter made his way to St. Louis where, stymied, he cast about for some enterprise to his liking.

> *How dull it is to pause, to make an end,*
> *To rust unburnish'd, not to shine in use!*
> *Ulysses*

Craving adventure, he sold some of his fancy wardrobe and also borrowed money to buy trade goods, then joined some Frenchmen in a wagon train bound in 1835 for Santa Fe, New Mexico.

Near present-day Great Bend, Kansas, the caravan began to follow the Arkansas River to be near water as they pushed through arid country. Beyond where Dodge City would crop up four decades later, they came to a vital fork, and chose the Mountain Route along the north bank of the Arkansas — 100 miles longer, but safer from Indians. They paused at Bent's Fort, which dominated the fur trade in the southern Rockies, and flew the only American Flag west of the Missouri. Its customers were bearded trappers and feathered Indians. Sutter, who one day would build his own fort, noted that bastions on northeast and southwest corners offered commanding views of the outer walls, so defenders could repulse scaling attempts.

From Bent's, the caravan trekked over rocky Raton Pass into New Mexico and Santa Fe, at the foot of the Sangre de Cristo ("Blood of Christ") Range on the rim of a great plateau rolling west to the Rio Grande. In a typical arrival, traders stood up in their stirrups, shot off firearms, and yawped their elation. Mules brayed and oxen lowed, infected by the high spirits. Santa Fe people rushed into the streets: "Los Americanos! Los carros! La entrada de la caravana!"

I will drink life to the lees.
Ulysses

Sutter picked up a smattering of Spanish and honed his skill at dickering over prices. He drank and gambled. He flirted with senoritas, who were taken by his blond hair and blue eyes. In the fall, he picked up the long trail back to Missouri, delighted with fat profits and a rousing adventure.

Now he entertained drinking companions with yarns of the Santa Fe Trail, and also began to embroider his military record. In Berne, he had risen to the rank of first lieutenant, but now he promoted himself, as it were, to captain and passed himself off as a veteran of the King of France's Swiss Guards who fought in the July 1830 revolution. Yet Sacramento artist-historian Ted Baggelmann rebuts this legend of how Sutter came to be called captain, declaring that caravan leaders on the Santa Fe Trail were commonly so designated.

As the 1836 Santa Fe season drew on, Sutter assembled his own outfit and a crew of 15, joint owners with Sutter of $14,000 in merchandise — bought largely on credit. Riding horses and mules, with goods jammed in four ox-drawn carts, they joined a caravan of 80 wagons. Again they arrived at the crucial fork. But this caravan was big enough to brave the Cimarron Desert, as forlorn as a dead sea. This shortcut would save them 100 miles, but posed dangers from thirst and Comanches, perennially on the warpath.

Alas, this Santa Fe expedition proved ruinous because of new, exorbitant taxes by the Mexicans and fierce rivalry by caravans from the new Republic of Texas. Moreover, Indian uprisings forced many New Mexican gold mines to close down, drying up the flow of gold into Santa Fe, where trade goods glutted the market. But Sutter banished care in his usual style — gambling, carousing and dallying with the ladies.

The now-pauperized Sutter and a partner quested for jobs, but found only clerking and cooking. Sutter was happy to chuck this drudgery when news of a gold strike galvanized adventurous hearts. An Indian had flaunted a nugget he said was found on an upper stretch of the South Platte River in the High Plains. Sutter and partner joined some French-Canadians on the mini-gold rush. But bitter cold, supply shortages and hip-deep snow dashed their hopes.

Spirits later revived, they charged out once more after gold, to scrabble in an old New Mexican diggins, with only wretched rewards.

North of Santa Fe in the adobe village of San Fernando de Taos, Sutter struck up a friendship with the alcalde, Charles (Carlos) Beaubien, a French-Canadian and naturalized Mexican. Beaubien's tales of travels in California as a young man stirred Sutter profoundly, inspiring a great notion: One day he would settle in California. One might say that in this out-of-the-way desert town, the Sacramento story became a gleam in Sutter's eye.

His belly full of Santa Fe, Sutter hired a Mexican to help him drive 100 wild mustangs and mules back to Missouri. Many escaped on the way. At journey's end, Sutter's hot-under-the-collar creditors relieved him of many more.

Opportunity seemed to beckon in boomtown Westport (later Kansas City), then rivaling Independence as a jump-off for westering journeys. Selling his remaining animals yielded Sutter a stake to begin construction of a posh enterprise, the Far West Hotel. Once more, living beyond his means undid him. He gave his creditors the slip at dawn on April 1, 1838 — a shabby April Fool trick — as he and his partner, a fellow Swiss named Westler, slunk out of town on ponies.

I am become a name, for always roaming with a hungry heart.
Ulysses

For security in Indian country, they attached themselves to the American Fur Company's annual expedition to transport supplies

Johann Sutter was born in this papermill in Kandern, Baden, Germany, where his Swiss father was employed. Today, a plaque on the mill calls Sutter the "Kaiser von Kalifornien." Photo courtesy Swiss National Tourist Office, San Francisco.

to its trappers in the Rockies. The caravan numbered 200 horses and mules, 17 carts and wagons, and more than 60 men — plus four new brides and their missionary husbands, bound for a mission in Oregon territory. The women would record the epic journey in classic diaries.

The Oregon Trail! Nearly two-thirds of the breadth of the continent lay ahead, a savage immensity of mountains and deserts and rivers to cross. Day after day the caravan lumbered across the prairie. The April grass was carpeted with wild flowers. Indians seemed to be everywhere — painted and ornamented, hair cut Mohawk-style. Each evening the expedition hauled its wagons into a circle and picketed horses and mules inside to keep them from being stolen by the red men, who weren't too persnickety about property rights. Sometimes the sun bathed the travelers in warmth, and sometimes rainstorms bathed them from wild skies. One day in early May, flames rampaged across the horizon — prairie fire! Luckily the wind was in their favor, so the danger evaporated.

The expedition trudged along the shallow Platte River, in some places an amazing mile and a half wide. On May 20, they forded the South Platte to follow the first river, which upstream from here was designated the North Platte.

Herds of buffalo speckled the plains, offering what seemed an inexhaustible larder. As cooking fuel, the travelers burned "prairie coal," or buffalo chips, a resource of marvelous abundance. Sutter spied Chimney Rock on May 26, soaring 500 feet from the prairie, a famous landmark on the trail. Four days later, they toiled across bleak plains to rest several days at palisaded Fort Laramie, a major trading post on the Laramie River near the North Platte. They splashed across the North Platte on June 11 to follow the Sweetwater upstream. Three days later, massive Independence Rock rose on the horizon, lifting abruptly at the Sweetwater. Farther, the Sweetwater criss-crossed the trail in numerous fordings to where it boiled over broken rock in a steep-walled gorge called Devil's Gate.

They crossed the Popo Agie River on June 23 and camped in a cottonwood grove — site of the mountain men's rendezvous, a three-week spree of drinking, gambling, brawling and wenching. Sutter gave a trapper $100 for an Indian guide who could speak English and Spanish. When the trappers adjourned their annual binge, scattering to the four winds, Sutter and several companions including the Indian and the missionaries resumed their trek on horseback along the Oregon Trail.

Three days later, south of the Wind River Range, they rode through a wide sage plain, 7,650-foot South Pass on the Continental Divide — gateway to Oregon. The vast Oregon Territory embraced present-day Oregon, Idaho, Washington, and perhaps expanses of Nevada, Utah and Montana. Even in the July sun, they shivered in chill blasts from snowy peaks as they labored through steep mountains. Now they crossed blistering deserts of southern Idaho to the Hudson's Bay Co. trading post at Fort Hall on "The Bottoms," a bend of the Snake River near today's Pocatello, arriving July 27. Fort Hall commandant Francis Ermatinger protested Sutter's idea of striking southwest to California, saying so small a party was sure to meet trouble from Indians. What to do? Sutter asked. Continue to Fort Vancouver, he said, as winter isn't far off, and snow and cold can be as deadly as Indians in a strange country.

I am a part of all that I have met.
Ulysses

Bellies were hollow with hunger August 15 when they pitched

camp at Fort Boise on the Snake, but roly-poly trader Francis Payette surprised them with a mouth-watering spread: salmon, sturgeon, sweet corn, turnips, milk, butter, melons, pumpkin pie and boiled pudding. This unexpected feast in the wilds may have helped inspire Sutter's legendary hospitality in California to all comers.

A fortnight later, Sutter said farewell to the missionaries at their journey's end, the Whitman Mission. He gave them his French-English dictionary — on display today in the museum at the Whitman National Monument. Sutter and companions rode on to Fort Walla Walla, where Walla Walla River mixes with the Columbia. Now the Oregon Trail took Sutter and companions along the Columbia to The Dalles, a French word meaning rapids running between steep rock walls. As the gorge here was nigh impassable, they struck across the Cascades, wildest and roughest mountains Sutter had ever laid eyes on, Alps and Rockies included. At times they lowered their horses down cliffs on ropes. Once a stream in flood seized their horses and swept them away, but one man managed to rescue them.

Recalled Sutter: "I crossed right strait through thick and thin and arrived to the great astonishment of the inhabitants." Apparently he set a record: "I arrived in 7 days in the Valley of the Willamette, while others with good guides arrived only in 17 days previous my crossing." They canoed down the Willamette to the Columbia and to immense Fort Vancouver, western headquarters of the Hudson's Bay Co.

October leaves were falling and Sutter was itching to rush overland to California before year's end. But 400 miles of merciless wilderness lay between him and the Sacramento River. Chief Trader James Douglas convinced him it would be foolhardy in winter because of deep snow in the Siskiyous and bellicose Indians; in other words, hazardous to his health. One can only speculate on what California's history might have been if Sutter had blundered into the snowy wilds and perished. Douglas, in other words, may have saved New Helvetia before it was even born.

Sutter wangled letters of introduction from Douglas and others and traded a beaver pelt to a visiting Frenchman for a French uniform glittering with gold braid. No ship was bound for San Francisco Bay, so Sutter and only two of his companions, the Indian and a German cabinetmaker, boarded a Hudson's Bay Co. supply bark, *Columbia*, for the Sandwich Islands, gambling that in Honolulu he could catch a California-bound ship. His other companions deemed that too far out of the way, and planned to wait for spring and good trails.

To sail beyond the sunset, and the baths
Of all the western stars.
Ulysses

The *Columbia* sailed past Diamond Head and the grass huts of Waikiki — and Sutter on arrival found he had missed a California-bound ship by six hours. The only ship in the Honolulu port was the 88-ton British brig *Clementine*, which wouldn't sail for nearly five months, then would go to California via, of all places, New Archangel, the Russian fur colony at Sitka, Alaska. Detour upon detour! But Sutter turned the setback into an opportunity to win friends and influence people. Sporting his chichi French uniform, he called on American consul John Coffin Jones, the British consul, and other notables, presenting his letters of introduction. His ingratiating personality augmented his letter portfolio and won him many friends, including King Kamehameha III.

The king, impressed by Sutter's purported military experience, urged him to stay in the islands and assume command of an army he planned to form, in the mode of European monarchs. Sutter regretfully declined, for his heart was set on California. One idly wonders: If he *had* accepted, would Hawaii have had a Sutter's Fort?

Yet the king assigned eight (or 10) Kanakas, including two wives, to go with Sutter to California and help establish his colony. It may seem strange that the king was willing to dispatch some of his people to unknown fates thousands of miles away. But for decades whalers and other captains had recruited Sandwich Islanders, superb sailors and eager for adventure, for voyages all over the Seven Seas.

Sutter also recruited an Irishman, a Belgian and a German. Mostly on credit, he bought provisions, tools, firearms, and three small brass cannon. One merchant allowed him $3,000 in credit, a bill never paid until a decade later when he caught up with Sutter in California. In exchange for his expedition's passage on the *Clementine*, Sutter agreed to serve as supercargo — in charge of commercial affairs. William French, a merchant, also went along, to serve as supercargo after Sutter debarked in California.

A score of friends gathered on the waterfront April 20, 1839, and a slim girl in a grass skirt draped a lei around Sutter's neck. Seconds before lines were cast off, a man with a large bulldog on a leash said he didn't need him, and gave him to Sutter. The valiant dog, whose name is lost to history, one day would save New Helvetia from catastrophe. Sutter yelled farewells as *Clementine*, under command of Capt. John Blinn, sailed away — bound from the tropics to the frozen mountains of Alaska.

The vessel puffs her sail:
There gloom the dark broad seas.
Ulysses

Approaching New Archangel (today's Sitka), the ship threaded an archipelago of green islets to the stronghold flying the double-eagle flag of the Russian-American Fur Co. Mustachioed Gov. Ivan Kouprianoff gloated at *Clementine's* cargo of fresh fruits and vegetables, molasses, salt, sugar, paint and other goods. While trading went on, he invited Sutter, French and Blinn to be his guests at dinner in Baranof Castle. Later they sipped wine and danced in the lofty ballroom. Sutter took the floor with the governor's wife, but felt clumsy, remembering: "I was obliged to dance Russian dances which I had never seen before."

When *Clementine* set sail, Russian cannon thundered a salute. As the ship coasted south, heavy seas pounded it.

It may be that the gulfs will wash us down.
Ulysses

Gale winds played havoc with sails and rigging. *Clementine* limped into San Francisco Bay July 1 with storm damage and dropped its hook in the mud off Yerba Buena (later San Francisco). A mere dozen buildings hunkered on shore. Recalled Sutter: "An Officer and 15 Soldiers came on board and ordered me out, saying Monterey is the Port of entry, & at last I could obtain 48 hours to get provisions (as we were starving) and some repairings done on the Brig."

Monterey, the capital, to Sutter was an unimpressive town of adobe houses teeming with dogs, cats, chickens and naked babies. He marched up a knoll to Gov. Juan Alvarado's imposing whitewashed adobe. Alvarado, 30, examined Sutter's flattering letters from well over a dozen dignitaries. Commented one of Alvarado's aides: "No one has, ever before, come with so many letters." When Sutter broached his plan for a colony, Alvarado told him to help himself to the land he desired, build his colony, come

Custom House where Sutter transacted business in 1839 still stands in Monterey, its interior chock full of typical merchandise of the era.

back in a year, and he would make him a Mexican citizen and give him a deed. Sutter later wrote: "Alvarado was very glad that someone had come who wanted to settle in the wilderness of the Valley of California, where the Indians were very wild and very bad."

> *Come, my friends,*
> *'Tis not too late to seek a newer world.*
> *Ulysses*

Sailing back to San Francisco Bay, Sutter dropped anchor on July 7. With Capt. John Wilson, a new friend from Yerba Buena, he visited Sonoma to call on Gen. Mariano G. Vallejo, military chief of Alta California. Vallejo tried to turn Sutter from his reckless notion, pointing out he could acquire land for a colony near settled areas. Wilson offered to sell Sutter his big ranch in the Sonoma Valley, but Sutter turned him down. "Well, my God!" demanded Wilson, "I'd like to know what you really want!"

Sutter later explained why he would not be swayed: "I wanted to get away from the Spaniards. I wanted to be my own master."

From Sonoma, he traveled to redwood-palisaded Fort Ross on the Sonoma coast to visit Russian governor Baron Alexander Rotcheff and bring salutations from Sitka's governor. Rotcheff, 26, who governed the Czar's most remote outpost in the New World, greeted Sutter cordially and presented him to his wife, lovely Princess Helena de Gagarin. Sutter outlined his plan to settle in the Sacramento Valley. Replied the gallant Rotcheff: "If I can be of service to you, command me."

Clementine was too deep-drafted for the Sacramento River, so Sutter sent it back to the Sandwich islands. From Yerba Buena merchants, he chartered two schooners, *Isabella* and *Nicholas,* and bought a pinnace, a small ship's boat, cramming them with provisions, tools, seeds, guns and powder, much of it bought on credit. Needing an experienced river pilot, Sutter hired Capt. William Heath Davis, age 18, a.k.a. Kanaka Bill because he was born in Hawaii, albeit of Caucasian parents.

Could anyone tell him where to find the Sacramento's mouth? No, not Davis, nor anyone else: "I could find Nobody who could give me information, only that they Knew that some very large rivers are in the interior." Yet he embarked his colonists, who now included several sailors and mechanics from Yerba Buena, and cast off. He didn't know where he was going — but he was on his way!

> *One equal temper of heroic hearts,*
> *Made weak by time and fate, but strong in will*
> *To strive, to seek, to find, and not to yield.*
>
> *Ulysses*

The expedition doubled San Pablo Point and, by the end of the second day, mastered the fast current in Carquinez Strait, entering the rough water of Suisun Bay. They moored at Rancho el Pinole while Sutter visited Ygnacio Martinez in his adobe ranch house. Martinez agreed to supply the new colony, once it became a reality, with food, livestock and other needs — on credit.

The expedition invaded Delta mazes. In the pinnace with four Kanakas on the oars, Sutter scouted ahead, exploring each channel and inlet they chanced upon. He tied pieces of colored cloth to trees to blaze his watery trail. Evenings they camped ashore so Sutter could appraise the terrain as a colony site. Recalled Captain Davis: "When stopping along the bank of the river at night, we could not obtain any rest on account of the immense multitudes of mosquitoes which prevailed." Probing channel after channel, the expedition sailed up the wrong river, the San Joaquin, perhaps as far as today's Stockton. "It took me eight days before I could find the entrance of the Sacramento, as it is very deceiving and very easy to pass by," Sutter wrote.

About 20 miles below today's City of Sacramento, the expedition "fell in with the first Indians which was all armed and painted & looked very hostile; they was about 200 Men," Sutter remembered. As expedition men raised their rifles, Sutter shouted to them to put them down, and not fire unless he gave a direct order. Sutter threw a friendly salute to the Indians and waded ashore, alone and unarmed. Thinking some runaway mission Indians from San Jose might be among them, he trotted out his fragmentary Spanish: *"Adios, amigos! Adios, amigos!"*

The befuddled expedition chief was telling them goodbye! But as he persisted in his friendly jabbering, the Indians no doubt got the drift. As last he remembered the correct greeting: *"Buenas dias!"* He rapped his chest. *"Amigo!"*

One Indian advanced toward Sutter and demanded in pidgin English: "You come in peace, or you come in war?"

Sutter swore he came in peace and wanted to live among them as a friend. As he displayed his farming tools and trade goods, the Indians seemed satisfied.

Farther upstream, the expedition maneuvered past the junction of the American River with the Sacramento. The American struck Sutter as a beautiful river to explore, but he gave orders to follow the Sacramento. Seventeen miles upstream, they reached the Feather where it pours into the Sacramento. After their first encounter with Indians far downstream, later Indians fled at sight of the expedition. Sutter said they "hided themselves in the Bushes, and on the Mouth of Feather River they runned all away so soon they discovered us." At this time, however, he believed the Feather was actually the Sacramento, as the Feather is wider at the mouth than the Sacramento here. And the Sacramento angles in from the west, while the Feather aligns with the Sacramento below the junction.

In the pinnace with Kanakas on the oars, Sutter explored up the Feather 10 or 15 miles until he became convinced they were no longer on the Sacramento. He and the Kanakas returned in darkness to the Feather's mouth, where the schooners lay at anchor. He found the white men in an ugly mood, recalling: "All the white Men came to me and asked me how much longer I intended to travell with them in such a Wilderness. I saw plain that it was a Mutiny." He promised to give them an answer in the morning. At daybreak, he grudgingly gave orders to turn back.

They drifted down to the junction with the American, and sailed up that river as far as the boats could navigate in the dry season. He gave an order, and his motley expedition landed in the heart of the western wilderness. The date: Aug. 12, 1839.

They lashed the boats to trees. Suddenly, potential danger: Several hundred painted Indians — paddling tule canoes and armed with bows and arrows — were approaching. Sutter's men leveled their rifles, prepared for attack, but none materialized. Sutter posted sentries and gave orders to unload and mount the three cannon. His people unshipped all the cargo, pitched tents and lit cook fires. Sutter handed out trinkets to the delighted Indians, then called all hands together. At dawn, he announced, he would send the schooners back to Yerba Buena to fetch more supplies. All who wished to return were free to go. He wanted no malcontents, even if he had to remain in the wilds with only his Kanakas. Six white men opted to return. This would leave Sutter with eight Kanakas, a German, an Irishman, a Belgian, and the Indian who had joined him in the Rockies. In other words, most of Sacramento's original colonizers were Sandwich Islanders, or Hawaiians.

As the sun rose, the schooners cast off. Sutter ordered a farewell salute. Cannon crashed like thunderbolts, firing nine rounds. The cannonade sent hundreds of waterfowl screeching aloft, sent startled wild animals charging to and fro, and staggered the Indians. Cheers rang out from the departing schooners.

Much later the Indians, when on good terms with Sutter, confessed that save for their dread of the big guns they would have murdered the party to get its belongings. Without the deterrence of the cannon, would New Helvetia have been overwhelmed by the Indians? To become only a tantalizing footnote in history, all clues to its fate swallowed by the wilderness, like the Lost Colony of Roanoke, North Carolina?

Sutter dispatched a hunting party, which came back with an elk. Foreseeing flood danger, he moved his band a mile inland to a knoll free of that hazard. The Kanakas began constructing two Hawaiian-style grass shacks, Sacramento's first structures.The king of the Sandwich Islands would be proud.

But Captain Sutter — the presumption of the man! By what right did a fugitive from the law — an outlaw, in short — set himself up as head of such an admittedly historic expedition? By right of sheer audacity, soaring imagination — and the inalienable right of self-appointment. Where did he get his inspiration and knowhow? At the ends of the earth. Whence his tools, weapons and supplies? At earth's ends. And the people to help him? The same.

The people to help him were the original colonists: The Indian, name unknown, the whites — Fredrick Hugel, Louis Morstein and Henry King — and the stout-hearted Sandwich Islanders, who will be delineated in the next chapter.

Commemorating the expedition's immortal landing, a bronze plaque mounted on a huge gristmill grinding stone stood for many years at 29th and B Streets, Sacramento. It was relocated in 1989 to a more agreeable site at 28th and C Streets in Stanford Park. But the actual site where Sutter and his people came ashore, in one of the most momentous landings in the New World, lies somewhere north of the marker, a site ingloriously buried by the city dump.

Chapter 8
The Sandwich Islanders

They (Hawaiians) were the most intelligent, interesting and kind-hearted people I ever fell in with.
*Richard Henry Dana, **Two Years Before the Mast***

Sutter later recollected how he had obtained the services of the islanders:

"The King gave me eight men, all experienced seamen — for three years. I was to pay them $10 a month, and after three years, I was to send them back to the Islands at my own expense, if they wished to leave me. These men were very glad to go with me and at the expiration of their time they would not leave me. Two of them were married and brought their wives with them."

Some people interpret that to mean Sutter was accompanied by 10 Hawaiians. But he wrote it while reminiscing for historian Hubert Bancroft — 37 years afterward. Did his memory play tricks after so many years? For the identities of only eight Hawaiians, including two women, have been established.

Sutter's reminiscence continues: "These women I found very useful in teaching the Indian girls to wash, sew, etc."

He then paid the Hawaiians the supreme compliment when he added: "I could not have settled the country without the aid of these Kanakas. They were always faithful and true to me."

Without the Hawaiians, he is saying, the New Helvetia story would have come to nothing. And what does that say for the whole Sacramento story?

These were the eight identified Hawaiians who came to California to help start his colony:

1. Kanaka Harry, who later became Sutter's head steward at the Hock Farm on the Feather River.
2. Manuiki, Harry's wife.
3. Sam Kapu.
4. Elena, Sam's wife.
5. Maintop, who became captain of Sutter's launch, the *Sacramento,* which linked New Helvetia with the Bay Area.
6. Kanaka Harry's brother, Hukui or Kukui, who drowned in Suisun Bay in 1847 while swimming after a boat.
7. Kanaka Harry's brother-in-law Manuiki, who for some reason bore the same name as his sister, Manuiki.
8. Ioanne Keaala o Kaaina, dubbed John Kelly, who later settled at Yankee Hill near Oroville, Butte County, and married a Maidu woman.

King Kamehameha III of the Sandwich Islands was instrumental in Sacramento's founding.

Sutter's favorite was Manuiki, Kanaka Harry's wife. He apparently appropriated her from Harry. Heinrich Lienhard, Sutter's chief clerk, claimed she was Sutter's common-law-wife and bore him several children. All died in infancy. Lienhard said that when Sutter got bored with Manuiki he gave her back to Harry, then took up with a succession of Indian girls residing in the Fort.

Some of Sutter's Hawaiians, and some Hawaiians who arrived later, established a fishing village at Vernon (today's Verona) at the junction of the Sacramento and Feather, on the east bank, in Sutter County. They called it Puu Hawaii — Hawaii Haven. They engaged in salmon fishing and shipped barrels of salmon to Hawaii and also supplied salmon to Sacramento and the mining camps, and later to local canneries. Few if any Hawaiians live today in Verona, once the scene of a thriving village of Sandwich Islanders so far from home.

Some of the valiant Sandwich Islanders who came with Sutter married Indians and whites of this region, and it is said that some of their descendants live today in Sacramento — the first colonizers of which were mostly the islanders from so far away.

Chapter 9

The Fort in the Wilderness

After the Hawaiians raised their grass shacks, Sutter directed his people to construct a large building. Gradually its thick walls rose as many hands clapped sun-dried adobe bricks into place. The building housed the colony's kitchen, a workshop, storeroom, and Sutter's living quarters. It was finished just as winter rains began to spatter the earth. As 1839 dwindled down, the colonists broke ground for sowing wheat, and also chopped out a road west to an embarcadero on the Sacramento River, and another road north to the American.

And eight more white men arrived to join the colony.

Other than Indians, Sutter and his people were the first permanent settlers in the valley. Sutter called his colony New Helvetia, or New Switzerland. Helvetii were Celtic people in Switzerland in Julius Caesar's time.

Sutter desperately needed food for his people to sustain themselves until they could harvest some crops. He needed horses and oxen to plow the ground, corn and wheat to sow, and cattle to propagate the immense herds he envisioned in his mind's eye. Urgently needing money to buy such essentials, he recruited local Indians to trap beavers, whose skins fetched high prices. One chief helped him train some Indians and dispatch them on winter trapping expeditions near and far. Alas, the Indians had either little talent or little motivation to be trappers, and harvested a pitifully small number of furs. To worsen the situation, scalawag trappers from the Hudson's Bay Co. — flouting laws barring them from California — sometimes cajoled some of Sutter's Indian trappers into swapping their season's accumulation of furs for a jug of whiskey. So Sutter's trapping venture netted only picayune profits.

Meantime, other Indians cleared more land for planting. Still others, to guard against attack by hostiles, began constructing a high adobe wall encompassing a large area around the big house.

To Sutter's numerous wheedlings and cajolings of Bay Area merchants and ranchers for vital supplies — on credit — they responded stintingly, if at all. Nobody had much confidence he would succeed with his lonely colony, beleaguered by wilderness and distance. On the expedition's upriver journey, Sutter had stopped at the ranch of Ygnacio Martinez, who had agreed to supply him with horses, livestock and other needs, on credit, once his colony became a reality. To Sutter, this seemed the time, so he sent two Indians to Martinez with a letter requesting the animals agreed on "so quick as possible." He also needed another yoke of oxen, 10 or a dozen bullocks, several horses and mules, two milk cows, and some young cows. He promised to pay for all these with produce —"goods with which you will be much pleased." He also requested two or three "old Sadles" (saddles). "The Two Indians have no saddles. Please give them some old Sadles." He also petitioned for dried meat, beans, and some Indian corn seed "if you please."

A month later, irked at having received neither goods nor reply, and in even more desperate need, Sutter fired off another letter to Martinez. Two weeks later, still ignored, he dispatched another. On October 23, Martinez at last responded by sending a pathetically small herd of cattle and horses, all in deplorable condition. Token amounts of other goods arrived: dried beef, a tub of tallow, some wheat and beans, all poor quality. In a further letter to Martinez, Sutter complained the wheat was alive with weevils. Martinez had put Sutter's two Indians to work for him during their sojourn at his rancho, but overlooked the matter of paying them for their labor. Sutter called Martinez' attention to that detail, saying gentlemen didn't behave like that. Martinez ignored the slur and demanded that Sutter pay his bill without further procrastination.

The few unprepossessing animals Sutter received on credit from Martinez would in time multiply into herds of tens of thousands.

Now the adobe walls around the Fort, three feet thick, rose to 18

Bastions on Sutter's Fort originally were two stories high, as shown in this drawing by Sacramento artist-historian Ted Baggelmann. One-story bastions prevail in today's restoration.

feet high. Sutter supervised construction of two-story bastions, or towers, with walls five feet thick, projecting at northwest and southeast corners, and with high-pitched tile roofs. Rows of embrasures, or rifle ports, perforated bastion walls on the upper level, while ports on the lower level in time would bristle with cannon. These projecting bastions would enable defenders to pour fire on any attacking force trying to scale the walls. Below each bastion lay a dungeon for punishing malefactors.

The main gate was reinforced by rows upon rows of iron bolts. As added protection, a double row of sharp iron saw-like teeth spanned the top of the gate, to cut the ropes of any grappling irons an enemy might hurl over the gate. Also at the main gate, an Indian sentinel stood by a cannon. At night, an armed squad patrolled outside the walls.

Sutter designed his fort so that only a small band, if that was all he could muster in an emergency, could defend it against legions. The fort would take him four years to complete. Though only half as large as immense Fort Vancouver, it was the biggest and best fort in California, and larger than either Fort Laramie on the Oregon Trail or Bent's Fort on the Santa Fe Trail. Captain Sutter was here to stay, and he had masterplanned his fort so no one could oust him, not multitudes of Indians nor an army with banners.

But Sutter's Fort was destined to never fire its cannon at an enemy, nor ever be besieged. Ironically, it would "fall" at last, but not to an enemy army. All resistance would collapse when the very men Sutter counted on to defend its walls in the hour of peril deserted to join the stampede to the goldfields.

Though the Fort would never be assaulted by a military force, it once almost fell to enemies who came by stealth in darkness. One night in his first winter, Sutter and a young aide Octave Custot, a Frenchman, were chatting in Sutter's quarters. Just then they heard someone cry out. Dashing to the door, they flung it open — and found Sutter's bulldog attacking an Indian. They dragged the dog off the terrified Indian. Very strange, they thought, and went back to Sutter's quarters. A bit later, another wild cry rent the night — and they nabbed another Indian under the same circumstances. Now truly alarmed, Sutter roused the whole Fort to put everyone on the alert. Recalled Sutter: "It appeared that a whole band of Indians had come to kill all of us and seize my settlement. I sewed up the wounds of the savages and told them I would forgive them this time but that further attempts would be met with severe punishment."

Unfortunately, the name of the stout-hearted bulldog that saved New Helvetia from disaster is lost to the record.

This story almost reminds you of how the geese saved the young community of Rome by sounding a raucous alarm as the Barbarians crept toward the sleeping city in the dead of night.

Not long after, Sutter got wind that Indian laborers were smuggling weapons into their quarters. Sutter surmised they were planning an attack, and recollected: "When I asked them why they wanted to kill me, who had treated them very well, they answered that they simply wanted to plunder."

In the spring of 1840, local Indians were growing ever more rambunctious, stealing horses, butchering cattle and giving other signals of mounting resentment. One day all of Sutter's Indian workers were nowhere to be found. Sutter had a hunch they were congregating with the bellicose Cosumnes Indians south of the Cosumnes River, 20 miles to the southeast, perhaps plotting a mass attack on New Helvetia. Sutter calculated that if he waited for them to make the move, he wouldn't have a chance: 10,000 Indians dwelt in the valley and foothills. A preemptive attack might teach them a lesson. He mustered a squad of eight stalwarts and led them, armed and mounted, in darkness to the Cosumnes. Just before dawn, Sutter and his band charged into the hideaway, where 200 or more Indians were sleeping. Blazing guns killed six Indians. "They ceased their resistance and asked for mercy." Sutter said. "None of my men had been killed or wounded. I told them that everything would be forgotten if they would come back to the village and attend to their work as before." The Indians went along with that proposal, and henceforth Sutter found them to be good and faithful workers. Many enlisted in the small army he was organizing.

Sutter loved to impress visitors with his "home guard" of Indian soldiers. He wrote: "The Indian boys were obliged to appear every Sunday morning for drill, well washed and neatly clad. Their uniforms consisted of blue drill pantaloons, white cotton shirts, and red handkerchiefs tied around their heads. They were very proud of this uniform."

Sutter ran his Fort by strict military rule. Not only was a sentry stationed at the gate night and day, but the 15-man home guard of young Indians, neatly dressed in their uniforms, made the rounds at night, marking each half hour with a stroke on the bell and an "All's well!"

In that same year of 1840, Sutter felt obliged to teach a lesson to another band of Indians. He led a mounted posse of 20 men, whites and Indians, in fast pursuit of an Indian raiding party. The miscreants had attacked an Indian rancheria, shot five defending Indians and dashed out the brains of some old women. When Sutter caught up with the villains, he ordered 14 shot by a firing squad.

August of the same year brought cause for celebration, and Sutter fetched his *aguardiente*, a cheap brandy, to do it right: Five white men who had crossed the Rockies with him, but separated in Oregon Territory, had now rejoined him at New Helvetia. That increased the number of people in his colony to 25 — 17 whites and 8 Kanakas.

As Governor Alvarado had told him, to qualify for his immense land grant he would have to become a citizen of Mexico. A year had elapsed since he founded New Helvetia, and it was time to see Alvarado again. Sutter and companions rode horseback over the Livermore Pass to San Jose, changed horses and continued to Monterey, capital of Mexico's Alta California province. Mexican officials no doubt were impressed by this man who boasted he had fought in a revolution as a captain in the Swiss army, and now was taming the Indians that Alvarado had warned him were "very wild and very bad." In a ceremony, Sutter swore allegiance to Mexico, and thus on August 29, 1840, became a naturalized citizen. Alvarado gave him the deed to 11 square leagues (nearly 100 square miles) in the fertile valley. His grant was bounded on the north by the remnants of three volcanoes called Tres Picos (Three Peaks), today known as Sutter Buttes; on the east by "the margins of" the Feather River; on the west by the Sacramento River, and on the south by the parallel of 38 degrees, 49 minutes and 32 seconds of north latitude. In other words, the southern boundary would be about five miles *north* of Sutter's Fort — a gross error that would give rise to no end of hassles when it surfaced during the turbulence climaxed by the Squatters' Riots in Sacramento.

Alvarado appointed Sutter an alcalde, with authority to issue passports, record land titles, and act as justice of the peace. He also designated Sutter the Mexican government's official representative in the Sacramento Valley, and charged him with enforcing laws "to prevent the robberies committed by adventurers of the United States, to prevent the invasion of savage Indians and the hunting and trapping by companies from the Columbia" — that last item being a reference to the Hudson's Bay Co. Sutter's new offices gave him the accouterments he relished: the dazzling uniform of a Mexican army officer, which slaked his thirst for martial pomp and gave authority to his military boasts. Alvarado authorized him to levy his own army, which he had already begun to do. His army in time would number 225 men, a motley band of 100 Indians and some of the wildest and most uncouth frontiersmen who ever wandered into California.

When Sutter and his men rode out of Monterey, homeward bound, half a dozen recruits rode with them. One was a barrelmaker, who became the first black man to settle in the Sacramento Valley, but his name is lost to history.

Sutter was not the first to receive a land grant in the valley. The better part of two decades earlier, John B.R. Cooper arrived in California in 1823. In 1833, having married Encarnacion Vallejo, he petitioned for a land grant, and was given one that straddled the American some miles east of present-day Sacramento. The American then bore the name Rio Ojotska, or River of Hunters, apparently because Russian hunters and trappers frequented this wild country. Two years later, Cooper renounced and forfeited his grant because for some reason he never settled on the land and thus failed to develop it. If Cooper had succeeded, the Sacramento story might have been considerably different. A copy of the map of the Cooper Land Grant, showing the Rio Ojotska, is in the State Archives, with the original in the National Archives.

A famous scientific expedition arrived at New Helvetia on Aug. 23, 1841. When Sutter's Indian fishermen brought news of its approach, a clerk was sent to the landing to identify the people. In six whaleboats, Lt. Cmdr. Cadwalader Ringgold with a company of seven officers and 50 men had rowed upstream from San

Francisco Bay, and stopped to visit Sutter's Fort. They were part of Lt. Charles Wilkes' scientific expedition, first of its kind authorized by Congress. In three years of travel, they had discovered Antarctica and reached California, where Ringgold and his men were detached to explore the Sacramento River.

When Sutter got the news of their approach, he sent them horses, donned his uniform, ran up his flag and fired his cannon — to honor the first official visitors from the United States. He promptly ordered up a banquet. "They were very much interested to find a flourishing establishment in this wilderness," recollected Sutter, "and it made a very good impression upon the Indians to see so many white men visiting me." Sutter entertained his guests by taking them on an elk hunt. The expedition then resumed its upriver journey as far as it could, descending in early September, and stopped here for another visit, camping on the American near the Fort.

Meantime, another Wilkes contingent struck out for Sutter's Fort from the north, from Fort Vancouver, after the expedition ship *Peacock* came to grief on a Columbia River sandbar. For protection in the wilderness, several families bound for Sutter's Fort had joined them. One family consisted of Joel P. Walker, his wife and children. The party rode horses south along Oregon's Willamette River, then crossed the mountains until they found the Sacramento River, and followed it to New Helvetia. Mrs. Walker, carrying her infant daughter Louisa, became the first American woman to reach Sutter's Fort.

Expedition mineralogist James Dwight Dana gave Sutter some vital news, but Sutter failed to recognize its importance at the time. On the trek south, Dana told him, he had seen rocks in many tracts of California that looked like gold-bearing rocks he had encountered elsewhere.

In that same notable year of 1841, the Bartleson-Bidwell party blazed a wagon path cross the Sierra — the California Trail — though they had actually abandoned their wagons in snowdrifts before reaching the Sierra. The party of 31 men, one woman and her infant daughter had been journeying with nine wagons drawn by mules and oxen. In the Forty-Mile Desert west of Humboldt Sink, Nevada, they had had to slaughter their oxen for food. Crossing the Sierra at Sonora, they wandered through bewildering Stanislaus River canyons and finally ate mule meat until they reached the game-rich San Joaquin Valley on October 30. Bidwell, 22, a former teacher, and three companions reached Sutter's Fort on foot from a ranch 100 miles south, where the others split off to trek to coastal settlements. The woman, Nancy Kelsey, carried her baby as she walked barefoot into Doctor John Marsh's ranch in the East Bay Hills near Mt. Diablo. The stalwart Bidwell would become one of Sutter's ablest assistants.

But the most momentous event of that eventful year of 1841 had occurred earlier, on September 4, when the Russian schooner *Constantine* docked at the Sacramento embarcadero, bringing Governor Rotcheff to make Sutter an offer he couldn't refuse.

Chapter 10
The Russian Connection

For a quick sale at only $30,000, the Russians would let Sutter have the whole works — their entire colony in California. Little or nothing was said about the land, as Russia never held title to it. Perhaps the Muscovites hoped Sutter wouldn't notice a trifling detail until too late. Sutter knew a good deal when he saw it. To seal the bargain, he sailed back to San Francisco Bay with Rotcheff aboard the *Constantine*. They landed at San Rafael where, Sutter remembered, "we found horses ready with Russian servants, ready to carry us to Bodega." They visited both the Bodega Bay settlement and Fort Ross, so Sutter could take inventory of what he was purchasing in both places.

The Russian presence in California had begun with high hopes. Colonies of the Russian-American Fur Co. in the Aleutian Islands and at New Archangel (Sitka) were remote from trade routes and were suffering food scarcities. As sunny California looked promising, Russians in 1805 sailed south to San Francisco Bay and even as far as the Channel Islands off southern California, questing for sea otters and fur seals. If they had found enough there, they might have clung to that California region, and it's not too far-fetched to imagine that Los Angelenos today might be addressing each other as "Tovarish" (comrade).

Count Nikolai Rezanoff, chamberlain of the Czar, found New Archangel's people starving when he arrived in 1806. He sailed to

San Francisco Bay — where the Spanish told him no foreigners were allowed to enter. But this was an emergency: He desperately needed food. At the Presidio of Yerba Buena, he tendered his petition seeking relief for Sitka. The Spanish greeted him courteously, but must have guessed he was up to no good — probably scouting the chances for a Russian colony.

In one of history's most poignant romances, Rezanoff won the heart of Concepcion de Arguello, daughter of the Presidio's commandante, and reputedly the most beautiful woman in California. After announcing their engagement, he got his needed supplies. The Russians were delighted: The betrothal was a diplomatic coup.

On May 21, 1806, a month and a half after his arrival, Rezanoff sailed back to starving Sitka with food. He then departed for St. Petersburg, today's Leningrad, apparently to seek the Czar's authority to wed Concepcion. Crossing Siberian wastes on horseback, he became ill. Approaching Krasnoyarsk, he fell off his horse, which kicked him in the head. He died March 8, 1807, and was buried there. One might say Concepcion's heart was buried there too, for she remained faithful to his memory, rejecting all other marriage offers, and became a nun.

At Bodega Bay in 1809, Ivan Kuskoff and his expedition of Aleut hunters dropped anchor. Their hunting tactic was to form a circle with two-man kayaks, and close in, harpooning otters as they surfaced to breathe. Sometimes they held a captive otter pup so its distress cries would lure mature otters into harpoon range. Laden with 2,350 pelts, they sailed back to Alaska. Kuskoff also confirmed Rezanoff's observation that this coast was unoccupied and seemed ideal for a Russian outpost. The Spanish had correctly divined Rezanoff's motive.

Kuskoff returned in late 1811 with an expedition of 80 Aleut hunters. He annexed the Bodega region for the Czar after the Indians signed an agreement to exchange their spacious Sonoma lands for four strings of beads, three hoes, three pair of breeches, and two axes — a transaction that calls to mind the famous Manhattan exchange. In 1812, a crew of 95 Russians and 40 Aleuts built a fort — Fort Ross — on a bluff overwatching a cove 10 miles north of the Russian River, then called the Slavianka. Ross was named for *Rossiya*, of course. Encompassed by a redwood stockade, the stronghold included two blockhouses defended by cannon, and scores of other buildings. It would serve as headquarters for the sea-otter trade, for growing crops to feed the

Alaskan colonies, and to expand their grip on the Pacific coast. For six months, no other nation including Spain got wind of what was happening at Fort Ross.

When the Spanish learned of it, they clashed with the Russians over the lucrative sea-otter trade. Deeming the Russians trespassers and fearing their encroachment, the Spanish closed San Francisco Bay to the Russians and prohibited anyone from dealing with them. Yet exchanges of goods and services took place anyway, with the Russians buying grain and beef for their Alaskan colonies and selling the Spanish kitchen utensils and other items crafted by Russians.

The Russians also laid out three ranches, one at the mouth of the Slavianka (Russian) River, and a warehouse at Russian Gulch, 65 miles north of the fort. Sebastopol in Sonoma County has no connection with the Russian occupation, having been named by enthusiastic Americans after a famous victory in the Crimean War of 1853-56.

The Czar in 1821 issued a ukase closing the coast north of San Francisco Bay to all but Russian vessels — the audacity of which precipitated the 1823 Monroe Doctrine declaring the New World closed to aggression and expansion by European powers. In that same year, Mexico won its independence from Spain and Mexican officials, like the Spanish, regarded the Russian toehold in California as a peril. But economics, not politics, spurred the Russian pull-out. From 1812, when they harvested 40,000 furs, the annual crop had dwindled to less than 400, a pitiful 1 percent of the first year. With otters near extinction, the Russians accelerated their farming efforts — in vain. They lacked a green thumb. Rabbits and gophers literally had a field day in their orchards and vegetable gardens. If the Russians had killed as many varmints as they did otters, they might have turned the corner. So varmints helped change California history by eating the Russians out of house and fort. Disenchantment with crop failures and meager harvests of furs added up to failure of the colony, so the Czar in 1839 ordered the colonists to sell out and go back to Alaska, ending 27 years in California. Sutter had not been aware of the Czar's decision to unload.

Now Sutter and the Russians got down to business. In exchange for buildings, livestock, implements, stores and the schooner *Constantine*, the Russians demanded a $2,000 cash down payment plus the equivalent of $30,000, mostly in produce, paid over four years, making $32,000 the actual purchase price. The contract expressly excluded the land, as the Russians didn't have title. Sutter, mortgaging New Helvetia as security, agreed to make payments as follows: first and second year, $5,000 in produce annually; third year, $10,000 in produce; fourth year, $10,000 in coin. Each produce shipment would consist of 1,600 bushels of wheat, with smaller amounts of peas, beans, soap, suet and tallow. The Russians each year would send a vessel to New Helvetia to embark the produce. With both parties agreeing on terms, they boarded the *Helena* anchored at Bodega. "We had a grand dinner on board," Sutter remembered. "Champagne flowed freely; the Emperor's health was drank and the health of the new owner of Ross and Bodega."

One wonders if the Russians laughed up their sleeves at finding a fool at last to buy this godforsaken territory, especially as negotiations with three other potential buyers had come to naught:

—In April 1840 they offered the colony to the Hudson's Bay Co. for $30,000, but the Canadians apparently weren't interested, for they neglected to respond.

—The Russians rejected a $20,000 offer from Jacob Leese, a Yerba Buena merchant.

—On Feb. 16, 1841, they offered it to the Mexicans for 30,000 pesos. But as the Russians held no title to the land, the Mexicans determined to wait for them to pull out, then seize whatever they left. The buildings also belonged to the Mexican government, argued General Vallejo in a letter to Governor Alvarado, "on account of having been constructed on national ground and with materials from the same land." Mexico "could not, without loss of dignity, buy what already unquestionably belongs to it," he added.

Alvarado expressed fear that the Russians — as they apparently had threatened — would burn down the buildings rather than leave without selling them. He called this "barbaric." When Sutter learned of that, he commented in a letter: "Nobody but a Russian would act like that."

This is what Sutter received in his momentous transaction with the agents of the Czar of Russia: 1,700 cows, calves and oxen, nearly 1,000 horses and mules, 1,000 sheep, numerous tools, plows, carts, corrals, a tannery, a dairy, a boathouse, two kayaks, a fishing boat, a canoe, two windmills, a millstone, a horse-powered mill and stone; two machines, one for beating tan bark and one for grinding it; houses, storehouses, barracks — all the lumber he needed to finish his New Helvetia Fort. He also received all the other moveable property at Bodega and three area ranches. He acquired an arsenal of weapons and ammunition, including several score French flintlock muskets said to have been abandoned by Napoleon's Grand Armee in its catastrophic 1812 retreat from Moscow. He obtained a fine brass field piece mounted on a caisson, cast in St. Petersburg in 1804 and fired in 1812 at Napoleon.

Also in 1841, Sutter bought six larger cannon from a friend, captain of an Italian ship, who had picked them up in South America. Sutter also purchased other cannon from other ships, and he had brought three cannon from the Sandwich Islands. One might say Sutter was well cannonized.

Sutter obtained so much ammunition in his deal with the Russians that he later boasted: "At times I had more amunition (sic) stored up than the whole California Government possessed."

As Sutter prepared to close his transaction with the Russians, a thought occurred. Recalled he: "I wanted some of the Russians to remain with me as hired men, but the officers told me I could do nothing with them, that they could scarcely manage them, & that they were sure I could not be severe enough." They embarked in a small boat and sailed into the Golden Gate to Yerba Buena. "The boat was manned by four powerful Russians," Sutter remembered. "Rotcheff accompanied me. The tide was against us, the sea ran high and we narrowly escaped drowning. I said to Rotcheff, your tyranny over your men is so complete that they will carry you to destruction if you tell them to."

Baron Alexander Rotcheff (or Rotchev), depicted in later life, was only 26 when he welcomed Sutter at the Czar's most remote outpost in the New World.

At Yerba Buena, they stopped at the Hudson's Bay Co. office where the town's alcalde joined them to witness execution of the legal papers. Sutter gave the Russians $2,000 in cash.

And the Lord of New Helvetia had gotten his hands on all the Czar's possessions in the most farflung outpost in the New World.

The Russians began to abandon their holdings, and finally evacuated Fort Ross in 1841, and sailed back to Alaska on Jan. 1, 1842.

Back in New Helvetia, Sutter dispatched John Bidwell to Fort Ross to take charge of what must be one of the world-record "moving days." The big move would take two years. Bidwell, 22, was the stout-hearted man who earlier in 1841 had helped pioneer the California Trail over the Sierra. Sutter assigned the schooner *Constantine,* renamed *Sacramento*, to ship everything but the livestock to New Helvetia. As early as Sept. 28, 1841, he sent some Mexican and Indian vaqueros to begin driving the horses and cattle to New Helvetia. All the animals made it except 100 sheep, drowned while fording the Sacramento River. Vaqueros recovered the bodies and salvaged the precious hides, then known as "California banknotes."

The big move included Princess Gagarin's cherished greenhouse, which she had implored Sutter to rebuild at the Fort, as she could not take it with her. Sutter swore he would. His workers shipped the dismantled sections to the embarcadero on the Sacramento, carted them to the Fort, and laid them out on the ground. For some reason, it proved to be a jigsaw puzzle nobody could solve, try as they might. Sutter rued breaking his promise, but salvaged the glass and installed it in various Fort windows — so the greenhouse did serve a purpose, if not the one intended.

Only one problem: Sutter delighted in firing his cannon for ceremonial reasons, and every time he did there was heard a cascade of tinkling glass.

Sutter said the Russians treated him liberally. The vessel that came to collect the produce installments brought him vital supplies such as iron, steel and ammunition.

The roguish Sutter had tried to slip one over on the Mexicans, but failed. Somehow he obtained a duplicate deed, never recorded, which said that Fort Ross and Bodega were "delivered to his indisputable possession with all lands." At some future time, he hoped to find a chance to switch deeds. He bragged about this in his 1876 memoir: "After I had bought Fort Ross, I informed the Mexican government of my purchase and asked for a title. I was informed, however, that the Russians had no title to the land and hence no right to sell it to me. If I had had a few thousand dollars of ready cash, I could easily have secured the legal title. Money made the Mexican authorities see anything."

Put the case that Sutter hadn't been here for the Russians to sell

Sheep graze today at Fort Ross where the Russian Bear ruled an empire yesterday.

out to, and time passed and no other buyer turned up — and suddenly it was 1848, the golden year. Would the Muscovite empire have girded itself to cling to this surprising land with all its strength? If so, who knows what California's history might have been?

Chapter 11
The Splendid Little War

Cry "Havoc," and let slip the dogs of war.
Shakespeare's Julius Caesar

On the frosty New Year's Day of 1845 at New Helvetia, Captain Sutter, sporting his natty French uniform *cum* gold-handled sword, swung aboard his silver palomino. Now he set about mustering some 220 men — some on whickering horses, some afoot — into a proper column. Shouting men and prancing horses exhaled white plumes. When everyone had fallen in, Sutter rode to the head of the column, unsheathed his sword and raised it high: *"Forward — Ho!"* Saddle leather creaked and spurs jingled as the expedition began its march, headed south.

Behind Sutter rode his aide John Bidwell and a squadron of men on horseback. Then came the men on foot, headed by a youth pounding a bass drum, three others rolling sticks on snare drums, and a lad tootling a fife. Next followed 85 riflemen in garb of trappers, settlers and assorted other adventurers, and they were followed by 100 Indian soldiers strutting in their uniforms. In the rear marched some artillerymen goading a yoke of oxen that dragged the brass field cannon, rumbling along on its caisson, and then more oxen lugging supply wagons. Sutter and his gallant little army were off to war, to join Gov. Manuel Micheltorena in his campaign to crush a nasty rebellion.

"We left the fort with music and colors flying," recalled Sutter.

They also left the fort garrisoned by 15 white men and 30 Indian soldiers.

The rebellion had been brewing for some time, and Sutter was indirectly to blame. In 1842, Mexico's president Antonio Lopez de Santa Anna — the same who overwhelmed the Alamo in 1836 —vexed by rising numbers of Yankees drifting into California, with their threat to Mexican authority, dispatched 500 soldiers to California under a new governor, Brig. Gen. Manuel Micheltorena. His orders were to seize the government from Gov. Juan Alvarado and strictly enforce laws that permitted only Mexican nationals to own land or settle in California.

Most of his 500 soldiers were fractious ex-convicts, sent to California not only to beef up its defenses, but at the same time to get rid of their obnoxious presences. Mexican officials also hoped to get rid of Sutter. Micheltorena departed for California with orders "to put Sutter in order or root him out."

But Sutter was not about to be rooted out.

His waxing strength and independence, plus his hospitality to all arriving gringos, made him the object of suspicion and hostility. Letting him settle in the valley — Mexican officials realized too late — enticed the very sort of rascals they most wanted to keep out: gringo trappers, hunters, sailors, and other unsavory adventurers. The overland migration into California was still only a small leak in the levee, but Sutter had put out the welcome mat for all newcomers, and was doing all he could to urge more to follow.

British as well as Mexicans regarded Sutter as a monumental nuisance. Sir George Simpson, western governor of the Hudson's Bay Co., wrote of him to the company in London: "Now that he has, I may say, defrauded almost every one with whom he has come into contact, he has seated himself down in a stronghold on the Sacramento, surrounded and protected by a body of runaway sailors, vagabond trappers from the United States, and other desperadoes, bidding defiance not only to creditors but even to the public authorities and the laws of the country."

By the time Micheltorena had traveled north to Monterey with his army of ex-convicts, known as *cholos*, in the autumn of 1842, death and illness had decimated his force to only 300. As the new governor, Micheltorena seemed a straight shooter: He returned church property appropriated a decade earlier, founded an educational system, and initiated reforms to ease political strains between northern and southern California. But his cholos nullified his good deeds by going on a stealing spree that got the whole population in a lather. So ex-governor Alvarado (Sutter's benefactor) and General Jose Castro hatched a conspiracy to rid the province of Micheltorena and his detested cholos.

Sutter had become friendly with Micheltorena, who had appointed him a general in command of the army of the northern frontier, and charged him with recruiting volunteers, promising them land grants. With the rebellion boiling, Sutter felt he had to cast his lot with Micheltorena. No doubt he felt guilt pangs in opposing Alvarado, who had bestowed on him the immense New Helvetia grant. Alvarado minced no words in his opinion of the man he had befriended, calling Sutter "an ungrateful villain."

Sutter wrote a letter to merchant Jacob Leese of Yerba Buena, confident Leese would transmit its contents to Alvarado and Castro. It was a letter replete with fine bombast and braggadocio, designed to daunt Alvarado and Castro, in case they might think he was a pushover: "I am strong enough to hold me till the couriers go to the Willamette to raise about 60 or 70 men. Another party I would dispatch to the mountains and call on hunters and Shawnees and Delawares, with whom I am well acquainted. The same party then to go to the Missouri and raise 200 or 300 men more. That is my intention, sir, if they let me not alone. If they will give me satisfaction and pay the expenses which I have had to make for my security here, I will be a faithful Mexican. But when this rascal, Castro, comes here, a very warm and hearty welcome is prepared for him. Ten guns are well mounted to protect the fortress, and two field pieces. I have also about 50 faithful Indians who shoot their muskets very quickly."

One can almost see the loyal fighting men, near and far — should they receive the call — picking up their muskets and setting out on the march to join their bold commander.

General Castro had assumed command of the rebels. Alvarado could have been the leader but, at one time a rapid-rising young politico, he had gotten his nose too far into the bottle and turned into a lush. Neverthless, he joined the rebels.

In November 1844 the rebels launched their campaign with surprise attacks. First they stole all the government horses from Monterey, hamstringing the governor by instantly converting his proud cavalry to disgruntled infantry. The rebels then captured arms and ammunition at San Juan Bautista, rallied Californians to the flag of rebellion, and laid siege to Monterey.

Sutter was now "in a state of war," he declared in a letter December 13, 1844, adding: "Every day, drilling goes on. I have a strong garrison and several thousand Indians who have all been notified and are ready for service in a moment."

And on New Year's Day 1845, responding to an urgent summons from Micheltorena for help, Sutter led his expeditionary force — the strongest ever seen in California — southward to relieve Micheltorena, besieged in Monterey.

The jittery rebels, getting wind that Micheltorena's force would be more than doubled when Sutter's army reached the scene, abandoned their siege of Monterey and lit out southward, headed for the pueblo of Los Angeles, a nest of rebel sympathizers. At the Salinas River on January 9, Sutter's 220 men linked up with Micheltorena's 180-man army, and took off after the rebels. They followed them in two columns, Sutter commanding one and Micheltorena the other.

Nearly a month elapsed as they trekked 200 miles from the Salinas Valley to Santa Barbara, vainly trying to catch up with the rebels. Rain fell in torrents. Meager food and nights spent in sopping blankets increased the disenchantment among Sutter's men. Everything was in short supply except rain, muddy trails and foul tempers. Many men deserted, returning to their valley farms or haunts. Worse, some sneaked away to hitch up with the rebels, reckoning they had more to gain there.

Micheltorena, to gain allies to help him pulverize the rebels, had promised numerous land grants to his supporters. In 1844, he had signed 33 petitions for land grants in the Sacramento Valley, to "buy" support for his teetering administration. For the same reason, he had also promised Sutter a big new land grant. Now, in Santa Barbara on Feb. 5, 1845, he kept his promise to Sutter, granting him 22 square leagues, or 229 square miles. Sutter with his original grant of 11 square leagues, and his sizeable holdings at Fort Ross and Bodega, now possessed an empire of formidable dimensions. The new *Sobrante* (surplus) grant tripled his holdings.

Over the mountain pass south of Santa Barbara, the weary soldiers of the Sutter-Micheltorena army dragged themselves and their arms and baggages, and at last tramped into the valley beyond. Desertions had dwindled Sutter's once-proud army to a mere 50 woebegone soldiers. But a bit of good news: Some of the stragglers were drifting back, bolstering Sutter's force — and his spirits. Sutter reckoned he and Micheltorena had about 300 men, and the enemy double that. Other reports, however, estimate about 400 on each side as a clash with the enemy loomed.

Sutter tells how it was: "During the night it rained very hard. The hills became slippery, men and horses fell and rolled down the ravines. When day broke I found myself in sight of the Mission Buena Ventura, but not more than half of my command had come up. A council of war was held." Capt. John Gantt, in command of the Yankee riflemen, believed that not half the guns would fire, because of rain-soaked powder, and Lt. Felix Valdez didn't think they were strong enough to attack. A man identified only as Estrada, probably an officer, deemed an attack in broad daylight inadvisable. Sutter continued: "Only the captain of the Indians, Ernst Rufus . . . was confident, and said that the muskets of his company were in good order, for his Indians had taken care of them."

It was now drizzling, but Sutter was eager to attack, believing the foul weather would help them take the rebels by surprise. Also, scouts reported that the rebels had danced a fandango at the mission the previous night, and were probably still half-drunk and asleep. Recalled Sutter: "Taking as many men as I could gather, I made a charge upon the town." Sutter led the cavalry, swinging his sword and yelling encouragement to his men as they galloped through muddy streets. "The merry-makers of yesterday were pamic-stricken and fled in every direction. Since we came out of the woods, they could not tell how strong we were; hence they did not stop running until they came to an open space about three-quarters of a mile away where they tried to form ranks. They began to swear at us, as was their fashion, calling us thieves and all kinds of bad names."

General Castro later said he ordered the withdrawal because the downpour on the previous night had wet his soldiers' powder, rendering their rifles temporarily *hors de combat*.

Sutter dispatched Bidwell to ask Micheltorena's permission to pursue the retreating rebels. Micheltorena declined permission, saying his infantry wouldn't be able to keep up with Sutter's cavalry, and it would be risky to divide the force. Sutter later lamented: "If we had followed up on our advantage, we could have easily routed them."

A few days later after this bloodless victory at Buena Ventura (present-day Ventura), the Micheltorena-Sutter army pitched camp near the old Cahuenga Adobe in the San Fernando Valley. Meantime the Castro-Alvarado army had retreated all the way to Los Angeles, where its soldiers fomented rumors that Micheltorena's cholos were coming on fast, committing atrocities, and would terrorize the whole population if they captured Los

Angeles. Almost every able-bodied man joined the rebel army, vowing to hurl back the invaders. This tripled the size of the rebel force. Among the new recruits were 75 Americans. On February 19, the bolstered rebel army marched out of Los Angeles, vowing to stop Micheltorena in his tracks. They found the Micheltorena-Sutter force encamped near the Cahuenga Adobe, near Lookout Mountain.

That night, with the armies bivouacked on opposite sides of an arroyo, soldiers on each side stared at the constellation of campfires on opposite hills. A sudden windstorm blew tents down and whirled burning embers far away into the darkness. None of the soldiers got much sleep that night, knowing daylight would put them to the supreme test of combat, as each army summoned up all its nerve, sinew and muscle in a desperate effort to annihilate the other. Sutter — in an imprudent moment, hoping for victory the next day — urged his men to give "no quarter" to rebels, once they got them on the run. It was almost a fatal mistake for Sutter.

As the winter sun gilded the hills on February 20, tendrils of mist rose from the cold ground. Horses whinnied and stamped, sensing the tension. Sutter on his palomino pranced around to keep his cavalry unit in formation. Feet pounded as Micheltorena's army shifted into position. Micheltorena spoke to an aide, who yelled a command: The fifer tootled, the bass drum boomed and snare drums rattled, martial airs to galvanize the soldiers forward — into the jaws of death. Foot soldiers tramped down the hill, rifles at port arms.

Micheltorena, on horseback, commanded the infantry and artillery, and Sutter the cavalry. The joint army picked its way down the hill, ever closer to the enemy. Micheltorena shouted another command. An artilleryman on the cannon caisson drew his oxen to a halt. Other gunners unlimbered the piece. One artilleryman loaded a charge into the muzzle, tamped it in, then rolled in a cannonball, and stood at attention. Micheltorena: "Aim at their artillery, when I give the word to fire."

Just then in the gray mist shrouding the opposite hillside, a spurt of flame and a cloud of smoke bloomed like a flower — and a *boom!* echoed across the arroyo. A cannonball screeched through the air and smacked into the hillside near Sutter's cavalry, spraying geysers of dirt. Horses screamed and men plunged to the ground, but neither man nor animal was hit.

Micheltorena's cannon opened up with an ear-shattering blast, and white smoke pungent with burnt powder wafted across the hillside. On the opposite hill, a rebel cannon collapsed, its wheel smashed. Good shot, Sutter thought, recalling: "The enemy became frightened and those in charge of the cannon took to their heels."

Now it became a duel between cannon, as the armies were too far apart for effective rifle fire. Micheltorena's cannon erupted with thunderclaps, firing 100 rounds of grapeshot. Castro's gunners responded with cannonballs, then apparently ran out of balls, for they began firing water-rounded stones. Incredibly, the cannonade killed no one, nor does the record list any injuries to men. A mule, beheaded by a cannonball, evidently was the only casualty. Micheltorena sent a message to Captain Gantt's Yankee rifles, ordering them to advance to a position along the river. As they approached within range of the enemy, the *pop-pop-pop* of musketry from both sides reverberated through the arroyo. Unbelievably, still there were no casualties. One report says Americans on each side perceived fellow Americans on the other — so they fired into the air.

Sutter thought things were going too slowly, and later rued another lost opportunity: "Had we rushed upon them immediately, we might have secured the victory."

Now the foot soldiers on each side were getting closer looks at the soldiers in front. Not only did each side descry fellow Americans opposite, many even spotted old acquaintances. The air rang with shouts of surprise, yells of recognition, and friendly jeers and oaths.

"Why the hell are we fighting fellow Americans in some Mexican squabble? It don't make sense!"

"It don't concern us!"

Some of Micheltorena's Americans told Americans on the rebel side of Sutter's "No quarter!" order.

"We'll nail him to a cross!" one yelled. Others loudly seconded the motion.

Meanwhile in Micheltorena's position, a puzzled Sutter said: "I'll go and see why Gantt doesn't advance."

He motioned Bidwell to follow. They worked their way down the hill. To Sutter's astonishment, rebellion was being hatched: "I found his men casting ballots to determine whether they would stay on our side or go over to the enemy."

He fixed Gantt with angry eyes. "What do you *mean* by not obeying orders?"

Gantt remained unfazed. "We're voting to see who wants to stay on this side and who wants to go over to the other side."

"Voting which side to fight on?"

An infection of democracy in the autocratic art of war? Oh, the shame of it! "This is the time to *fight,* not vote," Sutter spluttered. "I've never *heard* of anything so stupid!"

He continued to harangue Gantt and his confused men, explaining where their loyalties lay, that it would be better for them if they stuck with Micheltorena. "Don't forget, he's promised everyone a piece of land, for supporting him."

Yet the more the Americans pondered the dilemma, the clearer the answer in their minds: Americans were not about to shoot fellow Americans in a Mexican quarrel.

Gantt: "Some of the Yankees over yonder say they're gonna nail you to a cross, if they catch you."

"Nail me to a cross?" Sutter sagged, shocked and depressed by this unpredictable turn. The Americans had decided not to fight any longer —it was a hell of a way to run a war. "I'll have to report this to the Governor," he told Gantt.

He and Bidwell started to trudge back up the hill toward Micheltorena, their minds dazed by depressing thoughts. Just then they found themselves surrounded by a platoon of rebels, rifles at the ready. Exactly how they blundered into this contingent is unclear in the records. Resistance would have been folly. They raised their hands in surrender. They were prisoners of war!

Luckily at first no one recognized Sutter, who had promised the rebels "no quarter," or he himself might have received none. Just then a man named Antonio Castro came up and recognized Sutter — and it was a terrible moment for Sutter when he saw Castro, as the rebels had threatened to crucify him. Fortunately for Sutter, Castro had friendly feelings toward Sutter. "I'll take over your prisoners," he told the other men. Saluting Sutter — but without betraying his identity — he said, "I'm very glad you're here."

After a couple of seconds of silence, Sutter muttered the only words he could think of: "Yes, but I'm not."

As rebel guards escorted Sutter into a room of the Cahuenga Adobe, one guard tapped Sutter and motioned for him to leave his shotgun outside the door. The firearm was Sutter's cherished double-barrel piece. He would never see it again.

After a short imprisonment in the adobe building, a rebel patrol conducted Sutter, Bidwell and a few other prisoners to Los Angeles, where they locked them in the house of one Abel Stearns. Stearns, a naturalized Mexican citizen, and officer, and married to a daughter in the aristocracy, was a rebel sympathizer. As Sutter languished in a dismal chamber, suddenly a key turned and the door was flung open. An officer and a soldier stepped in, while another rebel remained outside on guard."Give me your sword, sir," the officer demanded.

Recalled Sutter: "As I handed it to him, I thought to myself that things really looked dark to me." He still dreaded being nailed to a cross.

Behind the officer, Sutter glimpsed a familiar face — an officer he knew well, Eugenio Montenegro, a cavalry captain. He crooked a finger at Montenegro, who stepped into the room. Evidently Sutter knew Montenegro also had friendly feelings toward him, and would not betray him. "You can do me a great favor," Sutter confided. "Tell your superiors that they know nothing of the usages of war, if they put an officer of my rank under common guard!"

It worked like a charm. The rebel soldiers, perhaps hypersensitive to any hint they were ignorant of the fine points of their profession, figured this spiffily-accoutered officer must know what he's talking about. They invited Sutter into another room to join some rebel officers, who were conversing and restoring their morale with generous libations of aguardiente.

Yet Sutter was still dreading that at any moment he might be identified as the "no quarter" villain, and be taken out to face a firing squad of short-fused rebels. Just then he remembered something. After all, Governor Micheltorena had *ordered* Sutter, a general in the Mexican army, to join him with a military force. By God, he was only following orders, and therefore shouldn't be treated as a traitor! He begged his captors to let him rummage in his confiscated saddlebags. Reluctantly they assented.

At last! The very written order — proof he had merely been following orders, like any faithful soldier! He waved the paper high in triumph. Would they like him better if he was a scalawag traitor? Now that the war was over, and Pio Pico, a Los Angeles politician, had already been elected the new governor by the rebels, why, he was perfectly willing to swear an oath of loyalty to the new government. That threw a whole new light on the situation. Castro and others scrutinized the order and pondered Sutter's case anew. At last they agreed to release him. By the terms of the release, Sutter agreed to uphold the new regime.

Meanwhile, desertions of Americans had reduced Micheltorena's already dwindled army to where he deemed further struggle futile. On the morning of February 21 (the day after Sutter's capture), he pulled back to a nearby rancho ironically named Los Feliz — an infelicitous place for Micheltorena — and ordered the white flag hoisted. A day later, surrender documents were signed by both sides.

So ended one of history's most unusual wars, in that every man lived to tell the tale.

The magnanimous victors gave amnesty to all the vanquished, promising not to punish any who had taken up arms against them. Micheltorena promised to lead the remnants of his cholo army to San Pedro, there to board a ship to take them back where they came from. Sutter, Bidwell and the others who had been locked up were released after swearing oaths of loyalty to Castro and Alvarado.

Jim Beckwourth, a black mountain man serving in the Castro-Alvarado army, later said he imagined the Americans who had threatened to crucify Sutter did it only to frighten him because of his callous no-quarter order.

In terms of materiel, Sutter complained he had been the big loser

Black mountain man Jim Beckwourth campaigned with the rebels. Fuming because he wasn't paid for his services, he stole thousands of horses from Mexican ranchers. In 1850, he discovered a new pass in the northern Sierra. Beckwourth Pass memorializes him. Courtesy Department of Parks and Recreation.

Los Angeles high-rises tower over the once-isolated Cahuenga Adobe where Captain Sutter cooled his heels as a prisoner of war.

in the war: "I had fitted out most of the men at my expense, and failing in my purpose, lost it all — money, horses, arms, and provisions." The campaign had cost him 150 horses, badly needed to transport the expedition back home. They were stranded 500 miles from New Helvetia, with nearly 200 men, without horses and food, and almost without weapons. The Mexicans had declined to give back any of the spoils of war, and Sutter had no money to buy horses with. Luckily he did manage to purchase some — on credit, as usual — from a Los Angeles man he had befriended in earlier times at New Helvetia.

In mid-March, Sutter's defeated army picked up the long trail home, all riding on Sutter's newly-acquired horses. But they had no food, or money to buy any. Yet somehow they made it back, living off the land, swimming rivers, and taking pains to avoid Indians, since they had few arms to defend themselves with.

On April 1, 1845 — precisely three months from their departure — they rode back into Sutter's Fort. "I was really the greatest sufferer," Sutter complained. "Defeat meant much more to me than to the Governor."

Perhaps Micheltorena, who lost his governorship in the ignominy of defeat, and was sent to the dreary outpost of San Blas, might have begged to differ. Micheltorena's defeat obviously jeopardized all of Sutter's immense holdings, yet for some reason the new government honored his land grants — even the Sobrante grant given him by the deposed governor, who had taken up arms against them.

Today the Cahuenga Adobe — where Sutter was briefly imprisoned, and near where the climactic battle of the splendid little war was fought — still stands, at 3919 Lankershim Blvd., Van Nuys, preserved by the City of Los Angeles in a memorial park, engulfed by the L.A. megalopolis.

With Spanish-tile roof, gardens and a fountain, the once-isolated Adobe huddles in the shadow of high-rises amid traffic's roar.

It is famous for another reason. A bronze plaque notes that Andres Pico, commanding Mexico's forces, and Lt. Col. John C. Fremont here in 1847 signed the Treaty of Cahuenga, whereby the United States acquired California — validated in 1848 by the Treaty of Guadalupe.

But to Sacramentans, it may be more intriguing as the hacienda where Sutter was held prisoner of war.

Happy as Sutter was to be back home in New Helvetia, he was dismayed to find nothing but trouble.

Chapter 12
The Captain and the Indians

Lo, the poor Indian!
Alexander Pope

Sutter's treatment of the Indians constitutes a dark and sorry chapter in the New Helvetia story. Sutter excused himself by saying that other whites and the Mexicans treated the Indians the same way in that time and, he said, some Indians treated their own race as shabbily.

Dr. G.M. Waseurtz, Swedish naturalist and artist visiting Sutter in 1842, described mealtime for the Indians: "I could not reconcile my feelings to see these fellows being driven, as it were, around some narrow troughs of hollow tree trunks, out of which, crouched on their haunches, they fed more like beasts than human beings, using their hands in hurried manner to convey to their mouths the thin porage which was served to them. Soon they filed off to the fields having, I fancy, half satisfied their physical wants." By contrast, Sutter served Waseurtz a lavish breakfast of "beefsteak, tea, butter with coarse bread, eggs, beans, etc., etc."

Even a mountain man, accustomed to the most rough-and-ready kind of mealtimes, was shocked by the way Sutter fed his Indian workers. A scene similar to that reported by Waseurtz was recounted in 1845 by James Clyman, Virginia-born mountain man. "The Capt. (Sutter) keeps 600 or 800 Indians in a complete state of Slavery and as I had the mortification of seeing them dine I may give you a short description. 10 or 15 Troughs 3 or 4 feet long were brought out of the cook room and seated in the Broiling sun. All the Labourers grate and small ran to the troughs like so many pigs and fed themselves with their hands as long as the troughs contain even a moisture."

Another observer: In 1847, William A. Trubody, whose father helped Sutter build a gristmill, wrote: "Sutter and Bidwell (the storekeeper and clerk) had lots of Indians .... Sutter used to kill a beef, take the best, and the poor cuts and things they'd give to the Indians — also some liquor .... One day father sent Josiah, my brother, and me to the Fort from our camp to get some meat. On the way we met one of Sutter's drunken Indians waving a big boo-ey knife and motioning us to go away. We went off another way, glad to be rid of him." The Trubodys believed that Sutter generously supplied the Indians with liquor in order to "control" them.

Sutter had to keep a close eye on his Indian work gangs so they wouldn't take French leave the first chance they got — proving they were adept in picking up sophisticated European customs. Except while on duty, the Indians were locked in a stockade, and freed only during working hours. Though this was said to be common treatment for Indians elsewhere on the frontier, it shocked many visitors to Sutter's Fort. The stockade had no beds or sanitary facilities. "The condition of the place after ten days or two weeks can be imagined," wrote Fort clerk Heinrich Lienhard.

Lienhard also offered revelations about Sutter's sex life: "Among Sutter's employees was an Indian Vaquero whose wife had a white child whom she exhibited with considerable pride. One day I asked the woman if Sutter was the father of the boy and she laughed with delight. If the captain had many half-breed children, I do not know of any who survived, and the native woman's white baby died not long after. Sutter kept a harem of young Indian girls in his ante room."

Worst of all accusations against Sutter is that he engaged in slave trading, using Indians as slaves. Indian historian Jack Forbes says Sutter's forces raided distant villages for captives to be sold to coastal rancheros, "thus supplying Sutter with perhaps his most reliable 'crop.' " His slave trade included kidnaping and sale of Indian children, noted 19th-century historian Hubert H. Bancroft: "From the first [Sutter] was in the habit of seizing Indian children, who were retained as servants, or slaves, at his establishment, or sent to his friends in different parts of the country." On one occasion Sutter discussed a shipment of kidnaped Indians for Bay Area ranchero Antonio Sunol: "Today I send 30 Indians. These are gentiles and have never worked with mission Indians. Therefore, keep them as long as you want, but provide a shirt for each of them and deduct its value from their wages."

Sutter later justified his role in the slave trade as being "common in those days to seize Indian women and children and sell them. This the Californians [Mexicans] did as well as Indians."

Then-Governor Alvarado eventually exposed Sutter's sordid business: "The public can see how inhuman were the operations of Sutter who had no scruples about depriving Indian mothers of their children. Sutter has sent these little Indian children as gifts to people who live far from the place of their birth, without demanding of them any promises that in their homes the Indians should be treated with kindness. Sutter's conduct was so deplorable that if I had not succeeded in persuading Sutter to stop the kidnaping operations it is probable that there would have been a general uprising of Indians."

Theodora Kroeber, whose book *Ishi In Two Worlds* told the poignant story of the last known wild Indian in North America, wrote: "The soberly estimated numbers of kidnappings of Indian children by whites in California to be sold as slaves or kept as cheap help was, between the years 1852 and 1867, from three to four thousand; every Indian woman, girl, and girl-child was potentially and in thousands of cases actually subject to repeated rape, to kidnapping, and to prostitution."

Chapter 13
Flag Of the Grizzly

A little rebellion now and then is a good thing.

Thomas Jefferson

Back home from the war in the southland, Sutter found New Helvetia plagued with troubles. Spring rains had watered the land copiously, but not an acre had been plowed so crops could be sown. Far behind in his installments to the Russians, Sutter had been banking on a good harvest to bring him current. Other problems clamored for energetic corrections: Foothill Indians had raided valley ranchos. Worse, many of his own Indians had joined them. When rampaging Indians killed his friend Thomas Lindsay and stole 300 of his cattle, that was going too far. Lindsay had served with him in the southern campaign, and Sutter vowed revenge.

He didn't need to call in a tracking expert to trace the marauders. All he had to do was follow the trail left by 300 cattle. Before long, he and his mounted party of avengers caught up with the miscreants. In a vicious fight, they routed them, punished them with dismaying casualties, and recovered the cattle. But for Sutter it was a hollow victory: "My clerk and loyal companion during the recent campaign, Juan Vaca, was shot at my side." Vaca was the only fatality in Sutter's party, though others were wounded. Sutter came close to getting shot out of the saddle, but his charmed life saved him: "I was, as usual, the first to charge, and a number of arrows pierced my clothing. Yet I escaped without injury."

In another case, rumors were flying that General Castro had suborned Chief Raphero of the Mokelumnes into taking up arms against Sutter. Sutter decided on a preemptive attack. Instead of waiting for Raphero to descend in full force, he tracked him to his lair, defeated his band and captured Raphero. In "court-martial" proceedings, Raphero received a death sentence. His head was impaled on a spike above the gate of the fort, as a grisly warning to any other Indians with mischief in mind.

Year 1845 witnessed more violent clashes between whites and Indians. For a time they caused pandemic anxiety among valley settlers. The threatening Indians were belligerent Walla Wallas from Oregon Territory, not the usually placid California Indians. A band of 36 warriors, with some women and children, journeyed down from the north and camped near Sutter's Fort. The chief was named Leicer, educated at a mission school in the Willamette Valley. Visiting the Fort, Leicer got into a ruckus with Grove Cook, the distillery boss, in a quarrel over who owned a mule. Gunplay ensued, and the upshot was the Indian lay dead. The rest of the Walla Wallas dashed back to Oregon — with horses stolen from valley ranchers. Next morning Sutter dispatched a posse to recapture the horses, but the posse returned, unable to catch up with the fast-moving Indians.

When the Walla Wallas arrived in Oregon and reported the death of their chief, Dr. Elijah White, missionary and Indian agent in the Willamette Valley — under whom Leicer had been a pupil —fired off hot letters of protest to Sutter, Governor Pio Pico, and American consul Larkin, demanding Cook be tried — and punished, if found guilty.

In a July 21 letter to Larkin, Sutter stoutly defended Cook, saying Leicer had threatened him with a rifle. Leicer, during his visit to the Fort, had behaved in "a very saucy and haughty manner," Sutter said, adding: "Dr. White says that Leicer was by no means viciously inclined, but we believe here all that Leicer was a great Rascal."

Officials ordered an investigation, but whether it ever took place is not known. The incident, however, festered a long time in memory. Walla Wallas remained hostile. Occasional rumors that they were planning vengeful maraudings alarmed settlers.

As 1845 dwindled down, Sutter's energy and acumen were paying off. His workshops spewed out hats, blankets and leather goods. Other products sprang from the hands of blacksmiths, gunsmiths, coopers and wagonmakers. His improved distillery trickled brandy again. As early as October 1840, he had begun distilling brandy from a mash of wild grapes. Several carpenters were wielding hammers and saws. One bore the soon-to-be-immortal name of James Marshall.

Sutter's Fort, Mexico's northern outpost in California, was the lair of a wildcat breed of Americans — trappers, hunters and settlers — who weren't losing any love over things Mexican. And in the East, ever more Americans, bewitched by rhapsodies of returning travelers, were journeying west. Mexican officials had given Sutter stern commands to discourage such immigration, and now blamed him for leaving the door wide open.

As Mexico's official representative on the northern frontier, Sutter was charged with enforcing Mexican laws that barred foreigners from settling here, but he was caught between a mire and a morass. He *wanted* to be a dutiful officer, but his ingrained hospitality inclined him to give hearty welcomes to immigrants, and let them stay at the Fort as long as they hankered to. Many found a permanent home there, being the very sort of craftsmen he craved to keep his workshops humming. Even if he had *tried* to keep foreigners out, he no more could have stemmed the resistless tide of westward migration than old King Canute could have held back the sea.

Two visitors arrived at the Fort in November 1845 to make Sutter an offer. Capt. Andres Castillero, a Mexican commissioner, and General Castro proposed to give him $100,000, or the entire mission lands of San Jose, in exchange for New Helvetia. The Mexicans hoped to take over the Fort without a military struggle, and thus cancel its threat of American invasion. Sutter declined their offer, he later explained, because there were too many Americans in New Helvetia who depended on him.

Sensing that war with Mexico was inevitable, Capt. John C. Fremont had departed in 1845 on his third "scientific" expedition to California. On an earlier expedition in February 1844, he and Kit Carson had discovered the pass that would be named after Carson, with midwinter snow almost 20 feet deep. At the pass, Carson carved his name and the year, 1844, on a red fir. When the tree fell in 1888, the section with the inscription was taken to Sutter's Fort — and is on view today in the museum gallery.

Fremont and Carson, having abandoned their cannon and baggages, got their horses over the mountains only by pounding a trail with wooden mauls. It took a month. Famished and exhausted, they reached Sutter's Fort in March 1844. Fremont explained he had been assigned to survey a wagon route to California. In November of that year, the Bartleson-Bidwell party struggled over that route, though they had to abandon their wagons in snowdrifts before crossing the Sierra. In 1845, six trains of covered wagons finished the arduous trek along this route, the California Trail.

Sutter's Fort became the destination of most pioneer wagon trains into California — and Sutter had become the most powerful man in California. With incoming people and animals exhausted by months on the trail, Sutter, no matter how bad his financial shape, welcomed them all with food, clothing and shelter. He invited them to stay as long as they cared to, and his hospitality won their gratitude.

Incoming wagons brought him skilled workers for his shops — and in time a market for the goods his colony produced.

Now, in early 1846, Captain Fremont — with 60 men including frontier scout Kit Carson — set up his headquarters near Tres Picos, today known as Sutter Buttes, on the northern boundary of New Helvetia, 40 miles north of the Fort. Above the craggy buttes, red-tailed hawks rode the updrafts.

About April 1, 1846, General Jose Castro issued a stunning order requiring all foreigners who had lived in California less than a year to leave — without their arms, other personal property, or even their beasts of burden. Before long, many disturbed Americans in the valley got wind of Fremont's presence near the buttes and guessed that some kind of showdown with Mexico was in the offing. In fact, William B. Ide, 50, a former teacher from Illinois, received this agitating announcement on June 8, delivered by an Indian: "Notice is hereby given that a large body of Spaniards on horseback, amounting to 250 men, has been seen on their way to the Sacramento Valley, destroying crops, burning houses, and driving off cattle. Capt. Fremont invites every freeman in the valley to come to his camp at the Buttes, immediately." No doubt many others received the same notice, for Fremont soon was reinforced by a large band of Americans. Among them was Ezekiel ("Stuttering") Merritt, a hard-drinking trapper who wore a foxtail cap and could neither read nor write. He had a reputation for bravery based on, according to John Bidwell, his "continual boasting of his prowess in killing Indians. The handle of the tomahawk he carried had nearly a hundred notches to record the number of Indian scalps." Fremont appointed Merritt his "field-lieutenant." Merritt's two dozen followers comprised an equally rough-looking, ugly crew of long-haired settlers and mountain men in greasy buckskins with knives in their belts. They carried long rifles and were spoiling for action.

If trouble with Mexico was brewing, Merritt and cohorts didn't think it was much sport to cool their heels. They wanted to go out looking for trouble, not merely wait for it to find them.

Opportunity arose one day in June when Americans learned that 200 horses, obtained from General Vallejo and earmarked for Castro, were being driven from Sonoma to Monterey. They were herded across the Sacramento River at William Knight's Landing 20 miles northwest of Sutter's Fort by two Mexican lieutenants, including Francisco Arce, and several vaqueros.

Merritt walked into Fremont's tent and saluted, though he knew civilians don't salute.

Fremont, studying a map, glanced up.

"G-G-General, I'd like to volunteer me and my men to go and do a little h-horse-rustling."

"I was just thinking about that. If *we* stole those horses — us being soldiers in uniform — there might be hell to pay for acting without orders. But you boys are civilians. Think you could pull it off?"

Merritt said he did, and rejoined his men. After fortifying themselves with whiskey and vittles, Merritt and a dozen men grabbed their rifles, sprang into their saddles and galloped southward.

Lieutenant Arce and his men herded the horses across the American and spent the night of June 8 at Sutter's Fort. In the morning, he laughed and said to Sutter: "California is like a pretty girl — everyone wants her!" Arce and his men passed the next night at Martin Murphy's rancho on the south bank of the Cosumnes River near today's Elk Grove, after driving the horses into Murphy's corral.

As dawn glimmered, Merritt and his band crept up to the corral and overpowered the sleeping Mexicans. With the situation in hand, Merritt released the Mexicans and let each man keep two horses, and even returned their firearms.

"Senor," Arce addressed Merritt, "for letting us keep our horses and rifles, *muchas gracias*. However, if we had not been asleep, you never would have captured us. *Jamas!"*

Merritt laughed. "Well, *senor,* you're awake now. Sh-sh-shall we do it all over again?"

Arce scanned Merritt's crew of heavily-armed ruffians, who badly outnumbered his own force, and his smile faded. "No, *senor.*"

"Didn't think so. And tell your G-G-General Castro — if he wants his horses back, he can come and try and take 'em!"

Though not a shot was fired during this horse-stealing adventure, historians regard it as the first battle in the campaign to capture California from Mexico because, unknown to everyone in the province, the United States had declared war on Mexico the previous month. A historical marker denoting the former location of Murphy's Corral, and recounting its significance, stands south of Elk Grove on the west side of the frontage road on the west side of Highway 99 just south of the Grant Line Road interchange.

Merritt and company, driving the horses, met Fremont as he was marching his force south, shifting his headquarters down to the American River. He arrived at Sutter's Fort June 12 with 100 men and pitched camp. If attacked in force by Castro, the Fort was the only valley stronghold they could defend.

Fremont gave Merritt and crew another assignment: Offense being the best defense, he dispatched Merritt and two dozen men to raid Sonoma. En route, they picked up a few recruits from valley settlers. At Sonoma, they planned to demand the garrison's surrender and arrest General Vallejo. To their surprise, the barracks was empty. Vallejo, fed up with maintaining soldiers at his own expense, had disbanded them the prior year.

It was a quiet Sunday morning in Sonoma on June 14 — until General Vallejo heard rude noises and peered out a window of his Casa Grande. He was startled to see a band of rowdy Yanquis, armed and looking dangerous. Some wore buckskin shirts and britches and some blue knee pants. Some had no shirts, and many didn't even have shoes. Several wore coyote or wolfskin caps, while others wore grimy straw hats or slouch hats riddled with holes. Vallejo slipped into his uniform, opened the door and asked what they wanted. Nobody knew what to reply. He asked if they had captured the place. They knew the answer to that: Yes, indeed. He disappeared for a moment, reappearing with his sword buckled on, and offered to surrender it. Nobody stepped forward to take it, so Vallejo returned it to his chamber.

After parleying with Merritt and Robert Semple at the door, he invited them in to draw up articles of capitulation. Vallejo sent a servant across the square to ask his brother-in-law Jacob Leese, an

American merchant, to come and serve as interpreter. Leese arrived with his wife Rosalia, who later remembered the Americans as being "as rough a looking set of men as one could well imagine."

With Leese interpreting, Vallejo began to comprehend: The Americans wanted everybody to surrender. Mrs. Vallejo wanted to clarify a point, so she asked in a friendly way: "To whom shall we surrender?"

Semple, a six-foot-six Kentucky dentist, a comical figure in fringed buckskin with too-short sleeves and trousers, later described by Mrs. Leese as the "least unhuman of that god-forsaken crowd," explained: Their goal was to free California from tyranny, and General Vallejo had a deal of arms and other property that would come in mighty handy.

Protested Leese: "You're not soldiers — you're not in uniform."

"We're only settlers," Semple said, "but we're all opposed to General Castro. He threatened to drive all Americans out of California, irregardless."

Vallejo called for a servant, who brought wine, brandy and glasses. The servant poured everyone a brimful glass of wine, then brought more bottles and set them on the table. Drinking made everyone feel friendly and, as time went by, the thirsty Americans began to grow befuddled. They could have lost the battle right there but their host had also imbibed heartily. Yet somehow they managed to draft capitulation terms.

To those cooling their heels outside, the parley inside seemed endless. Patience worn out, they chose John Grigsby to enter and find out the cause of the delay. Grigsby was gone so long that William Ide was assigned to go after him. Teetotaler Ide found everyone in a drunken condition, still perusing the written articles of capitulation with pie-eyes. Furious, Ide grabbed the papers and rushed outside to read them to the men.

Merritt, aroused from befuddlement, began arresting people: Jacob Leese; Vallejo's secretary, Colonel Victor Prudon; and Vallejo's brother, Captain Salvador Vallejo. He then committed the paramount insult by lashing General Vallejo to a chair. Vallejo later recalled the indignity with anger: "And they tied me to a chair! Me! Vallejo!"

Vallejo, vastly outnumbered and realizing there was nothing else he could do, reluctantly appended his signature to the surrender terms.

Merritt and eight men put the prisoners on horses and escorted them to Sutter's Fort, turning them over to Fremont. Ironically,

General Mariano G. Vallejo was confined in Sutter's Fort as a prisoner of war. Courtesy Department of Parks and Recreation.

the prisoners included people who were among the most favorably disposed toward Americans: Vallejo, a longtime friend of settlers, including Sutter; Leese, an American; and Colonel Prudon, a Frenchman who had become an American citizen and was trying to persuade Californians to favor United States annexation of the province. Other prisoners included the general's brother, Captain Salvador Vallejo; Jose Noriega, Vicente Peralta, Julio Carrillo, and Robert Ridley.

When the prisoner escort encountered Fremont, Vallejo stepped forward: "Captain Fremont, I am your prisoner."

"No," Fremont replied, gesturing toward the escorts, "You are the prisoner of these people."

Sutter was stunned when he saw who the prisoners were, and protested that the arrest was "wrong and unnecessary," because Vallejo was the best friend Americans had in California.

Two dozen Americans had been left behind to defend Sonoma. They had no leader, so they elected William B. Ide as commander. One man was William L. Todd, nephew of Mrs. Abraham Lincoln. Gazing up at the bare flagstaff in the Sonoma plaza, it struck him that he ought to make a flag to represent their new republic. Mrs. John Sears donated two yards of muslin she had brought across the plains in a covered wagon. William "Dirty" Mathews, an express rider, raced to his nearby home and grabbed from the clothesline a red flannel petticoat belonging to his Mexican wife. The red served as a border for the flag's lower edge. Henry L. Ford suggested a grizzly bear would make a good emblem. Somebody else said it should also have a star, like the Texas flag.

So the finished flag was adorned with a red star, CALIFORNIA REPUBLIC in red capital letters on the bottom, and a crude figure of a grizzly standing on hind legs. The grizzly symbolized strength and stubborn endurance, an apt symbol for these men — wild,

Bear Flaggers — most of them New Helvetia dwellers — are remembered in the plaza at Sonoma.

rough and dangerous. California's State Bear Flag was adapted in 1911 from the crude emblem devised by this motley bunch.

The men yelled with jubilation as they hoisted their new flag on the Sonoma plaza pole. Ide read the proclamation he had drafted for the new republic. It said immigrants had been invited to California by a promise of lands to settle on. But when they arrived they were denied even the right to buy or rent land from friends. And military despotism threatened them "with extermination, if they would not depart out of the country, leaving all their property."

Some of the Bear Flaggers were having second thoughts: Maybe they were stepping into something bigger than they could handle. If Fremont didn't back them up, they wouldn't have a chance against Castro's army. Maybe they should abandon Sonoma and forget the whole thing.

At this juncture, Ide stepped forward. According to his autobiography, he orated: "Saddle no horse for me ... I will lay my bones here, before I will take upon myself the ignominy of commencing an honorable work, and then flee like cowards, like thieves, when no enemy is in sight. In vain will you say you had honorable motives; who will believe it; flee this day, and the longest life cannot wear off your disgrace! Choose ye! Choose ye this day, what you will be! We are robbers, or we must be conquerors!"

A fine speech, but who can believe that's what he really said on the spur of the moment? "Choose ye," indeed. It has the smell of midnight oil, maybe oil a bit rancid.

At any rate, the Bear Flaggers rallied 'round their flag and declared Ide president of the new republic — he would be the only president California ever had.

In Monterey, two days after the Bear Flag rose over Sonoma, General Castro issued his own proclamation. He urged all loyal Californians to rise against "the contemptible agents of the United States in the north." Did they take him for a fool? Behind the rough hand of the Bear Flagger, he discerned the fine hand of some scheming Yankee high in government.

In Santa Barbara, Governor Pio Pico also was at no loss for words to express his displeasure. He issued a proclamation saying a "gang of North American adventurers with the blackest treason that the genius of evil could invent" had stolen Sonoma, just as they had stolen Texas. Marvelous invective. He urged Californians to take up arms "in pursuit of the treacherous foe."

In New Helvetia, Sutter found he couldn't treat the prisoners as anything but guests, for he regarded them as neighbors and friends. Later he told how he felt: "I placed my best rooms at their disposal and treated them with every consideration . . . The gentlemen took their meals at my table and walked with me in the evening. Neither did I place a guard before the door of the room, nor did I order any soldiers to accompany us when we were walking. I thought that it was wholly unnecessary to be more severe with them. They were men of property and there was no danger of their attempting to escape."

When Fremont learned that Sutter was coddling prisoners, he almost had a hemorrhage. Couldn't be bothered to mount a guard over them! Even fetched them brandy and tumblers! This was no way to fight a war!

Fremont stomped into Sutter's office; "Don't you know how to treat prisoners of war?" he demanded.

Sutter poured a glass of brandy and proffered it. "Captain?"

Impatiently Fremont waved his hand. "Answer my question!"

"Indeed I do, Captain. I've been a prisoner of war myself." He drank a swig of brandy, then cleared his throat. "If you don't like the way I'm handling 'em, take charge of them yourself. I don't want any more to do with them."

Capt. John C. Fremont threatened to hang Sutter to an oak tree if he didn't obey orders. Courtesy Department of Parks and Recreation.

Fremont spun on his heel and marched out. He found John Bidwell and appointed him the new warden. Sutter slapped his thigh and roared when he learned Bidwell was allowing the captives as many liberties as they had enjoyed before.

Nobody knew exactly where Sutter's loyalties lay. Perhaps he wasn't sure himself. Maybe he reckoned California in time would join the Union, but he was shocked by the Bear Flaggers, who had outraged all Mexican-Californians and wrecked chances for a peaceful solution to the mounting American presence in the province. He regarded them as "a band of robbers under Fremont's command."

But now Sutter's impasse was broken. By opening the gate of his fort to Fremont, he had willy-nilly cast his lot with the United States, abandoning Mexico — which left a bitter taste in his mouth.

Fremont was more than a little suspicious about where Sutter's loyalties lay, and he had a splendidly direct way of addressing the subject. He sent Sutter this message via Carson: "If you are on the side of the Mexicans, go down and join them." That shook Sutter up more than somewhat. What kind of a crack was that? Didn't

Fremont understand his position? It was like being caught in a cross-fire. Bidwell remembered how it was: "Sutter came to me greatly aggravated, with tears in his eyes, and said that Fremont had told him he was a Mexican and that if he did not like what he [Fremont] was doing he would set him across the San Joaquin River and he could go and join the Mexicans."

Such ingratitude! In 1844, Sutter had aided Fremont's distressed expedition, supplying its manifold desperate needs with everything at cost or below. In payment he accepted Fremont's drafts on the U.S. Topographical Bureau — and later found he could cash them at only 20 percent of face value. Rued Sutter: "In the goodness of my heart I thought I would do the American government a favor by not taking advantage of Fremont's distress, but I only cheated myself thereby."

Sutter continued to visit the prisoners. But one day Dr. John Townsend, the Fort's physician, apparently heard a rumor, for he cautioned Sutter to avoid being too friendly with the prisoners, or he might become a prisoner in his own Fort. His advice was timely, for a day or two later Fremont sent word that if Sutter visited the prisoners once more, he would hang him on the oak tree in the courtyard.

Sutter was deeply offended because, in opening his gates to Fremont's force, he had obviously renounced allegiance to Mexico and openly declared for the United States.

Almost all the fighting in the California conquest occurred in southern California, but Sutter's Fort played a major role. Being the only stronghold in the valley, it not only sheltered settlers from hostile Indians but sheltered them from the soldiers General Castro threatened to send against them. And the Fort was the staging ground for recruiting, training and outfitting volunteer companies for the campaign against the Mexicans. Fremont had to enlist volunteers to bolster his tatterdemalion force. He signed up so many of Sutter's workers that when he marched away, looking for a fight, he took nearly all Sutter's craftsmen, hunters, trappers and harvest workers. For Sutter, it couldn't have been a worse time. His workrooms and mills nearly stopped functioning. Crops rotted in the fields. Livestock roamed wherever they fancied. All this dashed Sutter's hopes of being able to pay off his ponderous debts.

At any rate Sutter, who didn't have to raise a wet finger to see which way the political winds blew, resigned his Mexican commission, and declared in favor of the campaign to liberate California from the Mexicans.

Not all persons today regard the Bear Flag Revolt as a big deal. One is J.S. Holliday, author of the bestseller about the Gold Rush, *The World Rushed In,* destined to become a classic. In a talk in Sacramento on Feb. 5, 1985, he said: "Too much has been made of the Bear Flag event. It was a most tawdry event of cattle thieves and bumpkins not knowing what they were doing." Fremont, he noted, quickly took over what they had started. "It would have been infinitely better for the United States' relations with Mexico if the Bear Flag event had never happened."

Tawdry or not, it was made much of at the time.

Bear Flagger Robert Semple went on to make a name in politics when, in 1849 as a delegate from Sonoma, he was elected president of California's first Constitutional Convention in Monterey — but he was fated to die a horrible death five years later.

The facts were supplied by State Parks ranger Tom Palmquist and author James B. Alexander, both of Sonoma, and Barbara R. Warner of San Juan Capistrano.

Semple, riding a horse on his ranch seven miles west of Williams, Colusa County, suffered a severe fall. Friends, unable to detect any vital signs, pronounced him dead.

"He's not dead! He's not dead!" screamed his wife.

"Yes he is. Yes he is," said the others, for they could find no clue to indicate otherwise.

Semple, 48, was buried on his ranch in a coffin beneath two cottonwood trees — and his distraught wife had nightmares that he had been buried alive.

Circa 1900, the family sold the ranch. When they dug up the coffin to move it to the Williams Cemetery, they decided to have a look at Semple's remains — and were horrified to find that he had *not* been dead when buried, as witnessed by his contorted body and the marks of desperate efforts to claw his way out of his tomb.

Chapter 14
War and Peace

There never was a good war, or a bad peace.
Ben Franklin

Unknown to the Bear Flaggers when they threw down the gauntlet with their June 14 raid on Sonoma, the United States had declared war against Mexico a month earlier, on May 12. Hostilities were precipitated chiefly because the U.S. had admitted Texas to the Union. And perhaps also because, to some U.S. officials pumped up on "Manifest Destiny," leaving a Mexican province blocking the road to the Pacific was like contradicting Divine Revelation.

War ripples soon would lap the shores of New Helvetia.

Commodore John D. Sloat, commanding a U.S. naval squadron anchored at Mazatlan, Mexico, got the war news in June. Following his standing orders in case of war, he set sail for Monterey. On July 7, 250 bluejackets and leathernecks in six boats from three warships hit the beach unopposed and hoisted the American Flag on the Custom House, while 21-gun salutes boomed from the ships. An officer read Sloat's proclamation declaring that "henceforth California will be a portion of the United States."

Two days later, the sloop *US Portsmouth* sailed into San

Francisco Bay, and unopposed bluejackets sent the Stars and Stripes fluttering above Yerba Buena. A detail led by Lieut. Joseph Warren Revere — grandson of Paul Revere — boated to Sonoma to strike the Bear Flag and hoist Old Glory. Revere handed another Flag to a man named William Scott and dispatched him to Sutter's Fort, where he arrived at sunset July 10.

Before daybreak next morning, most of the Fort's denizens gathered in the shadows at the flagpole where the Bear Flag had flown for three weeks. Sutter had loaded all his cannon with fresh charges. Someone let out a cry, and other voices echoed it. As the red sun peeped through oak trees in the east, the red-white-and-blue started to ascend. Remembered Sutter: "When the Star Spangled Banner slowly rose on the flag staff, the cannon began and continued until nearly all the windows were broken."

Paul Revere would have been proud — if he knew his grandson had sent Old Glory to New Helvetia, to go aloft over the Fort for the first time ever.

But not everyone was proud, as Sutter observed: "Some of the people around the Fort made long faces, because they thought they would have had a better chance to rob and plunder if they had remained under the Bear Flag. The Sonoma prisoners, not knowing what was going on, were greatly surprised. I went to them and said: 'Now, gentlemen, we are under the protection of this great flag, and we should henceforth not be afraid to talk to one another . . . ' They all rejoiced that the anarchy was over."

Humiliation for Sutter was not over, however, for the next day Fremont transfered command of the Fort to Ned Kern, his topographical draftsman, who renamed it Fort Sacramento. Fremont demoted Sutter to second in command — another bitter blow. Ever since he had founded his colony, he had been the unchallenged commander.

In the following month, August, the Sonoma prisoners were released, whereupon they rode home. One source says that Fremont evidently had misgivings, and ordered them turned loose, while another says they were ordered released by U.S. navy officers despite Fremont's opposition.

Year 1846 also was one of Indian troubles in New Helvetia. When Mokelumnes ran off the horses of his chief trapper, Pierson B. Reading, Sutter surmised that General Castro had instigated the raid. In June, he and Reading led a punitive raid into the Delta. Crossing the Mokelumne River, one of their rafts turned over, causing substantial loss in arms and ammunition. At the Calaveras

River, Sutter's band besieged the Indians in a cave, but he had to pull back when they exhausted their powder and ball. However, he set a price on the head of Eusebio, the leader, and later a friendly Indian, Chief Pollo (Chicken) brought in his scalp.

Rumors in the fall of 1846 prompted Sutter to beef up security at the Fort, as he feared another raid by the Walla Walla Indians. With most settlers soldiering with Fremont, the remaining settlers feared that hostile Indians might raid their half-deserted ranchos and steal all the livestock.

Near the end of 1846, a band of Walla Wallas did enter the valley. Reported Sutter: "They came down from Oregon to hunt and trade in the valley and to seek justice for the murder of a young chief, the son of Yellow Serpent, who had been killed some time before during a quarrel with one of my men." The young chief evidently is the man Leicer mentioned in a previous chapter. Continued Sutter: "Their appearance at the northern frontier caused some of the settlers to flee post haste to my Fort, and the exaggerated reports caused such a panic throughout California that a massacre of the Walla Wallas was just barely averted."

Sutter talked the Walla Wallas into enlisting in the war against Mexico, promising the federal government would pay for their services. "Being a warlike people, many of them were glad to go," Sutter said.

So, in the final phase of the campaign, a contingent of Walla Wallas soldiered in Fremont's army. The Walla Wallas turned out to be double trouble, as it were. Recalled Sutter: "When they returned to New Helvetia, they had not yet received their pay and, believing that I had deceived them, threatened to declare war on us. I pacified them by giving them a lot of old, broken-down government horses, stamped U.S., that were roaming about the Fort. On their return to Oregon, they behaved very badly and did a lot of damage. They caught and maltreated a number of Indians from California tribes and stole horses from me and the other settlers."

Late 1846 brought another threat to New Helvetia. With Sutter delinquent on his payments for purchase of Fort Ross and Bodega, the Russians took preliminary legal steps to foreclose. Sutter hired an attorney to fight the proceedings, and also made frantic efforts to save his colony from the Russians by unloading it on Uncle Sam. Main reason for his delinquency: three years of drought, which had cut severely into his wheat production, his principal medium of payment to the Russians.

Meantime, a great tragedy impended on the California Trail.

Two years earlier, the Trail had been officially opened by the Elisha Stevens party — first to drag wagons over the monstrous Sierra. Their 11 wagons had rumbled across Nevada deserts, trying to make it to California before winter snows. An old Indian told them of a river to follow into the mountains and they found it, naming it Truckee, after the Indian. They followed the river for miles and then hit a stone wall — the granite cliffs of the Sierra. Now the party split up. Six men on horses picked their way over the mountains seeking help. In a grueling ordeal, the others managed to raise five wagons up the cliff, with their oxen hauling from above and men pushing and pulling below. Gradually they worked their way through the gap, crossed the mountains, and straggled into Sutter's Fort.

In the two years of 1845 and 1846, hundreds of covered wagons of weary settlers groaned onward along the long, long trail to California. At the base of the awesome cliffs, so many wagons were ready to cross that they had to line up, waiting their turns to tackle the colossal wall. Most of them made it. Gold hadn't even been discovered yet, but a river of settlers was rolling into California. The river flowed fairly evenly, save for the tragedy of 1846-47, which would give its name to the pass.

Today, Interstate 80 sweeps over the Sierra at 7,240-foot Donner Pass, near where the pioneers labored with untold tribulations to hoist their wagons up the titanic wall.

At Sutter's Fort, the harbinger of the tragedy came in September 1846 when two exhausted travelers, one named Charles Stanton, arrived with disturbing news about a party of 87 people crossing Nevada. Many of their animals had died and their food supplies were dangerously low.

The party's leader was a man named Donner.

Sutter promptly dispatched five mules packed with beef, flour and other staples with Stanton and two Indian guides. On October 19, they found the Donners, who had struggled into Truckee Meadows near present-day Reno. Meanwhile, some of the Donner party made heartbreaking efforts to get help. Of one party of 15 who started, only seven made it to Sutter's Fort, where their ghastly appearance and tales of agony betokened a major disaster.

One mother had left her children with the marooned Donners to join a snowshoe party to seek help. John Rhoads, a member of the first rescue party, encountered the woman and promised he would save her children. But at the tragedy scene he found only her petite daughter Naomi Pike still alive. He packed Naomi on his back through an ordeal in the snow, to reunite her with her mother.

In another rescue effort from Sutter's Fort at January's end, 1847, several men — each with a heavy pack of food strapped on his back — slogged into the mountains, trudging day and night with only brief rests. On February 18, they spied the snow-covered makeshift cabins near Truckee (now Donner) Lake and were welcomed like angels from heaven. With all their food gone, the sufferers were cooking and eating shoes, oxhides and finally the flesh of those already dead.

Of the 87 Donner party members who left Fort Laramie, Wyoming, only 47 survived — worst tragedy in wagon train chronicles. All the rescue missions had been organized and outfitted at the Fort, with Sutter a magnanimous donor of supplies. When the 47 survivors reached the Fort in 1847, Sutter welcomed them with food and lodging. All told, his four rescue expeditions saved over half of the Donner party. Editorialized the *California Star*: "But for the timely succor afforded them by Captain J. A. Sutter, one of the most humane and liberal men in California, they must all have perished in a few days."

However, two modern-day Sacramento historians have shone a whole new light on the rescue of Donner Party survivors.

In their compelling book, *The Donner Party Rescue Site*, subtitled *Johnson's Ranch on Bear River*, Jack Steed and son Richard present convincing evidence that the four relief parties rendezvoused, outfitted and set out from Johnson's Ranch two miles east of present-day Wheatland, and not from Sutter's Fort, as most historians tell it. True, word of the dire emergency resounded from Sutter's Fort and Sutter and alcalde John Sinclair offered money to recruit rescuers.

The Steeds also establish that it was to Johnson's Ranch the rescuers conveyed the 47 wretched survivors to recuperate until they could travel on to Sutter's Fort.

Furthermore, this was the vital ranch where hundreds of wagon-loads of pioneers would reach the end of the arduous California Trail.

The very existence of Johnson's Ranch was almost lost to history. Even historians who knew of it assumed – because of an error in an 1851 map, copied in later maps – that it lay on the south side of the Bear River, in an area later devastated by hydraulicking. Discovering the original error, the Steeds spent four years researching. They dug up hundreds of artifacts on the north side, proving where it really lay.

Thanks to the Steeds, Johnson's Ranch will appear on the National Register of Historic Places.

A 12-year-old girl, Virginia Reed, sent some valuable advice for pioneers in a letter to a cousin after she and other Donner Party survivors reached the Fort: "Never take no cut-offs and hurry along as fast as you can." Virginia's younger sister, Patty, carried a small doll through the entire ordeal — on display today in the Fort's museum area.

During seed-time and harvest, Sutter had up to 300 Indians working as laborers. Some wore shirts and blankets, but many were "entirely naked," according to Edwin Bryant, who arrived overland in 1846 and later wrote a book, *What I Saw In California.* Sutter paid the Indians with tin coins, each stamped with the number of days worked, indicating the value of merchandise a worker could buy at the store. Cotton cloth and handerchiefs were the most favored.

Bryant tells what it was like to be a dinner guest at the Fort: "Captain Sutter's dining-room and his table furniture do not present a very luxurious appearance. The room is unfurnished, with the exception of a common deal table standing in the centre, and some benches, which are substitutes for chairs. The table, when spread, presented a correspondingly primitive simplicity of aspect and of viands. The first course consisted of good soup, served to each guest, in a china bowl, with silver spoons. The bowls, after they had been used for this purpose, were taken away and cleaned by the Indian servant, and were afterwards used as tumblers or goblets, from which we drank our water. The next course consisted of two dishes of meat, one roasted and one fried, and both highly seasoned with onions. Bread, cheese, butter and melons constituted the dessert."

Bryant painted a bucolic picture of the region that later became the City of North Sacramento (still later annexed to Sacramento): "We passed through large evergreen oak groves, some of them miles in width. Game is very abundant. We frequently saw deer feeding quietly one or two hundred yards from us and large flocks of antelope."

For Sutter, the times were becoming prosperous: "I found a good market for my products among the newcomers and the people of the Bay district. My manufactures increased and there was no lack of skilled mechanics." Mechanics were plentiful for the Mormon Battalion had been disbanded, releasing many skilled craftsmen. A contingent of 238 Mormons led by Sam Brannan had departed

New York in the ship *Brooklyn*, bound for California via Cape Horn. The group included 70 men, 68 women and 100 children. When they arrived in San Francisco after a stop at Hawaii, they doubled the city's population, turning it into a Mormon town. The Mormons had enlisted to fight in the Mexican War, but all the fighting was done by the time they reached California. Yet they got a free trip west for themselves and their families. Some came to Sutter's Fort seeking work and found it. "The best people which I has ever employed," Sutter said.

Crops were superb in that year of 1847. Several hundred Indians gathered the golden wheat with sickles, knives, or even bare hands. Groaning Mexican *carretas*, each with two huge solid wooden wheels, carted the harvest from the fields to a corral. Indian vaqueros on horseback drove 300 horses into the corral, whooping and hollering to spur them on, driving them in a circle, round and round. Then they charged in front of the galloping horses, and with loud yells turned the stampede the other way. Time and again they repeated this performance. Grain was thrashed and the straw ground into chaff. "In this manner I have seen 2,000 bushels of wheat thrashed in a single hour," wrote John Bidwell four decades later. "Next came the winnowing . . . It could only be done when the wind was blowing, by throwing high into the air shovelfuls of grain, straw and chaff, the lighter materials being wafted to one side, while the grain, comparatively clean, would descend and form a heap by itself."

Sutter's mule-powered gristmills ground out floor ready for the ovens. Enough grain remained from the 1847 harvest to send a big cargo back on the Russian brig *Baikal* as an installment on Fort Ross — first shipment of any size Sutter had made.

Indian women tended the gardens, festooned with berries and vegetables. From the pond in back of the Fort, they carried water for irrigating. Hour after hour through the long summer, long files of women carried water from the pond to rows of carrots, lettuce, potatoes, turnips, cabbages, peans, beans and melons.

Sutter was now employing 600 persons. To feed them, he had to kill four or five oxen each day.

Though the Indians were paid tin coins stamped out by a blacksmith, enabling them to buy clothes, tools, or food, some workers helped themselves to "fringe benefits." Lienhard cited two cases: "When slaughtering took place, I noticed that the choicest pieces of meat disappeared rapidly toward the rear of the fort . . . . so next time some animals were killed I kept an eye on the Indians.

They did not know I was watching them, for I pretended to be occupied with other matters. Soon the Indians began to sneak to the rear of the fort with large pieces of meat. I cornered them where they could not escape, and made them return their plunder to the meat room, slapping their thick, vermin-infected heads . . . .

"Our bakery was always being looted, too. Often, after bread had been made, I saw Indians leaving the room carrying large bundles. I began to watch, and one day when the bread was about to be taken from the oven, I sat where I could see every door that led outside. I confiscated one large package being carried off by a huge, overgrown boy, and thrashed him soundly."

Sutter by the end of 1847 was monarch of all he surveyed, and he surveyed an immense thriving empire. Besides the Fort and related buildings, 60 houses dotted the region, homes of 160 white men and 47 white women. A wide scope of industries flourished, with Sutter leading the way in trading, shipping, irrigation, large-scale wheat-growing, lumbering, milling, mining and fur trapping. He commenced California's fisheries, factories, tanneries and distilleries. Thousands of livestock browsed his fields. A bumper crop of wheat was harvested. The Fort had granaries, a dairy, a blacksmith shop, bakery, storerooms, an arsenal, sawmill, five flour mills and a tannery. Everything grown or manufactured in New Helvetia commanded an eager market. Sutter later estimated his 1847 livestock holdings as 12,000 cattle, 2,000 horses and mules, over 10,000 sheep, and 1,000 hogs. He could raise 40,000 bushels of wheat in a season. "My best days were just before the discovery of gold," he later lamented.

The war with Mexico officially ended Feb. 2, 1848, with the Treaty of Guadalupe, although in California the Mexicans had surrendered to Fremont more than a year earlier, near San Fernando. In the Treaty, Mexico ceded a vast territory, California included, and the United States agreed to pay Mexico $15 million. As the Treaty guaranteed property protection to Mexicans remaining in California, Sutter, both a Mexican and a U.S. citizen, felt twice safeguarded.

On January 24, only nine days before the Treaty was ratified, gold was discovered in the California foothills, but what could the Mexicans have done, even if they had known?

As Christmas 1847 approached, Sutter resolved to celebrate his prosperity with a feast his guests would remember to the end of their days. He invited everyone, including his Indian workers. Actually there were two parties — one at the Fort and one at the

Hock Farm he had established on the Feather River. The fattest cattle were slaughtered. Chief delicacy of the Indians was fried jackass meat, so Sutter killed several burros for them, even though one donkey was worth four horses.

At the Fort, the feast began at noon. Tables groaned with mountains of frijoles and tortillas, salmon baked, broiled and fried, and fruits of all sorts. Barrels of wine were drained by thirsty guests, and by sunset the Fort was littered with the comatose bodies of those who had indulged too freely.

At Hock Farm, Sutter entertained his personal friends and neighbors of the region. Guests came from as far as Sonoma and San Francisco. To hone their appetites for the banquet, the men fished and shot ducks and geese, while the ladies enjoyed a river excursion on Sutter's new stern-wheel steamer. The men appeared in full dress for dinner — wearing silk jackets, embroidered vests, and velveteen breeches with gold lacings, while the ladies in bare arms wore silk or crape gowns, bright sashes, satin shoes and red or flesh-colored stockings. Jewelry glittered on necks and ears.

Sutter's specially-trained cooks prepared a soup said to be the equal of anything in New York. They served salmon, perch, trout and barracuda. Now the entrees came in — pigs' feet, peppers, frijoles, chiles and tomatoes, fricassees of turkey and chicken; veal and sirloin, and the finale — ducks, geese, grouse, quail and pigeon. Liquids included wine from Sutter's full cellar, and champagne from San Francisco.

When the feast ended, everybody adjourned to the long room Sutter had built for assemblies. Musicians tuned up a guitar, violin and a French piano. In the first dance, a *jota,* Sutter took each lady in turn for a few steps on the floor, while she was required to simultaneously sing a verse she had improvised. Now for the other dances: *fandango, bamba, zorrita* and *jarabe.* Not until Sierra peaks glinted with gold did the musicians play the final number —the *contra danza* — after which everyone retired.

It was said to be the most extravagant Christmas party in early California history.

The year ended with the Lord of New Helvetia at the zenith of his prosperity. With the discovery of gold in early 1848, his empire would begin an irresistible slide toward disaster, gradually at first and then gaining momentum like an avalanche. Sutter's great banquet and ball — and then onrushing disaster. It almost makes you think of Napoleon's Grand Ball on the eve of Waterloo.

Sutter had correctly calculated that the end of the war with

Mexico would unlock the floodgates of immigrants. In his mind's eye, he saw himself greeting all of them at the end of their long overland journeys. But now he was also dreaming of a city nearer the Sacramento River, yet on high ground to avoid floods. To keep expanding his empire, and to build his planned city of Sutterville on the southwestern reach of what is today's Sacramento, he needed lumber a-plenty, and that meant he needed a new sawmill. One day he sent carpenter James Marshall up into the foothills to erect a sawmill, where tall pines could be transformed into lumber. On the South Fork of the American, 30 miles from the Fort, Marshall picked out a site in a well-timbered valley the Indians called Coloma.

Chapter 15
Gold on the American!

Put forth thy hand, reach at the glorious gold.
Shakespeare, Henry VI

Contrary to popular notion, gold had been found in California at various sites for years before James Marshall's famous discovery in 1848. In 1841, Jean Baptiste Ruelle, a French-Canadian who had toiled in New Mexican placer mines, discovered a small quantity in the mountains of present-day Los Angeles County, but few people seemed interested. The most noteworthy early find occurred the following year, on March 9 in San Fernando Valley's Placerita Canyon, northwest of Los Angeles. While rounding up stray cattle, rancher Francisco Lopez stopped to eat lunch under an oak tree. He dug up a bunch of wild onions to eat with his beef jerky. When he saw glittering particles in the dirt on the roots, he realized what he had found. With his knife, he dug more gold from the soil. Lopez and others worked the modest deposit, and the discovery was reported to Mexico City officials, but for some reason it had no noticeable effect, except for a small gold rush among the locals.

One day in 1843 Ruelle — the first discoverer mentioned above, now working for Sutter — showed Sutter a buzzard quill filled with gold flakes he said he found along the South Fork of the American.

Gold-finder James Marshall is portrayed at the Coloma museum.

He asked Sutter to stake him to a prospecting trip with provisions, tools, two mules and two Indian workers. Sutter suspected Ruelle's real intention was merely to travel to Oregon, so he refused. When Marshall discovered gold — on the American's South Fork! — Ruelle claimed credit as the original discoverer, but nobody paid him any mind.

Sutter inadvertently sowed the seeds of his own destruction when on Aug. 27, 1847, he drew up a contract with Marshall. Marshall, about 37, was a lanky, taciturn carpenter and carriage-maker from New Jersey. The contract called for construction of a sawmill on the South Fork 30 miles east of the Fort at Coloma — from an Indian word meaning beautiful valley. Sutter had purchased 12 square miles of Coloma land from local Indians, paying them with hats, shirts, flour and trinkets. The sale never would be validated by the U.S. Government, which didn't recognize the right of Indians to sell land to private citizens.

By the end of 1847, the mill was nearly complete, save for a glitch with the waterwheel. The tailrace was designed to shunt water back to the river, after turning the wheel. But water flowing through the tailrace was backing up, preventing the wheel from turning properly. To fix it, workers each day removed boulders and dirt to deepen the channel. Each night, they opened the sluice gate to let water run through to flush away loose sand and gravel.

On the morning of Jan. 24, 1848, while inspecting the tailrace, Marshall spied a golden shimmer — the nugget that would change the world.

This is how Marshall later recalled his momentous find: "One morning in January — it was a clear, cold morning, I shall never forget that morning — as I was taking my usual walk along the race after shutting off the water, my eye was caught with the glimpse of something shining in the bottom of the ditch. There was about a foot of water running then. I reached my hand down and picked it up. It made my heart thump, for I was certain it was gold. The piece was about half the size and of the shape of a pea. Then I saw another piece in the water. After taking it out I sat down and began to think right hard. I thought it was gold . . ."

Good thinking.

But he wasn't absolutely sure. He asked an Indian helper to fetch a tin pan from the cabin. Into it he scooped sand and gravel from the stream edge. Moving the pan in a circular fashion, he sluiced away the lighter material, leaving in the bottom a small quantity of yellow flakes "about as much as a ten-cent piece would hold." His heart was thumping, but he was still uncertain. He walked back to his fellow workers and said, "Boys, I believe I have found a gold mine." They laughed in his face.

Marshall placed some of the flakes in a pot of lye that Mrs. Peter Wimmer, the cook, had on the stove, using it to make soap. She boiled them in the lye all night, but they only gleamed brighter than ever. No one could suggest more tests, so Marshall walked back to the tailrace. "We all followed him." wrote Henry Bigler, one of the Mormon mill workers, "and in looking close, we could see particles here and there on the base rock and in seams and crevices. Conjectures were it must be rich, and from that time the fever set in and gold was on the brain."

Four days after his discovery, Marshall reached Sutter's Fort during a cloudburst on the evening of January 28. He rode through the gate, slipped off his horse and splashed through mud and water, looking for Sutter. He found him in the distillery. Marshall fussed with his sombrero as water dripped from his clothes and pooled on the floor. "Is there somewhere we can talk in private?" he asked.

Sutter closed the door and asked what he wanted.

"Are we alone?" Marshall asked.

"Of course."

Marshall demanded two bowls of water. Sutter, puzzled by the man's erratic behavior, nevertheless rang the bell, summoning a servant, who was sent to get the bowls.

"Now I want a stick of redwood and some twine and some sheets of copper," Marshall said.

"But Marshall, why do you need all these things?"

"I want to make some scales."

Sutter decided to humor him. "Well, I have some scales in the apothecary shop." He left, and returned with them.

Marshall pulled out a rag from his pocket and from it took a one-ounce glass vial containing metallic pebbles and grains, none as big as a pea, many no bigger than pinheads. He spilled the contents on the table. The tiny pebbles gleamed in the light. Marshall whispered to Sutter: "Those are from Coloma. I think they're gold."

Sutter scrutinized a pebble. "Well, it looks like gold. Let's test it." He fetched some aqua fortis (nitric acid) from his apothecary shop and poured it onto the metal — no reaction.

"Do you have any silver?" Marshall asked.

Sutter fished some coins from his pocket, and put some in the scales. The volume of gold needed to balance the silver was substantially less. At last Sutter took his *Encyclopedia Americana* from a shelf and studied the piece on gold. He clapped the book shut. "I believe this is the finest kind of gold," he said.

On March 22 of that epic year, the first shipment of planks from the completed Coloma sawmill was delivered to Sutter's Fort. With the mill complete, the Mormon workers headed for the river to prospect. The men had promised to keep the gold discovery secret until the mill was completed, but Bigler had written some Mormons at the Natoma gristmill, near the Fort, recounting the discovery. He urged them not to tell anybody — "unless it would be someone who would keep a secret."

That did it for the Natoma mill hands. The Gold Rush was on. Sutter in vain tried to keep the discovery secret, realizing it would be bad for his enterprises, now expanding more than ever. Once the presence of gold was bruited far and wide, his workers would quit the fields and workbenches and head for the hills.

James C. Ward, visiting Sutter in 1848, described him in this watershed year of his personal fortunes, when he was yet unaware that his empire was beginning its slide toward catastrophe. Ward says he was of medium height, "rather stout but well made," with hair cut close, short mustache, healthy complexion and neatly dressed in frock coat, pantaloons and blue cap. His polished manners impressed everyone. "With his gold-headed malacca in hand, you would rather suppose him prepared for a saunter on the boulevards," Ward said.

But Sutter was not just a boulevard dandy. He was a man of empire, captain of industry and agriculture, a man who had commanded cavalry on raids against hostile Indians and against an enemy army and who had conquered a wilderness. But he was not invincible, and Destiny sometimes spawns unforeseeable doom.

Before long, Sutter's entire work force joined the stampede to the hills, leaving "only the sick and lame behind," he remembered.

Sam Brannan helped to speed up the Gold Rush. A Mormon

James Marshall at Coloma forever points to the site near the American where he found the nugget that changed the world.

elder, Brannan had arrived in California in 1846 with the Mormon Battalion. In late 1847, he had arranged with Sutter to open a general store at the Fort, said to be the first general store in California. In May 1848, storekeeper Brannan decided to get some first-hand information to check out all the wild stories about gold. What he saw made him leap like a cat on a hot stove. He stuffed nuggets in a medicine vial, dashed to San Francisco and galloped all day through the streets, waving the vial and galvanizing everybody by hollering: *"Gold! Gold on the American River!"* One man recalled the frenzy that overcame him when he heard those words: He had visions of such boundless riches that the Rothschilds and Astors seemed paupers by comparison.

Brannan, before his day-long public relations stint in San Francisco streets, had had the mercantile shrewdness and avarice to buy up all the cooking pans he could find in the city, and anything else useful for panning gold. Back at his New Helvetia store, he hiked the price of pans from 20 cents to half an ounce to an ounce of gold dust, $8 to $16 each, and boosted prices on the rest of his stock to yield him comparable profits.

In a few days, San Francisco was practically emptied of able-bodied men, who had lit out for the golden hills.

Brannan owned a San Francisco newspaper, the *California Star*. The editor, Edward Kemble, 20, perhaps on orders from Brannan, published the following: "The whole country from San Francisco to Los Angeles and from the seashore to the base of the Sierra Nevada resounds to the sordid cry of Gold! GOLD! GOLD! The fields are left half-planted, the houses half-built. Everything is neglected but the manufacture of shovels and pickaxes and the means of transportation to Captain Sutter's Valley."

Kemble is a good example of a salesman who sells himself on his own spiel. As soon as his item appeared in print, on May 29, 1848, he closed the office, bought a shovel at an outrageous price, and beelined for the gold country.

He made the trip from Sutter's Fort to Coloma in company with Sutter, Major Pierson B. Reading and George McKinstry. At Coloma, Sutter announced: "These gentlemen have come to see the gold mines, Mr. Marshall." Seeing Marshall's face cloud up, Sutter assured him they were friends.

But Marshall resented visitors, for he hoped to extract a fortune here, and wanted no outside help. Least of all did he want to encourage a gold rush. So, when Kemble asked him to show the precise location where he had found gold, Marshall picked up a piece of wood and scratched an X on it with his knife. Jabbing the knifepoint into the spot where the lines crossed, he barked: "*Thar!*"

As for the rest of the workers there, Kemble said that, in comparison to prying information out of them, "opening oysters with a wooden toothpick would have been an easy task."

Poor Marshall never would profit much from his epic find. Gold-seekers hounded him wherever he went, thinking he had some psychic ability to locate gold, and would lead them to a new discovery. At first, Marshall refused to offer any suggestions. Finally, to get rid of pests, he sent them off on wild goose chases to distant gulches — where some actually found gold. Some who didn't came back wroth, threatening to hang him. In 1857, he returned to Coloma and eked out a living with odd jobs. He grew grapes there. He became a partner in a quartz mine near Kelsey.

His fortunes brightened when in 1872 the Legislature gave him a pension for two years. The pension was renewed twice. But when Marshall visited the Assembly in 1878, the story goes, a brandy bottle slipped out of his pocket and rolled along the floor — which may partly explain the Legislature's failure to renew his pension. The disenchanted man lived his last days in a cabin at Coloma, dying in 1885 at 75. He was buried on a hill overlooking his discovery site. His cabin is now part of the Marshall Gold Discovery State Historic Park, at Coloma. Crowning the hill, a tall monument overlooks the discovery site. On top, the bronze figure of Marshall forever points downward toward the river to the spot where he found the wonderful nugget. Near the river's edge, Sutter's Mill, washed away by 1862 floods, has been reconstructed. A nearby museum exhibits Gold Rush memorabilia and illuminates the hordes of hot-eyed fortune-seekers who took California by storm.

James Marshall ignited history's greatest gold rush — and died poor.

But, back to 1848 when the feverish news of the gold strike was rocking California: Rumors of fortunes being made in gold ran like quicksilver north and south along the coast. One report put it this way: "We have seen the gold with our own eyes, and it really benefitted our optics." Soldiers in Monterey went AWOL to the mines. In San Francisco, Colonel Richard B. Mason, the U.S. military governor, decided to reconnoiter — with his adjutant, Lt. William Tecumseh Sherman, later of Civil War fame.

Chapter 16
Stampede

There's plenty of gold
So I've been told
On the banks of the Sacramento.
Author unknown

The young lieutenant, William Tecumseh Sherman, later a Civil War general, recalled the time in his *Memoirs* many years later: "As the spring and summer of 1848 advanced, the reports came faster and faster from the gold-mines at Sutter's saw-mill. Stories reached us of fabulous discoveries, and spread throughout the land. Everybody was talking of 'Gold! Gold!!' until it assumed the character of fever. Some of our soldiers began to desert; citizens were fitting out trains of wagons and pack-mules to go to the mines. We heard of men earning fifty, five hundred and thousands of dollars per day, and for a time it seemed as though somebody would reach solid gold."

In June, Sherman's commanding officer Colonel Mason authorized him to reconnoiter. "I selected four good soldiers, with Aaron, Colonel Mason's black servant, and a good outfit of horses and pack-mules." One of the soldiers was Capt. Joseph Folsom, after whom a city would be named. Two civilians joined the group and Mason also decided to go along.

Recalled Sherman: "We reached the Sacramento River, then full of water . . . . The only means of crossing over was by an Indian dugout canoe. We began by carrying across our packs and saddles, and then our people. When all things were ready, the horses were driven into the water, one being guided ahead by a man in the canoe. Of course, the horses and mules at first refused to take to the water, and it was nearly a day's work to get them across, and even then some of our animals after crossing escaped into the woods and undergrowth that lined the river, but we secured enough of them to reach Sutter's Fort . . . where we encamped at the old slough, or pond, near the fort."

Sutter, ever the generous host, dispatched some Indians back to the river, and they recovered the lost animals.

"At that time there was not the sign of a habitation there or thereabouts, except the fort, and an old adobe-house, east of the fort, known as the hospital," Sherman wrote.

"Sutter was monarch of all he surveyed, and had authority to inflict punishment even unto death, a power he did not fail to use. He had horses, cattle and sheep, and of these he gave liberally and without price to all in need. He caused to be driven into our camp a beef and some sheep, which were slaughtered for our use."

By the time of Sherman's visit, Sutter was drinking more than ever. By the previous year, 1847, he had become a confirmed drunkard, according to his chief clerk Heinrich Lienhard, who said he would begin tippling early in the morning. At his Fourth of July party in 1848, with Sherman present, he apparently got loaded. General Sherman wrote in his *Memoirs*: "Before the celebration was over, Sutter was very tight, and many others showed the effect of *aguardiente*."

Nearly three decades later, after reading Sherman's book, Sutter contradicted the aspersion: "General Sherman says in his memoirs that I was 'tight' that day, but I was no more intoxicated than he. Men cannot drink liquor without feeling the effects of it. I believe it was in bad taste for an officer of the Army to partake of my hospitality and then make flippant remarks about it, accusing the host of drunkenness. I think that Sherman was later ashamed of his words; in a letter he wrote to me he took back everything and begged my pardon."

A man named John A. Stone, in the popular *Putt's Original California Songster*, penned some lines perhaps inspired by one of Sutter's pixilated episodes: "I went to eat some oysters/ Along with Captain Sutter/ And he reared up on the table/ And sat down in the butter."

To Sherman, Sutter related Marshall's arrival with news of his gold discovery. Sherman's account differs somewhat from the other version: As Sutter sat in his room, he heard a knock and called for the person to enter. Continues Sherman: "In walked Marshall, who was a half-crazy man at best, but then he looked strangely wild. 'What is the matter, Marshall?' Marshall inquired if any one was within hearing, and began to peer about the room, and look under the bed, when Sutter, fearing that some calamity had befallen the party up at the saw-mill, and that Marshall was really crazy, began to make his way to the door, demanding of Marshall to explain what was the matter. At last he revealed his discovery, and laid before Captain Sutter the pellicles of gold he had picked up in the ditch . . . .

"Marshall returned to the mill, but could not keep out of his wonderful ditch, and by some means the other men employed there learned his secret. They then wanted to gather the gold, and Marshall threatened to shoot them if they attempted it; but these men had sense enough to know if 'placer' gold existed at Coloma, it would also be found farther down-stream, and they gradually 'prospected' until they reached Mormon Island, fifteen miles below, where they discovered one of the richest placers on earth."

Sherman published his *Memoirs* in 1875, but said he retained a vivid memory of the Mormon Island diggins — now flooded by Folsom Lake — as if it were yesterday: "In the midst of a broken country, all parched and dried by the hot sun of July, sparsely wooded with live-oaks and straggling pines, lay the valley of the American River, with its bold mountain-stream coming out of the Snowy Mountains to the east. In this valley is a flat, or gravel-bed, which in high water is an island . . . On its edges men were digging, and filling buckets with the finer earth and gravel, which was carried to the machine made like a baby's cradle, open at the foot, and at the head a plate of sheet-iron or zinc, punctured full of holes. On this metallic plate was emptied the earth, and water was then poured on it from buckets, while one man shook the cradle with violent rocking by handle. On the bottom were nailed cleats of wood.

"With this rude machine four men could earn from forty to one hundred dollars a day, averaging sixteen dollars, or a gold ounce, per man per day. While the sun blazed down on the heads of the miners with tropical heat, the water was bitter cold, and all hands were either standing in the water or had their clothes wet all the time; yet there were no complaints of rheumatism or cold . . . .

"A few bush-huts near by served as stores, boarding-houses, and for sleeping; but all hands slept on the ground, with pine-leaves and blankets for bedding."

Mason and Sherman purchased some gold and dispatched it with a report to Washington DC, where in time it reached President James K. Polk.

Polk exhibited the gold in the War Office, incorporated Mason's report in his December 9 message to Congress, and declared: "The accounts of the abundance of gold are of such an extraordinary character, as would scarcely command belief were they not corroborated by the authentic reports of officers . . ."

Another version of the Mormon Island discovery site — second major gold strike in California — relates that in the spring of 1848 two Mormons, W. Sidney S. Willis and Wilford Hudson, set out from Sutter's Fort to hunt deer. They shot one, and camped for the night on a bar on the South Fork of the American near its junction with the North Fork. Bellies full, they sat on the granite shore and watched the river rush by. One pushed back his hat and scratched his head. "They're taking out gold above us on the river. Let's see if we can find some at this place." He grabbed a frying pan, scooped into gravel at the river's edge, then swirled the contents, washing out the lighter material — leaving a smidgen of shiny yellow. "Will you look at that?" He tried again, with similar results.

At daybreak they sprang into their saddles and backtracked to the Fort, feeling obliged to report their find to Mormon leader Sam Brannan.

Brannan galloped to the discovery site and established a preemptive claim, demanding a tithe of all gold taken out, purportedly for the church. Soon many Mormons began to work the claim, as well as non-Mormons lured by the feverish activity. As long as Mormons remained in the majority, the tithe continued to be collected for Brannan. But when Mormons became outnumbered, the tithe could no longer be collected from non-Mormons.

Mormon Island by 1853 had grown to a city of 2,500 people, with four hotels, three drygoods stores, five general merchandise stores, an express office and many small shops. Three years later, fire leveled the town. It was never rebuilt.

On completion of Folsom Dam in the mid-20th century, the ghost town of Mormon Island would lie at the bottom of Folsom Lake. A bronze marker at Vista Point, Folsom Dam Overlook, notes that the town lay half a mile to the east.

Brannan meanwhile amassed thousands of dollars, investing it in real estate, and in merchandise for resale to miners. After he bought out his partner C.C. Smith, he had a virtual monopoly in the valley, and his store at the Fort took in $150,000 a month, accelerating him on the way to become California's first millionaire. Nobody ever accused him of failing to look out for No. 1.

In Salt Lake City, Brigham Young sent an agent with a letter to Brannan, demanding the tithe, saying the money belonged to God. Brannan told the agent: "You go back and tell Brigham Young that I'll give up the Lord's money when he sends me a receipt signed by the Lord, and no sooner." Young dispatched several Danites to demand the money from Brannan. Danites — also known as Sons of Dan, or Avenging Angels — were Mormon enforcers. Brannan invited them to go to hell. The church excommunicated Brannan and laid a curse on him. Yet for a long time everything Brannan touched turned to gold.

By June 1848, thousands of fortune-seekers were swarming into Sutter's Fort on their way to Coloma, transforming the Fort into a wild frontier town. Loud-mouth hooligans congregated in the saloon. Knifings and murders were not unusual. Often the Fort was so crowded with "wet, poor, and hungry immigrants" that Sutter himself had trouble finding a place to lay his head at night. He didn't charge the gold-seekers for room or board, but he was making money. He was pulling in sizeable rentals from his storehouses, and the stores at the Fort were doing a frantic business in food, clothing and miners' supplies. Each voyage that Sutter's *Sacramento* and *Amelia* made up and down the river netted him an enormous profit. He also received a nice income from ferry service across the river.

In a visit to the Fort during July 1848, J.A. Moerenhout, French consul at Monterey, found it a situation of "frightful confusion." Men on horseback and afoot were milling around outside the walls, while loaded wagons trundled in and out of the gate, "some bringing goods from the Sacramento landing, others taking them to different mining regions." Within the walls stood heaps of merchandise for sale. Crowds of buyers made such a hullabaloo that "one would have thought himself either in a Turkish bazaar or in one of the most frequented market places in Europe."

Moerenhout said Sutter reported receiving total rentals of $1,800 a month, excluding that from some houses outside the walls. And Sutter hoped rentals soon would aggregate up to $3,000 a month. At this time, in short, his future looked bright.

But Sutter couldn't hold onto his gains. Penniless prospectors buttonholed him with wonderful proposals: If he would stake them to food and tools, when they struck it rich they would split the profits. Sutter always fell for it. If the prospector did strike it rich, Sutter never saw him again, as he most likely was squandering his poke in some Sacramento or San Francisco gambling dive. If he failed to get lucky, he came back to wheedle more supplies out of Sutter. Sutter was a born patsy. When somebody asked him for something, he just couldn't say no.

Summer of 1848 found Sutter in jeopardy of losing everything. The Russians exacerbated the crisis when they warned him that unless he paid in full they would foreclose. Sutter had always been tardy with the annual installments and in the past three years was in unmitigated default. Before the gold discovery, he had staved off the Russians and other creditors with one excuse after another —crop failures, a poor trapping season, and other bad luck. If they would just be patient until his next harvest, he would pay in full. he *wanted* to pay, and meant to pay. God knows he meant to pay. But when, for every dollar of income there might be, say, three dollars owing — well, some things are impossible. He needed time. Couldn't they understand? Even a child could understand. But Sutter's creditors stubbornly and willfully and adamantly *refused* to understand.

But now, with business at the Fort booming and other bellwethers of prosperity just around the corner, Sutter's alibis and pleas for more time fell on ears of stone. William A. Leidesdorff, the black entrepreneur who was the San Francisco agent for the Russians, began legal action to keep Sutter from selling any property until he paid off the $19,000 he owed. It appeared likely the Russians would be tough cookies. Consider how history might have changed if Russia actually had foreclosed. But finally, their patience exhausted, they turned the affair over to the U.S. Government, which arrived at the same conclusion: Sutter either had to pay off the Russians or give up his empire.

Suddenly, arrival from Switzerland of Sutter's son, John Jr., age 21, in the summer of 1848 offered Sutter a chance to avert catastrophe. Young Sutter found his father "on the brink of ruin . . . and surrounded by a parcel of rogues and immoral men, which, instead of helping him, would only accelerate and in a short period accomplish his utter moral, physical and financial ruin." He further noted: "Everything belonging to my father was at everybody's disposal." Merchants operating trading posts at the Fort were supplying goods to all comers including local Indians, and urging them to run up huge bills and charge them to Sutter's account. Young Sutter realized drastic action was needed to avert onrushing disaster. To keep the Russians from getting control, Sutter decided to transfer all his property titles to his son. Sutter and son contended they weren't trying to bilk the Russians — merely trying to preserve the interests of all their creditors. The father, hoping his son's youth and vigor would stem the tide of irate creditors, escaped to Coloma.

But the inexperienced youth, in California less than two months, suddenly found himself controlling property of enormous dimensions. Small wonder he felt inadequate, and disliked his new responsibilities. Yet somehow by early 1849 he managed to pay off the most urgent obligations. He transferred the property titles back to his father and resigned his position. Sutter Sr. was nettled to learn that his son, in straightening out the accounts, even paid off some people he didn't owe. Further disillusionment with his son was in store.

Some time after the gold discovery, Brannan had shifted his store to the Embarcadero, a convenient landing place on the Sacramento, and other businesses at the Fort began following him to that handier site. Earlier, Sutter Sr. — hoping to attract settlers — had laid out the town of Sutterville, safe from floods on high ground two miles south of the Embarcadero.

When Sutter learned that Sam Brannan had talked his son into having lots surveyed and sold at the Embarcadero — the beginning of the City of Sacramento — he was even more upset. In Sutter's opinion, Brannan had gotten too big for his britches and could not be trusted.

Like Sutter, Brannan wanted his own empire. He had seen Hawaii in 1846 with the Mormon party voyaging from New York to California. In 1851, figuring the island kingdom would be a pushover, he and a gang of 24 armed men sailed for the islands. They spent much of the voyage in a drunken stupor, but also spent time rifling U.S. mail bags aboard to see if word of their plot was en route to Hawaiian authorities.

Word had reached Hawaii earlier. As they stepped ashore, marshal William C. Parke put them under surveillance. That very afternoon, a gang member galloped a horse through town at a reckless pace. Stopped by a policeman, he pulled a pistol, but was knocked down and tossed in jail. When Brannan arrived to make bail, Parke told him his scheme to conquer the islands was no secret

— and carrying firearms was prohibited. Brannan and cohorts slunk back to California.

Brannan became California's first millionaire — and its first one to go broke. At one time, it's said, he owned most of the property on San Francisco's Market Street, one-fourth of the City of Sacramento that he had helped establish on the Embarcadero, and sawmills in Nevada. Another venture was a huge resort that became the City of Calistoga, Napa County. He issued his own paper money from his own bank, and served in local government and in the state senate. In his spare time, besides reveling in his riches, he chased actress Lola Montez. His restless career included land speculation, preaching, loan-sharking, newspaper publishing, storekeeping and vigilante-leading. As he grew older, Lady Luck began to give him the cold shoulder. By the 1880s, heavy drinking, love affairs, lavish spending and losing business ventures — plus the fact his wife divorced him, receiving an enormous cash settlement that forced him to liquidate his assets — wiped him out.

He retired to a land grant in Sonora, Mexico, trying to recoup, then returned to California to spend his last few years in poverty, living in a tent near Escondido, San Diego County. He died in 1889 in Escondido, Spanish for "hidden," ironic because he died in obscurity.

Meanwhile as gold-fever intensified, Sutter decided to try his own luck in the mines, hoping to strike it rich and reverse the decline in his own luck, and at the same time keep his labor force in one piece. It threatened to disintegrate because other Indians hired by white men to dig gold were paid off in gold and went on buying sprees in the stores, making Sutter's Indians jealous. "When my Indians saw this," Sutter wrote, "they too wished to go to the mountains to dig for the all powerful metal. At last I consented. I got a number of wagons ready, loaded them with provisions and goods of all kinds . . . and left with about one hundred Indians and a large number of Sandwich Islanders."

They camped on the South Fork of the American 10 miles above Mormon Island, remaining until it became so crowded with other prospectors that Sutter opted to move.

They relocated 25 miles to the south, near today's town of Sutter Creek. Sutter continues: "The work was going well for a while until three or four traveling grog-shops were established within one and a half or two miles from the camp." The gold the men found was spent drinking and gambling, and next day they were too sick to work. "My laborers, especially the Kanakas, became more and more indebted to me, and I found that it was high time to quit this sort of business in which I only lost time and money. I therefore broke up this camp too, and returned to the Fort where I disbanded nearly all the people who had worked for me in the mountains.... The whole expedition proved to be a heavy loss to me." Unkind critics assert that one reason for Sutter's failure was that he was one of the best customers of the mobile grog-shops.

He returned to a colony that was close to ruin. People had butchered his sheep, hogs and cattle and stolen his horses. His 200 barrels of salmon had disappeared, together with the Fort's cannon, gate-weights and bells. Buildings had been torn down for lumber to build miners' cabins. Fences were ripped off for firewood. Crops were trampled. "There is a saying that men will steal everything but a milestone and a millstone," Sutter rued. "They stole my millstones. The miners would not buy flower (sic) from me when they could more easily steal it." One observer remarked about the Fort: "Self-interest is so great here that they cannot take time to bury people when they die."

Of this chaotic time, Heinrich Lienhard said: "Most miners were so greedy, treacherous and unreliable that no man's life was safe. Law and order were unknown, fights occurred daily and anyone who could not protect himself with his fists was unfortunate. Every man carried a gun.... Robbery and murder were a commonplace because many men still preferred to steal gold rather than work for it." Even hardbitten frontiersman George Yount blanched: "There is nothing in all the history of the natives of America to equal the deeds of cruelty perpetrated by individuals who early immigrated to the Land of Gold.... The dregs and scum of the cities rushed into California and murder and rapine marked their every footstep."

Strong stuff, but statistics seem to bear him out: By 1854, no less than 4,200 murders had been committed in California — an average of 700 per year for the six years of the Gold Rush.

Ever hopeful, Sutter adventured into the mountains again, to Coloma, where he founded a partnership with Lansford W. Hastings in a firm called Sutter, Hastings & Co., developers of mining properties and dealers in miners' supplies. When that business also folded, he blamed his partner: "Hastings was unworthy of my trust. The business made good profits, but I lost money."

Typical of eastern news reports that whipped up the frenzy to go west was this in the New York *Herald* in January 1849: "All classes of our citizens . . . are rushing towards that wonderful California which sets the public mind almost on the highway to insanity . . . . Every day men of property and means are advertising their possessions for sale in order to furnish themselves with means to reach that golden land."

All told by the end of 1849, at least 42,000 gold-seekers had reached California by overland trails. Also, some 6,000 Mexicans from Sonora arrived in the mining camps. Also by the end of 1849, nearly 700 ships had debarked over 41,000 Americans and foreigners in San Francisco, bound for the mines. Fewer than 800 were women. The 89,000 gold-seekers differed from other westward migrants in that they came not to settle a new land. They came to get rich quick, then cut out for home to spend their fortune.

Those who struggled overland to California were better prepared for the rigors of existence in the mines, having received "survival training" during their grueling journey. Those who arrived by sea were almost totally unprepared. Some of these dudes actually took off for the mines in top hats and tails — dressed for a theater or a ballroom, but pitifully unready for the hardships of scrabbling for gold in a raw land far from civilization's amenities.

The ethnic mix by 1850 included 962 blacks who had come to California — some free men from northern states, and some slaves brought by their owners. A decade later, over 4,000 blacks had arrived. About 25,000 Chinese also had arrived in California by 1852, most of them bound for the mines. Some brought packets of seeds of their favorite tree, *Ailanthus altissima*, or Tree of Heaven, to plant, and give them a little reminder of home in this country of barbarians. Tree of Heaven grows today in nearly every Chinese camp along the rivers, and has migrated to countless other areas.

Some placer mining areas — such as Negro Bar on the American near Folsom — were worked wholly by blacks, slave and free. Settled about 1849, Negro Bar declined a year later when Virginia Mining Co. appropriated so much river water it made it impossible for the blacks to continue mining. But Negro Bar became the nucleus of the City of Folsom.

Although blacks with gold dust were welcome at gambling tables, they faced discrimination elsewhere. Often a sizeable mining town had a hotel and restaurant solely for blacks and other nonwhites. The Emancipation Proclamation of 1863 didn't bolster blacks in California because it liberated slaves only in Confederate states. Two years later, when the 13th Amendment abolished slavery nationwide, California's blacks could begin to regard themselves as free.

Strangely enough, countries on the Pacific Ocean rim heard of gold in California before the east coast of the United States. News of gold lured fortune-seekers from Chile to China.

Whoever wrote that ditty about "plenty of gold . . . on the banks of the Sacramento" was a bit off on geography, but no matter. If a miner from Chile or China or Europe or the eastern United States reached the banks of the Sacramento, anyone could point him in the general direction — up the American River, or anywhere toward the foothills. Even if, by unlikely chance, he couldn't scare up anyone in Sacramento to give him directions, he'd have no trouble finding his way, if we can believe an argonaut from Chile. Vicente Perez Rosales, with his three brothers and other Chileans, left Sacramento for the mines. Somebody had given him directions, but he didn't need them, explaining: "We soon realized not knowing the road would have been no handicap to us. There was a trail of bottles strewn along the whole way. If you want to locate a Yankee, all you need to do is follow the empty cognac bottles and you are sure to find him."

At Sutter's Fort, even attic rooms of the two-story central building were turned into sleeping quarters for miners heading for the hills. For $1 a night, a miner got floor space, where he could wrap himself in his blanket, with his boots for a pillow. Sometimes 250 men jammed into the confined quarters.

"The men were packed in like sardines," a Forty-Niner recalled. "They were dead tired, cross and cranky, they swore at each other and all swore at the late comer for disturbing them. Being sworn at wasn't so bad. It was the atmosphere that tried the stoutest stomach — the combined smell of boot leather, tobacco smoke, sweaty clothes, sweating bodies, garlic breaths . . . If you raised up on your elbow and looked around, it was just like looking over a rolling ocean of men — twisting, squirming, turning over, talking in their sleep, some mumbling prayers, others sobbing, other cussing, some all of these. And good Lord, how they snored!"

Sutter's overly generous nature, plus the fact that gold-seekers were ripping him off of every valuable they could lay their hands on, only hastened his journey on the road to ruin. If a miner wanted a horse, he grabbed the first he laid his eyes on, most likely one of Sutter's. If he craved a thick steak, he butchered a steer, which often belonged to Sutter. Supplies kept vanishing from the Fort. Men awoke in the morning to discover that some sticky-fingered lout had made off with a valued possession.

As the invasion continued into the spring of 1850, Sutter kept his Indians at work, plowing and tilling and sowing, hoping law and order soon would bring things back to normal. "Before the crops come up, we will have better times," he said hopefully. But his Indian workers dwindled in numbers. Many had been beaten and some killed by gold-seekers. Many a boozed-up prospector murdered an Indian for no reason other than being trigger-happy, and knowing he could get away with murdering an Indian. When strangers stalked into the fields, Sutter's Indian workers fled. Sutter felt completely helpless.

At first, the Fort was the major entrepot for the horde of fortune-seekers bound for the hills, and prices of tools and supplies leaped to giddy heights because they couldn't be transported in fast enough to fill demand. But now the stores in ever-growing Sacramento City were luring ever more business from the Fort. The Fort lost its distinction as the only commercial center in inland California. One at a time, Fort merchants packed their stock, closed shop, and headed for Sacramento City, where saloons, theaters and gaming houses enlivened the hardships of the mining life.

By mid-June 1850, all the storekeepers had gone, and Sutter's income from Fort rentals dropped to zero. Some of his faithful Indian workers were still tending gardens, and the hot sun was ripening the grain. But the empty Fort no longer rang with blacksmith's hammer and anvil, or echoed with shopkeepers' cries and yells of roistering customers. The only "customers" now were thieves who sneaked in at night to loot whatever struck their fancy.

To salvage what he could from the debacle, Sutter sold all the Fort's usable appurtenances, rather than let looters rob him blind. Tools and equipment were carted into Sacramento City and auctioned, netting him less than $40,000.

Crops now were ripe for harvest, but a week later they were gone — strangers with rifles drove their cattle (some stolen from Sutter) to feed on his wheat. Bullets killed some of Sutter's Indians while they worked in the fields. Sutter could only boil with rage: "It can't go on! By Jupiter, it can't go on!"

That winter, five enterprising rogues armed with rifles and equipped with boats organized a partnership on an island in the Feather River near Marysville. They slaughtered Sutter's cattle and sold the meat in Sacramento. The thieves split $60,000 in profits, then split the scene.

In San Francisco during the summer of 1850, more than 200

abandoned sailing ships created a forest of masts as passengers and crew lit out for the gold country. The city's population doubled every 10 days during one period of several months. Acres of tents sprouted like mushrooms on the sand dunes west of town. From a drowsy hamlet of fewer than 1,000 people in early 1848, the city exploded into a boomtown of 40,000 in 1850, a dizzy increase of 4,000 percent in two years!

One might call Sutter "The man who built San Francisco — accidentally." Listen: Sutter contracted for a sawmill with Marshall, whose discovery triggered the stampede that detonated the explosion of San Francisco from a sleepy little town to a roaring boomtown. Without Sutter, where would San Francisco be? Come to think, where would Sacramento be?

Chapter 17
Boomtown

Change is not made without inconvenience, even from worse to better.

Richard Hooker

The Gold Rush brought dizzy changes to the little town hunkering on the Embarcadero. As argonauts from all over the globe rushed in, Sacramento exploded seemingly overnight from almost nothing to a boomtown gone berserk. In 1848, E. Gould Buffum arrived and called Sacramento "an untenanted plain." Less than a year later, in 1849, the town had mushroomed into one of 12,000 people, according to one report.

By early 1849, a number of log cabins and frame buildings had risen on the waterfront. As the Gold Rush accelerated in the late spring of 1849, the town soared. In mid-June 1849, Sacramento had 100 wood and canvas houses. Two months later, in August, prospector William L. Schooning reported that the city had upwards of 1,000 houses. His eyes popped at some of the marvels of growth: "Yesterday we drove our teams into the streets about 9 o'clock in the morning; they stood there for perhaps two hours. In the evening of the same day I passed along, and on the very ground (where the horses had been) there stood a baker's shop in full operation selling bread and receiving money for it!"

On Sept. 1, 1849, J.A. Moerenhout, French consul at Monterey, wrote the Minister of Foreign Affairs at Paris about Sacramento

City: "The growth and importance this new settlement has exhibited are among the marvels that are happening in this country. Last year I was at this place at the same season and there was not a house or even a tent there. Only a few schooners lay in the port and the only business of any importance was a trade or barter carried on at the fort of New Helvetia. Now there is a town of 3,000 to 4,000 inhabitants there, with a quay lined with fine buildings, streets laid out and with a large volume of business that increases as communication with the placers and the interior becomes more regular and easy, and where . . . thirty-five ships were at anchor, the smallest of which was fifty to sixty tons."

The town grew so rapidly that by October 1849, according to another report, it rose to over 6,000 people, of whom 4,000 were transients, all crowded into 45 wooden buildings and 300 canvas houses. The transients, of course, were mostly gold-seekers getting ready to make tracks.

Note that the figures of 45 buildings and 300 canvas houses for October 1849 contradict the "upwards of 1,000 houses" reported for June 1849 by Schooning. Somebody was wrong, but there was no doubt that Sacramento was on the rise. As to the city's population for 1849, one source estimated it at 12,000, but others put it in 1850, a year later, as variously 2,000 to 3,000 and 6,000 and 9,000. Confusing. Could it have fluctuated that much?

Perhaps so. Daniel B. Woods, who arrived June 27, 1849, reported that each hot flash of a new discovery in the hills triggered an exodus from Sacramento, emptying half the town, which then began to refill with new arrivals.

River traffic also was escalating. On one day in 1850, somebody counted 65 steam and sailing vessels ranged along the city's waterfront.

Year 1850 also was notable because Sacramento became one of California's original 27 counties.

California's population was increasing so fast that the Legislature ordered a special census in 1852 — which put Sacramento *County* at 12,589, including 9,457 white males and 1,739 white females; 804 Chinese, of whom only 10 were females; and 80 "domesticated Indians."

Chapter 18
Going For the Gold

I'm bound for Sacramento
With a washbowl on my knee.

When Stephen Foster composed "Oh, Susannah!" he never dreamed that thousands of gold-seekers would sing its tunes, with fractured lyrics, as they streamed toward the Far West. In one of the lines of the argonaut's version, he announces that when he sees the gold dust there "I'll pick it off the ground." Gold actually was picked off the ground in some cases in the earliest days of the stampede. An army officer spotted a nugget on the ground —before he even got off his horse. In other cases, it was dug out of rocky crevices with knives.

Legions of prospectors, in their mad search for riches, left no stone unturned in Sierra foothills. They christened their diggins with pungent monikers, many hinting of stories lost to the record: You Bet, Whisky Slide, Poverty Flat, Loafer Hill, Grub Gulch, Gouge Eye, Slapjack Bar, Port Wine, Sweet Revenge, Greenhorn Creek, Git-up-and-Git, Black Gulch Camp, Murderer's Bar, Railroad Flat, Boneyard Meadow, Hangman's Bridge, Hell's Half Acre, Henpeck City, Slaughter Bar, Groundhog's Glory, Bogus Thunder, Red Dog Camp, and Sucker Flat. But three gold towns yielded stories by Bret Harte in his famous tales, "The Luck of Roaring Camp," "An Episode of Fiddletown," and "The Outcasts of Poker Flat." And Angel's Camp, named after a man named George Angel and which retains its name, became famous as the site of Mark Twain's immortal yarn, "The Jumping Frog of Calaveras County."

Macabre holding pattern: Perhaps no more shocking illustration of the catastrophe the Gold Rush visited on the Maidu Indians of northern California can be imagined than this painting, "The Burial Tree," once exhibited in Sacramento History Center. It is the work of the late Frank Day, a Maidu Indian who frequented the Folsom area, and is based on the account told by his grandfather. The Maidus buried their dead under this oak tree in Butte County. Even in death, they could not rest in peace. Gold-seekers tore up the ground while prospecting, turning up the Indian remains. As long as miners continued to dig there, skeletons and bodies were lashed to tree limbs, out of reach of animals until they could be re-buried. Permission to publish this photo is courtesy of Institute of American Indian Arts Museum, Santa Fe, N.M.

Some picturesque gold town names became permanent communities but adopted more dignified appellations: Hangtown became Placerville; Bed Bug became Ione; Humbug became North Bloomfield.

Panning was, in 1848 when the rush started, the most popular way to recover placer gold — gold washed downstream from the fabled "Mother Lode" of gold-laden quartz in the Sierra. Miners preferred stamped-iron pans 18 inches in diameter, just under three inches deep, with flat bottom and sloping sides. The prospector would fill it half full of earth, plucking out the pebbles. Then he'd fill it with water, swirl it around, letting water spill over the rim with each swirl, while he scrutinized the contents for any "color" — flecks of gold. When he had swirled all the water out, any gold would remain, usually mixed with sand. But panning required many hours of hunkering in icy water and endlessly and wearisomely swirling the pan in a circular motion. A good worker could do over 50 pans a day. Even so, sometimes he netted zilch for his pains. While working, he usually had to stand in frigid water, which was conducive to pneumonia and rheumatic maladies. Scurvy often broke out among miners deprived of fresh fruits and vegetables for months while scrabbling in icy streams.

"Dry washing" meant tossing the muck in a blanket after plucking out the stones and drying it. The wind blew away the lighter stuff. But this was inefficient and resorted to only when pans were lacking. Pans were expensive, and miners guarded them from thieves.

Miners soon constructed various labor-saving devices that operated on the same principle as the gold pan, but boosted production. They included the cradle, the long tom, and the sluice box. Streams have been called "nature's sluiceboxes" because they erode gold-bearing strata and wash the gold downstream, where it often settles behind little ridges in the bedrock, just as in sluicebox riffles. Miners labored mightily to ferret out those secret caches of riches in submerged or buried bedrock.

Daniel B. Woods said the lack of pure water was a problem: "Our drinking water comes down to us thoroughly impregnated with the mineral substances washed through the thousand cradles above us."

In 1850, miners took $41 million in gold from the foothills and the gravel beds of the Sacramento, the American, and their tributaries. The take became $75 million for 1851, and $81 million for 1852.

The American's Middle Fork proved the richest of all, having more producing bars, several of which yielded millions. Mud Canyon and American Bar are credited with $3 million each, and Horseshoe Bend, Greenhorn Slide, Volcano Bar and Yankee Slide ranged down to $1 million each.

All told for the first decade, 1848-57, at least $400 million in gold was extracted in California — not too shabby, considering the low price of gold in those times. California's gold would help the Union win the Civil War, help finance the transcontinental railroad, and

In Old Sacramento, Edwin Morgan shows how the earliest argonauts separated the yellow metal from dross.

help a few people get very rich. The Gold Rush accelerated the epic of westward expansion. It was history's greatest gold rush because it was the first big one and stirred up the greatest emotions. Few events have impacted American history with such raw energy.

Prospectors at first were paid $16 to $18 for an ounce of gold. Later in 1848, so much gold was mined that the price plummeted, and miners had to take almost anything they could get. With the price $15 an ounce in Monterey, for instance, one buyer in the mining camps bought 36 pounds at a mere $3 an ounce. Late in 1848, Indians who found gold were cheated by being paid as little as 50 cents an ounce, and white miners at times were shorted for $1. Miners selling gold dust often were given short weight, and some complained that buyers blew away some of their dust. After 1848, the price climbed to $10 an ounce, and later, up to $18. However, some 10 per cent of the gold found in California contained other metals, which knocked the price to $17.

Most miners failed to find the bonanza they dreamed of. By August 1850, only one in 100 was netting a reasonable profit. But only one in 1,000 was compensated for all the tribulations of the journey to California and the hardships endured here. Only a few found a pot of gold, but many saw the rainbow..

In 1850, only eight women were among the 30,000 Gold-Rushers who sailed back home from California following the 1849 stampede, according to J.S. Holliday, author of *The World Rushed In.* He said one woman with an entreprenurial talent went home with $18,000 — earned by baking and selling pies to miners at $10 and $12 each. When Holliday told that anecdote to one audience, a skeptical voice rang out: "Yeah, that's what she told her mother back home!"

By 1853, gold recoverable by panning, rocker or long tom was getting harder to come by. Stream-beds with their easy pickings were petering out, so many miners shifted their attack to new ground. Some tried lode mining, or vein mining. Each miner would dig his own hole in a hillside, questing for veins or fissures harboring gold-bearing quartz, and follow them wherever they might lead, sometimes hundreds of feet through solid rock. Sometimes an entire hillside — known as a coyote diggins — would be riddled with holes, each housing a busy miner. If any unusual sound rent the air, dozens of miners popped out of their holes like big-eyed ground squirrels, gaping around to check out the disturbance.

Chilean miners built ore crushers, or *arrastres*, like those in

South America. Huge stone wheels on a common axle were rotated by a horse or mule, crushing ore on a rock bed as the wheels rolled over it. Some Mexican miners carted stamp mills into the Mother Lode, and other miners adopted this device for crushing ore. The din from the hammering of these mills resounded for miles through Sierra canyons.

To separate gold from pulverized rock, miners either washed the crushed ore in a rocker or added mercury, which amalgamated with the gold. They then distilled off the mercury, reclaiming it for further use.

Miners soon figured out that riches of placer gold might be found in the dry gravel deposits of buried ancient rivers and streams. The problem: The ancient waterways long ago dried up or changed course, and the gravel beds were covered by accumulations of soil and rock — or even raised and shifted about during the mountain-building epoch that created the Sierra. How to get at these buried gravels? Some lay under 200 feet or more of worthless rock.

"Ground sluicing" offered a beginning. Miners dug a small gully down a promising hillside, then channeled water to the hilltop via flume or ditch, and let it wash down the gully. Now they shoveled earth into their man-made stream. As the water rinsed away mud and silt, the irregularities along the stream-bed would trap gold, just as in a sluicebox.

In 1852, a Frenchman named Chabot improved his ground-sluicing project by using a hose to shoot water where he desired it. A year later, one Edward Matteson further improved the idea by affixing a nozzle to the hose. No explanation is available as to why it took a year for someone to think of putting a nozzle on a hose. At any rate, Matteson is credited as the father of hydraulicking, which would move veritable mountains of ore.

Mining was now becoming an organized business. Many miners, outclassed by the new techniques and with no desire to work for someone else, drifted back to the valley and took up farming. The organized-business miners were inheriting the earth — turning rivers out of their courses and hosing away hillsides in their mad quest for gold.

Chapter 19
The Mountain-Movers

Bring me men to match my mountains.
Sam Walter Foss; legend enscribed above the portals of the Jesse M. Unruh State Office Building, Sacramento.

Edward Matteson's hose nozzles evolved into the huge cannon-like monitors that, in a spree of hydraulicking, attacked the lush landscape like a battalion of artillery, laying it waste. Beginning about 1853, numerous small hydraulic mining companies operated at the Malakoff Diggins near North Bloomfield, formerly Humbug, northeast of Nevada City. One or two men could handle hundreds of tons of earth a day, making it economical to exploit gravels yielding as little as a nickel's worth of gold in a cubic yard.

Hydraulicking also scarred the hills near Sacramento. More on that later.

Hydraulicking required immense volumes of water, channeled in from reservoirs via ditches and flumes at a high enough elevation so it would fall to the mining site at high pressure. Powerful jets from the monitors blasted away at hillside gravels and riverside terraces, ripping away soil and rock, literally washing away entire hillsides. Debris-laden water was channeled through sluiceboxes, their bottoms lined with wooden blocks to trap the gold. Water exiting sluiceboxes flushed vast quantities of mud and silt into Humbug Creek, then into the Yuba River, then into the

Sacramento system. Hydraulicking at Malakoff, when going full bore from 1866 to 1884, grossed $3.5 million in gold from 30 million cubic yards of gravel, which averages more than 10 cents a yard.

It also grossed out a lot of people because it despoiled immense areas of the landscape. It caused floods in the valley, as tailings glutted streambeds. It ruined farmlands by depositing immense layers of sand and silt and clay. Water overflowing riverbanks transformed great areas of cultivated floodplain into swamps and marshes. Farmers were quite naturally incensed. In the Wheatland area, slickens piled up so deep they covered houses, says historian F.D. Calhoon. At Marysville, the Yuba River bottom rose higher than the town. Levees of course had to be raised. Even today in the Yuba and Bear Rivers, streambeds are higher in some places than the adjoining land.

For years the shipping business on the Sacramento system enjoyed a brisk commerce—until hydraulicking blockaded it with shoals and sandbars. It raised the riverbed more than five feet, making it mandatory to raise levees all the way down to the Delta, to guard against winter floods. Hydraulicking blocked the mouth of the American with a sandbar, closing it to most traffic.

Farmers were graveled by all the mud and gravel, and steamboat captains were, of course, steaming. But hydraulickers ignored the sound and fury as long as they could. Tailings not only crippled navigation in the Sacramento by closing its upper stretches to river traffic, they hampered navigation as far down as the Carquinez Straits. Silt traveled all the way to the Golden Gate, and impaired navigation in San Francisco Bay. It's been estimated that hydraulicking sent one billion cubic yards of tailings down the Sacramento. Incredible! If all those cubic yards were laid end-to-end, they would reach to the moon and back. Yet if they were dumped all in one pile, they would aggregate less than a fifth of a cubic mile.

The problem in the Sacramento River became so acute that in 1875 some 70 business companies and landowners signed petitions urging construction of wing dams to deepen the Sacramento channel at the bend below Sacramento City, "as nearly all transportation by water is being cut off." For some reason, the dams were never built.

Legal action by those chafing at the destruction seemed to get nowhere because the mining companies enjoyed popular support: They bolstered the economy by providing jobs. Yet there were many angry dissenters. When the English Dam, water source for

Malakoff Diggings was devastated by the mountain-movers.

Milton Mining Co., gave way, most people suspected it had been dynamited by somebody who had had it up to here with hydraulicking wastes.

At last in 1884, a California Supreme Court decision outlawed the dumping of tailings into streams. Some operators built tailing dams or reservoirs, to prevent stream pollution, and continued hydraulicking on a smaller scale. But the court's decision closed the spigot on most hydraulicking, and thus sharply reduced the state's gold production, cutting it almost in half. Since, then, most floodplain farmlands that were transformed into swamps have been restored to agriculture, and the badlands carved out of the lush landscape by the relentless monitors have been softened by erosion and the healing by many years of green growth.

Yet some badlands remain. Malakoff is an enormous pit that yawns 7,000 feet long, 3,000 wide, and nearly 600 feet deep in places, though some has been filled in by erosion. The site is now Malakoff Diggins State Historic Park, 2,777 acres. It includes a museum, the ghost town of North Bloomfield, and the yawning pit.

Although Malakoff hydraulicking hosed away countless millions of tons of earth and rock, the enormous cliffs of the pit, with their pillars and spires, lend a certain grandeur to the scene —

a badlands effect not unlike something one might admire in Yellowstone where nature, not man, wreaked the havoc. You also can see the 8,000-foot tunnel drilled to improve drainage so as to mine deeper gravels, and to flush the tailings into the South Yuba river.

Contrary to brochures from California State Parks and Recreation Department that bill Malakoff as the world's largest hydraulic gold mine, Don Dupres, associate geologist with California Division of Mines and Geology, Sacramento, says it isn't so. He says Malakoff is surpassed by the North Columbia hydraulic mine on San Juan Ridge, Nevada County, a few miles east of Malakoff. It mined gravels deposited by an ancestor of the Yuba River.

Another immense hydraulicking operation, the Stewart Mine, main gold source in the Gold Run district, is traversed by Interstate 80 between Gold Run and Dutch Flat, Placer County. This enormous pit — three miles long, one mile wide and up to 400 feet deep — yielded $6 million in gold from 1865 to 1878.

Hydraulicking also tore up the landscape on the Bear River and at You Bet and Rattlesnake Bar. Closer to Sacramento, it ravaged lands to the east. One site lies off Jackson Road in eastern Sacramento County near the Amador County line. After hydraulicking ended here, clay was mined from the Ione formation mentioned in the "Genesis" chapter. Remnants of the original landscape stand like outcroppings, around which countless tons of earth were hosed away.

Another hydraulicking operation laid waste the terrain around Michigan Bar, also in eastern Sacramento County. This town site on Michigan Bar Road, half a mile or so north of Jackson Road, today consists of only a private farm residence and outbuildings. A state historical marker on Jackson Road formerly identified the scene, but the bronze marker was missing at this writing. The lush grass that mantles the land round about, with a sprinkling of trees and schrubs, fails to conceal the broken look, corrugations and cocked-hat formations that identify this terrain as a onetime scene of hydraulicking.

Closer to Sacramento, a hydraulicking landscape can be seen today in Fair Oaks where the ravaged cliffs flank Illinois Avenue as it runs south to the entrance of Sailor Bar Park on the American River.

Chapter 20
River of Treasure

For many years, people driving Highway 50 between Sacramento and Folsom crossed a lunar-like terrain of nearly 30 square miles of rock-piles. For six decades until 1962, snorting, steam-breathing mechanical dinosaurs lorded it over this American River floodplain. Greedily they gobbled their way across the land, dumping behind them their endless acres of excretions —or tailings, if you prefer. These bucket-line dredges dug as deep as 100 feet — as deep as a 10-story building is high —bringing up the gold-bearing gravels and cobbles, burying the rich topsoil, literally turning a small world upside down, leaving a badlands in their wake. They left the soil on the bottom and gravels and cobbles on top, varying in size from a pea to 20 inches in diameter.

Prospectors mined placer gold with a dredge in early years of the Gold Rush. The first was described by J. Wesley Jones, writing in the *Pantoscope of California* in the early 1850s. He told of the *Phenix* dredging machine, a "cumbrous arrangement" designed to dredge sand from the bed of the Yuba River, in the hope of extracting large quantities of gold. Added Jones: "It was soon found, however, that this machine dredged more money from the pockets of the owners than it did from the bed of the Yuba, and this kind of dredging was soon abandoned."

But dredges were not abandoned for keeps. On the Lower American, mechanizing the quest for gold, dredging devices were first used in 1878, unsuccessfully. But success of floating bucket-line dredges in New Zealand before 1890 proved their worth. A New Zealand-type dredge began operating in California in 1898, not too successfully. By 1900 a rugged, economically successful dredge was developed for California placers and went to work on the American. By 1905, four companies operated five dredges here. One was the Natomas Company. By 1908, several dredging operations had merged to form Natomas Consolidated, later reorganized with its original name, Natomas Company. Came 1913, and 10 dredges ranged along 12 miles of the river between Sacramento and Folsom. Dredging peaked in the 1930s and 1940s when as many as 13 clanking leviathans were mucking along the river, assimilating gold. Some measured as long as 200 feet, two-thirds of a football gridiron. The largest had 17-cubic-foot buckets.

Before dredging a new area, operators first prospected with test borings to find locations with likely concentrations of gold. Workers on a dredge dropped its spuds to anchor it at a promising site. When they finished at that spot, they lifted the spuds. Workers stretched a cable to winch the dredge ahead to a new site, then dropped the spuds again. Dredges toiled around the clock, shutting down only for Christmas and July 4, and once or twice a day for maintenance.

These steam-powered dredges churned up over one billion cubic yards of gravel in their clangorous search for treasure. One billion cubic yards equals 27 billion cubic feet, or five cubic feet of gravel for every person on earth.

A dredge floated in a pond of its own creation. Its endless chain of buckets scooped up the gravel and dumped it into sluiceboxes, where riffle devices separated the gold. Mercury in the riffles captured the gold by amalgamating with it, whereupon it settled to the bottom. Workers ladled up the gold-laden mercury, or drained it off into buckets. In a retort house in Sacramento, the mercury was distilled off, collected, and used again. The gold was melted into bars.

The conveyor belt dumped the gravel tailings behind, leaving rows of giant mounds and furrows as the dredge masticated its way through the landscape. In some places, piles of tailings were heaped as high as 40 feet above surrounding non-dredged land — high as a four-story building.

For years many people thought the dredges had wrecked the land forever, for any use. But today most of it has been reclaimed

Members of the local Real Estate Association in the 1920s inspect a mammoth dredge on the American. Maybe they're touring it because one of them listed it for sale. Photo courtesy Sacramento Museum and History Division.

for use in one way or another. In 1951, Aerojet-General Corp. purchased 7,300 acres of the dredged area, and in 1956 another 4,200 acres, for development and testing of missile propulsion systems, and even moon rockets. In short, Aerojet turned the lunar landscape into a testing ground for — lunar rockets.

As years passed, residential subdivisions and light industry crept across the man-made badlands — reclaimed by removing or leveling the tailings, then grading. Top soil was imported.

About 1,900 acres of tailings lie in parks, where trees, grass and shrubs now garnish the once-sterile wasteland. American River Parkway embraces 736 acres of tailings; Folsom Lake State Recreation Area has 827, and Prairie City Off-Highway Vehicle Park, 300. World-Turned-Upside-Down has become a Brave New World. The strange mounds and furrows offer park visitors reminders of the time when dredges literally turned a small world upside down in their night-and-day scrabble for gold.

Dredges in Sacramento County clanked to a halt in 1962 when they no longer could recover enough gold to make it pay. Prices of everything else had gone up, but gold remained controlled at $35 per ounce.

Between 1900 and 1962, over $125 million in gold was dredged from the 17,400 acres of gravels along the Lower American between Sacramento and Folsom. This was in the days when gold was priced at $24 to $35 an ounce. Today that gold would be worth a billion or more, depending on market value, which in recent years has fluctuated up to nearly $800 per ounce.

During the heyday of dredges, protestors charged that the tailings permanently destroyed agricultural land. Proponents argued that dredging employed thousands of workers in California and paid millions of dollars in wages annually, and that dredged land was only a trifling percentage of California's arable land.

Hardly anyone knows that even today gold is mined commercially from American River gravels near Sacramento. It's a by-product of gravel production by A. Teichert & Son and Granite Construction Co., says Don Dupres, associate geologist, California Division of Mines and Geology, Sacramento. But mum's the word. "When it comes to gold, they clam right up," Dupres said. "They don't even have to tell how much they produce. But I know they produce a lot of gold — and a little bit of platinum."

But the big question remains: With a billion-dollar treasure (today's value) of that yesteryear gold already recovered by dredges from gravels of the Lower American, could an equally staggering treasure still lie in the never-mined, buried gravels of the American channel that courses from Folsom to Elk Grove? At least one local geologist regards it as possible. Chris Hulbe of Sacramento City College explains why those gravels were never exploited: Gravels of the other channels were visible on the surface — signal flags to prospectors. But those of the Elk Grove channel are buried under 60 feet of soil. How do we know they exist? Explains Hulbe: from data on water-well drillings compiled by State Department of Water Resources.

Could a billion dollars lie buried in the gravels of the ancient American?

Chapter 21
In Old Sacramento

The city is one great cesspool of mud, offal, garbage, dead animals and that worst of nuisances consequent upon the entire absence of outhouses.

From an 1849 letter by Jonas Winchester

To stave off his father's creditors John Sutter Jr. decided to map out a city near the Embarcadero and sell lots. He and Sam Brannan hired two army officers — Captain William Warner and Lieutenant William Tecumseh Sherman — as surveyors. Creator and destroyer: Sherman, who helped create Sacramento, later destroyed a famous eastern city when, as a Civil War general, he burned Atlanta. But now the two officers, working from December 1848 to January 1849, mapped a gridwork of streets oriented to compass points, and numbered and lettered, just as they are today. They earmarked many blocks for public use. Today these lots ornament the city as one-block parks. Lots were priced at $500 each, or $250 at some distance from the waterfront. In early 1849, proceeds from lot sales enabled young Sutter to make his final payment on Fort Ross and pay other claims from the Hudson's Bay Co., Ygnacio Martinez, and Don Antonio Sunol.

But he had a problem with George McDougal, who the year before had leased from Captain Sutter rights to inaugurate a ferry service on the Sacramento. When McDougal converted a vessel into the first store on the Embarcadero, young Sutter thought he was going too far, so he tried to re-negotiate the ferry lease. That got McDougal in an uproar, and he claimed exclusive right to use the riverbanks for 400 yards south of the junction with the American. He then transferred his enterprises three miles south to Sutterville and triggered a trade war by selling merchandise at cost. This jeopardized other businesses on the Embarcadero and at Sutter's Fort. McDougal, to coax merchants to locate in Sutterville, offered 80 free lots. Counterattacking, young Sutter offered 500 free lots to merchants willing to open shop in Sacramento City. Sutterville lost the real estate war, and was destined to die on the vine.

When the elder Sutter, snowed in at Coloma, got the news of the new town on the waterfront, he waited only until the snows thawed to fling a saddle on his horse and gallop to Sacramento, to discharge his son. But he was too late to clamp the lid on boomtown Sacramento. The furious captain later told historian Hubert Bancroft: "Had I not been snowbound in Coloma, Sacramento would never have been built."

The Sutterville name today designates a suburban area in rolling ground south of Land Park Zoo. Sutterville Road on the south edge of the park is another reminder of the early community.

As early as April 30, 1849, city officials convened to name 11 men to a committee to propose a proper form of government and establish city boundaries. The committee went hog wild — proposing as boundaries the Coast Range on the west, the Sierra in the east, and the length of the valley on north and south. All told, 7,000 square miles — or a city nearly as large as the State of New Jersey!

By the summer of 1849, gold-seekers by the thousands from all over — the Forty-Niners, they were called — were bursting the seams of the ramshackle riverfront city. They thronged in from the east coast, from San Franscisco and from earth's far corners, jamming through Sacramento on their race to stake a claim in the hills, pausing here for supplies and a belt or two of John Barleycorn.

The notion of a saloon on the Embarcadero had been conceived as early as 1841 when a man named McVickar announced plans to build a grogshop up in a sycamore tree, 20 feet above the ground, with access via a ladder. He never did translate his vision into reality, perhaps because he may have had another vision — one of juiced-up customers trying to make their way down 20 feet of ladder in darkness.

Sacramento's first saloon-keeper was a fast-working entrepreneur who — only an hour after he hit town — fetched a sail from a ship on the waterfront, wrapped it around three trees, slapped a plank across two barrels and hollered "Bar's Open!" or words to that effect.

Zadock Hubbard, said to be one of three persons who constructed the first theater in Texas, brought his showmanship talents to Sacramento. On J Street at the Embarcadero, he erected a circular tent 50 feet in diameter, calling it the Round Tent Saloon. Enormously popular, it featured live music, a handsomely ornamented bar, gambling for every taste, and paintings of women in various stages of undress, to titillate lonely miners. Though other saloons cropped up, the Round Tent reigned for months as the town's most popular watering hole. Dr. John F. Morse, physician and journalist — and brother of telegraph inventor Samuel F.B. Morse — offered this observation about the Round Tent: "The toilers of the country, including traders, mechanics and speculators, lawyers, doctors, and some apostate ministers, concentrated at this gambling focus, like insects around a lighted candle at night; and like insects, seldom left the delusive glare until scorched and consumed by the fires of destruction." Tens of thousands of dollars in gold dust changed hands there in an evening, just as dust changed hands in every Sacramento saloon. The usual price for a drink was a pinch of dust, with the bartender measuring. Saloonkeepers who wanted to hire a bartender would ask each applicant: "How much can you raise in a pinch?" The man with fat fingers got the job.

After the Round Tent's popularity waned, for some reason, it was succeeded by the Gem, a frame building at 2nd and J Streets owned by Joseph McKinney, later the sheriff. Others were the Humboldt, Mansion, Empire, Diana, Lee's Exchange and some of lesser fame. Gambling went on at fever-pitch. Every saloon was jammed, and every table ringed by hot-eyed plungers.

There seemed no end to the incoming tide of thousands who stopped here to buy provisions, guzzle whiskey, try their luck in games of chance, and dally with painted ladies — then off to the hills merrily. The Forty-Niners also were known as Argonauts, after the ship *Argo* in which Jason and his band of Greeks sailed in their legendary quest for the Golden Fleece. No doubt many California Argonauts perceived the irony: Instead of finding the Golden Fleece, they were fleeced of their gold in Sacramento's gambling halls.

Before long, Sacramento was hosting another type of itinerant, those whose golden dreams had turned to lead. Some prospectors had found gold, but for most it was disappointingly scarce. Few found real riches. Many who had failed in the mines were ashamed to go back to their faraway homes, to confess defeat. So they retraced their steps only as far as this lusty town on the river, where they poured whiskey down their throats to numb the pain of failure. If they could afford more than painkiller, they looked for other diversions such as gambling, and they gambled even if they couldn't afford it. Lonely miners looked for still other diversions. A bit of doggerel of the time memorializes one diversion:

The miners came in '49,
The whores in '51,
And when they got together
They produced the native son.

Actually the advent of the first ladies of the evening to Sacramento occurred earlier than 1851, but the versifier was reaching for a rhyme.

City Hotel — first hotel in Sacramento — began to rise in June 1849 when Sam Brannan and John Fowler transported the remnants of Sutter's unfinished Brighton flour mill to the Embarcadero, using them to build the new hotel. Only two weeks after groundbreaking, Sacramentans staged a grand ball there to celebrate the Fourth of July, 1849, though the three-story building, destined to become the town's center of fashion, would not be complete until September.

Promoters of the ball spared no cost to offer a gala commensurate with their new prosperity. Organizers scouted far and wide to recruit ladies to embellish the dance floor. They ransacked tents, cabins, ranches and wagon beds for females, the upshot being that 18 women were gathered into the ballroom. Some 200 men paid admission. Tickets sold for $32 each, and gents had to wear swallow-tail coats and white vests. Commented Morse of the belles of this ball: "Not all were amazons, but replete with all the adornments and graces that belong to bold and enterprising pioneers of a new country."

Some time that summer, Stephen C. Masset of the *Placer Times*—Sacramento's first newspaper, born April 28 of that year at Sutter's Fort — found lodging in City Hotel. He didn't like it even a trifle. He complained in print about the heat, the smell, mosquitos, fleas, and bedbugs who "came in myriads to greet and congratulate me upon my arrival." Itching and scratching kept him awake most of the night. The noises — swearing and snoring of occupants, cries of children, and the yells and hee-haws accompanying departures of mule train after mule train — added up to "a perfect pandemonium." Just as sheer exhaustion dragged him into a doze, he felt a heavy bump against the board that screened him from the street: "To my astonishment the head of a big ox presented itself, and with its cold and moist snout commenced rubbing against my knee! I leaped from my slat."

With City Hotel flourishing, construction of other hotels followed. But prospectors looking for a place to flop for a night or two found nothing intended for the persnickety. A man named Hinton R. Helper remarked on Sacramento's "dozens of miserable, filthy little hotels," adding: "Blankets, which have never been submitted to any cleaning process, are provided for the guests to sleep on; and when they retire, they seldom remove any of their clothes, except their coats, and sometimes not even those. In the morning, when they rise to perform their ablutions, a single wash-pan answers for all, and one towel, redolent of a week's wiping, serves every guest."

Unfortunately, too many arrivals were not even lucky enough to find lodging in such woebegone quarters. Many were arriving sick and destitute. Many suffered from scurvy after long ocean voyages, and more scurvy victims were arriving overland. Morse wrote: "Sacramento became a perfect lazar-house of disease, suffering and death, months before an effective city government was organized."

It seemed to some observers that the more common these sad conditions became the more indifferent other men became to pleas from the suffering. Fathers paid little heed to their sons, and sons deserted their fathers — if they needed troublesome care. When sickness came, brother abandoned brother. An old man, starving after a voyage around Cape Horn, arrived in Sacramento in the last stages of scurvy, and was abandoned by a son and other relatives on a levee to await death, which soon came. By July 1849, such scenes were not infrequent.

The first association for relief of the sick was organized about that time by the fraternity of Odd Fellows, when several members started to do what they could to relieve the suffering.

Some of Sacramento's destiny arrived in the person of a rare individual. Architect Nathaniel Goodell came to California in 1849 to try his luck in the goldfields, then returned to Sacramento — not intending to stay, because he didn't like this village of tents and mud roads. And the few women in town were "not of the best reputation." But he did stay — and he dominated architecture here for two decades, designing hundreds of houses, including the old Governor's Mansion and Heilbron House. He also worked on the first city hall and waterworks, designing the top portion housing a reservoir. The building has been reproduced to serve as the Sacramento History Center. All told, he would design 400 to 450 buildings — churches, businesses and homes.

A letter he sent home in 1849 tells what the city looked like to him while he was en route to the goldfields: "August 12 I took passage on board the Mary Taylor from Sacramento City. As we passed up the Sacramento River, we saw some of the moast (sic) beautiful scenery on its banks that I ever saw. The land on which [Sacramento] is located is almost perfectly level as far as the eye can reach, and is studded with live oaks about one to 10 rods apart. When I was there, there was about 3,000 inhabitants. Now they number 6,000 or more. They have put up a great many houses during the fall, and they still keep building."

As sounds of hammering and sawing echoed from every direction, the city continued to grow. Only 100 houses stood here in mid-June 1849, but two months later William L. Schooning saw more than 1,000 houses. He recounted how he parked his horses for a couple of hours on one street, and returned in the evening to find a bakery selling bread on the very site. The proprietor may have been one of those who fared badly in the mines, but were discovering gold in the many businesses that sprouted in boomtown Sacramento.

Hundreds of men were returning from the mines by October of that year. For many, dreams of riches had vanished into empty air. They straggled down from the hills to seek surcease from hardship and drown their sorrows and take the edge off the poignant ache for home and loved ones, thousands of miles away. Other disappointed miners chose to seek their fortunes in another way, by providing supplies and services to the incoming flood of tenderfeet eager to squander their grubstakes.

Sacramento's noisy saloons and crude entertainment helped to alleviate the crashing boredom of life in the mines, but the gambling halls — or "gambling hells" — were not for the faint-hearted. Many a miner saw his hard-won pile of dust vanish in the spinning wheels of fortune, like a tiny sandcastle washed away by the sea. The canvas-walled saloons offered poor entertainment —usually two or three musicians competing with the hullabaloo from boisterous boozers.

As boomtown Sacramento seemed to be turning into a roaring Sin City, preachers from afar arrived to bring religion, to keep everybody from going to hell in a handbasket. One of the first ministers was the Rev. Isaac Owen, who arrived with his family on October 23, 1849, impoverished by an accident. He and his family had driven their ox-team across the plains en route to his appointed field in San Francisco. At Benicia, he learned he had been re-appointed to Sacramento, so they embarked on a schooner for this river city. The crew got drunk and the schooner tipped over, plunging the Owens into Suisun Bay. All survived, but they lost everything but the clothes on their backs. Ironically, their journey on a "prairie schooner" ended without accident, but the real schooner brought them misfortune. Five days after arriving in Sacramento, Owen preached under an oak at 3rd and L Streets, and organized Methodist Episcopal Church — one of the city's earliest churches — the same day, with 72 members. He did it all wearing the only suit he had — the bedraggled one he had worn across the plains, because the good one he had saved for sermons was marinating at the bottom of the Bay.

As Christmas 1849 approached, hundreds of prospectors drifted in from mining camps to buy supplies, or embark on a spree, or hibernate the whole winter here. For many who had come west overland, it was their first visit to Sacramento. Among them was Isaac Lord, who from the Feather River paddled a boat down the Sacramento, reaching the city Dec. 22, 1849. "The first view we had of the city," he noted in his diary, "was where a line of ships stretches along the river for nearly a mile, then a few houses loom up mistily in the fog among the trees." The moored ships were serving as storehouses. "We paddled our craft into a kind of pool, tied up to a tree on the bank and stepped into the street . . . . The first that strikes one's attention . . . is the want of order — the utter confusion and total disorder which prevail on every hand . . . . The whole town plot is covered with boxes and barrels, empty or filled with all kinds of goods, in passable, indifferent, or bad order, or totally ruined; and wagons, lumber, glass bottles, machinery, and plunder of all sorts, heaped and scattered and tumbled in the most admired confusion."

On the same day (December 22), Jonas Winchester wrote a letter home: "The streets are half a leg deep in filth and mud, rendering getting about awful beyond description . . . . The city is one great cesspool of mud, offal, garbage, dead animals and that worst of nuisances consequent upon the entire absence of outhouses."

Isaac Lord further noted in his diary on December 22 that Sacramento's taverns generally had a large barroom in front with "more display of bottles, cigars and liquors than in three or four of the largest liquor taverns in Chicago." Adjacent to the barroom stood several tables "and a man behind dealing monte, and this at all hours from breakfast to midnight." He wrote that Sacramento merchants evidently were preparing for the Christmas invasion from the hills: "The whole city is literally stuffed, crammed with eatables of every description, so exposed that almost every kind must suffer more or less damage and hundreds of thousands of dollars' damage is already done. I saw at one establishment alone over 200 boxes of herrings rotting in one pile; any amount of spoiled pork, bacon, cheese, moldy and rotten; pilot bread; and most everything else. The destruction and waste of property here is almost or quite equal to that on the plains, with not half the necessity, and a thousand times the recklessness." Many goldseekers crossing the plains had had to abandon wagons and loads when their oxen died, littering the entire way with abandoned property.

On Christmas Day 1849, Isaac Lord observed that a number of buildings were under construction, and the builders all do as they please, "taking possession of the land where it is not actually occupied by improvements and building and improving in defiance of all show of authority or law .... Whoever wishes to build gets his lot surveyed and has it registered and up goes a house at once. They are running them up rapidly on Front Street, facing the river, and within a short stone's throw of the river and the shipping. A small house costing $2,000 will rent for $500 a month on this street."

The day after Christmas, Lord noted in his diary the remarkable lack of theft in Sacramento: "I think there is less of what is ordinarily called stealing here than any place I was ever in; and yet there can be little difficulty in stealing to almost any extent. A vast amount of property, easily movable, is daily and nightly exposed without a watch, or even a lock."

Sacramento was incorporated as a city in February 1850, after the Legislature enacted the appropriate measures. The action also called for election of a mayor and a city council. More than 2,500 votes were cast in the city's first election, and Hardin Bigelow won the office of mayor in a landslide, polling 1,521 votes.

Also in 1850, Sacramento County was established as one of California's original 27 counties — compared to today's 56. The county embraces some 995 square miles. The only boundary alterations since then have been occasioned by minor shiftings of the courses of the Sacramento and Mokelumne Rivers, on respectively the western and southern borders.

Slavery in old Sacramento: Slaves resided in the city during Gold Rush days, and some were bought and sold here. Item: This ad appeared April 1, 1850, in the Sacramento *Transcript:*

> For Sale — a valuable negro girl, aged 18, bound by indentures for two years. Said girl is of amiable disposition, a good washer, ironer and cook. For particulars, apply at the Vanderbilt Hotel of J.R. Harper.

Southern slave-owners envisioned profits by working their slaves in the goldfields, and brought many to California. By 1852, some 2,200 blacks were in California, mostly slaves. If they failed to find gold, or if their owners needed money, they often sold their slaves. This ad for an auction appeared in the June 1852 *Democratic State Journal*, a Sacramento newspaper:

> Negro for sale. — On Saturday the 26th inst., I will sell at public auction a Negro man, he having agreed to said sale in preference to being sent home. I value him at $300, but if any or all of his abolition brethren wish to show that they have the first honorable principle about them, they can have the opportunity for releasing said negro from bondage by calling on the subscriber, at the Southern House, previous to that time and paying $100 . . . . If not redeemed, the sale will take place in front of the Southern House, 87 J St., at 10 o'clock of said day.

Sacramento's future eminent architect Nathaniel Goodell wrote a letter June 2, 1850: "All kinds of business is lively and most kinds is good. As you land on the banks of the Sacramento River, you can see every kind of thing imaginable coming off from the vessels, such as lumber in its rough state, houses all framed, sashes, blinds, doors, bricks, nails, glass &c. in the building line. I need not write all the things that are constantly coming here, for you can hardly name the article that is not here, more or less of it. When you find a thing that there is not much of here, the price is enormous." Later this year, Goodell opened a carpenter shop.

Another view of Sacramento in 1850 was offered in San Francisco's *California Courier* by a writer identified only as "F.M." F.M. could be Frank Marryat, an English writer mentioned later in this chapter. In the San Francisco paper, F.M. wrote that he had had only modest expectations of Sacramento: "You can imagine my surprise at seeing a great and thriving city, with a broad levee, where vessels of considerable burthen could discharge their cargoes at once, without any heed of the caprice of wind and tide . . . . Immense trees covered, with their graceful shade, this scene of busy industry; for here vast quantities of goods were landing, and crowds of merchants, traders and laborers were actively employed in the various pursuits of business . . . . Here were water carts constantly at work, with the characteristic inscription 'Down with the dust; the dust of Ophir!' "

The water service had been inaugurated this year with the arrival of William E. Henry, who noticed that good drinking water was in long demand but in short supply. He created a job for himself by filling buckets with river water and peddling water door-to-door. Another new arrival envied Henry's profits and emulated his enterprise, bailing water out of Sutter Slough to sell house-to-house.

F.M. found the river water sweet and clear. "One thing that surprised me very much," he said. "I visited a plantation just across the river from Sacramento and saw melons, tomatoes, corn, potatoes etc. growing luxuriantly without irrigation, as on the most cultivated lands."

F.M. further observed that in Sacramento strangers were treated with such consideration they forgot they were strangers. He added: "But this is a general feature of the place; the people all seem to partake the generous character of the climate. If the soil is rich in untold wealth, the hearts of the people who inhabit it seem to have acquired, in equal profusion, those fine mineral qualities, without which all this prosperity would be a curse . . . . They have an Operahouse, Theatre and Circus so well patronized as to prove that gain is not an all absorbing pursuit; but that amusement and relaxation are wisely intermingled in the common business of life."

Yet this was a time in Sacramento when lynch mobs took the law into their own hands. In this year of 1850, a gambler named Roe shot a merchant named Meyers, as Meyers tried to break up a fist fight. Roe had no defense attorney and, being locked in jail, was tried in absentia. The jury, intimidated by the threats of 2,000 irate spectators, found him guilty.

The mob stormed the jail at 2nd and J Streets, tore out awning posts to use as battering rams, and smashed the door down. Deputy Sheriff Harris and a small posse put up a brief struggle, but were overwhelmed. The mob dragged Roe to a large oak on 6th between K and L Streets and hanged him.

More than 200 Sacramentans in the following year organized a Vigilance Committee — later blamed for at least one necktie party:

When a court found four men guilty of robbing and beating a citizen — a capital crime then — the four were sentenced to hang. While a crowd collected at 4th and O Streets to witness the hanging, word came that the governor had reprieved one man. Irate vigilantes surrounded the man and refused to let him go. After the three others were hanged, the crowd cheered as vigilantes strung up the pardoned man.

Sacramento's lawless atmosphere was deplored by architect Goodell in a letter April 18, 1851: "All kinds of wickedness is carried on to a great extent throughout the state. Murders, robberies, horse stealing &c &c and lynch law reigns."

After a time, the Vigilance Committee lost favor with most Sacramentans, and passed into history.

Sacramento was taking on the aspects of a proper city, according to one A.C. Sweetser, who wrote this in a letter on May 24, 1850: "Many of the blocks are not inferior in appearance to eastern cities, with buildings painted to imitate granite." Both architecture and traffic were remarked on by William T. Parker in his diary on Sept. 3, 1850, saying that many Sacramento buildings were substantial frame and brick constructions, but there were drawbacks: "The streets are not paved and in most places without sidewalks, but these are being built of boards in many places. Everything has the aspect of hurry and temporary. Everybody appears intent on his own business and generally lets others alone. Those who ride horseback go on a full run through the streets."

Amos Batchelder observed in his diary Oct. 23, 1850, that J Street, the main business route, stretched back from the Sacramento River some two miles and was "completely filled with teams and people coming in from and going out to the mines, loaded with provisions and mining apparatus."

Isaac Lord, our previously-quoted visitor, painted a word picture of the pullulating Sacramento waterfront in his diary entry on Nov. 26, 1850: "Along the bank of the river, fastened by chain and rope cables to the huge oaks and big sycamores, are a number of dismasted ships on which are built storehouses one to two stories high .... Steamers and ships and other craft haul up on the outside and pass the goods over the decks of these store ships, on to the levee. From thence they are carted to the stores and to the mines .... The levee is a tangled mess of Mexicans, Chinese, Chileans and Kanakas; also horses, mules, asses, oxen, drays, and lumber; flour, potatoes, molasses, brandy, pickles, oysters, jams, cabbages, books, furniture and almost everything that one can think of."

River traffic was hectic because Sacramento was the hub of commerce between San Francisco and the mining camps. On one day in 1850, somebody counted 65 steam and sailing vessels congregated on Sacramento's waterfront. A sandbar at the entrance of the American blockaded most vessels from closer approach to the mines.

The English writer Frank Marryat, 24, toured Sacramento in June 1851 and found much to delight and astonish him: "The houses are gayly painted, and the American flag waves in every direction. The streets are wide, and some trees that have been left standing in the town give it a cheerful appearance. It is an American town at the first glance. An immense quantity of sign-boards stare at you in every direction; and if anything would induce a man to purchase 'Hay and grain,' 'Gallego Flour,' 'Goshen Butter,' or any other article for which he has no want, it would be the astounding size of the capital letters in which these good things are forced upon his notice.

"Every other house is an hotel or boarding-house . . . and in hard times, when cash is scarce, one half the population may be said to feed the other half gratuitously, or on credit, which often amounts to the same thing . . .

"Sacramento is terribly dusty. The great traffic to and from the mines grinds three or four inches of the top soil into a red powder that distributes itself every where. It is the dirtiest dust I ever saw, and is never visited by a shower until the rainy season sets in, and suddenly converts it into a thick mud . . .

"A levee, or sea-wall, has been built in front of the city, to protect it from the river when it rises with the high spring tides; but the river generally undermines these works, and flows over the surrounding plain as it has been wont to do for ages past.

"A large number of old dismantled hulks, now converted into floating houses, are moored along the front of the levee, and it is from these, probably, the rats first landed that are now so distinguished at Sacramento for their size and audacity. These animals come out after dark in strong gangs, as if the town belonged to them, and attack any thing that may happen to have been left on the wharf during the night; being very numerous, the destruction they cause to merchandise is a serious loss."

In the same year of 1851, a man named Carl Meyer claimed he counted 30,600 rats in Sacramento as he walked 10 square blocks at night. Perhaps he counted some more than once. The city advertised for a Pied Piper.

Continues Marryat: "Ten thousand dollars were offered, I was told, to the man who should clear the town; and, seduced by this bribe, some one in the rat-catching line volunteered to draw all the rats into the country, and there inclose them in a paddock, to be publicly exposed previous to a massacre; but whether the rats thought it best to leave well alone, and be content with the comfortable quarters and nice pine-apple cheeses they enjoyed in the city, or whether they objected to country air, does not appear; but they never went out to the paddock, except one."

That particular heroic rat dared to approach the rat-catchers. Standing on hind legs, and scratching its nose with its paw as if cogitating, it apparently decided discretion is the better part, for it turned tail and skedaddled for the city. Five terriers took after it in hot pursuit, in vain.

Disastrous fires in San Francisco had been attributed to arsonists, so Sacramento organized a volunteer night patrol to guard against firebugs and, Marryat wrote, "to protect the inhabitants from the wholesale plunder of organized bands of burglars."

This contradicts the observation a year and a half earlier by diarist Isaac lord that "there is less . . . stealing here than any place I was ever in" . . . though a "vast amount of property" was exposed day and night. Times do change.

Marryat and companions rode in a spring-wagon to Brighton, five miles east of Sacramento, near today's 65th Street and Folsom Boulevard: "The road was straight and level, and on either side, inclosed by fences, were well-cultivated farms; numerous dwelling-houses lined the road, and it was difficult to believe that the signs of civilization and industry that met us on all sides, were the result of two years' occupation of the country by gold-hunters.

"As we left Brighton we overtook long lines of wagons, heavily laden with stores for the mines; and these, drawn by innumerable oxen, plowed up the deep dust to such an extent as obliged us to cover our faces as we passed them. We met wagons coming in, containing miners, on whom, to judge by their appearance generally, a bath, a shave, and a new suit of clothes would not be thrown away; and I have no doubt they indulged in these luxuries on their arrival at Sacramento."

Marryat went back to England, but returned to California in 1853 with his bride. Both contracted yellow fever on the journey. They sojourned in California only briefly before returning to England, where he wrote a booklet about his travels, *Mountains and Molehills.* Weakened by the fever, he died there in 1855 — at age 29.

The ships Marryat had seen along the 1851 waterfront included at least one prison ship, its hold partitioned into cells — the answer to the jail-space shortage. First of these floating jails, the bark *Strafford* served as the county jail March-May 1850. It was succeeded by a hulk, *Stirling*, which foundered and sank. For *La Grange*, third and last of the floating jails, $2,500 was spent to partition the hold into cells and add a topside superstructure. Moored to the riverbank, *La Grange* was easy to escape from. To insure that escapes were not facilitated by lax or bribable jailors, the Court of Sessions in 1851 ruled that $500 would be deducted from money allocated to the Sheriff for each escape. This tactic seems to have had some effect. Prisoners were shackled each night to long iron shafts embedded in oaken planks. Jailors riveted a ball and chain to a leg of each prisoner.

But in summer 1852, three convicts escaped by removing a bar from a port, using a hand-made windlass. Despite their leg irons, they started to swim to shore. One drowned and two escaped, but were later recaptured. Many other escapes were attempted, and four or five a year succeeded.

When the 1855 Grand jury inquired into the number of prisoners confined on *La Grange* to await trial, it found 39 men charged, and this was the breakdown: grand larceny, 11 charged; petty larceny, 3; assault and battery, 6; robbery, 4; rape 3; breach of peace, 3; passing counterfeit money, 3; assault to murder, 1; assault with a knife, 1; burglary, 1; possessing burglary instruments, 1; forgery, 1; keeping a gambling house open on Sunday, 1. *La Grange* housed four other convicts awaiting transportation to the state prison. One man had been entenced to a year for stealing a gold watch; another, four years for trying to burn down a house; a third man, seven years for burglary; and the last, 10 years for assault to murder. To defray costs of running the jail, some prisoners were put out to work for hire — on occasion as a chain gang doing road-work.

Near-disaster ended the floating-jail experiment on November 18 after a series of heavy rains. About 6 a.m., jailors were jolted awake by prisoners yelling "The ship is sinking!" Water was flooding the cells. *La Grange* was so tightly moored at bow and stern as to prevent it rising with the rising river. By the time jailors heard the alarm, it was too late to loose the moorings. But they swiftly rescued the prisoners, transferring them to the Station House in the new city hall. The 33 prisoners included two women.

But it was too late to save the ship. Floodwaters surged ever higher until only two flagpoles showed above the muddy current. When the waters finally subsided, mud filled the hold and cabins.

Although *La Grange* died, most of its corpse was resurrected. Salvaged timbers went into the crafting of wagons and saloon bars, benches, tables and other furniture. Colonel John T. Hall bought the two cabins and moved them to his Elk Horn ranch up the river, where they remained until leveled by fire.

Flood and fire — the ordeals of early Sacramento.

Chapter 22
First Major Disaster: Flood

Sacramento's early history was a catalog of disasters — terrible fires, a cholera plague, squatters' riots, and flood after flood, costly in lives and property. But days dark with calamity were not without bright glints of courage and humor.

The 1850 flood was Sacramento's first major catastrophe. By mid-November 1849, rain-swamped roads brought wheeled transportation virtually to a halt. Freight wagons north of Sacramento bogged down in the mire, their oxen struggling in mud up to their bellies. "Some were being pulled out with chains around their horns by other cattle," one man reported, "while bundles of hay before those waiting their turns showed them to have been mired some time."

December came on with no end of dirty weather. Day after day —rain, rain, rain. By January the saturated earth could absorb no more. Like many valley floods, this was aggravated by warm rains that melted heavy snow in the mountains. Both rivers ran brim-full. On an evening early in January, the dark heavens loosed another deluge. At night, both rivers leaped their banks, turning Sacramento into a lake four feet deep, catching many people in their beds. People fled to high ground or rooftops. Nobody knows how many drowned. Dead animals and debris of every sort floated in the streets. Ten city hospital patients, moved to high ground and left exposed to the elements, died.

Boats replaced horses in Sacramento streets during the 1850 flood. Lithograph courtesy California State Library.

In the Hotel de France, Stephen Masset of the *Placer Times* gazed out of his window and saw merchandise of every kind afloat. Rafts and boats laden with people and property filled the streets. Wrote Masset: "Those persons who were lucky enough to own a house lived and slept on the roof — cooked on the roof — made calls on the roof — drank on the roof — prayed on the roof — laughed and joked on the roof — sang on the roof — took a bath on the roof — cursed the gold fields on the roof — wished they were back in New York on the roof — got married on the roof — wrote letters on the roof — and thought they'd never get off the roof."

Lorenzo Hamilton of the People's Market told how he rescued his merchandise during this flood: "There was apprehension that the water would come over, and I went up to my store in a cart, placed pork and beef barrels on end, and platforms on these, and on these platforms placed my goods. Before I got through, the water was around my waist. I had large quantities of pork, beef, and pilot-bread [hardtack] in front of my store; the bread during the ensuing night and next, mostly floated down to some higher ground near O Street, in the direction of the burying ground. The man who saved it charged me salvage."

One man thought Sacramentans seemed to be having a good time. Franklin Buck, in a letter Jan. 13, 1850, wrote: "Instead of the people wearing long faces as you would suppose, the city never was more lively. The streets were filled with boats, and everyone was for having a frolic." Another man dissented. Jacob Stillman, in a letter the same date, said it was not all peaches and cream: "The yelling for help by some men on a roof or clinging to some wreck, the howling of a dog abandoned by his master, the boisterous revelry of men in boats who find all they want to drink floating free about them, make the scene one never to be forgotten. After dark we see only one or two lights in the second city of California." He also saw a variety of makeshift transportation: "All sorts of means are in use to get about — bakers' troughs, rafts and India-rubber beds."

As might be expected, small boats for sale or hire commanded premium prices, noted E.W. Morse in his diary on that same January 13: "A common-size whaleboat brought $30 per hour and sold readily for $1,000. But in an incredibly short time every particle of lumber that would answer for a boat or raft-making was thus appropriated, and in a few days the people were enabled to emigrate to the adjacent hills." Boat operators made tidy profits by ferrying marooned customers to high ground, charging $5 to $8.

On the same day, Jacob Stillman wrote in a letter: "The weather is cooler and the water is falling a little. The vessels on the river are all crowded with people, and some cases of typhus or ship-fever have occurred. The high ground near Sutter's Fort is covered with tents, dogs, and cattle . . . . Cattle have perished in immense numbers." Franklin Buck mentioned the cattle in a letter the same date: "It is a hard sight to see them swimming about or lying in heaps on some little hill."

James Eaton, 18, joined some men in using a flatbottom boat to rescue marooned livestock — horses, cows, mules and oxen — standing in water two or three feet deep. "Many of the animals were beginning to drown because of their weakened condition from standing so long in the cold water and for want of food," he wrote several days after the levee break. The men embarked 10 or 12 animals at a time. "In a short time we had a good-sized herd of stock of various kinds on the island." This apparently refers to Sand Hill Cemetery, today's City Cemetery at 10th and Broadway.

When they rowed the boat close to an animal, two men would get out and lift its forefeet into the boat. "The animal always helped itself as much as it could, but some of them were in such weakened condition they were barely able to stand up," Eaton noted. The men grabbed an animal's hind legs and boosted it in, with the animal helping: "It seemed as if the stock understood that we were trying to befriend them and they offered no resistance whatever. The men stated that the stock would stand perfectly still on the boat and that they could walk right over their backs and they would not even flinch."

Eaton and companions had been flooded out of their cabin located in a "Cut Off of the American River" between the American and the Sacramento River. A hospital also lying in the same low-lying area was a harrowing scene when the levee broke, Eaton said. The water "came down with a rush and it wasn't long until the water was up in the hospital, then in the lower tier of berths." He continues: "Soon it was over them and the sick on the opposite side in high berths could only see the water covering and drowning their sick companions who were unable to help themselves, neither could they render any assistance to them. It was awful! As the water rose higher it came on those in the second, then the third and even the fourth tier of berths and many of the poor, unfortunate sick in these hospitals came to an end, not through disease, but by drowning, and nobody able to help them."

A sexton lived on Sand Island, used as a city burying ground. Eaton resumes: "The next day after the flood, he began bringing in corpses on a boat and burying them and he kept this up for several days bringing over as many as he could carry in his boat. After working this way for several days it seems as though his mind became unbalanced from seeing so much desolation and heart-rendering scenes, and as he neared the cemetary (sic) — a corps (sic) in his boat for burial — he jumped overboard . . . and was drowned."

When the cattle on the island began dying, the men knew they had to find pasture for the rest. Seven men and Eaton drove them off the island, then through floodwaters toward high ground near Sutter's Fort. But first: "All of these men took a big drink of stimulants, excepting me . . . . After a while the stimulants began to tell on the men and soon they were so drunk they could hardly go, and had to walk holding to each other to keep on their feet . . . . Already the cattle in the lead were swimming and these men were so drunk that they could not swim if they had wanted to. They were beginning to realize their danger . . . . One of them in the moment of despair . . . cried out, 'What in the name of God will we do?' . . . We saw a man some distance off in a boat and the men began to hollow out to him for help and as soon as he heard them he started toward us . . . . When he came up along side of us I put my hands on the stern of the boat and easily jumped in but when the other men tried it, none of them could get in by their own effort, so the man who came to our rescue, and I, dragged them in the boat and they were so drunk that they couldn't sit up on the boat but laid down in the wet bottom and laid there until he got them on dry land .... The cattle did not have to be directed .... When they came to the dry land and pasture they all went to eating the grass raviniously (sic)."

Physician-journalist John F. Morse recorded a horror story. He helped rescue some sadly neglected patients from a canvas shelter serving as a makeshift hospital. They hadn't had a bath in weeks, until immersed by the chilling flood. One man, swathed in a filthy blanket, died soon after being succored. Noted Morse: "The blanket was with difficulty detached and when drawn off presented a shirtless body already partly devoured by an immense bed of maggots."

As might be expected, many other invalids died. The firm of Boyd & Davis fashioned coffins for them. They would send a man — identified only as a "Dutchman" — and another man in a boat to bury them. The Dutchman, who didn't trust anybody, carried all of his gold, $2,000 worth, in a "belly bank," or money belt. One day he placed a coffin athwart the smallest boat. The two men climbed in and reached deep water, whereupon the boat began to careen, and then sank. The Dutchman cried to the other man to hold on, and he would swim ashore and fetch another boat. He plunged in — but the weight of his gold dragged him down. With a supreme effort he managed to surface, and struck out for shore — only to sink. Several more times he rose in desperate struggles. At last he sank, and rose no more. His companion floated to safety on the coffin —recalling the ending in Herman Melville's *Moby Dick*, where Ishmael saved himself by clinging to a coffin, while all others were lost when the ship was sunk by the great white whale. Like Ishmael, the Dutchman's companion could have said, "And I alone survived to tell the tale." But the Dutchman's companion's story is not fiction.

The flood destroyed an incalculable amount of Sacramento property. On the Embarcadero alone, hundreds of thousands of dollars worth of merchandise was swept away by raging waters. This was a time when 300 or more persons were engaged in business in the city, yet only half a dozen or so had second stories in which to warehouse goods safe from floods. All the others had to watch their cherished merchandise ruined by rising waters, or float away.

After the waters subsided in January 1850, Hardin Bigelow

started building a levee on the waterfront and pestering everybody to help. Having lived in the Mississippi Delta, Bigelow was no stranger to floods. He knew a floodplain when he saw one, and knew what to do — build a levee. Many pitched in, yet regarded him as a bit loco. Swiftly the toilers raised a levee three to five feet high, stretching from high ground near Sutterville, west to the bank of the Sacramento, then north to the American, then along the American two and a half miles to high ground. Stubborn-headed Bigelow was credited with saving the city. Maybe he wasn't so loco after all.

In March, when another cloudburst began drenching the city in that stormy year of 1850, Bigelow directed construction of an improved levee. Night and day he rode his horse here and there, urging workers to greater efforts. It came to pass that for the second time Bigelow was credited with saving the city from floodwaters. And grateful Sacramentans rewarded him by electing him their first mayor in the city's first election ever, on April 1, 1850.

Only three days later, still wobbly from the flood disaster early in 1850, Sacramentans suffered another disaster on April 4 — when eight buildings on Front Street were ravaged in the city's first bad fire. Fires were frequent in Gold Rush days because open flames were used for lighting and heating. More on this in the "Trial By Fire" chapter.

The safety belt of levees bulwarking Sacramento lulled the people into a feeling of security — until the great flood of 1852-53. In March 1852, rising rivers broke through levees and inundated the city with chilling waters. Levees and other high ground were jammed with people, tents, wagons, horses and cattle in great profusion. For days Sacramentans had to endure the misery of being marooned in cold weather, and everything they needed to make life bearable was in short supply, or gone. Boats cruised everywhere, a somber regatta of people mourning their losses. Strange spectacles were reported: Someone sighted a sailboat far out on the flooded prairie, bound in the direction of Stockton across what normally was dry land.

Workers repaired the break — in vain, for on Christmas Day of the same year the Sacramento crested at 22 feet, flooding the city once more.

But life went on, somehow. Even business went on. Very early in January, while wagon roads linking Sacramento with the mining country lay under water, a little town sprang up overnight on high ground a mile east of Brighton, near the present campus of California State University, Sacramento. It was named Hoboken, perhaps by homesick people from New Jersey. Undaunted by high waters, Sacramento merchants set up temporary branches at Hoboken, so customers from the mines could reach them. Previously, only one structure stood there, a roadside inn named Four-Mile House. By January 10, some 40 houses and tents and several hundred people doing business populated Hoboken. Steamboats made four round trips daily between Sacramento and the new town. But ephemeral Hoboken was destined to endure only three months. When the waters went down, the town died, its lease on existence having expired.

During this flood, as in the earlier flood of 1850, many of the refugees who had raised tents and shanties on levees and other Sacramento area high ground refused to evacuate when the waters went down. Long-smoldering anger flared up into what became known as the Squatters' Riots, which were punctuated by two bloody shoot-outs.

Chapter 23
The Riots: Death in the Afternoon

In the January 1850 flood, the only sections of town not inundated were the high ground at the Fort, the Plaza on J Street between 9th and 10th Streets, and the levees. These islands suddenly blossomed with tents and shacks. When the water dropped, many occupants refused to vacate their humble abodes. The clutter they created on the levees hampered merchandise unloading and other shipping business.

Businessmen called a meeting, the upshot of which was they vowed to forcibly remove the obstructions. One of those who had built a shanty on the I Street levee, deemed public land by the businessmen, was Dr. Charles Robinson.

With a band of men resolved to dispossess the squatters, Sam Brannan rode up in a lather to Robinson's edifice. Brannan seized a timber of the rickety dwelling and yanked on it. Robinson popped out the door, brandishing a shotgun. "Hold on, sir!" he yelled. "You touch this house at your peril! It's mine, and I intend to defend it!"

Brannan turned to the nearest of his wrecking crew. "Warbass," he bellowed, "cover that damn scoundrel, and if he raises his gun, shoot the hell out of him!"

In minutes, the shanty lay in ruins.

Nearby, another building came under assault by the dismantlers. They grabbed a pole supporting the eaves, and struggled with it for a few minutes. Whenever they tugged at it, it kept springing back.

Just then a rancher cantered up on a mustang and began to laugh. "What's so funny?" Brannan demanded. "Get down here, damn you, and lend a hand. Don't just stand looking on!"

The horseman casually uncoiled his lasso from his saddle-bow and threw the looped end to Brannan. "Throw that over the end of the pole," he said.

He took a turn of the lasso around his saddlehorn and put the spurs to his horse. Down tumbled pole, roof and one side of the house, amidst applause of bystanders. The rest of the house soon was leveled.

By sunset, Brannan's wreckers had demolished every obstruction on the levee and every squatter's shanty in town.

Squatters, being outnumbered, offered no physical resistance, but their curses and threats sounded a menacing counterpoint to the huzzahs and raucous laughter of other spectators.

Bitter feelings mounted daily. Squatters, also known as free-soilers, first organized in 1849 when they crowded into the house of a man named Kelly on Front Street near J Street, where speakers whipped them into a frenzy with denunciations of speculators, widening the rift between squatters and people who had purchased land from the Sutter grants.

The angry issue was exacerbated by the thousands of immigrants pouring into California each week, hungry for land. They saw no fences or boundary markers, so they settled on the land, claiming it by right of frontier tradition. When they learned that someone else claimed title, they argued that the original titles were clouded by Mexico's cession of lands to the United States, and they asserted the land belonged to whoever settled it. Further, they couldn't stomach the fact that Sutter and a favored few other early arrivals had glommed onto so much prime land, and they rankled at the fact that whenever parcels of it were put up for sale, it was only at outrageous prices.

In Sacramento, some new arrivals settled on some lots that other people had bought from young Sutter, but hadn't improved yet. The latter based their ownership claims on Sutter's land grants and called the unwelcome settlers "squatters" — illegal occupants. They argued that Sutter's titles were valid because — in the 1848 Treaty of Guadalupe that ended the war with Mexico — the United States had guaranteed that land titles granted under the Spanish-Mexican system would remain intact. Sacramento area squatters raised another challenge: In the legal description of Sutter's land grant, the southern boundary was defined as latitude 38 degrees, 41 minutes, 32 seconds. But a later survey by Fremont showed this latitude as five miles north of Sacramento and Sutter's Fort. Sutter had sold land that didn't even belong to him! The imbroglio would not be resolved without many years of litigation.

The error apparently was perpetrated by a merchant sailor Sutter hired to draw the map, according to Sacramento historian Joseph McGowan. McGowan told the author he can't understand how a sailor "who had been sailing up and down the coast for 17 years could have made such an error." He posed the possibility of fraud. On the other hand, sailors who do nothing but "coast" — navigating only by recognizing familiar landmarks — might be inept in the use of charts and instruments.

The squatters were supported by two newspapermen, Richard Moran and James McClatchy. The latter would become the first editor of *The Sacramento Bee*. Squatters demonstrated by openly settling on lots in various sections of Sacramento, thus increasing the strife. Some squatters were ejected from time to time.

The hot summer sun brought the pot to a boil as some angry Sacramentans organized an Anti-Squatters Association. Toting firearms to strengthen their arguments, they confronted squatters who had moved in on the disputed lots and told them to get out and stay out, if they wanted to stay healthy.

A judge ruled that one John T. Madden was an unlawful occupant of a lot between N and O and 2nd and 3rd Streets, where he had built a house. The judge ordered him dispossessed. Sheriff Joseph McKinney, a man in his early 20s, evicted Madden, apparently despite some resistance by Madden and supporting squatters.

Squatters convened at the levee with two leaders, Robinson and James Maloney, a Mexican War veteran. The meeting heightened their resolve: They determined to plead their case to the public in posters that declared squatters were prepared to "appeal to arms" to protect their "sacred rights" — with their lives, if need be — and disregard all court decisions in land cases. Those who physically opposed them would "share the fate of war."

Next day, Sheriff McKinney issued warrants for arrest of several men who had opposed him as he dispossessed Madden. McClatchy and Moran were named in the warrants, as the sheriff had recognized them among the resisters. McClatchy and Moran turned themselves in to authorities and were incarcerated in the prison brig *La Grange*, charged with rebellion. Being confined, they took no part in the ensuing bloodbaths, the first of which occurred three days later, on Aug. 14, 1850.

Some 40 mounted squatters, led by Maloney with Robinson second in command, forcibly reinstated Madden on the disputed lot from which he had been dispossessed.

Now the squatters' band launched another rash act — they vowed to march on the *La Grange*, moored at the Embarcadero, to release McClatchy and Moran, contending they had been illegally deprived of their rights.

Meanwhile, Mayor Bigelow appealed to all good citizens to help suppress what he feared was imminent riot.

The showdown took place at 4th and J Streets, where the squatters were mustering for the assault on the *La Grange*. Bigelow, Sheriff McKinney and others confronted the group: Bigelow ordered them to surrender their arms and disband.

James Maloney yelled: "Shoot the mayor! Shoot the mayor!"

The sun was shining but some of the brightness went out of the day. Squatters raised their rifles. Crashes rent the air as a volley scourged the sheriff's group. Four bullets struck the mayor, who was on horseback. One gouged his cheek, another tore through his thigh, one ripped his thumb and shattered his hand. The fourth passed through his abdomen. As his horse bolted, Bigelow clung to its neck a few moments, then thudded to earth like a sack of grain. He struggled to his feet, stumbled a few steps, then dropped.

City Assessor J. W. Woodland, who had been standing near the mayor, was hit by a ball that passed through his groin. He died moments later.

The squatters' gunfire was instantly returned by citizens loyal to McKinney. Squatter Jesse Morgan, one of those who had fired at the mayor, fell dead from a ball through his neck. A recent arrival from Ohio with his wife and child, he was the proprietor of the Oak Grove House.

One squatter fired his revolver six times at Sheriff McKinney — who remained miraculously unscathed.

Squatters' captain Maloney's horse was shot from under him. Fleeing, Maloney dashed up an alley, but was shot dead as bullets thudded into his arm, back and head. One other squatter, name unknown, was killed.

Robinson, wounded, fled the scene as fellow squatters scattered in all directions. Witnesses said Robinson had been one of those who fired at the mayor.

J. W. Harper, in the heat of the fray, emptied his revolver at squatters, then flung the weapon at them. As squatters fired back, he raised his hands to his chest to protect himself. One ball penetrated his hand and struck his side, severely wounding him. Two other men with the sheriff suffered leg wounds when hit by bullets — a son of Mr. Rogers of Burnett & Rogers, and a Mr. Hale, of Crowell, Hale & Co. on J Street.

In this first shoot-out, four persons were killed — three of them squatters — and five wounded, all five being with the sheriff's group. Mayor Bigelow, badly injured from wounds and from the fall from his horse, was carried to the Columbia Hotel, where doctors attended him.

Later that day, a rumor flew that squatters were assembling at Sutter's Fort. Sheriff McKinney and a posse galloped out there, but found no trace of them. Other patrols canvassed the city for clues to their whereabouts.

General A. M. Winn, commander of the militia, declared the city under martial law, and ordered all law-abiding citizens to organize into volunteer companies and report to headquarters. Five hundred men were called for duty as policemen, and a contingent of soldiers arrived from Benicia. By evening, quiet prevailed everywhere in the city.

On the following morning, August 15, as citizens expressed admiration for Sheriff McKinney's "perfect coolness and composure" in the melee of the day before, McKinney set about organizing a posse of 20 armed men. Word had just reached him that squatters involved in the shooting spree were holed up east of Sacramento at Brighton in the Five Mile House, an inn owned by a man named Allen. Brighton lay near the present intersection of Highway 50 and Folsom Boulevard.

Hooves pounded, raising dust clouds, as McKinney and posse hit the road to Brighton. Just before they approached within sight of Five Mile House, McKinney halted the posse. One of the men with him, McDowell of Mormon Island, was well known at the roadhouse, so McKinney calculated it would be prudent if McDowell checked out the place while the posse remained secluded, then come back to report whether squatters were present.

For some reason this plan was aborted — McKinney didn't wait for McDowell's return. Instead, shortly after McDowell rode up to Five Mile House, the impatient McKinney and posse galloped up. They surged into the barroom, where they confronted owner Allen and eight or 10 armed squatters. McKinney identified himself and ordered them to lay down their arms.

Allen, standing behind the bar, started to talk in a casual manner, saying he knew the man the sheriff was seeking — and at that instant Allen whipped out a heavy duck gun and blasted away. In the same instant, other squatters behind the bar fired too, scourging McKinney. Dr. Brierly, a posse member, dove to the floor and fired his revolver several times at Allen, wounding him. Gunfire thundered in the barroom as both sides raked each other.

As the smoke cleared, two squatters named Kelly and Henshaw lay crumpled on the floor, dead. McKinney's amazing luck the day before had run out. He also lay dead. Two other squatters were wounded, and two more raised their hands in surrender. The wounded Allen and the others had fled.

Another version of the sheriff's death relates that in the confusion he exited the house at the front door, whereupon a tall man inside the house raised a long gun and fired a load of buckshot. McKinney threw up his hands, exclaiming: "I'm dead! I'm dead! I'm dead!" He stumbled a few steps, collapsed and died.

Brierly fired at the tall man, who dropped his gun and fell, wounded but evidently not fatally, because reports list only three persons killed at Five Mile House — the sheriff and squatters Kelly and Henshaw.

The four captured squatters, one a black man, were taken in a horse-drawn omnibus to the prison-ship *La Grange*. Three of the prisoners were John Hughes, John R. Coffman and William B. Cornogg. It is not clear if one of these was the black man.

The body of Sheriff McKinney, escorted by a guard of horsemen, was conveyed to Sutter's Fort for burial preparations. Only in his early 20's, the highly-respected McKinney was Sacramento County's first sheriff. He also operated the Gem, one of the city's numerous gambling halls.

The funeral cortege set out from the Fort the following day. Many friends on horseback and in carriages and many others on foot filed along in the procession. McKinney was buried in the Sacramento City Cemetery, as was City Assessor Woodland and later Mayor Bigelow — who died some months after he was wounded. On the day of the funeral for McKinney and Woodland, two companies of soldiers arrived in Sacramento by steamer from San Francisco and placed themselves under General Winn's command, ready to enforce his declaration of martial law.

But Robinson, who had escaped after the first riot, was still at large. Dr. J. D. B. Stillman, deputized by city officials to take Robinson dead or alive, set out on horseback with two other men, all armed with double-barrel shotguns.

As they crept cautiously into a house in which Robinson was rumored hiding, the proprietor — standing at the top of the stairs and brandishing a shotgun — threatened to shoot if they ascended. One of Stillman's men advised him to put down his gun — "unless you want a large hole made in your body." Facing three shotguns, the proprietor decided he was outgunned, and complied. The men shut him up in one room and ransacked the house — and found Robinson lying on a bed in a back room, wounded. Stillman examined him and found a small bullet-wound in his left side, apparently not a critical injury, and judged he could be moved without harm. He found a cot to use as a stretcher. Rounding up four men, he ordered them to carry Robinson to the prison-brig. Robinson was charged with murder in connection with the August 14 riot fatalities.

Meanwhile a posse on horseback set out on the trail of other squatters, who had fled up along the river on horses. Five miles farther, they overtook a man named Caulfield who, glimpsing his pursuers, spurred his horse into a furious gallop. One pursuer, a man named Latson, caught up and veered close enough so he could grab hold of Caulfield, while both horses were charging along at full gallop. Caulfield lunged away, breaking Latson's grip, then jerked out his rifle, aimed at Latson and pulled the trigger. The rifle misfired. Latson whipped out a pistol and swung it, knocking Caulfield off his horse. The stunned Caulfield was quickly trussed up, swung over his saddle and lashed there.

The posse raced back to town along J Street with their prisoner, his face a mask of blood and dirt. Vowing to string Caulfield up a tree, they galloped down to the levee. Apparently the lynching threat was only a bit of theatrics, for they delivered Caulfield to jailors on *La Grange*.

Mayor Bigelow, despite his wounds, issued a proclamation announcing restoration of peace and order, and declaring that discharging firearms in the city was forbidden. But Bigelow's injuries forced him to resign his office. More than three months later, on November 26, still weak from wounds, he would succumb to cholera in San Francisco, where he had gone to recuperate. He died there at age 41.

Before long, the squatters' movement died out, ending a bloody chapter in Sacramento history. While Robinson was still a prisoner, friends nominated him for the State Assembly from Sacramento County. He was one of 18 candidates for the post in the fall election. Still behind bars, but thanks to concentrated allegiance by squatters and sympathizers, he won the election. Never brought to trial on the murder charge, he was released to serve as an Assemblyman. In later years, he would serve as Governor of Kansas.

Chapter 24
The Plague Year

To live in Sacramento during 1850, you had to be a glutton for punishment. It was a horrendous year, with a disaster for every season, plus one. In winter, Sacramentans entered the New Year reeling under one of the worst floods in city history. Spring brought the first serious conflagration. Summer brought double trouble, a banking panic (see "The Moneymen" chapter) and the squatters' riots. Autumn came with a cholera plague to devastate the city.

Flood — fire — bank panic — bloodbath — and now cholera. Was there no end to it?

At 2 a.m. on October 15, the riverboat *New World* steamed into Sacramento with thrilling news — and a terrifying passenger. The news was the long-awaited tidings that California had been admitted to the Union. In Washington, John Bidwell gave the documents to Elisha Crosby's daughter Mary Helen, bound for California. While crossing the Isthmus of Panama, she hid them in her umbrella. The news was a warning to Mexico and other powers that big trouble loomed for any power that embarked on aggressive tactics in California.

The dread passenger carried by the *New World* was the cholera virus, although Sacramentans didn't know anything about viruses in those days. All they knew was that on October 20, five days after the steamer arrived, an immigrant who had been aboard the steamer was found dead on the levee, diagnosed as a cholera victim. It was the first case reported in the epidemic that would terrorize the city. The *New World* had earlier arrived in San Francisco from Panama on October 7 with 22 known cases of cholera, including 14 passengers who had died. Failure to quarantine the steamer there allowed the disease to run wild. In Sacramento on October 23, Amos Batchelder wrote in his diary: "The cholera has just commenced its ravages here, and the citizens are actively engaged in cleansing the city. It is in a filthy condition — piles of rubbish are burning in the streets in every direction, filling the air with suffocating smoke." Another diarist on the same day, Isaac Lord, said the fires were set to burn anything believed contaminated by cholera, and added: "The lurid fires, shining in the murky air, burn old shoes and boots and clothes by the ton and cartloads of bones and raw hides and putrid meat and spoiled bacon — so that the end of the matter is worse than the beginning."

The next day, October 24, the city physician reported seven cholera cases, five of them fatal. On October 27, he reported six cases; on the 29th, 12 cases; on the 30th, 19. The secret — if it had been one — was out. Street fires burned cast-off garments and bedding and furniture and whatever else had been contaminated. Fires by day raised a dark pall of smoke over the city. Fires by night illumined the town with weird flickering lights, like some antechamber of hell — which it was.

Four-fifths of the population fled the city. Cholera panicked Sacramentans with its sudden onslaught and, said Dr. John F. Morse, the "hopeless rapidity with which it hurried its victims into eternity." Some heroic Sacramentans, however, remained here to aid victims. They included John Bigler, later elected governor. Dr. Morse said Bigler "could be seen in every refuge of distress that concealed the miseries of the dying and destitute . . . He braved every scene of danger that presented, and with his own hands administered relief to his suffering and uncared-for fellow-beings."

Physicians worked day and night. One of them was Dr. Thomas Logan, who came to Sacramento in August — with rain gauge and gold pan. First he tried panning at Coloma, but it didn't pan out, so he returned to Sacramento to practice medicine — arriving just in time to help cholera victims. Later, he measured rainfall, temperatures and humidity here. Some say this makes him the operator of the first weather bureau west of the Rockies.

But the cholera: Not one physician here ducked out during the city's hour of agony. All remained to minister to the stricken, and

As many as 800 cholera victims of 1850 may lie beneath this tombstone, installed in 1852.

17 died of cholera by the time the plague was over — almost one in three of city doctors. Others who remained to help victims included members of the newly-organized Odd Fellows and Masonic lodges.

A Sacramento correspondent for San Francisco's *Alta California* newspaper reported November 4: "This city presents an aspect truly terrible. Three of the large gambling resorts have been closed. The streets are deserted, and frequented only by the hearse. Nearly all business is at a stand-still. There seems to be a deep sense of expectancy, mingled with fear, pervading all classes. There is an expression of anxiety in every eye.... The daily mortality is about sixty. Many deaths are concealed, and many others are not reported. Deaths during the past week, so far as known, 188." Years later, Dr. Morse wrote that 150 cases occurred in a single day at the peak of the epidemic.

The precise number of deaths is unknown because many cholera fatalities were ascribed to dysentery, fever, and whatnot, to allay public apprehension. But public apprehension was not allayed by that ruse, as is seen by the fact that 80 percent of the town escaped to distant parts.

The daily mortality rate dropped to 12 on November 14, and on the 17th the plague was reported entirely subsided, having run its course. The ordeal lasted about a month. When it was over, the city was nearly depopulated — virtually a ghost town. Some people thought the catastrophe's impact on the city was a greater affliction than it could ever recover from. But they proved wrong — far sooner than anyone could have imagined.

Soon those who had fled the city began to trickle back. And those who had stayed in the city and somehow lived through the terror took heart and were reinvigorated by their new lease on existence. Sacramento began to act like a city again. Merchants once more engaged in brisk business, and what was good for the merchants was good for the community, they no doubt explained. As the beautiful weather of this winter came on, it seemed to put everyone in fine spirits, instilling a vitality that never could have been foreseen by anyone who had endured October's purgatory. It brought a lovely finale to a calamity-laden year, which included a bad fire — but the worst fire of all was yet to come, two years hence, in 1852.

Chapter 25

City of the Dead

"See you later" — epitaph on Old City Cemetery tombstone of Robert Samuel Spear, who died in 1971 at age 17.

Some 35,000 people are buried in the Old City Cemetery at 10th and Broadway, a multitude that, if living, would populate a fair-sized town. Many constituted the hordes of immigrants who had funneled into Sacramento from all over the globe, only to end their long journeys in this 48-acre graveyard.

Even though people who lived in what we think of as historic times make up the bulk of local burials, it may not be common knowledge that even today people are buried in this cemetery.

"Now let's see if I got this straight," a visitor said to Virginia Marsh, who has been researching this cemetery since 1985. "To be buried in Old City Cemetery, either you've got to be a member of a family that owns a lot here, or maybe you can buy a gravesite here, if some family is willing to sell one. And the third requirement for being buried here is — you gotta be dead."

"No, that's the *first* requirement!" put in docent Dorothy Mills.

"People are dying to get in here," quipped Marsh.

Famous and notable residents of this Sacramento necropolis include John Sutter Jr., Judge E.B. Crocker, three Governors, Sacramento's first mayors, and William Hamilton, son of U.S. Treasury Secretary Alexander Hamilton.

Hamilton, who died Oct. 7, 1850, at age 42, was buried here three different times in three different plots. First, he was interred in a frontal area near Broadway. Twenty years later, a friend back east

Mass grave in East Lawn Cemetery holds the remains of 4,685 Sacramentans.

inquired about the condition of the grave, then asked that Hamilton be moved to a more suitable site, which was done. When the city opened a new section in 1889, officials felt Hamilton deserved a spot in it, and transferred his remains.

Rumor has it that Hamilton's body was moved to the third site to sell gravesites in what became known as Hamilton Square. Who wouldn't want to be buried near the son of Alexander Hamilton?

"The story of Hamilton is fraught with mystery and contradictions," said tour guide John Bettencourt. "Some say he was indigent, yet it is known that he sold gold pans to miners in Weaverville, and came to Sacramento with $13,000. What happened to the $13,000, nobody seems to know."

The initial mortuary report says he died of dysentery, Bettencourt said, yet some historians insist he died of cholera. But cholera apparently hadn't arrived in Sacramento until October 15 of that year, when borne in by a passenger on the *New World* steamer.

A weird episode links Old City Cemetery with East Lawn Cemetery, 43rd Street and Folsom Boulevard, and a third cemetery.

Over 5,000 early Sacramentans lie in limbo — in mass graves in the first two cemeteries, after being exhumed in 1955-56 from the Old New Helvetia Cemetery at Alhambra Boulevard and J Street. Originally known as Fort Sutter Burying Ground, it was the first formal cemetery in New Helvetia. Many people had been buried there only a few inches below the ground, with only crude wooden markers to identify them. Sutter Middle School, built in 1958, occupies the site today.

Many of New Helvetia's residents had migrated long and arduous distances to reach Sacramento, and never could have foreseen that even in death they would "migrate" from one cemetery to another.

Reporting on the exhuming, *The Sacramento Bee* on March 30, 1956, said City Manager Bartley Cavanaugh told the City Council that 5,235 bodies were found in the New Helvetia Cemetery — instead of the 1,500 anticipated.

Records indicate only 1,200 were buried there, he said.

Many of the unaccounted-for bodies were discovered in single excavations where mass burials apparently took place during one of the early-day cholera epidemics here, Cavanaugh said.

Discovery of the thousands of additional bodies adds a shocking new dimension to what we know of Sacramento's cholera epidemics, which harvested the population at a terrifying rate.

Unidentified remains from New Helvetia Cemetery were reburied in individual redwood "bone boxes" in East Lawn and Old City Cemetery. A bone box measured 12x12x28 inches, just big enough to contain skeletal remains.

A total of 4,685 were transferred to a mass grave at East Lawn, and another 424 were buried in three mass graves in Old City Cemetery.

Back in 1917, remains of 1,000 Chinese were exhumed and sent back to China, after the Chinese tongs who owned the graveyard land on the northeast corner of New Helvetia Cemetery deeded it to the city.

The mass graves in East Lawn and Old City Cemetery remained unmarked by any headstones until History Week in August 1989 when monuments were dedicated to honor the "misplaced pioneers."

Another mass grave at Old City Cemetery ensconces the remains of some 500 to 800 who died either in the 1850 or 1852 cholera epidemic.

One thinks of mass graves in connection with wartime atrocities, but these mass burials may have been the city's only practical answer to epidemics, which slew Sacramentans with whirlwind velocity, and piled up bodies so rapidly they could be disposed of only in wholesale interments.

In the 1955-56 transfer, some markers in New Helvetia Cemetery were lost, some were trucked to a dump, and others were carted off for use as stepping-stones and other garden ornaments.

When Pat Stanford of Sacramento County Historical Society gave a talk in California Middle School about local cemeteries and told of the missing headstones, she was taken aback when a boy raised his hand and said, "We have some of those stones in our yard!" The boy's mother, unaware of the markers' origin, had been using them as stepping-stones in her lawn.

Bob LaPerriere, M.D., chairman of the historical society's Old City Cemetery Committee, reported similar cases: "A beautiful marble headstone from 1885 was returned. Somebody had it in his garden." Also, he said, a woman in Curtis Park called to say she suddenly realized that 16 stones in her yard were headstones.

"When the bodies were moved in the 1950s, the stones were piled up and not moved with the bodies," LaPerriere said.

"Some were assimilated into the neighborhood as stepping-stones in back yards."

The story of the gravestones gone astray may recall the jest about the ad supposedly placed in a newspaper: "For sale cheap, used tombstone. A wonderful bargain for somebody named O'Toole."

Why didn't the stones accompany the bodies, in the transfer of remains from New Helvetia Cemetery?

Explains Bob Herberger of Miller-Skelton & Herberger, whose predecessor firm, Miller & Skelton, had the contract to move the bodies: Because of confusing conditions in the mass burial, it was impossible to match gravemarkers with unearthed bodies.

"We had no idea who any of them were," he said. "We just removed the remains. All we were responsible for was transferring them. We have no idea who took them out of the ground."

In East Lawn, some flat gravemarkers lie inside the two corner angles in the south area of the mass grave. And a five-and-a-half-foot tombstone rises in the center.

In Old City Cemetery, plaques inscribed with names of the dead transferred here were dedicated. Two are in the frontal area near Broadway. The one with by far the largest number of remains is in the middle area 150 feet or more east of the Chapel.

The only one here with an individual headstone is that of Phillipina Keseberg, a Donner Party survivor who died in 1877. Her marker stands in mid-lawn, under which a yard or so deep lie bone boxes containing remains of over 200 other Sacramentans.

The mass grave at East Lawn lies in a 60- by 70-foot rectangle of lawn, with a three-foot-high concrete block structure marking each corner. In the center stands the black marker.

"Eventually we'll put up a plaque with as many names as we can come up with," LaPerriere said.

He notes that J.W. Reeves "had a beautiful underground vault in New Helvetia Cemetery, and now is buried in Old City Cemetery without even a stone."

Most graves in that cemetery were identified with wooden markers but Reeves, his wife and five children were buried in the only tomb there. A marble headstone graced the oval-shaped, $4,000 tomb, and 10 marble steps led down into the 11-foot-deep interior.

Reeves was the undertaker and superintendent of New Helvetia Cemetery, founded by Capt. John Sutter in 1849. Reeves purchased the 20-acre cemetery in 1857.

The magnificent Reeves vault was opened March 5, 1956, and the Sacramento County Recorders Office issued this report on June 30:

"The bodies of John Wesley Reeves and 18-month-old Ella T. Reeves were in iron caskets and found to be in perfect condition. These have been buried for 90 years. The bodies were still a natural color and had the appearance of smooth wax. The clothing was in perfect condition also. The caskets had a small removable iron lid over the upper part of the body and a glass seal beneath this."

They were reinterred at the Old City Cemetery.

The Sacramento County Recorders Office report added: "All remains which were unmarked, unidentified and unclaimed by heirs were reinterred at East Lawn Cemetery, at 43rd and Folsom Blvd., in an area containing all those designated as 'unknown.'

"All remains having identification name markers, but no claiming heirs have been reinterred at the City Cemetery, 10th and Broadway...

"Other remains having identifying markers and claimed by heirs, have been reinterred in various other" local cemeteries.

Old City Cemetery is the final resting place for many people with intriguing stories, and cemetery tours conducted during good-weather months offer opportunities to hear some, at no charge.

Tour guide John Bettencourt tells about locomotive engineer William C. Brown — "Sacramento's Casey Jones" — who died Sept. 26, 1880, saving the lives of perhaps hundreds of passengers by sacrificing his own.

After attending the State Fair in Sacramento, members of the First Infantry Regiment, California National Guard, caught the train to go home to San Francisco.

As the locomotive chuffed into the Oakland waterfront, Brown, leaning out of the cab, spied an open switch — which would send train and passengers onto the wharf and into the Bay! (This track was intended to embark a train on a ferry — but no ferry was waiting.)

No time to throttle down! No time to brake!

Brown could have jumped and saved himself. Instead, he slammed on the airbrakes and disengaged the engine from the cars. The airbrakes automatically brought the cars to a grinding stop, while Brown rode the hurtling engine into Bay waters.

When the locomotive next day was raised from the Bay, Brown's body was found in the cab, hands still on the controls. He was buried in Old City Cemetery, where his grave is marked by a column with a bas relief of a locomotive.

The real Casey Jones was driving his *Cannon Ball* express at a headlong pace from Memphis, Tenn., to Canton, Miss., one day in 1900. He was late, but swore he would catch up. Suddenly he spotted a standing freight train — dead ahead! He slammed on the brakes, ordered his fireman to jump, then crashed and died — but saved his passengers.

Casey's heroism *followed* Brown's. So, instead of calling Brown "Sacramento's Casey Jones," it would be more accurate to say that

Casey Jones is "Tennessee's William Brown."

Tour leader Fran Pendleton tells about "the most unique monument in any cemetery" — a do-it-yourself monument for Georgia Fisher by her fiance, local pottery-maker Martin Leonard Bergman. Not yet 20 years old, Georgia died in 1875 of diphtheria.

Bergman fabricated all the tiles — 4x4, rusty-brown — and designed the monument, which included one tile bearing a picture of Georgia. Alas, in 1951 imbeciles vandalized the monument and stole the adornments, including her picture.

Pendleton tells about Sophia Pleasants Comstock, born in 1872, died in 1915. Having often fretted about horses suffering from thirst, she willed a handsome sum for installation in downtown Sacramento of water troughs for the refreshment of Dobbin.

For some reason decades passed and nothing was done. Meanwhile horses vanished from downtown, and now it didn't make sense to waste money on water troughs. So a special committee deemed it fitting, because of her fondness for horses, to spend her $11,000 on an equine statue, as one local commemoration of America's bicentennial in 1976. The inscription on Sophia's tombstone explains: "A gift from her estate provided the nucleus of a fund to erect in Old Sacramento State Historic Park a memorial to the Pony Express."

Tour guide Pat Stanford tells of "The Mayflower Family" — their progenitors arrived on that ship and were descendants of Miles Standish. "This is the saddest story," Stanford said.

The jinxed family of Marcellus Crane Tilden and his wife Elizabeth is memorialized here with a marble shaft.

First to die of unnatural causes was Elizabeth's father, James Harvey Ralston, who had served as a state senator from Sacramento. After the silver discovery in Nevada, he was named a probate judge there. One day he left his home in Austin, Nevada, to visit his ranch out in the country. When he failed to return, searchers set out — and found the feeble old man dead, presumably having perished in a recent snowstorm.

But mystery remains: Since his ranch was only 30 miles from Austin, why was his body found 120 miles from Austin?

Elizabeth married Marcellus Crane Tilden in 1861 and they became parents of six kids including twins Mary and Elizabeth, born in 1876, after the births of the other children.

Four months after the birth of the twins, Elizabeth, the mother, died "in extreme distress from a mysterious ailment," dropsy of the heart, Stanford said.

One twin, Mary, age 22 months, died of accidental poisoning. Since the death of the mother, Judge J.T. Landrum's wife had been taking care of the Tilden twins.

The Landrum house was infested with rats, so Mrs. Landrum mixed strychnine with mashed potatoes. The judge thought she was preparing food for the twins.

At night, the twins awoke. As Mrs. Landrum attended to one, the judge fed the other — with the deadly potatoes.

Mrs. Landrum screamed: "Oh, Judge! That's poison! You've killed the baby!"

A doctor arrived double quick and gave the infant mustard and water to induce vomiting, but it was too late.

Two years later, a son Charles, 16, was drowned while boating with a friend in San Francisco Bay.

Another son, Ralston, 29, an apprentice railroad engineer, was killed in 1890 on the San Francisco peninsula when a farm wagon failed to stop at a crossing signal.

A son Frank, on an elephant hunt in Africa, was killed when a wounded elephant charged.

Daughter Laura May, an early Sacramento attorney with her father, later practiced law in Colorado where, in 1926, she was killed when she lost control of her car and it plunged off a mountain road.

The other twin, Elizabeth, and her father, Marcellus Crane Tilden, both ruined the family reputation — by dying of natural causes.

There are 35,000 stories in the City of the Dead, and the foregoing have been only a few of them.

Many people who know this cemetery are convinced many graves are yet to be found. Researcher Virginia Marsh seeks for clues in old records.

David Abrams, anthropology instructor at Cosumnes River College, and his volunteers use what he calls "low-tech remote sensing" — poking rods in the ground to try to find something.

Abrams once worked with famed anthropologist Richard Leakey, seeking clues to early man in Africa. Now he is seeking clues to early Sacramento man.

When Virginia Marsh was asked what are some of the interesting things she has found in her research, she said: "Every day there are discoveries of all kinds. For example, today I copied this information from a stone: 'Created by himself.' " She explained that, as many people do, the man had specified the words he wanted

Virginia Marsh, researcher in Old City Cemetary, shows a tombstone in the shape of a tree stump, marking the grave of Woodmen of the World member Ernest Rupa.

on his stone. But this was unusual in that he wanted the public to know he had created the work himself. Gave himself a byline, as it were.

Marsh told of the monument that looks like a tree stump — for a member of Woodmen of the World fraternal organization.

She has written and published a book of 100 epitaphs on markers here.

To raise funds to restore this long-neglected burial ground, history buffs buried a Time Capsule here during History Week in August 1988, and collected $1,000, reported Mory Holmes, cemetery committee treasurer.

Pallbearers wearing plug hats and black frock coats toted the Capsule — a regular burial casket — out of Mory Holmes' Victorian at 917 H Street and hefted it into a horse-drawn hearse. A parade of horse-drawn vehicles and antique cars escorted it to the cemetery.

With LaPerriere emceeing, the Capsule was stuffed with business cards and other mementos. Mayor Anne Rudin contributed a gold-plated key to the city.

Other donations: a newspaper, the swimsuit issue of *Sports Illustrated,* and a copy of this *Sacramento* book that you are now reading — minus this "City of the Dead" chapter, which wasn't included in the first printing.

For a donation of $1, anyone was invited to place a business card with a message in the Time Capsule, which is scheduled to be dug up and opened in 2088. This author contributed a card with a note: "I regret that a previous engagement will prevent me from attending the reopening of the Time Capsule."

Pallbearer Rick Stevenson noticed a woman whose hand was hovering over the coffin, tendering a check to Treasurer Holmes on the other side, to pay for the card she wanted to contribute. For a second, Stevenson thought she was about to place the check in the Capsule.

Inspiration! He dashed off to fetch his checkbook, and ran back. Chomping on a cigar, he showed photographers a $1 million check he had written out, payable to his great-grandchildren. He committed it to the Capsule and quipped: "I don't have any kids, so I'm safe."

Volunteers have put in countless hours in restoration here, notably of the Volunteer Firemen's Plot, with about 149 graves, and the Garden of Peace, where most of the interments were in the 1920s. Numerous broken tombstones have been repaired, and several individual plots restored through the "Adopt-a-Pioneer" program.

The beautiful old Chapel, long used as a storeroom, has been converted to a mini-museum and archives center.

Another cemetery figures in the Sacramento story, because it's not far away and harbors the remains of a member of the greatest exploration expedition in American history.

In Franklin Cemetery 15 miles south of Sacramento lies the body of Alexander Hamilton Willard, of the 1804-5 Lewis and Clark Expedition. Willard was one of a few good men chosen from 400 applicants eager to set forth on the grand adventure authorized by Pres. Thomas Jefferson, to seek a Northwest Passage.

They did indeed find a passage to the Pacific — an arduous overland route, not the mostly water passage hoped for. Yet its result was momentous: It opened the gates to westward expansion.

Willard was cited for his talents as gunsmith, blacksmith and hunter. Returning from the 6,000-mile adventure, he married, worked as a blacksmith, farmed and fought in Indian wars.

At age 74 in 1852, he set out for California, driving his ox-drawn wagon with his wife and several children. They settled on a ranch in Georgetown, today's Franklin.

Willard died March 6, 1865. In 1957, California Chapter, Daughters of Founders and Patriots of America, placed a bronze marker on his grave — honoring him as the Last Surviving Member of the Lewis and Clark Expedition.

Only one problem: According to author Dayton Duncan, who followed the Lewis and Clark Trail and wrote a book about it — *Out West, An American Journey,* published in 1987 by Viking — Sgt. Patrick Gass outlived all the others, dying in 1870 at age 99.

Chapter 26
Trial By Fire

A mere two months after the first big flood, Sacramentans had to weather their first big fire, on April 4, 1850, when no less than eight buildings on Front Street between J and K Streets turned into an inferno. The worst was yet to come. Two and a half years later, in late 1852, Sacramento was still an unholy gallimaufry of ramshackle wooden structures lighted by candles and lamps — a collection of the worst kind of firetraps. Small wonder fires sometimes ran wild.

Sacramento's worst fire began shortly after 11 p.m. on Nov. 2, 1852, a Tuesday night, when someone sounded an alarm after seeing smoke billowing from Madame Lanos's millinery shop on the north side of J Street near 4th. Lanos was ill in bed. A northerly gale fanned the blaze throughout the city. As hungry flames crackled, feasting on dry wood shacks, the wind escalated to hurricane force. It tore away flaming planks and whipped them far. Some landed on roofs of buildings a block downwind, igniting new blazes in a dozen different places. It was a conflagration impossible to control. The fire demon had seized the city.

Sacramentans fled to open spaces to escape the terrific heat and menacing flames. The roaring blaze turned night into day as it ravaged over 40 square blocks — nine-tenths of the city. Six people died, including Madame Lanos. The others included a woman who lived next door to Lanos, and three firemen on the roof of a brick building, who burned to death when the roof caved in. A contemporary report adds: "The number scorched is enormous." Damage was estimated at $10 million.

Dawn glimmered on skeletonized ruins. The wind still blew strong, whipping away coils of black smoke from the charred, still-smoking rubble of buildings that were no more. Almost everyone was homeless, as well as heartsick at the appalling losses. Thousands of Sacramentans trudged debris-laden streets, staring at the devastation, picking among the ruins, stunned by personal losses, stunned by the staggering losses of the entire populace. Virtually the whole city had been carbonized. On every countenance, shock and confusion and dismay were written. Not a few vented their grief in unabashed tears. As the day wore on, and the sun rose to high noon and then began to dip into the western sky, the chill wind still blew from the north, though not as fiercely. Despair by degrees began to be succeeded by a resolve not to be conquered by catastrophe.

Night descended on stricken Sacramento. Everywhere in town, people huddled around fires, warming themselves, cooking and eating what food they had managed to salvage from the holocaust, or obtain from kind farmers on the outskirts. Now they dared to talk about rebuilding the city. Once before they had built the city, and they could do it again. If each person assumed responsibility for rebuilding his own house or business, while other citizens lent a hand with whatever materials or labor they could spare from their own rebuilding chores, they could do it. The daunting task of rebuilding could be reduced to manageable dimensions.

Today, the brick-constructed Lady Adams building on the north side of K Street between Front and 2nd is the only building still standing in Old Sacramento that survived the 1852 fire. Its brick came around the Horn as ballast in the brig *Lady Adams*, hence the building's name. The Lady Adams building taught fire-blighted Sacramentans an unforgettable lesson. It didn't take a genius to notice that bricks survived fire, while wood didn't make it.

Another building that rounded the Horn, but went up in smoke during the 1852 fire, was the prefabricated Orleans Hotel, one of Sacramento's toniest hostelries, on 2nd Street between J and K. The hotel was assembled in Sacramento from pre-cut wood that arrived by ship from New Orleans, thus its name. It lent a Creole accent to Sacramento. After the fire, construction of a new, three-story brick Orleans Hotel began at once and was finished only 20 days later. It would become the most eminent Sacramento hotel of

Firestorm whipped by hurricane-force winds wiped out nine-tenths of Sacramento in 1852. It was the city's worst fire. View is from the levee. Courtesy Sacramento Museum and History Division and California State Library.

its era. A saloon occupied the entire ground floor. Ads boasted about the saloon, a billiard room, a reading room and "second and third stories . . . set apart for parlor, family rooms and chambers." Catering to well-heeled travelers, it was said to be the biggest and most commodious of its kind in the state. A fourth story was added in the 1850s, increasing capacity to 300 lodgers. One famous lodger was Horace Greeley, who arrived after taking his own advice to "Go west, young man."

Within 30 days of the 1852 fire, an incredible 761 buildings had risen in Sacramento, 65 of them built of brick, most of it manufactured in local brickyards. Also, new city ordinances mandated that fireproof materials be used in construction of all commercial buildings. But most home-builders constructed wood frame dwellings, no doubt for economic reasons.

By 1854 — year of another big fire — some 500 new brick and 2,000 frame buildings had risen in the city. On July 13, the mercury had risen to 100 degrees when somebody in a furniture store tipped over a spirit lamp being used to heat a glue-pot, igniting the city's third big conflagration. Many large buildings were consumed as most of 12 blocks was leveled by flames that roared along I and J Streets and ravaged the north side of K between 3rd and 17th. In front of the courthouse, serving as the temporary State Capitol, a frantic Gov. John Bigler hollered at passersby, begging them to help save the building. Several men halted to lend an ear, but didn't tarry long enough to lend a hand.

"Gotta save my own property," one said, and scurried off.

"Me, too," another said, taking off on the run.

A fine portrait of George Washington hung in the courthouse. "See!" Bigler said, jabbing his finger at the doors, through which the portrait was visible. "Will you let the Father of your Country be destroyed?"

Well said, for several men promptly rushed through the doors and rescued the portrait and scooped up a few other portables. But the inferno was now out of control. The courthouse was fully engulfed and there was no way to save it.

The City Directory of 1854 reported: "So rapid was the spread of the fire, and so intense its heat, that step by step they (the firemen) were forced to retreat before it, until they were driven entirely beyond its reach."

This 1854 fire did not burn as many blocks as the fire two years earlier, but was every bit as costly in damage because many more large buildings standing in the city at this time fell before its onslaught. Over 200 wood frame houses were destroyed.

In San Francisco, telegraph keys clattered with news of the Sacramento Fire. Firemen of San Francisco's Monumental Engine Co. were sitting down with their friends to a banquet when the alarm came in. But there was no hesitation among those brave men in Sacramento's hour of need. Abruptly they left the groaning board, yelled farewells to their guests and departed San Francisco on the *Wilson G. Hunt*; 83 men and their beautiful red engine voyaged to succor Sacramento. Not until the following morning did they arrive in Sacramento — too late to help knock down the fire, because Sacramento's firemen had it under control. Sacramentans, however, grateful for the goodwill shown by San Francisco, accorded the visiting firemen a hearty welcome.

Like the story of the doughnut and the hole, there were two ways of regarding Sacramento's fire: A pessimist would lament that half of the city was destroyed; an optimist would take courage that half was saved. Half a city is better than none. Especially was it good news when compared to the disaster two years earlier, when practically the whole town was wiped out. The difference was largely owing to the new City Water Works, a 240,000-gallon reservoir atop the new city hall, even though not yet fully operational. The gravity-flow, pressurized system was the first municipally-owned water system in California. Harrowed by the 1852 nightmare, Sacramentans had designed the new system so pressurized water would be available in an emergency. The city also had a system of about 10 elevated cisterns, probably brick reservoirs, at various locations from which firemen could pump water.

After the first big fire in 1850, irate Sacramentans had clamored for fire protection. And Sacramento in that year became the first city in California to form a volunteer fire-fighting group — Mutual Hook and Ladder Co. No. 1. In the next decade, 13 more companies organized, with 400 volunteers. Stationed at strategic points in Sacramento, they were equipped with carts, hoses and other "modern" fire-fighting apparatus. Each company had a formal name, a nickname, and a motto. Each fireman wore a uniform: red shirt, fireman's hat, and belt identifying his company.

The first three engine companies, which operated hand pumpers, were formed in 1851: Confidence Engine Co. No. 1, with motto "Douse the Glim"; Protection Engine Co. No. 2, "Duty tho' in Peril"; and Sacramento Engine Co. No. 3, "Always Ready." Its house on the west side of 2nd Street between K and L is still preserved as The Firehouse restaurant.

The companies solicited the public for urgently-needed financial support. To those who didn't come across, denunciations and dire warnings appeared in the newspapers. For example, *The Sacramento Union* printed this report from one fire company: "Resolved, as Messer McNulty and Co., who exult in having $75,000 worth of goods in their store, and who refuses positively to subscribe a dollar toward the organization of a fire department, that in case of fire in their building, the energies of the citizens are requested to be directed to the saving of adjoining property, and not of theirs."

It's a bit of an embarrassment that an out-of-town fire company — from San Francisco — was prepared to extend unstinted aid to Sacramento firemen, yet Sacramento's own fire companies didn't cooperate noticeably well with each other. Some firemen were not above turning in false alarms, having first alerted their own companies so they could be first to respond, and be so credited in the newspapers. Rivalry between companies went too far in other ways. Item: Knickerbocker Co. No. 5 and Confidence Engine Co. No. 1, rushing toward a fire at Jefferson School, simultaneously entered a narrow bridge over a slough and sideswiped each other. One engine crashed into the slough. While the two companies of hot-headed fire-fighters mixed it up in a wild flurry of bare knuckles, Jefferson School turned to ashes.

And sometimes, while firemen squabbled over whose jurisdiction a building stood in, flames leveled it. History is silent on whether any departments were arguing over jurisdictions during the terrible fires of 1852 and 1854. Perhaps it's better that we never know.

Sometimes overzealous competition even led to arson — by firemen! Consumed by desire to be first at a fire, which was always good for their image in the public prints, some firemen engaged in a bit of "harmless arson" — so their knowledge of its whereabouts would give them a head start in reaching the fire first. These certain individuals were later denounced as "unprincipled rowdies . . . who are a curse to the Company they represent."

When someone spotted flame or smoke, he ran to the nearest firehouse to sound the alarm bell in the tower. Hearing the alarm, the unpaid volunteers dropped whatever they were doing and dashed to their firehouse, clapped on fire hats, seized the hose cart and pumper's drag rope, and sallied forth. With the foreman bellowing orders through his trumpet, they manhandled their ponderous engine toward the alarm.

Smoke, flame, or some passerby often would give them the direction to the fire. Other times, firemen sprinted to the nearest intersection and eyeballed in all directions for some clue to its whereabouts. If no one could spot the fire, each company rushed pell-mell in a different direction, in a frantic effort to come upon it.

Sometimes, when a volunteer at some distance from his company sighted a fire, he ran to his own outfit, even if another company was closer. One volunteer was so loyal to his Young America Co. that he ran from 2nd and J Streets to his firehouse on 10th Street to sound the alarm — when he could have sounded it at any one of five companies that were closer.

In winter, muddy streets were often impassable to the heavy engines, so firemen rushed their pumpers and hose carts along the board sidewalks. *The Sacramento Bee* took a dim view of this because "it forced men, women and children to rush into nearby stores in fear of their lives." Pioneer Flour Mill was totally destroyed in 1860 because of the miserable condition of the streets, preventing firemen from hauling their apparatus to the scene speedily enough.

When in 1857 an engine company from San Francisco stopped at Sacramento, awaiting a steamboat for Marysville, they apparently added a whole new dimension to the expression "visiting firemen." *The Sacramento Bee* recorded the antics, but was not amused:

"A portion of our fire department gave them a hearty welcome. They drank and sang together and made the night hideous with their wild and terrific yells. They even went so far as to make bonfires in the street, to ring with fearful violence the fire alarm bells and thus awake the whole city and call out the entire department. What with the yells of some 100 intoxicated men, who acted like demons, with the barking of dogs, the ringing of bells etc., the whole city seemed turned into a pandemonium. We are ashamed, grieved, disappointed at the behavior of our firemen. Their conduct was a disgrace to the whole city."

But to the firemen it must have seemed that a good time was had by all.

Civil War recruiting depleted Sacramento fire companies of many young and strong hands, and shifted the burden of fire-fighting to a smaller number of older and tired volunteers. The foreman of the Young America Co., harassed by the difficulties of extricating older men out of snug beds in the wee hours to fight fires, may have lost some of his patience, but apparently didn't lose his sense of humor. Two entries in his 1861 logbook:

"October 21, 1:45 a.m. Six men [only] took the engine down and back. The old story. The beds stuck too tightly to the members. They could not leave without taking them along; not wishing to do that they remained with the bed . . . .

"November 7. As many of our members are possessed of constitutions which require considerable sleep, we would suggest that bell ringing be dispensed with and that the Foreman be appointed a committee of one to wait on members at every night alarm and ascertain if they have secured sufficient sleep, and if their health will permit their exposure to the night air."

An 1872 act of the Legislature established a paid fire department in Sacramento, thus professionalizing it.

During the big fires, one of the many floods that paralyzed early Sacramento would have come in handy, but the timing was wrong — but not by much in one instance. November 1852, the same month as the city's second big fire, heralded (later in the month) another flood disaster, as 19 inches of rain soaked the city in the November-December period — more than the average for an entire year. Would floods never cease?

Ninety percent of Sacramento went up in smoke during the 1852 fire. But in only a month, undaunted Sacramentans raised an incredible 761 new buildings. Courtesy California State Library.

Chapter 27

Neither Can the Floods Drown It

Sacramento is a doomed city.
Comment in the ***Nevada Transcript*** *during our 1861-62 floods.*

Samuel Norris in 1850 had tried to establish a small town on the south bank of the American River opposite his immense Rancho Del Paso. Modestly he christened the town — located near the present H Street Bridge — Norristown. It took on a transient glory in the winter of 1852-53 when floods drove merchants out of Sacramento to higher ground. The temporary residents renamed the town Hoboken. It consisted of tents and hastily-built shacks and was patronized by customers from mining towns desperate for supplies, who found Sacramento isolated by rampaging waters. Steamboats from Sacramento made four daily jaunts up the American, unloading supplies at Hoboken, where they were picked up by mule teams hauling giant wagons that had rumbled down from the mountains.

Hoboken even had a mayor, E. L. Brown, elected in January 1853 during spirited voting in which town founder Norris came in third behind J. B. Starr. Mayor Brown had a pragmatic attitude toward his mayoralty. In his inauguration address, he swore to faithfully perform his official duties — "provided I am paid for it." By mid-February, floodwaters ebbed and roads to Sacramento reopened. Little Hoboken, after only six weeks of glory as a stand-in for Sacramento, was abandoned as its citizens trooped back to Sacramento and its transient precincts reverted to cropland.

The floods had arrived after great volumes of warm rains melted heavy snows in the mountains. But rainfall in the next nine years measured less than average. In near-drought conditions year after year, who worries about floods? But after nine years of only mild winter rains, December 1861 and January 1862 brought the worst floods ever to Sacramento. Citizens were caught off guard by the staggering floods, floods so immense they took on the character of legend. Like the 1852-53 floods, they arrived after heavy inventories of snow in the Sierra melted under immense volumes of warm rains. Nevada City, for example, measured 109 inches of rain, over twice its annual average. Sacramento was washed with 23 inches in only December and January, well over the annual total.

At 8 a.m. on December 9, 1861, the swollen American breached the levee on the city's eastern boundary, sweeping in on the city with "the strength and speed of a hurricane." Many persons died, but no casualty list is available. More might have died if the sudden flood had struck at night, with everyone abed. Many houses were toppled, floating off on the current with shrieking women and children clinging to doors and windows.

The emergency brought out the worst side of some Sacramentans: On a pretext of rescuing persons in danger of drowning, they borrowed boats from the Front Street levee, and took advantage of the crisis to extort money from victims. One man had ensconced his wife on the roof of a house that was tottering, and had to pay a rogue $75 in gold to ferry her to safety. In another house, a man stood in water up to his chin, begging help from a passing boatman, who demanded $15. The man said he had no money. "Then," said the pirate, "I'll leave you to drown." And he did leave, but the victim luckily was soon rescued by a boatman who was not charging his passengers. In several instances, flood victims had to pay $15 to $20 just to ride a block or two. A young lady paid $35 to ride from uptown to 2nd and L Streets, partly by carriage, the rest in a boat. A man had to pay $25 for a boat ride from the levee to the city hall, on K Street near 3rd.

The Front Street levee was jammed with people and animals. One woman landed there in the afternoon and at once delivered a baby, which survived only moments. Another woman who found

Sacramento streets looked like the canals of Venice during the 1862 flood. Photo courtesy California State Library.

refuge at the Pavilion, 6th and M Streets, said she had given birth earlier in the day, but had no idea where either the baby or her husband were.

To allow floodwaters to flush out of the city, the jail's chain gang cut an opening in the R Street levee. Some houses, including two-story structures, floating near the cut were sucked through on the current and smashed into kindling on the down side. By December 11, floodwaters receded, leaving many boats stranded on mud flats.

But the worst was ahead. Beginning in January 1862, relentless rains combined with melting snows in the mountains scourged an already-groggy Sacramento. Rising rivers were flooding the whole valley — and on January 9 the American overflowed its banks. Merchants frantically tried to raise their goods onto platforms they hoped would be above the clutch of floodwaters. Stock owners herded horses and cattle onto high ground. Yet even now, not all Sacramentans suffered a dampening of their spirits. As hundreds of boats floated by, loaded with passengers, many relished the novelty of a boat trip through the city's major streets, and their obvious pleasure was applauded by jovial spectators on balconies.

All bridges on the American had been washed out, save for the railroad bridge at Folsom. But three-fourths of a mile of the railroad to Folsom was washed out. Swift currents of the American had swept the steamer *Gem* of California Steam Navigation Co. through the levee break at 28th Street, stranding it in a peach orchard at 23rd and Z Streets, from which it was not extricated and relaunched until a month later. Twenty-five houses had been seized by raging waters and carried away.

Tops of telegraph poles crossing the valley were submerged, reported William Brewer of the State Survey, who added: "Steamers ran back over the ranches 14 miles from the river, carrying stock, etc., to the hills." Five dead bodies were discovered floating on the American. On 18th Street near R Street, two dairyman lost 70 cows.

The waters began to abate — but on January 22, another levee break occurred, and high water bashed the city's business section. Governor Leland Stanford could enter his mansion, at what is now 800 N St., only by boat at the second floor. The Legislature packed its bags and adjourned to San Francisco. Most Sacramentans could not adjourn to San Francisco — 5,000 miserable citizens huddled on levees and other high ground such as City Plaza, Sutter's Fort and Poverty Ridge, the hill rising east of 20th Street.

Real estate developers one day would change its name to Sutter's Terrace, as a more euphonic label with which to lure home buyers.

Waters had risen higher than ever in the 1862 floods because upstream riverbeds were clogged with hydraulicking debris.

When the waters subsided, people had to wade through mud stinking with bodies of drowned animals. All boats and barges were put to work rescuing thousands of starving cattle marooned in various places. Throughout the emergency, steamboats arrived each day from San Francisco, laden with cooked food for flood victims. Folsom people set up an aid station and invited all flood victims to enjoy the town's hospitality. Howard Benevolent Society, wrote one historian, "cannot be too greatly extolled" for its work in assisting the suffering.

Calamity-howlers found Sacramento's devastation laden with omens of future doom. The San Francisco *Morning Call* editorialized: "It is simply an act of folly for the people of the town of Sacramento to endeavor to maintain their city on its present location." The *Nevada Transcript* bewailed: "Sacramento is a doomed city." Other newspapers said Sacramento had no business being the site of the State Capitol, with all those flood problems.

Sacramentans literally had had it up to here with floods, and the time had come to do something drastic.

Chapter 28
The Moneymen

Whilst here in Sacramento I can every moment expect to be murdered or robbed.

Heinrich Schliemann, Gold Rush banker

Successful miners returned to Sacramento to exchange their gold dust with merchants for more supplies, and with banks for gold coin. Merchants gladly accepted dust at a discount, and bankers happily bought dust at a discount. The bankers naturally were adept in the art of tapping the financial circulatory system to draw off a steady golden stream, and they did it of course by following the Golden Rule: He who has the gold makes the rules. By mid-1850, they customarily offered 5 percent interest *monthly* on deposits. Barton Lee then offered 6 percent.

As the fever heated up the economy, some banks if we can believe it went as high as 10 and 15 percent a month. To pay such reckless interest, banks naturally had to loan money out at even more reckless rates, which they frequently couldn't do without taking reckless chances.

The piper had to be paid. Pipers just don't take no for an answer. Not surprisingly, August and September 1850 saw three major banking institutions in Sacramento lock their doors. What might be called Black Summer began with the collapse of Barton Lee, representing capital of almost $1.5 million. Others followed like falling dominoes: Henley, McKnight & Hastings, then Warbass & Co., and some prominent merchants who dabbled too deeply in banking. The chain of failures sowed mistrust in the monetary value of all sorts of property and mediums of exchange — except gold. Also, it dismantled public confidence in bankers. The *Sacramento Directory* for 1853-54 doubted that "there was a single individual who was really competent" in banking. And *Sacramento Illustrated* in 1855 recalled: "The most wild and moonshine speculations were indulged in, and all seemed to forget that the day of reckoning must surely come — when monthly, ten and fifteen percent interest must be paid." Before long, however, the ailing Sacramento economy managed to make a sturdy recovery from its wild excesses of 1850 — probably because it had the vigor and resilience of youth, and there was no holding it down, any more than Lilliputians could hold down Gulliver.

The Mills Brothers of banking: A shining exception to the dismal litany of failure in Black Summer was the bank of D. O. Mills, which didn't lose a nickel of depositors' funds, then or ever in its history. Darius Ogden Mills, arriving in Sacramento in 1849 at age 24, had already demonstrated his fiscal acumen as part owner of a bank in Buffalo, New York. He came to California via the Panama route, having dispatched a shipment of trade goods around Cape Horn. Before long, he was joined in Sacramento by brothers James and Edgar, who had left the East Coast long before Ogden, but took longer because they voyaged by way of Cape Horn.

Darius's first marketing venture took him up the San Joaquin River with a boatload of goods for miners -- a hands-down success. He tried the same thing on the Sacramento, with even greater success. He returned home to join his cousin and business associate Elihu Townsend in shipping more merchandise to California.

He and Townsend arrived in Sacramento in May 1850 and got out their rakes, as it were, to rake in fat profits. Sensing a need here for a bank, Mills opened D. O. Mills and Co. — said to be the first bank on the Pacific Coast. He and brother James closed their merchandise store so as to channel all their energies into banking, with Townsend, as Mills, Townsend & Co. The bank proved such a capital success that many other envious entrepreneurs plunged into banking. Plunged is apt, for many soon "took a bath" in the business and got cleaned out, much to the dismay of their depositors, who would have preferred they remained filthy with lucre.

Statue of Columbus and Isabella that graces the Capitol rotunda was a gift from banker D.O. Mills.

Townsend sold out to his partners and went home to New York. James took his share and also went home, while Edgar Mills and Henry J. Miller remained partners in the D. O. Mills bank. The firm erected a banking house at 228 J St., a small frame structure with stone facade, destroyed in the 1852 fire, then rebuilt. The bank busily collected bills for eastern creditors, financed shippers and bought gold dust.

Getting wind of the gold strike at Columbia, Tuolumne County, D. O. Mills lost no time in opening a branch there. The following year he financed Tuolumne County Water Company's project to deliver water to the mines. Upshot: From one square mile of the Columbia area, $55 million in gold was recovered, more than from any similar area in the western hemisphere. When the boom petered out in a few years, Mills sold the branch to a local financier.

After the 1862 flood, the bank shifted to more commodious quarters in Heywood's Building (restored), 2nd and J Streets. Mills in 1865 purchased the building, and while he owned it it housed not only his bank but these other pioneer businesses: The Fashion Saloon, Pacific Union Express, Hatch and Carey, opticians, gunsmiths and jewelers; and Pacific Mutual Life Insurance Co. —which became one of the West's largest insurance companies.

Mills's reputation for acumen and integrity caught the eye of tycoon William C. Ralston, founder of the Bank of California, San Francisco, who appointed Mills first president of that new bank. Brother Edgar remained to handle Sacramento affairs. As time went by, D. O. Mills acquired a series of hand-over-fist moneymakers, including Virginia Truckee Railroad, vital link to Nevada's Comstock Lode golconda.

Thirty years after arriving in California, Mills, 54, decided to pack it in, so he packed his bags and returned to New York to spend what would be the final 30 years of his life. He became prominent in the Bank of New York, and also renowned for his generosity in establishing three Mills Hotels for poor and homeless men in New York. While affiliated with New York's Metropolitan Museum of Art, he purchased the marble Columbus and Isabella statue that today — a donation from Mills — graces the rotunda in the California State Capitol.

Mills has been credited with having done more than anyone else of the area to make Sacramento a financial mecca and commercial entrepot. Also profoundly concerned over the moral effects of his work, he has been hailed as "California's greatest banker."

The last Sacramento home of the Bank of D. O. Mills — and the least known of Sacramento's architectural marvels — stands on the northwest corner of 7th and J Streets. The magnificent colonnaded building was constructed in 1912 as a D. O. Mills bank even though Mills had died in 1910, age 84. Later it was occupied for decades by state offices until 1966 when Bank of Sacramento moved in, having purchased the building. In 1970, Bank of Sacramento merged with Security Pacific National Bank, the present occupant. In a 1979 restoration, the lobby ceiling was cleaned for the first time, illuminating its decor of gold-leaf rosebuds. This ceiling, the most striking feature of the interior, soars 42 feet high — high as a four-story building. In the ornate fifth-floor board room, scenes were filmed for two movies — "The Jericho Mile" and "Chattanooga Choo-Choo."

Sacramento's most astonishing banker has to be Heinrich Schliemann. At age 8, according to a nigh incredible story, Heinrich decided to prove there really was a Trojan War, that the City of Troy existed, and that *Homer's Iliad*, the epic story of the war, was based on fact. It is nigh incredible because Schliemann did exactly that, in later life as a wealthy amateur archeologist, confounding all the scholars who said Troy was a mythical city and those hoary legends of the Trojan War were hokum.

The Gold Rush had lured Heinrich's brother Louis to California in 1849. Three months after arrival of his last letter, Heinrich received from California a newspaper clip saying: "On 25th May, 1850, Mr. Louis Schliemann, of German nationality but latterly of New York, died from typhus in Sacramento City, at the age of 25 years." A letter with the clip indicated his brother had left a substantial estate. Heinrich, 28, already wealthy as an importer in St. Petersburg (today's Leningrad), then capital of Russia, sailed for America to search for his brother's grave. In New York, he quizzed Louis's partner, but found him strangely close-mouthed. From another source he learned that Louis, arriving in the Mother Lode, bought dust in Placerville, profiting enough to open a tavern in Sacramento, where he prospered, but fell ill. Schliemann suspected the partner of theft, but reckoned it would be difficult to prove in court, and a waste of time. He determined to go to California to find his brother's grave and erect a tombstone.

But first, not lacking chutzpah, he journeyed to Washington DC to interview President Millard Fillmore and query him on the economic state of the nation.

Arriving in Sacramento in April 1851, he failed to find Louis's grave, so he boarded a riverboat for San Francisco. En route, he narrowly escaped drowning in a watery mishap. Lodging in San Francisco, he narrowly escaped death in a raging fire that gutted two-thirds of the city. Back to business again: He called on a Rothschild bank there, and was pleasantly surprised to find it managed by a man named Davidson, whom he had known in Italy. Schliemann proposed to establish a Rothschild branch in Sacramento. Brilliant idea, Davidson said, or words to that effect.

Yet, before a final decision to commit time and money in Sacramento, Schliemann toured the Gold Rush region to check out its economic potential. Traveling by stage, he visited such mining towns as Coloma, Placerville, Rough-and-Ready, Nevada City, Grass Valley and Marysville, confiding in his diary: "Gold was glimpsing everywhere and even in the mud which clung to my boots I saw many particles of the precious metal."

Confident that Sacramento was going places, he opened the banking house at Front and J Streets, leasing space in a fireproof building, and hired two clerks. From the recently-collapsed bank of Barton Lee, he bought a massive fire-and-theft-proof safe that required a score of men and a dozen yokes of oxen to drag from Barton Lee across the street to his office, and a day to do it.

Open for business, he bought nuggets and dust, melting them into bullion. Schliemann, a short and wiry man, scrutinized customers through gold-rimmed glasses and could speak with them in any of eight languages. He could write well in 11 languages. His command of languages and phenomenal diligence — he worked in his office from 6 a.m. to 10 p.m., eating only one meal a day — piled up the profits.

On some days he handled up to 180 pounds of gold — and this was a time when desperadoes prowled the streets and the air reeked of danger. Dreading robbery, Schliemann and his clerks went armed day and night with Colt revolvers and Bowie knives. He seemed to expect the worst when he wrote to a friend: "Whilst here in Sacramento I can every moment expect to be murdered or robbed .... Never a Negro slave worked harder than I did. But that is all nothing to the danger of sleeping the night alone with so immense amounts of gold. I always spend the night in a feverish horror and loaded pistols in both hands. The noise of a mouse or a rat struck me with terror."

Came April 1852, and it was time to turn his business over to the Rothschild representative in San Francisco. En route to Europe, he sailed for Panama City on the steamer *Golden Gate* with a fortune that one biographer has reckoned at $2 million.

Schliemann returned to Sacramento in September 1865, to search once more for his brother's grave, now desiring to send the body home to Europe for a proper burial. Once more his search was fruitless. Astonished at Sacramento's complete transformation since he had last seen it, Schliemann wrote: "It is impossible to recognize . . . not a single house seems to stand of those which were here 14 years ago."

Sacramento banker Heinrich Schliemann astounded the world when he unearthed the lost city of Troy, proving it was not mythical.

Now the greatest adventure: Sacramento gold would help finance his search for the fabled lost city of Troy, a lifelong dream. Troy — scene of the Trojan War in *Homer's Iliad*, starring the beautiful Helen ("the face that launch'd a thousand ships," in Christopher Marlowe's poem), her lover Paris, warriors Hector and Achilles, the great wooden horse, and a supporting cast of thousands of Greeks and Trojans. All mythical, scholars sneered. Even Troy is mythical, they scoffed.

Near the Dardanelles in present-day Turkey, Asia Minor, Schliemann in 1868 hired a gang of 100 men and gave them shovels. Following clues in Homer, he told them where to dig a trench. Wonder of wonders, he found what he sought — the fabled buried city, and 8,700 gold articles, the golden hoard of Troy's King Priam, at that time the greatest lost treasure ever found – thanks in part to Sacramento gold. But if the city was real, perhaps the stories were too. In the *Iliad*, Greeks — wrathful because Paris had abducted Helen — set sail and besieged the walled city of Troy for 10 years. The siege ended after some Greek warriors hid themselves in a colossal wooden horse they had fabricated. Curious Trojans dragged it into their city. Creeping out at night, the Greeks opened the gates to their army, which captured the city and burned it.

But the phenomenal Schliemann — what to do for an encore? He went ahead and discovered an even greater treasure, the gold of Mycenae, in Greece, by digging exactly where scholars said it couldn't be found.

Although Schliemann unearthed an entire buried city in Asia, he never was able to find where his brother was buried in Sacramento.

Chapter 29
Jacking Up the City

Did you ever hear of the dementia that possesses Sacramentans?
Correspondent for a Nevada newspaper in 1865.

Levees alone just didn't do it. That was only too obvious. Somebody had to come up with a better idea. Luckily someone did. Amid all the early agonizings over flood problems, the *Daily Union* in 1853 had published an anonymous letter from a local merchant, outlining a scheme to save Sacramento. If floods can't be contained by levees, he said, then let's lift the city above the floods! This could be done, he elaborated, by dumping enough fill atop the main streets to raise them above the high-water mark, thus creating a business district that would remain high and dry amid the worst floods.

The audacity of the idea captured the imagination of Sacramentans. More flooding in the spring of 1853 spurred them to do something. They resolved to raise I, J and K Streets from the river to the knoll at 10th and I Streets (today's Plaza Park). Then, let the rivers do their worst. Merchants and others would remain lofty and undampened on their tight little flood-time island. Undaunted that such a thing had never been done before, citizens rolled up their sleeves and went to work. With pick axes and scrapers, they dug the fill, transported it to the streets in wheelbarrows and one-horse dump carts, and tamped and smoothed it down. They worked through long months. By Thanksgiving, the main business stretches of I, J and K Streets had been raised three to five feet. So far so good.

For the next eight years, however, Sacramento kept growing in near-drought conditions. Not much work on street-raising projects was accomplished, as few people think about floods in dry times. Then came the horrendous onslaught of 1861-62, described in a previous chapter. On Dec. 9, 1861, the American overflowed its banks on the northeast section of town, rampaging down 13th and 14th Streets until blockaded by the R Street levee. Floodwaters piled up and backed up into the city, surging toward the Embarcadero. This was the time the *San Francisco Morning Call* and the *Nevada Transcript* sounded their doom prophecies.

Sacramentans had to show the world they weren't going to knuckle under. *The Sacramento Bee* editorialized that the city was here to stay, contrary to the San Francisco paper's suggestion that Sacramento pick up its chips and find another place to play. Even when floodwaters submerged *Bee* printing presses a couple of weeks later, its editorial composure remained undampened.

The battle cry resounded through Sacramento precincts: Raise the streets higher! Vowing to prove the calamity-prophets wrong, city officials got off the dime and spent a barrel of dollars. In other words, the city in January 1863 allocated $200,000 for the astounding engineering job — raising city streets 10 feet or more above their original levels, or two feet or more above high water marks.

This decision had by no means been unanimous, nor without vociferous opposition from many Sacramentans. For years, townspeople had debated how to combat floods. Some opted for better levees, and some proposed moving the city to higher ground. Property owners in the city's southern areas feared that raising the streets north of them would drain water onto them. So the decision to raise the streets ran into a stiff counterattack, and was enfiladed by volleys of petitions and legal sniping. But the day came when the city ordered each property owner to construct a brick bulkhead along the street fronting his property.

Thousands of cartloads of sand and gravel were dredged from river bottoms, dumped on the streets between bulkheads, and tamped down. By degrees the streets rose higher and higher. It seemed never-ending, and was a staggering task, yet achieved with such simple tools as one-horse dump carts, small-team wagons,

Sunken courtyard at Fulton's Prime Rib restaurant, Old Sacramento, reposes at the original street level before streets were raised to combat floods. Note pedestrians on today's level.

and scrapers, wheelbarrows, picks and shovels.

A correspondent for a Nevada newspaper wrote in 1865 that this process called high-grading had gotten out of hand: "Did you ever hear of the dimentia that possesses Sacramentans? They are what is called grade crazy. They commenced raising the town to keep out the freshets, and they have kept on till the passion has got beyond their control."

Gravel and sand fill had to be left in place for months, to allow settling before paving with cobbles or macadam. Teamsters found that ascending or descending the steep unpaved ramps between high and low grades was irksome and hazardous. Sometimes two or three teams a day tipped over. In winter, streets turned into muddy sloughs that bogged vehicles. Came summer, the muddy corduroy channels and potholes in the unpaved roadbed dried out and created a rock-hard, dipsy-doodle ride for wagons. All too often, underneath the vast deposits of fill, vital necessities such as fire hydrants, cisterns, and water and gas lines lay buried, with scant clues to their locations.

In October 1865, a water line under newly-raised 2nd Street broke. Without warning, all water in Sacramento was shut off at 5 p.m. Laborers toiled until 11 p.m., struggling through 10 to 12 feet of new fill to reach the break. For a time, water had to be turned on again, to fight a fire. As workers delved, the new fill kept caving in, so they had to dig a very wide hole. After a day or so the original break was fixed — but two more breaks occurred. Water had to be pumped out of the excavation to find the leaks. And so it went. Sacramentans sometimes had to do without gas and piped water for weeks.

Yet Mark Twain, writing in the *San Francisco Bulletin* on Nov. 30, 1866, perceived fringe benefits in the temporary disaster area: "The grade has proved of salutary importance to Sacramento; nothing else could have so happily affected the health of the city as the new grade. Constant exercise on the dead level is too monotonous — the human system eventually ceases to receive any benefit from it. What the people there needed was a chance for uphill and downhill exercise, and now they have got it. The more the grade progresses the more the people are exercised and the healthier they become."

But one might also speculate that some people got so exercised over the mess that it wasn't too healthy for their blood pressure.

Next step: Property owners had to jack up their buildings — or convert the first floor into a basement, and the second floor into a new first floor and entrance. They also had to raise sidewalks in front of their properties. Each owner had to pay for raising the building and sidewalk. The most common and cheapest way of raising buildings was by jackscrews, similar to the old auto jacks. Early on, in 1864, hydraulic machinery was used to raise some buildings. But by the end of 1865, jackscrews were in wide use, being far cheaper and more readily available. Besides countless jacks, the project also demanded immeasurable volumes of perspiration.

Sometimes building owners didn't coordinate, in that one raised a building to one height, and others to another height. One man got too uppity, raising his building much too high, whereupon city officials told him to get that dang thing back down where it belongs. Which he may have done, as the historical record doesn't indicate otherwise.

Mark Twain elaborated on that problem: "You see, they have raised some of the houses up about eight or 10 feet, to correspond with the new grade, and raised the sidewalks up accordingly; the other houses remain as they were before, and so do the sidewalks in front of them; the high walks are reached from the low ones by inclined staging similar to the horse stairways in livery stables. This arrangement gives infinite variety to a promenade there, now."

Business suffered mightily during the seemingly endless ordeal. Most merchants closed shop during raising of their buildings. For those that didn't, customers found it vexatious to navigate streets that were crowded with workers dumping fill, and where other workers were raising stores and cluttering the route and getting in the way of traffic.

A Sacramento visitor, writing in the *Overland Monthly* of July 1870, described the spectacle at the east ends of J and K Streets: "At the outer ends of these streets, many buildings, not yet raised, seem to be dropped down, as it were, into a cellar, so that their eyes are only on a level of the street."

Sidewalks — raised in front of one store and remaining for a time at the original level in front of another store — posed hazards to pedestrians, especially at night, although makeshift stairs connected the different levels. Yet every so often somebody would absentmindedly or drunkenly walk off a raised sidewalk — onto a vacant lot or unraised sidewalk. Continued the *Overland Monthly* writer: "Various isolated buildings near these streets [J and K] have lifted themselves up, and have a piece of pavement several feet higher than other people's. Everybody here in Sacramento builds his pavement on a different level from that of his neighbor, and does not always drive down his nails well. Consequently there are innumerable little shoulders or steps which are so exquisitely unexpected that you drop off with one foot, and plump down with the prettiest possible little nod, and a 'thank-ee.'" Scarcity of street lights added to the chances wayfarers would "get hopelessly wrong end up."

By the time street-raising had reached several blocks east of the river, workers had learned their business well enough to avoid creating the gentle sea-swell effect still discernible in some Old Sacramento streets.

All told, workers raised more than 200 buildings using jackscrews, and Sacramento became a city roosting on stilts. Some buildings required an inordinate number of jacks. A three-story building was dubbed the "Iron-Legged Centipede" as it perched on 150 of them. The St. George Hotel, one of the largest buildings in the city, estimated to weigh 2,000 tons, needed all of 250. Dozens of men worked on that job. Painstakingly they inserted the jacks until all were in place by August 1865. Turning them began, inch by inch. By October, the ponderous structure had been jacked up the required eight feet — surviving the ordeal without a scratch. But the job cost $7,450, a lot of scratch. But it wasn't the record. The *Overland Monthly* writer reported it took $16,900 to raise the Courthouse, then doing duty as a temporary Capitol, which didn't include the cost of raising street and sidewalk in front.

Not all were as lucky as the St. George owners, to get off without a scratch. Nor were all buildings vacated while being hoisted. During gale winds, a wooden tenement in the Chinese section on I Street was being raised — when it tipped over, scattering its occupants. No casualty list is available. One night, as the K Street Annex of the Union Hotel roosted eight feet in the air on dozens of jacks, the building collapsed, leaving bricks, furniture and fixtures in a hopeless jumble. In a near-miracle, the occupants escaped without injury.

Workers paved most of the raised streets with cobbles quarried from the Folsom area, transported on the Sacramento Valley Railroad. By 1870 macadam was increasingly used.

Mark Twain was confident that some day all the trouble would be worth it: "The patience, money and energy required to prosecute the work to a successful completion are fearful to contemplate but I think the citizens are equal to the emergency. Sacramento, with its broad, straight avenues, shadowed by stately trees and bordered with flower gardens, is already handsome, and someday will be beautiful."

The tremendous undertaking, an ordeal for all, was mostly done by 1873. Sacramento never again was seriously flooded. By the 1880s it was clear that raising the city and filling many lots also helped make the city safer from the malarial-type diseases associated with swampy areas, such as those the citizens had filled in.

Sacramentans evidently put their faith in the axiom: "Make no little plans, for they have no power to stir men's blood."

In other flood-control projects, Sacramentans excavated new channels for the American, one to straighten out a problem-prone curve, another to ease pressure at the mouth by cutting it into the Sacramento a fourth of a mile north of the original confluence.

To tie all flood-fighting efforts together, a master flood control plan was approved in 1910, with federal, state and local agencies cooperating to reinforce existing levees and build new ones. Next, a sequence of escape channels for high water was excavated. One was the Yolo Bypass west of Sacramento, to take pressure off the river where it flows past the city. To shunt floods into Yolo Bypass, the city in 1917 built Sacramento Weir. Farther upriver, Tisdale, Fremont, Moulton and Colusa Weirs were finished by 1933. The final stage in putting a hammerlock on rampaging rivers was construction of the great dams — Shasta, Folsom and Oroville.

After Sacramento's streets and buildings were elevated, nobody thought to fill the spaces under the raised sidewalks. This left underground passages connecting one building with another. For decades, they formed a subterranean domain known as the "catacombs." Legends grew about these secret caves. Some said they ran for many blocks, as far as the river, where robbers, smugglers and illegal immigrants could surreptitiously enter, then make their way into the heart of town. Such legends may be mostly fabrications, because filling in the streets surely blockaded any subterranean corridors that would have led from one block to another, although one could probably circle an entire block in this fashion. But there would be no way to travel from one block to another without surfacing.

In numerous places, one could creep from one building's basement to another's basement, a condition that tended to lure burglars. Many decades later, to foil burglars, many businessmen built separation walls from their buildings to the street, choking off the passages.

Chapter 30

Meanwhile Back At the Fort

Frank Bates, alcalde (magistrate) at Sutter's Fort, had some unorthodox ideas about fines. For a petty crime, he usually fined the miscreant six to 12 bottles of ale, depending on the gravity of the offense — and depending on the thirst of those in the court. Six bottles was worth $48 to $50, each being valued at half an ounce of dust. The wrong-doer had to pungle up the dust at once to pay for the ale, which was promptly guzzled by court officials.

A slight case of murder: In late 1848 or early 1849 — when the Gold Rush had yet to reach full bore, and things at the Fort were still only in a mild upheaval — Charles Pickett, a merchant, killed a man. Pickett was renting part of the northwest bastion of the Fort. Another part was occupied by a man from Oregon, Isaac Alderman. Pickett, an eccentric writer of pamphlets, claimed the right to use certain storage space. Alderman took umbrage, and they quarreled. Alderman, brandishing an axe, advanced on Pickett who, armed with a shotgun, retreated to the wall, warning Alderman not to come farther. When Alderman ignored the warning, Pickett pulled the trigger.

Pickett claimed self defense, but merchant Sam Brannan said he should be tried in court. Brannan asked Alcalde Bates for a warrant, whereupon Bates promptly resigned for some reason. John S. Fowler, the second alcalde, also resigned, as did the sheriff. A strange situation, which the records don't explain.

Brannan called a meeting of all Fort residents to ponder the case. First on the agenda was the need to appoint an alcalde — but everyone nominated respectfully declined, until Brannan accepted. Nominations for prosecuting attorney went the rounds without acceptance — until Brannan accepted. In short, Brannan served as both judge and prosecuting attorney, a bit irregular. A. M. Tanner, designated sheriff, ordered defendant Pickett to consider himself under arrest.

Brannan seated himself as judge, and the trial began. The eight-man jury included Captain Sutter. Pickett, represented by his counsel, a man named Payne, pleaded self-defense. Pickett made his appearance with a revolver strapped on, and a Bowie knife in his belt. Someone protested that a murder defendant shouldn't be armed to the teeth during his trial, so Pickett was persuaded to surrender his weapons. They were placed on a table beside a jug of brandy intended for the sustenance of all.

With security precautions taken care of, Sheriff Tanner called for a round of drinks for everybody, and the jug was passed around. Someone proposed that cigars also make the rounds. Someone else objected to this as highly irregular. But Judge Brannan opined that since California ladies were smokers, it could not be inappropriate anywhere, even in court.

Brannan deemed it needless to begin the trial with a tiresome statement of particulars, as everyone already was apprised of the facts.

Every time defendant Pickett questioned a prosecution witness, his counsel angrily ordered him to be quiet, and let *him* ask the questions. Pickett just couldn't understand why *he* couldn't get into it, and he got exercised over that. Twice the sheriff had to call a recess and order a round of drinks while the squabblers cooled off.

Brannan — switching to his alternate role as prosecuting attorney —began examining a witness.

"Hold on there, Brannan!" Pickett yelled. "This won't do. You're the judge, not the prosecuting attorney."

"I know I'm the judge — and I'm prosecuting attorney too."

Picket scratched his head. "All right, go ahead," said the befuddled defendant.

By the time Brannan finished examining the witness, it was after midnight. Sutter and another juror were leaning against the wall in their chairs, eyes closed, apparently asleep. Another man, testifying to Alderman's character, mentioned that he had killed two men in Oregon — a strange character reference. Sutter evidently was not asleep, for his eyes popped open, his chair dropped back to the floor, and he scrambled to his feet. "Gentlemen, the man's dead. He's atoned for his faults, and I won't sit here and hear his character traduced." Sutter staggered toward the door, but was prevailed upon to remain.

After all testimony was complete, Brannan called on the defense counsel to sum up for the defense. But at this late hour, defense counsel was "too far gone" to continue — whether from sleep or brandy or both is unclear. So defendant Pickett had to offer his own summation.

The jury exited — and re-entered as daybreak gleamed. The spokesman said they had been unable to reach a verdict. Judge Brannan discharged them. "Mr. Sheriff, " he said to Tanner, "the prisoner is remanded to your custody."

"What am I to do with him?" Tanner asked.

"Put him in close confinement."

"I *haven't* any place to put him in."

"Then put him in irons."

"There *ain't* any irons about the place."

After debate on whether the defendant should be released on bail, the entire court, including jurymen and spectators, voted on it, in the affirmative.

At a later trial, with everyone in a more sober condition, Pickett was acquitted.

In spring 1849, John Sutter Jr. contracted with Heinrich Lienhard, his father's clerk, to go to Switzerland and bring the rest of the Sutter family to California. Lienhard, a Swiss emigrant who had been at the Fort since 1846, departed San Francisco aboard the Pacific Mail steamer *Panama* on June 20.

By the summer of that year, young Sutter had somehow managed to extricate his father from his quagmire of debts. He did it in great part by hiring as his agent Peter Burnett, destined to become California's first governor. He ordered Burnett to sell as many Sacramento lots as he could, letting Burnett keep 25 percent of proceeds as his commission. Young Sutter even paid off the Russians.

Captain Sutter in the fall of 1849 helped draw up the first state constitution during the convention in Colton Hall, Monterey. Friends urged Sutter to run for governor. At first he declined. Later he changed his mind and tossed his planter's hat in the ring. On election day, Nov. 13, 1849, he trailed in third place with only 2,223 votes. Peter Burnett, the man who had helped him out of his financial mess, became California's first governor. One man demanded: "How can a man in his senses think that responsible men would ever vote for a man like Sutter, who is drunk more than half the time?" It might or might not be an exaggeration to say there were times when Sutter didn't know whether he was afoot or on horseback.

Poor John Sutter. Gold-seekers swarmed over his land, looted his storehouses, butchered his cattle and ripped him off of whatever took their fancy. Robbing Sutter became a regular business. Sometimes rustlers held off his Indian workers at gunpoint as they butchered his cattle by the hundreds. One gang stole a herd of horses from Hock Farm and drove them to Oregon. Slaughter of Sutter's cattle, increasing for more than a decade, climaxed in the winter of 1849-50. The Feather overflowed, flooding grazing lands and driving cattle to refuge on some knolls. Recalled Sutter: "People from the surrounding towns approached by boat and killed hundreds of animals." This was the winter in which five men formed a partnership for the express purpose of slaughtering Sutter's cattle, and netted $60,000. "The country swarmed with lawless men," Sutter wrote. "Talking with them did not do any good. I was alone and there was no law."

He was also victimized by a more sophisticated breed of sharpers, who stole by means of pen and paper. "I was so foolish," Sutter confessed. "I understood so little about business. I gave men powers of attorney to sign deeds and they swindled me on every side." Sutter claimed that Sam Brannan owed him $50,000 for some Sacramento lots gotten by browbeating his son. Swindlers were fighting with dirty tricks and berserk energy for shards of the empire that was slipping through his fingers. "I was the victim of every swindler that came along," Sutter rued.

Reunion in San Francisco: On Jan. 21, 1850, Heinrich Lienhard returned on the steamer *Panama* with Sutter's wife, Anna, their two sons and a daughter, and Mrs. Sutter's sister, Mrs. Schlaffi, and her son. Captain Sutter met them in San Francisco, then escorted them to his Hock Farm on the Feather, installing them in the new two-story house built under direction of John Bidwell. Lienhard later said young Sutter paid him $4,000 for his services in bringing the group from Switzerland, plus $8,000 for their traveling expenses.

Meanwhile, as the Fort's commercial tenants shifted their businesses to the more convenient location on the Sacramento waterfront, the Fort by degrees began to assume a lonely and forlorn aspect. Weeds flourished in the courtyard, walls crumbled, roofs sagged, and debris strewed the ghostly vacant rooms that once echoed with the towering drama of early California.

Sacramento area settlers cannibalized bricks and other materials from the Fort for their own buildings. Some historians blame the high cost of lumber — $1 per board foot — for the depredations. Also to blame, no doubt, is that an abandoned building is a magnet for yahoos with sticky fingers or a penchant for vandalism.

Before long, houses, workshops, corrals and even the massive walls came tumbling. Some of the cannibalized materials went into buildings in what is now Old Sacramento. Other Sutter properties also, including his unfinished flour mill at Natoma — at today's Brighton area, site of the city filtration plant — on which Sutter said he spent more than $30,000, were torn down. Lumber from the mill was assimilated into construction of the City Hotel, Sacramento's leading hostelry.

Disintegration of the Fort went on, as scavengers, squatters and weather continued their pillages. By 1858, only the large central building with its thick adobe walls and hand-hewn timbers had

When Gold Rush madness drove Sutter from his Fort, he retreated to his idyllic Hock Farm on the Feather river. But an ingrate put the great house to the torch. Courtesy Department of Parks and Recreation.

survived years of neglect and vandalism. Doors and windows were gone, and plaster peeled from the walls, exposing adobe bricks. In succession, the central building served as a trading post, gambling casino, hospital, boardinghouse, storehouse, private home, and lastly and most ingloriously, as a stable, chickenhouse and pigpen, until finally it was abandoned.

One of the first who urged the Fort be restored was local poet Lucius Hardwood Foote, who put his petition in verse:

Sutter's Fort

I stood by the old fort's crumbling wall,
On the eastern edge of the town;
The sun through the clefts in the ruined hall
Flecked with its light the rafters brown.

Five more verses followed. But nothing much happened until 1888, when Sacramento city trustees revealed a plan to open a new street — which would pass through the center of Sutter's Fort. That would mean demolishing what was left of it. This threat aroused historically minded citizens. General James G. Martine of Sacramento on June 4 published a letter in the *Record-Union* addressed to "The Pioneers of the Pacific Coast," pointing out that the famed old landmark faced total destruction. He proposed establishing a fund to buy and restore it. Response was so heartening it launched a campaign to raise $20,000 to buy the site, consisting of two blocks encompassed by K, L, 26th and 28th Streets. Success of the campaign was guaranteed when the family of railroad tycoon Charles Crocker donated $15,000 — and former Governor Leland Stanford vowed to pay any deficiency.

In the fall of 1889, the full amount was raised by public subscription. Title to the property was vested in 1891 with the State of California. The Legislature agreed to provide funds for rebuilding and maintenance. Reconstruction got under way in 1891 to restore buildings and grounds as closely as feasible to the Fort's high noon of historic grandeur.

Chapter 31
The Last Days of Captain Sutter

It is a wonder that I am alive.
Captain Sutter, reminiscing on his turbulent life

Sutter picked a lovely setting for his Hock Farm retreat. It lay on the west bank of the Feather some miles below its junction with the Yuba. Thinking of making it his permanent home some day, he had started developing it in 1841. Lieutenant George H. Derby of the U.S. Topographical Engineers and his expedition camped across the river from Hock Farm on Oct. 15, 1849, while mapping the region.

"This is the most beautiful situation I have seen in California," he reported. "The river, which at this place is about 600 yards in width, is lined on either bank with majestic sycamores, in a fine grove of which, upon the west bank, is situated Captain Sutter's farm-house, a remarkably neat adobe building whitewashed and surrounded by high and well built walls enclosing out-houses, corrals, etc. There are about 100 acres of excellent land enclosed and cultivated upon the west bank, which yields the most astonishing crops of wheat with very little labor. The river is filled with salmon; and we observed two seines drawn across the river, about a mile apart, from which I was informed the occupants of the farm-house obtain a plentiful supply."

From the Fort, Sutter moved into the Hock Farm in 1850 with his family, and with what remained of his cattle from the Fort region. Even here, Sutter couldn't escape curious strangers. Each day, four steamers passed his landing, often stopping to unload visitors who wanted to cast eyes on "the Pioneer of Pioneers." Even at isolated Hock Farm, squatters still plagued him, and refused to be ejected except by due process of law, a long and irksome procedure. In December 1853, Sutter wrote to Ned Kern: "The squatters are loose in my fields; all is squatted over. So long as it [his land claims] is not decided, I am in debt and cannot sell a foot of land at present. Our government did not act right with us Californians."

Writing to a friend, Jacob Hess, Sutter remembered that only four houses stood in Yerba Buena when he arrived in California. "I built miles of the inner part of California, with a sword in my fist, and through my labors gold was discovered . . . . I commanded the 2nd Division under General Micheltorena, was in many a hard battle and was once a prisoner of war and was to be shot but was rescued and often I had bloody battles with the Indians. In short, it is a wonder that I am alive."

The Legislature in February 1853 appointed Sutter a major general commanding the California militia, an honorary post with no duties or compensation, but Sutter was proud of the honor. Two years later, a full-length portrait of him in his general's uniform tricked out with gold braid was purchased by the Legislature for $2,500. The work of pioneer California artist William S. Jewett, the portrait hangs today in the Capitol.

Bad news in 1858: The U.S. Supreme Court confirmed his New Helvetia grant but denied the Sobrante grant, reducing Sutter's real estate from 230 to 75 square miles. Because he had long ago sold off parcels of the Sobrante grant, he was forced to use much of his remaining assets to repay those who had bought the Sobrante parcels, and whose titles in turn went by the boards. Before long, bankruptcy again threatened.

A reprieve came in April 1864 when the Legislature voted him $15,000, to be paid at $250 monthly for five years. Austerity forced him to curb his former extravagances, which at times had erupted into sprees that legends are made of. In one four-week binge in San Francisco, Sutter spent $15,000, then borrowed $1,000 more, spent that, and offered a note for $10,000 — all due in two weeks.

Disaster ended the Hock Farm idyll in June 1865. Sutter had allowed a vagrant ex-soldier to loaf about the place. When the clod

John Sutter swaggers in his uniform as a major general of California Militia. Courtesy General Don Mattson, California National Guard.

repaid the Good Samaritan with thefts, Sutter ordered him bound and lashed. Once he was let go, the rascal took revenge by setting fire to the Great House. Sutter and his wife escaped just in time as the inferno leveled their beautiful home and destroyed all their belongings — clothing, art objects, relics, documents — except a few prized items Sutter managed to save.

Five months later, he sailed for the East with Anna, nevermore to return to California.

For several years the Sutters lived in Washington D.C. area hotels or boardinghouses. When Congress recessed each summer, they relocated to drowsy villages in Pennsylvania to flee the capital's steamy heat. One town they kept returning to was Lititz, Pennsylvania, a postcard-pretty village founded in 1757 by the Moravian Church. Sutter admired its well-kept houses and tree-lined streets; it nestled in hills studded with handsome farmhouses with stone barns. Lititz reminded him of the towns of his youth, and the people were congenial to his Old World background. German was widely spoken by older residents. Lititz also had some fame as a health resort, whose springs mollified his rheumatic ailments.

Finally the Sutters chose Lititz as their permanent home. Sutter built a house there — a well-made two-story brick building with green shutters, steep-pitched slate roof, and a brick-paved patio where Sutter entertained guests.

Each year until his death in 1880, Sutter petitioned Congress to reimburse him for some of his losses: For his aid to California immigrants, for his expenses when the Supreme Court declared his Sobrante grant invalid, and for his help in colonizing California. In the mid-1870s, Sutter supplemented his claim by declaring he could have sold New Helvetia for $100,000, but turned down the offer because it would have left American settlers in the lurch. In 1845, he related, General Jose Castro and other Mexican officials desiring to discourage immigration had tried to buy him out with a $100,000 offer. Sutter retreated to his office to consult with John Bidwell, Pierson B. Reading and a man named Locker. "They all thought that it was a very large sum," recalled Sutter. "After they had discussed the matter for some time, their thoughts turned naturally upon their own interest. 'What shall we do?' they said. 'And what will all the settlers in the valley do if you abandon us to the Mexicans?' "

That did it for Sutter: "I felt that I was in duty bound to continue my protection of the immigrants. Had it not been for this

The dapper Captain Sutter is portrayed at age 63 when he lived near Washington DC. Courtesy Swiss National Tourist Office, San Francisco.

consideration, I should have accepted the Mexican offer. Often I have regretted not having sold New Helvetia at that time, because for this great sacrifice I have been rewarded with nothing but ingratitude."

Historian Hubert Bancroft concluded that Sutter's claim of being offered $100,000 was unsupported by other sources. He pointed out that the claim was made while Sutter's bill for compensation was before Congress. If Sutter had been able to convince Congress he had rejected such an enormous amount, to safeguard American settlers, it would count heavily in his favor.

Despite disappointments, friends who assured Sutter his services to California and America were not forgotten helped him keep his courage up. In 1877 at the annual meeting of Associated Pioneers of the Territorial Days of California, in Long Branch, New Jersey, the whole program was devoted to the bold colonizer, present as the guest of honor. The 200 persons attending — all former Argonauts, with a splash of dignitaries — heard a series of speakers and guzzled endless toasts. When the band whomped out "Hail To the Chief," Sutter lurched to his feet to acknowledge a thundering ovation. Ex-Californian Samuel E. Upham recalled the emotion: "General Sutter . . . with a suppressed voice expressed his inability to respond adequately to the remarks which were so flattering to him, and which he so thoroughly appreciated. 'It is not possible,' he said — but there his words failed him, and he sat down, and the assembled Argonauts rose up as one man, and waving their glasses in the air, gave three cheers that utterly drowned the music of the band."

Sutter was elected president of the association in its January 1878 meeting. But he didn't attend the annual banquet a year later, and sent a message to explain why: "Sick at heart and body, in vain appealing to Congress to do me justice and to return only part of what was wrongly taken from me, and with little hope of success unless you my friends by your influence will aid my cause, I could not feel cheerful as your guest at table tonight, and did not want to mar your pleasure by my presence. Remember old times without me."

Stirred by the oldtimer's gloom, association members vowed to employ "all honorable means" to persuade Congress to approve Sutter's legislation, by then hanging fire for 15 years.

Sutter's spirits soared when Senator Daniel W. Voorhees of Indiana on June 11, 1880, introduced a joint resolution to award him $50,000 for his losses and services.

Even as Congress's time for adjournment neared, Sutter stayed in his room at the Mades Hotel, not far from the national Capitol, ready to rush home as soon as the good news came. But this was an election year. As the lawmakers scurried toward adjournment, Sutter's measure was one of those that got sidetracked in the confusion.

When Sutter learned June 16 that Congress had adjourned without acting on his bill, it was too much. He plunged into a depression that sent him to his bed. His apprehensive friend Colonel Frank Schaefer pleaded with Senator Voorhees to call on Sutter at his hotel and promise him he would give top priority to Sutter's bill in the next session. Voorhees had to delay his meeting with Sutter for a day. For the old veteran, it was one day too late. When Voorhees called at the hotel, he found that Sutter, 77, had died the day before, on June 18, 1880.

At this time, Annie Bidwell, wife of John Bidwell, was visiting her parents in Washington. She went to Lititz to console Mrs. Sutter, then wrote to her husband: "I think we ought to take care of Mrs. Sutter if she does go to Cal. until a good home can be secured for her . . . There is something very distressing to me in the thought of her dying from neglect, when her husband rescued so many from similar situations."

Anna Sutter died less than a year later. In the Moravian Brotherhood Cemetery at Lititz, they lie in a joint grave topped with a marble slab. The house Sutter built still stands at 17-19 East Main St. After Anna's death, the building was sold and remodeled. Today a hardware store occupies the first floor.

In 1939 at Lititz, a bronze tablet was unveiled to memorialize the 100th anniversary of the founding of Sutter's Fort — 3,000 miles away. It reads:

JOHN A. SUTTER
1803-1880
Eminent Pioneer of California, who
founded Sacramento in 1839
and over whose lands poured
the Gold Rush of 1849,
lived his last years in
Lititz and is interred in an
honored corner of the nearby
Moravian Cemetery

Sutter has been the target of detractors, and has been accused of things he was perhaps not innocent of. His ambition knew no bounds, he was insensitive to Indians, he fled creditors as if they had leprosy. But what an adventurer and colonizer!

Did he perhaps save California from the Russians, albeit inadvertently? Put the case that the Russians *hadn't* found a qualified buyer for their colony before 1848 — before news of the Coloma gold strike galvanized the world. Would the Russians then have loosed their grip on California for several shiploads of wheat and beans, and chickenfeed in terms of cash? Or would they be thinking of wealth beyond the dreams of avarice? Gold would have gotten their attention fast; it would have inspired them with berserk energy, just as it did the legions of hot-eyed fortune-seekers who took California by storm. Instead of decamping, the Russians likely would have reinforced their garrison and entered the contest for a chunk of the Mother Lode, perchance the lion's share. And Californians today might be pledging allegiance to the Hammer and Sickle.

That is speculation — but it is not speculation that Sutter, more than any other, developed our agricultural and mineral wealth. He had dreamed of an immense empire in California — and his dream came true, for California today is recognized as one of the world's greatest agricultural and commercial empires.

Consider that, without Sutter, California might never have become part of the Union. Put the case that there had been no Sutter's Fort. What then? Though Sutter's Fort never fired its cannon at an enemy, the bold presence of this wilderness stronghold made it the western anchor of America's Manifest Destiny. General William Tecumseh Sherman, who had served in California as a young officer, immortalized Sutter's role with these words: "To Captain Sutter, more than any single person, are we indebted for the conquest of California with all its treasures."

Sutter had come to America to seek his fortune, and how he found it is a marvelous story: Found it in the heart of the western wilderness after a journey to some of the uttermost places on earth; found it by building an empire with, as he said, a sword in his fist. And then at the last had to watch it wash away, as New Helvetia was inundated by a flood of gold-seekers and swept downstream to the dead sea of lost empires.

Chapter 32

Sutter's Fort Today

Today a State Historic Park, Sutter's Fort reposes on two square blocks, an area that doesn't hint of the 230 square miles of New Helvetia's maximum dominion. Reconstruction has achieved what some archeologists say is an authentic restoration, but at least one other authority says it is not quite right.

Sacramento artist-historian Ted Baggelmann says his research has uncovered noteworthy discrepancies, and cites these sources:

1. In 1850, an unknown artist chanced to come upon the southeast bastion when its facade had caved in, enabling him to sketch the interior. His pencil sketch — now in the State Library — reveals that the original bastions were two-story and oblong in floor plan, not the one-story square structures of today's restoration. And the originals had high-pitched tile roofs, not the low-pitched roofs of today. The unknown artist also sketched rows of embrasures, or rifle ports, on the bastion's second-floor level under the eaves. No rifle ports perforate the reconstruction.

2. Earlier, Lt. Joseph Warren Revere (Paul Revere's grandson) of the U.S. Navy in 1847 made identical observations about the bastions when he inventoried the Fort's defenses. Revere also noted that the main gate was reinforced by rows upon rows of iron bolts, to strengthen it against assaults by battering rams. As added protection, a double row of sharp iron saw-like teeth spanned the gate's top, to cut the ropes of any grappling irons an

Sutter's Fort today is a magnet for tourists, whereas in yesteryears it was a magnet for immigrants exhausted after their arduous overland journeys.

enemy might hurl over the gate. Today, the gate is topped by wooden beams, one straight and one curved, with spikes that replicate the iron teeth.

These construction details only further demonstrate Sutter's iron resolve not to be "rooted out" of his wilderness stronghold — not by a horde of aborigines, nor an army with banners, nor the Devil on horseback. Captain Sutter against the world.

Baggelmann says Sutter's design was influenced by the medieval architecture of Burgdorf Castle, in Switzerland, and the town's 12th-century fortifications. Other historians conjecture Sutter also garnered ideas from the many forts he saw on his long, long trail to California.

But don't let these scholarly quibbles about the reconstruction diminish your enjoyment of this marvelous Fort — the immortal evidence of its builder's magnificent audacity.

Wilderness of course was not restored so it may be a bit difficult to fully grasp that the Fort was built here when wilderness abounded in every direction for at least 100 miles. Yet this is the fabled Fort (restored) that Sutter had had the genius and temerity to plant here when this was hardcore wilderness.

The Fort stands in an older section of Sacramento, crowded on all sides by buildings — commercial and public edifices, including the namesake Sutter General Hospital, the State Indian Museum, and many Victorian-era residences. Perhaps it is this commonplace setting that makes it difficult to comprehend the full impact of what Sutter did here in the wilds.

Located at 2701 L St., the Fort is open from 10 a.m. to 5 p.m. daily except Thanksgiving, Christmas and New Year's Day. For group reservations, call 445-4209; hearing impaired call 324-2667. The Fort is under jurisdiction of California Department of Parks and Recreation. Rangers generally fire the antique cannon daily at 11 and 2. If they forget, ask them and they'll happily comply.

You can go on your own tour of the Fort, armed with a "wand" that broadcasts recorded messages as you stroll from place to place. It takes an hour to do it properly, because there are so many things to hear and see about the frontier life depicted here.

In the cooper's shop, you'll see a black manikin making barrels — first black man in the Sacramento Valley. On an underground level in the southeast corner, look for the dismal prison room, now

Captain Sutter in bronze greets sightseers in perhaps the same open-handed gesture the real Captain greeted arriving pioneers. Sculptured by Spero Anargyros, the statue stands in front of Sutter General Hospital, facing Sutter's Fort.

occupied only by two surly manikins. This dungeon in times of yore incarcerated a variety of rogues. Moving along, you'll see a weaving room with loom and spinning wheels, with Indian manikins busy making blankets. Yonder lies the bakery: It dispensed bread made from some of the vast wheat crops grown on Sutter's land. It was a coarse-ground whole-grain product that persnickety visitors called "adobe bread." In another room, you'll see the great still that produced liquid cheer in the form of "Pisco Brandy," named after the grape, for Sutter and friends. Have a look at the grist mill, gunsmith shop, and candle shop. And the kitchen, from which Sutter fed hundreds of Indian workers at a time.

In the museum gallery, a glass case displays a tiny wooden doll that Patty Reed, 7, carried in the pocket of her dress from Illinois to California as she and her family traveled with the Donner Party in 1846-47. No one knew she had the doll until she pulled it out of her pocket on arrival at Sutter's Fort.

Docents donate time and talents to enrich the experience of visitors. On Living History Day, five times a year, docents and staff gussy up in period costumes, turn back the clock to 1846 to become pioneers, and chat with visitors. Some bake wholewheat bread, carrying out the entire process from starting the fire, to mixing and kneading the dough, and then baking it in the "beehive" oven, which emanates mouth-watering aromas. Visitors get to taste this pioneer bread — the same kind the Captain relished.

At night in the Fort in the old days, candles were the main source of light, so other docents practice the art of candle-dipping, from melting the wax to drying the finished candles. Visitors get a chance to try their hands at it.

The Fort is equipped with spinning wheels, looms, drop spindles and wool carts, so docents can demonstrate weaving basics. A few sheep roam the enclosure, and a pamphlet notes: "The Fort has a few resident sheep who are happy to provide us with raw wool." How do docents know the sheep are happy? Don't ask.

Slowolf, a king-size professional blacksmith, ran the blacksmith shop for seven years from 1979 until his death.

Many people, said Stan Mortensen, a later blacksmith, think old-time blacksmiths were mainly horse-shoers. Not so. "Anyone who traveled clear across the country would be able to shoe his own horses."

For Captain Sutter, he said, blacksmiths probably manufactured hoes and plow-blades and did other welding. So today's smithies here are portrayed mainly as fabricators – turning out door hinges,

Sutter's Fort was journey's end for this cavalcade and wagon train from Carson City.

fire steels (for starting fires), candleholders, cups, forks, knives and S-hooks for hanging pots over fires. Mortensen has since moved to Oregon.

At this writing, Mike Carson, a professional blacksmith near Woodland, does duty at the Fort, demonstrating the making of horseshoes and nails. Carson admits his family has a tradition that links them to pioneer scout and adventurer Kit Carson.

Mike Carson is paid during the "History Live" summer programs, but works as a volunteer docent the rest of the year. A docent there since 1994, he has also operated the blacksmith shop at Cal Expo since 1993.

At the Fort, others who share smithy duties are Dennis Brehm ("Biscuits") and Robert Benson ("Little Scotch"). Brehm acquired his monicker at a mountain men's rendezvous when he burned the biscuits so badly that their only use was as hockey pucks, he confesses. Robert picked up his nickname because one time a little scotch whiskey rendered him hors de combat.

Sacramento actor Victor Larson used to do impersonations of Captain Sutter at the Fort, once in a planter's outfit, recalling Sutter's role as an agricultural pioneer, once in black uniform with yellow sash and gold epaulets, reminding of the Captain's fancy taste in uniforms and his military adventures. Larson's monologue included the tale of the Russian from Fort Ross, who came here to dun Sutter for a late payment of wheat. Larson stepped into his Sutter persona: "As he and I ambled on a friendly stroll, the Russian glimpsed what he thought was a cat, and ran to catch it. It was a skunk – which caught the Russian with a full barrage. We had to bury his clothes." Larson stepped back out of his persona and said history doesn't record whether the Russian obtained other clothes, or had to go home in a barrel. Larson has since died.

George R. Stammerjohan, one of the founders of the Fort's Living History Days, also plays Captain Sutter. A historian with California Department of Parks and Recreation, Sacramento, Stammerjohan has this nameplate on his desk:

CAPTAIN JOHN SUTTER
a.k.a. GEORGE STAMMERJOHAN

The Living History Day idea was concocted at Asilomar. "Then we struggled for two years to get it planned," Stammerjohan said. "We had our first one in June 1980 as a one-shot experimental plan. Ninety percent went wrong." Nevertheless, it took off. He and Eileen Hook, a state park interpreter, recruited a volunteer band of history buffs, many from the department, to run the program. The Fort now stages five Living History Days a year, usually five typical days during the momentous year of 1846, when the Fort flew three flags: Mexican, Bear Flag, then the Stars and Stripes.

As Sutter, Stammerjohan chose a costume that is basically civilian, because the type of uniform Sutter may have worn at times is moot. For day wear, he dons a royal blue frock coat. His favored hat is a straw with four-inch brim. To represent Sutter at more formal occasions, he slips into an out-of-date tail-coat, gray-green with black cuffs and black collar — out-of date because frontiers of course were never au courant with the latest fashions on Parisian boulevards.

Eileen Hook plays Eliza Gregson, an actual pioneer woman who arrived here in 1845 with husband James. The Gregsons later settled in Sonoma County.

Hook is pleasantly surprised by occasional visits from a Gregson descendant — Augusta Gregson Cunningham, granddaughter of

George Stammerjohan as Captain Sutter and Eileen Hook as a pioneer woman originated Living History Days at the Fort.

Eliza. Cunningham, 88 years old in 1987, calls Hook "Grandma."

"And I call her Granddaughter," Hook says with a smile.

The story of Captain Sutter seems so far back in our past that who could imagine he had any link with the aeronautics age — only five years after he arrived in California? Yet Stammerjohan cites this believe-it-or-not fact: Sutter witnessed the first manned flight in California. Explains Stammerjohan: In 1844 while visiting the Mexican governor in Monterey, Sutter watched the manned balloon ascension that was part of the festivities.

James Birch, who became president of the world's biggest stagecoach empire, drowned at age 29. Courtesy Department of Parks and Recreation.

Chapter 33
Stagecoaches West

I have found in travelling in a stage-coach, that it is often a comfort to shift one's position and be bruised in a new place.

Washington Irving

Staging in California was born in Sacramento.

For two years, James E. Birch had driven a stage in Rhode Island, and was engaged to the comely Julia Chase — who told him of her dream of living in a mansion filled with beautiful things, and with servants. Birch knew that would take plenty of gold, so he took off for California, because everybody knew there was plenty of gold on the banks of the Sacramento.

Arriving in Sacramento in midsummer 1849 Birch, 21, observed that prospectors had no way to reach the mines save by horse or shank's mare. He saw a need and filled it — inaugurating a stage-line route from Sacramento to Coloma via Mormon Island, starting with a farm wagon, he as the driver. Soon he added a second driver and another coach. The *Placer Times* editor tried the novel enterprise and found it "highly satisfactory." The wiseacre newspaperman added: "The horses . . . dashed through sloughs and gulches in a remarkably knowing style. These California horses seem to know about as much as most folks."

Birch kept adding stages and drivers, running lines to all the hotspots in mining country.

In November 1851, he sold out — and went back home with a fortune, and built a mansion for Julia. They were married in it in less than a year after he left California.

J.D. Borthwick, arriving in Sacramento in 1852 to catch a stage to the mines, sojourned a night in "a large hotel, which was also the great staging house." In 5 a.m. darkness, he joined 100 persons in a candlelight breakfast. At daybreak, it was time to go adventuring: 24 four-horse coaches filled the street in front of the hotel, all bound for different places.

"Crowds of men were taking their seats, while others were fortifying themselves for their journey at the bar," Borthwick wrote.

Half the crowd were passengers. The rest were "runners" for the various stages, charged with recruiting passengers. "And each was exerting his lungs to the utmost," Borthwick wrote. "'Now then, gentlemen,' shouts one of them, 'all aboard for Nevada City. Who's agoin'? Only three seats left — the last chance for today for Nevada City?' Then catching sight of some man who betrays the very slightest appearance of helplessness . . . he pounces upon him, saying, 'Nevada City, sir? — this way — just in time,' and seizing him by the arm, he drags him into the crowd of stages and almost has him bundled into that for Nevada City before the poor devil can make it understood that it is Coloma he wants to go to."

California had gotten into James Birch's blood. A wealthy man, he returned in March 1853 and purchased stagelines — and telegraph lines. Because of grievous competition, he and other stageline magnates agreed in December 1853 to pool their resources to form a corporation — California Stage Co. — which swiftly became the biggest and richest staging company in the world, with assessed value of $1 million — and with Birch, 24, as president.

From its headquarters in the Orleans Hotel on 2nd Street, each day at 5 a.m. up to a dozen coaches rolled away. Carrying 10 or 12 passengers, they rattled along at four or five miles an hour, bound for major mountain towns, and Marysville on the north and Stockton on the south.

Ads of California Stage Co. listed such destinations as the following; many of these poetic earthy names still survive on today's maps: Charley's Rancho, Clear Creek, Red Bluff, Cotton Wood Creek, One Horse Town, Pit River Diggins, Diamond Springs, Log Town, Mud Springs, Forty Mile House, Deer Creek, Rail Road House, White Rock Springs, Gold Springs, Gold Hill, White Oak Springs, Green Springs, Negro Hill, Willow Springs, Alder Springs, Middle Bar Bridge, Mokelumne Hill, Frenchman's, Kentucky House, Angel's Camp, Murphy's, Carson Hill, Robinson's Ferry, Shaw's Flat.

By 1855, the company's lines were reaching all over northern and central California and as far south as Los Angeles. By 1856, California Stage Co. owned 1,100 horses, 80 Concord coaches and 125 Concord wagons.

James Birch, unfortunately, did not live long enough to fulfill his early promise as an entrepreneur. This pioneer of a giant land transportation combine was destined to drown at sea — only a year hence.

In 1855 Birch, sensing he was ready for even bigger ventures, pulled out of California Stage Co. as an active participant, yet remaining the company's biggest stockholder, and went back East.

Two years later, several staging tycoons — and Birch as a lone contender — submitted bids to the government for "the great overland mail contract." While awaiting the decision, Birch accepted a four-year contract to carry mail on a new route between San Antonio and San Diego — then was dismayed to learn that President James Buchanan had awarded the great overland contract to John Butterfield and associates.

The *New York Times,* which agreed with the decision, nevertheless had this to say on July 7, 1857: "Mr. Birch is a gentleman of large capacity, much experience and more competent than any other single man in the United States to execute this great mail contract . . . ."

It may be that the government reckoned that the resources of Butterfield's group outweighed those of Birch as a lone-wolf entrepreneur.

The chagrined Birch switched all his energies to his San Antonio-San Diego contract. Knowing Butterfield wouldn't begin his operation until September 1858, Birch vowed to establish the first *through* stageline to the Pacific, beating Butterfield to the coast — a victory of sorts.

Birch sailed to California on July 6, 1857, to set up his western

Racing toward sundown, a Wells Fargo stagecoach relives a thrilling epoch. Photo courtesty of Wells Fargo & Company.

terminus — then sailed back to New York to establish his headquarters there.

He never reached New York. Aboard the *Central America* when it foundered off South Carolina on Sept. 12, 1857, he was one of hundreds who drowned. He was 29 years old.

Julia Chase Birch did not have to wear her widow's weeds for long. To settle her husband's estate, she journeyed to Sacramento — where she met Birch's good friend, Frank Stevens, vice president of California Stage Co. They were married in Sacramento July 24, 1858.

Wells Fargo, later a giant in the staging business, shipped mainly bullion and other freight in the early years, graduating into passengers in years to come. Organized by tycoons Henry Wells and William Fargo, it began as a banking and express firm in Gold Rush-era San Francisco.

In Sacramento, Wells Fargo opened its doors at 45 2nd St. in 1852, with this brief announcement: "Wells, Fargo & Co. is now ready to undertake a general Express Forwarding Agency and Commission Business and the purchase and sale of Gold Dust, Bullion, and Specie." In 1854, the firm moved to the Hastings

Building at J and 2nd Streets. That was the year Angus Frierson took over as agent here, and built up a reputation for diligence and magnanimous donations to charities.

When he died suddenly in 1855, the community was saddened — and shocked several months later when Wells Fargo directors discovered that he had embezzled $195,889. This apparently explained his generous charitable contributions — a Robin Hood working an inside job.

Wells Fargo operated in the Hastings Building until 1857, catering to miners who brought nuggets and bullion in for exchange or safekeeping. Today this Wells Fargo office, catty-corner from the Pony Express statue in Old Sacramento, is open as a museum. Typical of an Old West banking office, it contains the basic tools of the early banker's profession — a balance, a clock and a letter press. These simple tools helped Wells Fargo agents get the job done.

The handsome copper-and-brass balance on view was built by the distinguished Boston firm of Howard and Davis. Fewer than 100 of these rare scales were manufactured. Their primary purpose was to weigh gold brought in by miners. Each balance, meticulously crafted to precise specs, was hermetically sealed in metal containers and shipped around the Horn to California. These balances were so renowned for accuracy that miners asserted they could register the weight of a pencil mark on a piece of paper.

Howard and Davis also fabricated the famed "banjo" clock, named for its shape, that hangs on the wall here. It is a weight-driven, seven-day type — a familar sight in Wells Fargo agencies.

A 19th-century letter press, also on view, was used to copy important documents. The complicated chemical process required three minutes to produce a finished copy. But who needed a copy faster than that?

Wells Fargo stages halted here at the Hastings Building to take on supplies bound for all points in the gold country. It cooperated with several other stage companies, including California Stage Co., Holladay Lines, and the Overland Mail Co. Overland offered the first regular transcontinental stagecoach service. In 1866 these companies linked up, with Wells Fargo as the dominant principal. This blazoned the Wells Fargo logo on the entire Overland Mail route from the Missouri to the Pacific — plus thousands of more miles of stagelines nearly everywhere else in the West. Almost overnight, Wells Fargo was visibly the world's largest stagecoach empire.

Stagedrivers favored the rugged and stylish Concord coach, the brand name in rolling stock. Its design was borrowed from the English mail coach, but revised to adapt it to the rugged terrain of the American West. To give it more roadability, it was built lower to the ground, so it could take sharp curves at hair-raising speed. Most Concords had upholstered seats to accommodate nine passengers inside. Half a dozen or more could ride on top. The topside seat next to the driver, if not occupied by the shotgun, was most popular with passengers. At every stop, this passenger was expected to host the driver to drinks and cigars. Tipping drivers was an unpardonable sin, but they would never turn down a gift of cigars, or a new whip, or boots.

Roof passengers spent most of the journey desperately clinging for their lives. Yet it seemed as if there was always room for one more. This item appeared in 1858 in the *Butte Record* of Oroville: "A stage from Shasta passed through town yesterday, about one o'clock, with an enormous load. The coach was of the biggest size. We counted thirty-five passengers on and inside of it, besides the driver and one Chinaman."

To carry mail and baggage, the Concord had a leather-covered platform, or "boot," in the back, and a compartment under the driver's seat for strong-boxes. Most Concords were painted pomegranate red, then varnished to a high gloss. Wheels were painted yellow. Interiors were overlaid with damask. Ornate paintings and gold scrollwork decorated the vehicles.

Leather curtains made a poor shield against the elements. In winter, rain poured in — or snow blew in. In summer, the coach commonly was engulfed in dust clouds churned up by the horses' hooves, while inside temperatures often sizzled up to 100 or more. For men passengers, whiskey helped to kill the pain, but women were forbidden to imbibe in public. One passenger, after traveling across the country in a stagecoach, wrote: "I know what hell is like. I've had twenty-four days of it."

The isolated way stations would not have been recommended by Duncan Hines. A correspondent for the *San Francisco Evening Bulletin* reported that meals consisted of "tough beef, beans, greasy potatoes, venison and an occasional dried apple pie with coffee strong enough to float a mule shoe." Mark Twain noted that some stations dispensed a beverage that "pretended to be tea, but there was too much dishrag and sand, and old bacon rind in it to deceive the intelligent traveler."

Sometimes a traveler recalled a captivating moment. Mrs. Rebecca Yokum, who came west on a stage in 1860, remembered:

"Somewhere after we got into California we were all one forenoon going through the mountains. The road was very narrow and every few minutes the conductor would play a little tune on a bugle to warn any other travelers that the stage was coming. The long notes of his bugle echoing through the mountains sounded very romantic."

There was only one guarantee of safety from Indians, according to John Butterfield, operator of a stageline between Mississippi and California, who warned passengers: "You will be traveling through Indian country and the safety of your person cannot be vouchsafed by anyone but God." God helps those who help themselves, so stagelines urged passengers to arm themselves with rifles and pistols and plenty of ammunition. To discourage bandits, passengers were advised not to carry valuables.

Desperadoes often found bullion-laden stages a temptation greater than they cared to resist. Wells Fargo's biggest headache was Black Bart, who robbed 28 company stages. This versifying "gentleman bandit" often left a sample of his doggerel at the scene of a crime. In one rifled strongbox, he contributed these lines:

I've labored long and hard for bread
For honor and for riches
But on my corns too long you've tread
You fine-haired sons of bitches.

Just what grudge Black Bart held against Wells Fargo is unknown; he apparently didn't rob any other company's stages.

Black Bart's luck fizzled out on Nov. 3, 1883. On the Milton-Sonora run, driver Reason McConnell's strong-box contained $5,000 in gold, and his only passenger was young Jimmy Rolleri, armed with a rifle. Jimmy planned to go deer hunting, so when the stage toiled up a long grade, he hopped off, saying he'd hunt along the trail and catch up on the other side of the hill.

As the stage neared the hill-crest, a hooded figure stepped out of manzanita, covering McConnell with a sawed-off shotgun: "Get down from there so I can get to the box!" Just then, Jimmy blundered onto the scene, not realizing the situation until the last moment. He threw up his rifle and squeezed — missed! He fired again as the bandit leaped off the stage and hit the ground on the run. McConnell grabbed Jimmy's rifle and fired. The bandit went sprawling, scrambled to his feet, and plunged into brush.

In Copperopolis, the sheriff telegraphed Wells Fargo in San Francisco. Meanwhile, a posse found sundry articles apparently abandoned by the holdup man, including a handkerchief with a laundry mark — FX07. James Hume, chief of Wells Fargo detectives, assigned a man to check out San Francisco's 91 laundries. On the eighth day, he got lucky. Laundryman Thomas C. Ware identified it as belonging to a patron, retired mining engineer Charles E. Bolton, who lived in Webb House on 2nd Street. Hume took Ware along to introduce him.

After exchanging amenities, Bolton began to fidget and refused to answer questions. Hume summoned police who, over Bolton's protests, ransacked his room. The damning evidence was a letter in the identical handwriting of the verse Bart had left at holdup scenes. The law put the collar on him and Bolton finally confessed to 28 Wells Fargo holdups in eight years. Sentenced to six years of compulsory retirement in San Quentin, he was released in 1888 for good behavior after four years and two months.

Only unverifiable rumors account for what happened to Bolton in later years. Most persistent rumor: Wells Fargo agreed to pay him an annual pension if he would desist from his pesky habit of robbing stages. But Wells Fargo says it has never found evidence in its records that Bolton was on its payroll. If the rumor is true, it means Bolton reckoned that honesty was the best policy. Wells Fargo would never admit it was bribing a bandit — it might give other bandits ideas.

Besides Black Bart, two other figures in the Wells Fargo saga had literary proclivities. Bret Harte came west in 1857 at age 21, rode shotgun on Wells Fargo stages in Humboldt, Trinity and Siskiyou, switched to teaching school, then came down with the itch to write. He contributed to *The Sacramento Union*, then went on to become an acclaimed writer of Gold Rush stories, including "The Luck of Roaring Camp."

Actor Dale Robertson, memorable for his detective role in the TV series "Tales of Wells Fargo," became intrigued with stagecoaches, turned writer, delved deep into history, where he detected some rousing stories, and surfaced with a fascinating book, *Wells Fargo, the Legend.*

Stage-drivers were regarded by passengers as heroes, and of course regarded themselves as heroes, looking down on lesser mortals with unconcealed disdain. In *Roughing It,* Mark Twain wrote: "In the eyes of the stage driver, station-keepers and hostlers were a sort of good enough low creature, useful in their place, and helping to make a world, but not the kind of beings which a person of distinction could afford to concern himself with." The driver "had but little less contempt for his passengers than he had for his hostlers."

Drivers had to be an elite breed, because their job was so demanding: They were sent out to drive strange horses on strange roads in unpredictable weather. Butterfield's general order to drivers: "Remember, boys, nothing on God's earth must stop the U.S. Mail." Nothing seemed to daunt the drivers, but careening hell-bent around hairpin turns daunted the passengers, who were helpless to do anything but send up their most fervent prayers.

Temperance was not the average driver's long suit. One driver was legendary for his intemperance: Hank Monk, a sometime driver for Wells Fargo, is said to have had his only accident in three decades when he took his team out while sober. Another time, he got so drunk he "whiskeyed the horses and watered himself," thereby sobering up long enough to manage his pixilated ponies.

En route to Sacramento, newspaper editor Horace Greeley transited the Sierra in 1859 with Hank Monk at the reins. Mark Twain immortalized the ride. In Carson City, Greeley told Monk he was in a hurry to get to Placerville, where he had an engagement to lecture. Twain tells it: "Hank Monk cracked his whip and started off at an awful pace. The coach bounced up and down in such a terrific way that it jolted all the buttons off of Horace's coat, and finally shot his head clean through the roof of the stage, and then he yelled at Hank Monk and begged him to go easier — said he warn't in as much of a hurry as he was awhile ago. But Hank Monk said, 'Keep your seat, Horace, and I'll get you there on time' — and you bet he did, too, what was left of him!"

At Placerville, Greeley staggered out of the coach and into the Cary House, and a banquet in his honor. The battered and bruised Greeley, responding to numerous toasts, had to rise from a couch rather than a chair. Evidence that Twain's story wasn't fiction: The Cary House proprietor vividly recalled that the stage roof was broken in three places and that Greeley's hat was mashed in.

Finally arriving in Sacramento, Greeley chose the Orleans Hotel on 2nd Street as his home base for further adventures in the Wild West.

But the most improbable stage-driver has to be Charlie Parkhurst. Tobacco-chewing "Old Charlie" was nearly 40 when he came west in 1851. He drove many a stage for James Birch's California Stage Co. You could always count on Charlie — whip a-cracking and cheek a-bulging with tobacco — to bring the stage through along the treacherous roads of the gold country. He had a rare talent for handling horses, a talent so uncanny the stable hands could explain it only as "some kind of hoodoo." His New England twang supported the rumor he had once driven stages on the Boston Post Road, but nobody knew anything else about him.

One black-as-sin night on the Hangtown run, the passenger riding next to him on the box demanded: "How in the world can you see your way?"

Charlie let fly a stream of juice into the void, and wiped his chin: "I've traveled over these mountains so often I can tell where the road is by the sound of the wheels. When they rattle, I'm on hard ground. When they don't rattle, I generally look over the side to see where she's going."

Charlie never got mad at anybody — except a road agent who had the gall to jab a pistol into his belly and order him to surrender the strongbox. Charlie nearly exploded: "Next time you try and stop me, I'll be ready!"

He was ready the next time. When some bandits yelled "Halt!" Charlie tore out a pistol and killed the leader in his tracks. He lashed his horses and escaped the others and was never bothered again — evidence that capital punishment is a deterrent.

One time an ornery horse kicked him in the face and put out one eye, so he reckoned he must be getting old and it was time to hang up his whip. Ending 20 years of hustling stages in California, he retired to another job — operating a combined saloon and stagecoach stop on the road between Santa Cruz and Watsonville. Then he tried cattle raising. But rheumatism forced him to hang up his saddle. After moving to a small abode near Watsonville, he died Dec. 29, 1879.

As friends prepared to dress him in his best outfit to lay him away properly, they were flabbergasted to discover that — Old Charlie was a woman.

Besides pioneering as a woman stagedriver, Charlie voted in one or more elections, making her the first American woman ever to cast a ballot, if she voted before Wyoming women won voting rights in 1869 — and unless some other transvestite beat her to it.

With completion of the transcontinental railroad in 1869, overland stagelines began to roll into history. But smaller stage outfits continued to lurch in and out of California's mining communities late into the century.

The next chapter will look at stages that remain in one place.

Chapter 34
Comedies and Tragedies

Flushed with success of his Round Tent Saloon, proprietor Zadock Hubbard decided to build a theater and import some actors. Construction of his Eagle Theatre — first western theater built as a theater — began in July 1849 on the second lot north of J and Front Streets and was soon completed. A stepladder on the exterior led patrons to the second tier. In respect to the ladies, canvas was tacked strategically around the ladder, so no one could catch a glimpse of unmentionables. The Eagle had a tin roof to shed rain and falling branches. Its wood frame was overlain with blue canvas that, when wet with rain, hampered ventilation, fostering a hot and stifling atmosphere.

The Eagle opened to a full house on Oct. 18, 1849, with a production of "The Bandit Chief, or The Spectre of the Forest." Tickets were $3 for the pit and $5 for the box tier. Many patrons paid their admissions with gold dust. Some fine-looking ladies graced the "dress-circle," according to the *Placer Times* reviewer. Another reviewer at this performance was author Bayard Taylor, sent by Horace Greeley's *New York Tribune* to write about the Gold Rush. Spectators wore heavy overcoats, felt hats, and knee-high boots, Taylor wrote in his book *El Dorado*. He said the orchestra was composed of five persons "under the direction of an Italian" and performed "with tolerable correctness." The *Placer Times* reviewer, on the other hand, said the orchestra consisted of a violin, a large drum, an iron triangle that did double duty in announcing meals at a nearby boarding house, and an instrument he described as "a very cheezy flageolet" (a small flute) tootled by a one-eyed musician.

The drop-curtain depicted a landscape of dark-red forest against lilac mountains and a yellow sky. The red trees apparently hinted of bloody scenes to follow, Taylor said. The play starred the eminent Mrs. Ray of New Zealand's Royal Theatre. Taylor's review continues: "The bell rings; the curtain rolls up; and we look upon a forest scene, in the midst of which appears Hildebrand, the robber, in a sky-blue mantle.

"The other characters are a brave knight in a purple dress, with his servant in scarlet; they are about to storm the robbers' hold and carry off a captive maiden. Several acts are filled with the usual amount of fighting and terrible speeches; but the interest of the play is carried to an awful height by the appearance of two spectres, clad in mutilated tent-covers, and holding spermaceti candles in their hands. At this juncture Mrs. Ray rushes in and throws herself into an attitude in the middle of the stage: why she does it, no one can tell."

Taylor doesn't describe the "attitude." Whatever it is, Mrs. Ray repeats it several times in three acts. Taylor said it had no connection with the tragedy, and apparently was incorporated in the play only to show the audience a real live female performer. The delighted audience of mostly miners, starved for a glimpse of a comely woman, greeted her antics with wild applause. Taylor goes on: "In the closing scenes, where Hildebrand entreats the heroine to become his bride, Mrs. Ray shone in all her glory. 'No!' said she, 'I'd rather take a basilisk and wrap its cold fangs around me, than be clasped in the hembraces (sic) of an 'artless robber.' Then changing her tone to that of entreaty, she calls upon the knight in purple, whom she declares to be 'me 'ope — me only 'ope!' We will not stay to hear the songs and duets which follow; the tragedy has been a sufficient infliction." In short, Taylor didn't like it.

Unfortunately, the theater venture ended in calamity for Hubbard, who had overextended himself in its construction. He became so ill his sanity was in doubt. Creditors forced him to sell out. His partners Gates Brown and Madison Pruett, trying to stave off bankruptcy, filed a cross petition with the court, in vain. The theater was sold for $4,350 to Clinton Hastings and Samuel C. Bruce. After minor repairs, it reopened November 13 with "Douglas," a popular tragedy.

The 1849-50 winter brought heavy rains, beginning early in November. Violent storms in December interrupted the schedule when hurricane winds toppled the three-story building Sam Brannan was erecting at Front and J Streets, crashing part of it onto Eagle Theatre. But Eagle reopened on December 24.

But the theater's final curtain, as it were, was drawn prematurely by the 1850 floods, breaking up a performance in midpoint. On the night of January 4, the Sacramento River sundered its levees, flooding the whole Embarcadero. Water rose inches deep in the pit of the Eagle before the doors opened, and the play had gone on only an act or two when the benches were awash.

For the most part, the audience ignored the water. Between acts, patrons gambled on the rough-board benches. Sometimes a rowdy miner, pretending wild excitement at some aspect of the play, yelled and applauded, then flung out his arms, striking customers on each side, knocking them into the water. Everybody thought that was hilarious, except those ignominiously dunked. The latter arose soaking wet and with fists flying, contributing a little drama that momentarily upstaged the actors.

Water kept rising and the play came to a sudden end. The theater company lost all its costumes and scenery and other appurtenances.

The flood-damaged theater was purchased by McDougall, Fowler and Warbass and shifted 200 feet east, so it faced 2nd Street between I and J. The new owners replaced its canvas sides with lumber and added private boxes. Reported the *Placer Times:* "The internal fixins of the house were made tasteful and pleasant in all respects."

Renamed The Tehama, it opened March 25, 1850. Famed tragedian James Stark performed some of Shakespeare's works on its boards, including "Hamlet," "Macbeth," "Othello," and "Richard III." But fire, scourge of many early theaters, demolished it Aug. 14, 1851, ending Sacramento's first theater.

Meanwhile, four more Sacramento theaters succeeded the drowned Eagle: Lee's Exchange, New Hall, National Arena, and the Pacific. At the Pacific, Italian dancer Signora Fanny Manten presented Sacramento's first ballet. This program also featured magician-ventriloquist Signor Rossi, whose most sidesplitting act was his conversation with, supposedly, a drunken man locked in a trunk.

Even Captain Sutter had a brief fling on the stage — playing himself in command of his military force in Dr. David Robinson's extravaganza, "Past, Present and Future of San Francisco," presented in that city. But the play aroused derisive laughter with its painted backdrop of San Francisco Bay — spanned by a bridge.

World-famed Edwin Booth — who would be acclaimed the greatest actor of his time — honed his early thespian years in Sacramento theaters. All the famous Booths played in early Sacramento at one time or another — except the notorious John Wilkes Booth, Lincoln's assassin. Other luminaries such as Lotta Crabtree, David Belasco, Maude Adams, and scores of other renowned troupers tramped over the local boards and tore up the scenery with melodramatic emotions.

But perhaps no shooting star left such a dazzling trail across the Sacramento firmament as did Lola Montez.

Born as Marie Gilbert in Ireland in 1818, she married an army officer, but the marriage ended in divorce. Claiming Spanish descent, she adopted the name Lola Montez and headed for Paris to try her luck on the stage. Though her singing and dancing were said to be nothing special, Lola's smoky beauty made her a sensation that lured, as moths to a flame, such notables as Franz Liszt, composer, and Alexandre Dumas *pere,* author of *The Three Musketeers* and *The Count of Monte Cristo*, among numerous other lovers. Commented the disillusioned Dumas: "She has the evil eye. She will bring bad luck to every man who links his destiny with hers."

King Ludwig I, age 60, of Bavaria became enamored of her in 1847 when he saw her dance in Munich and sent agents to France bearing jewels and love-notes. She became not only his mistress, but a countess and his chief political advisor, virtually ruling Bavaria. Ludwig squandered the national treasury on her. The people of Munich, incensed at being governed by a courtesan, rioted in the streets: "Down with the whore!" Montez fled to Switzerland just ahead of the 1848 revolution she had helped start. Ludwig was forced to abdicate, in favor of his son, later famous as "The Mad King of Bavaria."

Touring the United States, she spent a year in San Francisco, dancing in theaters by night and challenging people to duels by day. She performed her acclaimed "La Tarantella, or the Spider Dance." She and Patrick Hull, young publisher of the *San Francisco Whig* newspaper, were married July 2, 1853. She was 35 and it was her fifth marriage.

That afternoon they sailed to Sacramento on the steamer *New World* and registered next day at the Orleans Hotel. She gave her first performance July 6 in the Sacramento Theatre on 3rd between

Lola Montez is portrayed in a painting that hangs in her Grass Valley home.

I and J Streets. The *Whig* newspaper had described her "Spider Dance" as a rapid whirling number from Italy, which Lola performed in a multi-colored costume: "She unwittingly gets into one of those huge nests of spiders . . . She commences to dance and the cobwebs entangle her ankles . . . . The music is a slow-measured but fascinating amalgamation of polka, waltz, mazurka and jig. The spiders accumulate and the danseuse stamps. They appear in myriads . . . about the stage, invading the edge of milady's petticoats and taking such unwarrantable liberties that the spectator imagines an inextricable mass of cobwebs and enraged spiders, and would sympathize with Demoiselle, but she seems to take it so easily herself that one jumps to the conclusion that she is enough for them. It is Lola versus the spiders. After a series of examinations and shaking dresses, she succeeds in getting the imaginary intruders away — apparently stamps daylight out of the last ten thousand, and does it with so much naivete that we feel sort of satisfaction at the triumph. The picture winds up Lola's victory, and she glides from the stage overwhelmed with applause, and smashed spiders, and radiant with parti-colored skirts, smiles, graces, cobwebs and glory."

In Sacramento for some unexplained reason she got off on the wrong foot, so to speak, with her audience. As the curtain rose, she appeared in a costume decorated with large spiders. Pretending terror, she whirled madly, snatching off the spiders and flinging them to the floor and stamping on them. For some reason the audience began to laugh, but Montez intended the dance to be taken seriously. Imperiously she strutted to the edge of the stage, eyes flashing. "Ladies and gentlemen! Lola Montez has too much respect for the people of California not to perceive that this stupid laughter comes from a few silly puppies."

Again the audience burst into laughter.

"I will speak!" she shouted over the tumult, eyes glaring. The laughter died. She extended her arm, beckoning, and shouted: "Come up here! Give me your men's trousers and take my women's skirts and wear them! You're not worthy to be called men!"

Laughter became uproarious.

"Silly puppies! Lola Montez is proud to be what she is, but you haven't the courage to fight with her — yes, this woman, who has no fear of you all, who despises you!"

Hitherto merely boisterous, the crowd now turned ugly. Lola tried to continue, but the uproar drowned her voice. Rotten apples and eggs flew through the air, pelting the stage and forcing her to duck behind a curtain.

In his loge seat, violinist Miska Hauser — whose diary recorded this unscheduled drama — could only stare in shock. The manager, wringing his hands, rushed up to Hauser and begged: "Please play something to save the show! Play anything!"

Hauser hesitated — the audience's mood was terrifying.

"A hundred dollars!" the manager pleaded. "I'll give you that, but just play anything to save the show!"

Hauser's diary recorded his dismay: "O wretched moment! Never did a concert giver find himself in a more painful position. I would rather have endeavored to silence the rage of a tempest-swept sea than this audience. But the distress of the director and the $100 which he in his misery offered me for the service touched my heart."

Trembling, Hauser clambered onto the stage and stood up, facing a crowd whose wrath was volcanic. Trembling more, he raised his violin and bow. To his immense relief, the crowd greeted him with a burst of applause. Calmer now, he played. His violin sang with the lovely notes of "The Bird in the Tree."

The audience grew ecstatic: "Encore! Encore!" Hauser happily obliged.

From the audience, a loud and imperious voice started to speak, and all was still: "Theater director, we have paid our dollars! The dancer Montez is unworthy to appear before us! The much esteemed Miska Hauser with his magic bow has just performed wonders, appeased an outraged audience and made happy again our angry hearts. Theater director! We do not want to see Lola Montez again — we want to hear Miska Hauser!"

Stormy applause followed. Behind the curtain, Lola heard the insult and rushed out and began to dance again. The crowd starting boiling with anger. Men rose to their feet en masse, yelling, then began to surge toward the stage, toppling chairs and benches. As the press of bodies lurched against the walls, window panes crashed. To Hauser, it was the fury of a hurricane.

"Scoundrel!" the crowd roared. "We want our money back!"

The manager, dreading the mob's wrath, disappeared from view, while Hauser tried to calm the crowd with diplomatic words — in vain. It was impossible to make himself heard over the tumult. He raised his violin and began playing. He played "The Bird in the Tree" again and other "foolish things" such as "Carneval" and "Yankee Doodle." For a long time he kept playing. By degrees the crowd simmered down.

From behind a curtain, Lola burst forth — and again began her Spider Dance. This time, for some inexplicable reason, the audience let her continue to the end of her performance.

Later that evening, 40 or 50 men armed with pots and pans convened under her window at the Orleans Hotel and launched into what Hauser called "a serenade of awful cat-cries, broken pots and old kettles, flutes and drums . . . an ear-splitting symphony." Montez stuck her head out the window to see what the hullabaloo was all about, then stepped onto the balcony, holding a lamp and screaming: "You cowards, low blackguards, cringing dogs and lazy fellows! I would not despise a dirty dog so much as I do you!"

Loud applause greeted that statement. Perhaps they admired her spirit and her way with words. Patrick Hull tried to calm the crowd by inviting everyone into the barroom for a drink.

One man climbed up on the balcony and blew out Lola's lamp, and who knows what might have happened then if suddenly a band of men had not dashed onto the scene, dispersing the rowdies with death threats, emphasized with brandished rifles and pistols.

In her performance the following evening, Montez appeared in a penitent mood. But to her astonishment and delight, instead of rotten apples, cabbages and other flying groceries, the audience flung wreaths.

Afterward, she skipped up to Hauser and said laughingly: "Believe me, dear Hauser, last evening was worth more to me than $1,000. I was delightfully amused and I have added another to my list of adventures."

Her mood turned to fury two days later when Sacramento's *Daily Californian* rolled off the press with a jab at her: "The house might be called full, but looking it over, we could distinguish only a few, a very few of our citizens present. To strangers impelled by mere curiosity and the free use of free tickets, is she indebted for an audience."

Lola was enraged at the insinuation that the crowd's fervor was due to a lavish hand-out of free tickets. The nerve of the wretch! Steaming, she wrote a letter challenging the editor to duel: "After such a gross insult, you must don the petti-coats. I have brought some with me, which I can lend you for the occasion. You must fight with me. I leave the choice of two kinds of weapons to yourself, for I am very magnanimous. You may choose between my duelling pistols or take your choice of a pill-box. One shall be poison and the other not, and the chances are even. I request that this affair may be arranged by your seconds as soon as possible as my time is quite as valuable as your own."

The editor declined the opportunity to meet Montez on the field of honor, and the duel never took place.

After five more Sacramento performances, to capacity crowds, Montez moved to Grass Valley. Despite reports she had tossed Patrick's bags out the window of the Orleans Hotel to end their marriage, he accompanied her to Grass Valley, where they bought a house. But the marriage soon ended in divorce.

In her Grass Valley sojourn, she raised eyebrows by smoking in public, hosting noisy all-night parties, and keeping "a remarkable collection of animals: 4 dogs, a goat, sheep, lamb, Grizzly bear, horse, 3 canarys, a wild cat and a Crazy German who follows her all over the country, " somebody wrote. And for horsewhipping a newspaper editor.

The Sacramento Union in 1854 printed an account of Lola's horsewhipping of Henry Shipley, editor of the *Grass Valley Telegraph*: "With a lady's delicate riding whip in one hand and a copy of the *Telegraph* in the other, 'her eyes in fine frenzy rolling' vowing vengeance on that scoundrel of an editor," she rushed through town to the Golden Gate Saloon, with a crowd following her.

"Lola struck the editor with her whip, but he caught it and wrest it from her before she could hit a second blow.

"She then applied a woman's best weapon — her tongue. Meanwhile her antagonist contented himself with keeping most insultingly cool. Finding all her endeavors powerless, the 'divine Lola' appealed to the miners, but the only response rendered was a shout of laughter. Mr. Shipley, the editor, then triumphantly retired, having by his calmness, completely worn out his fair enemy. The immediate cause of the fracas was the appearance of sundry articles, copied from the *New York Times*, regarding the 'Lola Montez-like insolence and affrontery of the Queen of Spain.' The entire scene was decidedly rich."

Lola told her side of the story in the *Alta California* Dec. 1, 1854, saying she went to the saloon armed with a "whip which was never used but on a horse, this time was to be disgraced by falling on the back of an ASS." When she found Shipley, she "quick as a flash of lightning laid the said whip on his shoulder and head four times, on my word of honor, before my enemy could remember that he was sitting on a chair."

Montez is credited with discovering child star Lotta Crabtree, whose mother had enrolled her in dancing classes held in a Grass

Valley tavern annex. Montez taught Lotta to dance the fandango and the highland fling. At 8 years of age, Lotta captivated audiences with her dancing, singing and comic routines in Sacramento theaters and elsewhere.

The Montez house (reconstructed) at 248 Mill St., Grass Valley, now contains a museum and offices of Nevada County Chamber of Commerce. The Crabtree house, not open to the public, is two doors north, at 238 Mill.

Several other child stars also were box office biggies of this era in Sacramento. Susan Robinson, 8, "The California Fairy Star," beguiled Sacramento spectators in 1853 with performances of "Annie Laurie," "Whiskey In the Jug," and a burlesque of Lola Montez doing her Spider Dance.

Montez gave additional performances in Sacramento in late 1856, following an Australian tour. Reported *The Sacramento Union* September 12: "The management seems to have struck a rich lead in the engagement of Madame Lola Montez; a full house having been in attendance each evening of her performance."

Patrick Hull died in 1858 in Marysville after a long illness. Montez in 1859, having begun a new career in New York as a lecturer, suffered a stroke, and the next year an attack of paralysis. She died Jan. 17, 1861, at age 42.

Early Sacramento theater patrons arrived loaded with "ammunition" to demonstrate their displeasure, if the play warranted it. In The National (later Metropolitan) Theatre on K Street between 4th and 5th, *The Sacramento Union* covered a performance of Shakespeare's "Richard III" on Dec. 6, 1856, with Hugh McDermott in the title role. The stabbing of King Henry was, the reviewer opined, "too much." He described the carnage as the audience launched a barrage: "Cabbages, carrots, pumpkins, potatoes, a wreath of vegetables, a sack of flour and one of soot, and a dead goose, with other articles, simultaneously made their appearance upon the stage.

"Richard looked aghast, but held his ground; the dead Henry was the first to flee, a potato intended for his murderer having, by its rough contact, roused him from his death slumber."

That was only the first act. In the next, the audience again got into the act, as it were, with a storm of shouts and exploding firecrackers. As Richard III fled the bedlam, "a well-directed pumpkin caused him to stagger; and with still truer aim, a potato relieved him of his cap, which was left upon the field of glory, among the cabbages."

Seven people were killed when the floor collapsed in Moore's Opera House, above Pacific Stables on 2nd Street.

It was no make-believe tragedy when seven people were killed during a theater performance in early Sacramento. The entire floor collapsed during a performance in Moore's Opera House, occupying the second floor of the building known as Pacific Stables and State Armory on the west side of 2nd Street between K and L. Erected in 1855 with an ornamental plaster facade, it was one of early Sacramento's most distinguished buildings. Basement and first floor served as carriage depot and 100-horse-capacity stable. Other occupants of the building were offices of the State Adjutant General, Sacramento Guard, and Sutter Rifles.

Impresario George Moore leased the second floor in October 1876 and renovated it into "Moore's Opera House." Two years earlier, the State Armory had moved out because its officials were alarmed by ominous structural conditions. Reported *The Sacramento Bee* on Nov. 18, 1876: "The second story . . . has been transformed into a neat, compact and well appointed theater, capable of seating 1,000 people . . . it will be thrown open to the public this evening with a first class variety troupe, every member of which is an artist in high standing in the profession, just from the East, and including the renowned Peak Family of Swiss bell ringers, twelve in number."

An opening night audience applauded the first act — minstrels with banjos and blackened faces. As the minstrels exited, sounds of timbers cracking were heard over the tumult of applause. The theater floor began to sway! Suddenly the floor and stage gave way with a thundering crash, sending the audience plunging to the stable floor, with theater boxes and other seats crashing upon them. Dust and smoke filled the air. Pipes carrying illuminating gas ruptured, spewing torches that inflamed stage settings and curtains. Screams and moans arose from agonized heaps of victims on the stable floor. A stable boy quickly switched off the gas supply, and the nearby fire department, alerted by the new electric Fire Alarm Telegraph, responded at once and swiftly controlled the blaze.

Besides the seven fatalities, over 200 were injured. Witnesses were amazed at the low death toll, considering the number of people caught in the meat-grinding avalanche of timbers and furniture.

Next day, a coroner's jury probing the cause found that the building had sustained extensive damage from the heavy floods of 1861-62 — and more damage when jacked up to its present level during the street-raising era. It was also revealed that the State Armory had moved out two years earlier because its officials were alarmed by sagging floors and bulging walls. The walls had been fixed, but corrective efforts failed to solve the sagging floors. It was also disclosed that, when Moore leased the second floor, the leasing agent falsely asserted that repairs had been effected and the floor was sound.

The shocking coroner's jury report led to more stringent state legislation on building construction. It also led the city to establish stricter building codes, and appoint a building inspector to police them.

Chapter 35
Mail From St. Joe: The Pony Express

Boot, saddle, to horse, and away!
Robert Browning

The first ride began simultaneously at both ends of the route. In San Francisco at 4 p.m. on April 3, 1860, James Randall, riding a pony trimmed with miniature flags, trotted away from Alta Telegraph Co. on Montgomery Street, carrying the first eastbound *mochila*, or mailbag. As spectators cheered, he rode to the waterfront and delivered the mail to the Sacramento-bound steamer *Antelope*, queen of the river packets. Randall was not a regular rider.

Meanwhile at St. Joseph, Missouri, the first horse and rider dashed away from the Pike's Peak Stables and boarded a ferry to cross the Missouri.

At Sacramento, *Antelope* docked in a rainstorm at 2 a.m. April 4. Young Sam Hamilton picked up the mochila and draped it onto his horse. Except for someone from the Express office, not a soul was on hand to give him a send-off. The mochila contained 56 tissue-thin letters from San Francisco, and now another 13 from Sacramento, prepaid at $5 per half ounce, plus U.S. postage. The mochila was a leather rectangle with four weatherproof cantinas, or boxes, one at each corner, each secured with a small padlock.

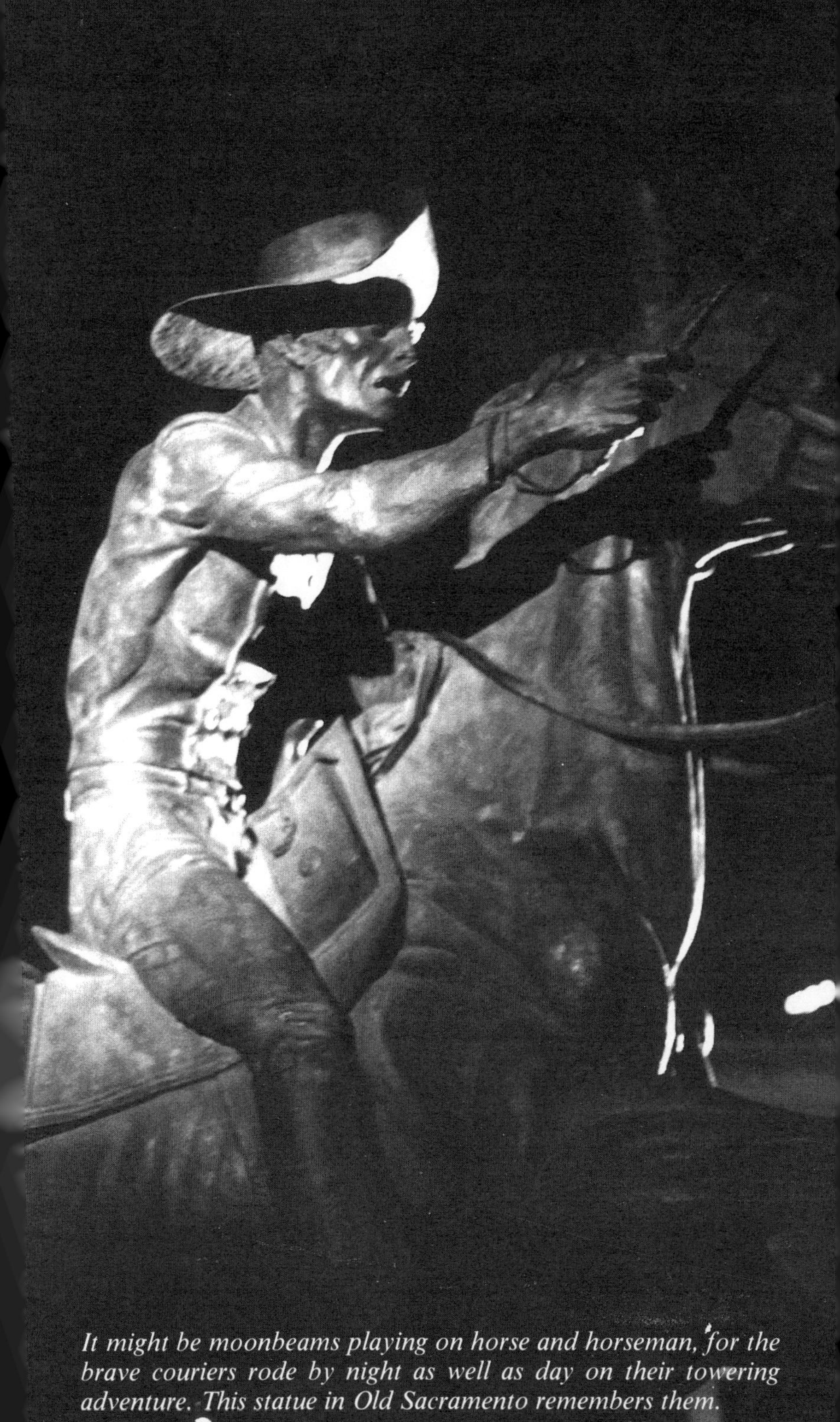

It might be moonbeams playing on horse and horseman, for the brave couriers rode by night as well as day on their towering adventure. This statue in Old Sacramento remembers them.

With a creak of leather, his horses' hooves splashing in mud and water from two days of rain, Hamilton galloped off to the east, following J Street out of town, thence along the American River, inaugurating the 1,966-mile route, just as his counterpart was doing from St. Joe. In the darkness and rain, it was difficult to follow the soggy road along the river, but Hamilton had been hired because he knew the route and was a superb horseman.

Changing horses at Five Mile House, Fifteen Mile House, and Mormon Tavern, he arrived in Placerville at 6:45 a.m., half an hour under schedule. Each time he changed horses, he flung the mochila on the fresh horse. From Placerville, he dashed off for Sportsman's Hall, 12 miles farther, and made it in an hour. In a bit over five hours, he had galloped along 60 miles of storm-lashed trail. Three times his horse had stumbled and fallen, but he jumped clear and suffered no injury.

Worse was in store for Warren Upson, who picked up the mochila for the run beyond Sportsman's Hall. Upson, son of *The Sacramento Union* editor, continued up the American River canyon, tracking through a Sierra blizzard in an ordeal that has taken on the aura of legend. Upson had learned to ride among Mexican vaqueros, had performed in rodeos, and had roamed and hunted the Sierra. And he had picked out a trail-smart pony. Well that he did, for ahead lay the worst section of trail on the route — steep, rugged and storm-swept. Heavy snow had fallen in the mountains, holding up stages on the Carson City line, that hadn't missed a run in three years.

From Sportsman's Hall, the trail worsened at every yard. For days, neither vehicle nor horseman had passed that way, so Upson's mustang had to break trail through snow. At times Upson had to dismount and break trail for his horse. Though he knew the trail, snow shrouded landmarks, and at times he risked plunging into a canyon. Freezing winds funneled through the pass, sweeping snow into his face. As Upson fought through drifts up to 20 feet deep, the difficulties seemed at times nearly insuperable.

At last he reached the summit — the worst was over. From here, the road was downhill. Late that night he rode into Carson City — having changed horses at Strawberry, Hope Valley, Woodbridge, and Genoa, Nevada, covering 85 miles under conditions that would have daunted born mountaineers.

On Sunday, April 8, somewhere east of Salt Lake City, east- and west-bound riders passed each other.

The first westbound mochila reached Sportsman's Hall at 1 p.m.

April 13, where Sam Hamilton was waiting to pick it up. A cheering crowd greeted him, but a big surprise awaited him as he neared Sutter's Fort.

Not a person had seen him off in the miserable rainy darkness 10 days before. But this time it was a sunny afternoon and, at the Fort, a cavalcade of nearly 100 citizens formed a double line along the road, to escort him in triumph into Sacramento.

J Street was hung with flags and lined with people, some watching from balconies, others from rooftops, all ecstatic. At 5:25 p.m. somebody on J Street spotted the cloud of dust far out on the road to the east. Hark! A faint tattoo of hooves and scattered huzzahs wafted from the outskirts. *"Here he comes!"* The words flew from mouth to mouth down J Street. *The Sacramento Union* of April 14 reported: "First a cloud of rolling dust in the direction of the Fort, then a horseman, bearing a small flag, riding furiously down J Street, and then a straggling, charging, band of horsemen flying after him, heralding the coming of the Express."

Sam Hamilton was coming back with the mail, just as he had dashed out of town with it 10 days before: But he rode behind the cheering horsemen spurring into Sacramento. Mounted on fresh horses, they easily forged ahead, forcing Hamilton and his tired pony to "eat dust" the rest of the way.

As he galloped down J Street, festooned with flags and banners, the town went wild. Delirious crowds erupted with cheer on cheer. Church bells and firehouse bells rang. Firemen boomed a salute with a cannon, and an anvil chorus augmented the din. *The Sacramento Union* also noted: "Amidst the firing and shouting, and waving of hats and ladies' handkerchiefs, the pony was seen coming at a rattling pace down J Street, surrounded by about thirty of the citizen deputation. The little fellow stretched his neck well to the race and came at a fast pace down the street, which was wild with excitement. Out of this confusion emerged the Pony Express, trotting up to the door of the agency and depositing its mail in ten days from St. Joseph to Sacramento. Hip, hip, hurrah for the Pony Carrier!"

Hamilton later complained that his overzealous escorts put spurs to their fresh animals and took the lead, creating a great dust, which was not only annoying to him but injurious to his pony.

More wild enthusiasm heralded his arrival at the Express office, where he hauled on the reins of his foam-flecked horse, which halted with a clash of hooves and a whinny. He handed over the mochila to the Express man. Mail for Sacramento was speedily sorted out, and the mochila handed back to Hamilton. Remounting, he galloped to the dock and clambered aboard *Antelope*, pony and all, for the final leg to San Francisco where, at 12:37 a.m. on April 14, sounding bells and soaring rockets greeted him. Across the land, newspapers hailed the triumph.

Later, pony mail for San Francisco was sent in a regular mail pouch, leaving horse and rider behind, so that the living chain of riders ended at Sacramento.

Fast as the ponies hustled, they could have shaved more time off the run — if they had boarded the train. The superintendent of Sacramento Valley Railroad had offered a special engine to speed the mail on the 22 miles between Folsom and Sacramento. But Pony Express officials wouldn't hear of it. Perhaps arrival of a rider on a train in Sacramento would diminish the glamor evoked by mail arriving across the continent on thundering hoofbeats. It was not until July 1, 1860, nearly three months after the service was inaugurated, that Express and railroad people worked out a schedule enabling riders to tote the mail on rails along the Sacramento-Folsom leg.

Up to 1860, the fastest messages took 25 days to get from rails' end in Missouri to Sacramento and San Francisco. The Pony Express abridged the time to a mere 10 days, a feat that stunned the nation. Would wonders never cease? Alas, it also stunned its investors when it went bankrupt 18 months later, cleaning them out of their life savings.

The pony mail idea wasn't exactly new: Romans and Incas had used similar arrangements to communicate with distant parts.

How it began in America: The story goes that U.S. Senator William McKendree Gwin of California, desiring closer links with his constituents, broached the idea of a pony mail to W. H. Russell, Alexander Majors, and William B. Waddell. These three operated an express outfit called Central Overland California and Pike's Peak Express Co., or COC&PP for short. Disenchanted employees dubbed it "Clean Out of Cash and Poor Pay" Express Co. — also an apt characterization of the new subsidiary, the Pony Express.

With the nation on the brink of Civil War, Russell, Majors and Waddell hoped their pony mail would help keep California in the Union, and also prove feasibility of a year-round central route to California. It took $100,000 in gold coin to establish the route. They bought 500 of the finest horses — mostly tough, speedy California mustangs for the western divisions, and superb

Kentucky stock for the eastern divisions. About 190 stations 10 miles apart bracketed the nearly 2,000-mile route; they hired a staff of 400 men.

A home station every 75 to 100 miles gave a rider a brief rest before starting back with the return mail. Each rider covered the road between two home stations, changing horses six to eight times at smaller relay stations. Stations varied from a small corral where two men guarded some horses, to cozy roadhouses with bunks, stables and blacksmith shops. In Sacramento County, stations included Five Mile House near the town of Perkins, at today's California State University, Sacramento; another at Fifteen Mile House on White Rock Road, and one in Folsom. Next came Mormon Tavern, just across the El Dorado County line.

Most stations had dirt floors. Beds were pole bunks. Boxes made do as furniture. Food was bacon, beans, molasses, pickles, corn meal, dried fruits, bread, and coffee.

About 80 riders and 500 horses did the mobile job. The company recruited riders with newspaper ads: "WANTED — Young, skinny, wiry fellows, not over 18. Must be expert riders, willing to risk death daily. Orphans preferred." One report says the youngest rider was only 11 years old, but he may have been a stocktender who subbed as a rider in an emergency, as they often did.

Riders were housed and fed at company expense and paid a lucrative $25 a week. Each rider had to sign a pledge that: "I will under no circumstances use profane language; that I will drink no intoxicating liquors; that I will not quarrel or fight with other employees of the firm . . . So help me God."

In *Roughing It*, Mark Twain at a stagecoach stop thrilled at the sight of an approaching Express rider: "Away across the endless dead level of the prairie a black speck appears against the sky, and it is plain that it moves. Well, I should think so! In a second or two it becomes a horse and rider, rising and falling, rising and falling — sweeping toward us nearer and nearer — growing more and more distinct, more and more sharply defined — nearer and nearer still, and the flutter of the hoofs comes faintly to the ear — another instant and a whoop and hurrah from our upper deck, a wave of the rider's hand, but no reply, and man and horse burst past our excited faces and go swinging away like the belated fragment of a storm.

"So sudden is it all, and so like a flash of unreal fancy, that but for the flake of white foam left quivering and perishing on a mail sack after the vision had flashed by and disappeared, we might have doubted whether we had seen any actual horse and man at all, maybe."

Riders rode day and night in all weathers. They rode through the nauseous heat of summer, horse and man dusty and sweat-streaked, and rode through the aching cold of winter, horse and man spouting vapor, rider chilled to the bone.

The company saw to it that a Bible was packed with each rider, but most riders also packed a Colt revolver, doubly insuring themselves. Yet they relied mainly on the swiftness of their fine horses to outrun trouble from Indians and road agents. Alas, sometimes they couldn't outrun it. In Ruby Valley, Nevada, the arrow-studded corpse of Billy Tate, only 14, was found among bodies of seven Indians he had killed with his pistol before dying. Still, most deaths of Pony Express personnel involved those manning relay stations. Usually far out in the wilderness, they presented weak, tempting targets to Indians and outlaws. An arriving rider who found a station burned down and horses stolen just had to keep going on his fatigued animal. "The mail must go through," said the Express motto. One rider covered 300 miles on one horse — which collapsed and died at journey's end, an equine hero.

The ponies learned so well what was expected of them that riders could grab some shut-eye as they tore along. Perhaps the ponies also realized the mail must go through. Thomas Owen King, a rider out of Fort Bridger, Wyoming, told an interviewer: "Many a time I went to sleep in the saddle, and the pony would keep his pace. Other riders would sleep, also.

"I remember once I came into Bear River after a night ride of 80 miles from Salt Lake, and reported to the station keeper that I had not passed Henry Worley, who was riding in the opposite direction. Worley had reported the same thing about me at the other station. We had both been so sound asleep in our saddles that we didn't know when we passed each other."

J. G. McCall was not a Pony Express rider, yet made a pony mail ride into Sacramento. On the run between Folsom and Sacramento, Wells Fargo agent McCall rode on a stagecoach as it approached the scene where the pony rider had been thrown from his horse and broke his leg. McCall volunteered to finish the run, and Sacramentans greeted him with the proper enthusiasm.

In Nevada and Utah, the route sliced through the most dangerous Indian country in the west, hunting grounds of Paiutes and Shoshones — who resented the rise of stage and pony traffic through their lands. Stationkeepers and stocktenders knew that, but coolly ensconced themselves in the nearly defenseless posts that the Indians could overwhelm any time they wanted to.

The Paiute War began May 7, 1860, with an Indian surprise attack on William Station, killing five Pony Express employees. For 30 days, service was interrupted. Full-scale war was averted, but the company lost 150 horses, seven stations, and 16 men killed. Raids continued for a year by small bands of young braves seeking a reputation.

William Finney, pony agent in San Francisco, hurried to Carson City, where he appealed to Sacramentans for help, no doubt sending his letter by Pony Express: "Will the people of Sacramento help the Pony in its difficulty?" he wrote June 6, 1860. "We have conferred some benefits, have asked but little, and perhaps the people will assist. Can anything be done in your city towards paying expenses to furnish arms and provisions for the twenty-five men to go through with me to Salt Lake to take and bring on the Express?

"I will be responsible for the return of the arms, will have transportation of my own, and can get men here. What is wanted is $1,000 for the pay of the men, $500 for provisions, and twenty-five Sharp's rifles and as many dragoon pistols. I will guarantee to keep the Pony alive a while longer."

Sacramentans swiftly ponied up, so to speak, the $1,500 and most of the arms asked for. Destroyed stations were rebuilt and restocked. Five well-armed men remained to occupy each until the Indian troubles ended. Rebuilding the stations, pay to increased personnel, and other expenses totaled $75,000 — a heavy blow to a company that, even in favorable circumstances, had been bogging down ever deeper in deep stuff. The pony schedule resumed July 7.

President Lincoln's vital inaugural message reached California in March 1861 via Pony Express — with "Pony Bob" Haslam running an Indian gauntlet across the most dangerous stretch, 120 miles of Paiute-pullulating western Nevada. Anticipating ambush, Haslam several times approached what seemed likely terrain for it, but wise Old Buck, his horse, showed no alarm.

As they galloped on, Old Buck suddenly pointed his ears forward and snorted, sensing Indians. Haslam looped his reins on his saddlehorn and, firing a pistol with each hand, charged right into it. As he hurtled through a hail of arrows and bullets, one arrow savaged his mouth, knocking out five teeth and breaking his jaw. Another pierced his left shoulder.

Several Indians on horses took after him, but he turned around and fired, dropping them.

At the next relay station, Haslam stopped only long enough to have the arrow pulled out of his shoulder. "Fetch me a clean rag to hold in my mouth," he grunted. "I'm going through."

John Wayne couldn't have done it better. Or said it better. In fact, John Wayne as Rooster Cogburn in the movie "True Grit" pulled the same caper, firing pistols with both hands in a solo charge on horseback against a gang of varmints. But Haslam did it for real.

When the final rider galloped into Sacramento with Lincoln's message, Haslam's death-defying charge had been the most precarious link in the living chain of riders carrying the message. One arrow or bullet hitting Haslam in a vital spot could have shortstopped the message in Nevada — and perhaps changed history.

It was vital to speed Lincoln's message to California. With the nation on the precipice of Civil War, and California teetering toward the Confederates, whether this state remained with the Union hinged partly on the President's policies as spelled out in his speech, and how fast it could reach California to win the people's hearts and minds here. California's vast resources would go to whichever side, North or South, could seize them.

Just maybe the pony mail turned the tide for the North and kept California in the Union. If California's treasure of bullion — most of which did in fact support the Union cause — had been grabbed by the Confederacy, who knows how the war might have ended?

Yet another war intrigue: *Sacramento Bee* founder James McClatchy sent a Pony Express message to President Lincoln warning him that General Albert Johnston was scheming to divert army war materiel in California to the Confederates. Swift removal of the general thwarted that conspiracy.

A revelation: The Pony Express demonstrated that the central trail over the Rockies, and Sierra, was passable in winter – an astonishment to all who remembered the tragic Donner Party.

Folsom became the western terminus of the pony mail on July 1, 1860, as the Sacramento Valley Railroad began to transport the mail between Sacramento and Folsom, saving an hour's time.

Placerville became the western terminus from July 1, 1861, to Oct. 26, 1861, when the service died of a sudden illness called bankruptcy, leaving a deficit of $200,000.

Only 18 months after the first rider galloped into Sacramento, telegraph linemen working from both east and west connected their wires at Salt Lake City, and the brass key's *dit-dit-dah* spelled *The End* for Pony Express investors. Though the amazing enterprise had captured the fancy of the nation and had seemed a sure bet for the investors, betting on the ponies, so to speak, had cost them a bundle. Grumped one disgruntled investor: "No way a horse can compete with lightning."

Today in Old Sacramento, at 2nd and J Streets, a horse and rider dominate the intersection, their dynamic figures spellbound forever in bronze, symbolizing the audacity that won the west — the work of sculptor Thomas Holland. The rider lashes his horse with a quirt; the horse's nostrils flare. Hooves plunge forward — but horse and rider remain forever immobile. Yet you can almost hear the clash of hooves and the horseman's cry — the thrilling cry that echoed down the cobbled streets from mouth to mouth, from door to door: "Mail from St. Joe!"

The Pony Express — dead but not forgotten. The Pony Express dead? No, it still lives — after a fashion. Each year, members of the National Pony Express Association, a group of aficionados headquartered in Pollock Pines, El Dorado County, re-enact the epic enterprise. Donning the traditional uniform — red shirts, yellow bandanas, blue jeans, leather vest, widebrim hats — they gallop out of Sacramento in one year, bound for St. Joe. In alternate years, the chain begins with a rider leaving St. Joe for Sacramento. At each end of the line, cheering spectators, many in western garb, greet the arriving horseman — greeted also by news media.

Today their mochilas carry commemorative envelopes, coveted by stamp collectors, sale of which will help pay for trail markers when the old route is established as a historic trail.

Today's riders, where the route follows pavement, have to cope with the hazards of horseless-carriage traffic, and it may be they envy the original riders, who had only Indians and outlaws to fret about.

But Pony Express riders also carried "real mail" in modern times —when an enormous mudslide blockaded Highway 50 east of Pollock Pines for two months in spring 1983. Association members were delighted when postal officials accepted their offer to pack the mail on horseback to isolated hamlets. They did it for only a nominal $2 per day.

When word got out through news media that Pony Express members were saddling up for a genuine ride, the Pollock Pines post office was swamped with letters from stamp collectors around the world. They sent envelopes to be hand-cancelled with Pony Express symbols, then carried via pony mail. From the average 1,200 letters daily, post office volume rose to nearly 2,000.

Members from 14 to 72 years of age rode five-mile intervals on the 40-mile route — two-thirds along Highway 50 and the rest on trails encumbered with mud, snow and fallen branches, following part of the original trail — and saving mail trucks a 114-mile detour along twisting roads. They rode through a bizarre mix of weather — "sleet, hail, thunderstorms, snow and, yes, even sunshine," said rider Malcolm McFarland.

On the far end of the historic route, St. Joe, like Sacramento, has a statue of the famous rider. Another oddity: Both ends of the route began with water trips. From St. Joe, the first rider crossed the Missouri on a ferry. In San Francisco, only the mochila rode the steamer to Sacramento, where doughty Sam Hamilton grabbed the mochila and galloped eastward in a rainstorm. But on his return trip, both Sam and his horse boarded the steamer for San Francisco.

Chapter 36

Messages By Lightning: The Telegraph

Strange as it seems, when Pony Express rider Sam Hamilton was galloping back to Sacramento from Placerville, Sacramentans already knew that he was leaving on time with the return mail from St. Joseph.

They had gotten the message by telegraph from Placerville and, earlier, a telegram from Carson City, Nevada, had given them similar information about the pony rider on that leg.

Furthermore, Sacramento was already connected by telegraph with San Francisco and other points.

In other words, even at the very origin of the Pony Express, its doom could have been foreseen in the expanding network of telegraph wires.

Telegraph service in Sacramento was inaugurated as early as Oct. 19, 1853 — over six years before the beginning of the Pony Express — when the first message from this city zipped to Marysville along wires of California State Telegraph Co. This firm had been set up the previous year by two New York promoters, Oliver Allen and Clark Burnham, who obtained a franchise from the Legislature for a 210-mile line connecting San Francisco and Marysville. It ran south around San Francisco Bay through San Jose, then through Stockton and Sacramento.

Meanwhile, the aggressive Alta Telegraph Co. was continually adding miles of wire and opening new offices throughout the gold country. No conflict arose between the two companies because neither encroached on the other's territory — until July 1856 when Alta, expanding its network to 420 miles of wire, strung a line into San Francisco. Officials of California State Telegraph bristled at this invasion of their bailiwick.

In 1859, Alta Telegraph began operating in Sacramento's Hastings Building, but collided head-on with telegraph inventor Samuel F.B. Morse, who filed a lawsuit charging patent infringement, and won, swiftly putting Alta out of business.

Agitation for a transcontinental telegraph was building up to fever pitch, and many telegraph companies wanted to build the western section — not least of all because the tremendous enterprise would mean juicy plums in the form of government subsidies.

By this time, four telegraph companies were operating in California, and all wanted the prize. Besides California State Telegraph, they were Northern California Telegraph, on a line between Marysville and Yreka; Pacific Atlantic Telegraph, between San Jose and Los Angeles; and Salt Lake Company, between Placerville and Fort Churchill, Nevada.

Hiram Sibley, president of Western Union, proposed to the Federal government that the rivalries be contained by consolidating all four companies, to build the western section of the transcontinental. The Feds, because of rising tensions between North and South, agreed. Jeptha Wade, another Western Union official, came to California to consolidate them.

The governmental money for the consolidated firm included $6,000 a year that the California Legislature allocated starting in 1859, and a Federal subsidy of $40,000 a year, starting in 1860. Each was for a 10-year period, for construction and maintenance.

Just as the railroads one day would build toward each other from east and west, telegraph construction crews labored toward each other, installing poles and wires.

In Nevada, Paiute Indians worked in construction — barehanded, whereas white workers donned heavy leather gloves. Once a thunderstorm broke over the landscape, charging the wire with high voltage. Some of the Indians, called upon to help tighten the wire, grabbed it — and the charge bowled them over like tenpins. Word of the mysterious "bad medicine" in the wire flew around among the Indians. Afterward, when an Indian had occasion to ride under a telegraph wire, he whipped his horse to a full gallop and warily kept his head low.

The new telegraph by 1861 was sending Civil War news to California. The daily bulletins clicked to the telegraph's westernmost station, then transferred to the Pony Express, which relayed them to the easternmost station of the western crew. As outer stations on each end of the line approached, the Pony Express played an ever shorter role. But the pony riders gave valuable help during construction by reporting breaks in the wire: Some of the younger Indians, unafraid of the mysterious wire, would destroy it to show their contempt for the white man.

The crew moving from the east finished connections to Salt Lake City on Oct. 18, 1861. Two days later, workers from the west completed the line between the Pacific coast and Salt Lake City. From Sacramento, the first transcontinental message flashed out from the California State Telegraph office in the Hastings Building, 2nd and J Streets, when State Chief Justice Stephen Fields wired President Lincoln, assuring him of California's loyalty to the beleaguered Union. Ironically, this building also housed the Pony Express office, whose death-knell echoed in the telegraph wires.

Chapter 37

Epic Adventure: Rails Across the Nation

If you want to jubilee in laying the first spike here, go ahead and do it. I don't. These mountains look too ugly and I see too much work ahead. We may fail, and I want to have as few people know it as we can.
Collis P. Huntington, one of the Big Four, explaining to associates why he planned to be absent during the Jan. 8, 1863, Sacramento groundbreaking for the transcontinental railroad.

The story begins when Colonel Charles Lincoln Wilson came to California from Maine during the Gold Rush. By 1852 he had been a miner, riverboat operator, and builder of a plank road crossing San Francisco's sand dunes. On August 16 of that year, he incorporated Sacramento Valley Railroad, first railroad west of the Rockies, and became its president. Lincoln, Placer County, would be named after him.

His vice president was William Tecumseh Sherman, who had helped map out the City of Sacramento in 1848 and one day would win fame as a Civil War general. As their chief engineer, they hired Theodore Judah, 26, to survey a route from Sacramento to Folsom. Judah, already an accomplished engineer, had constructed a railroad through Niagara Gorge.

It was that remarkable feat that brought him to the notice of

New York Governor Horatio Seymour, who commended him to Colonel Wilson of the Sacramento Valley Railroad, a track designed to capture the immense freight and passenger traffic between Sacramento and foothill mines.

Arriving in Sacramento, Judah electrified his new bosses by forecasting a transcontinental future for their railroad — at a time when its first engine and iron rails had yet to be shipped around the Horn.

While building Sacramento Valley Railroad from 1854 to 1856, Judah kept dreaming of a railroad over the Sierra, the biggest hurdle of the transcontinental job. At his own expense, he made barometric surveys of several Sierra passes, convincing himself such a railroad was feasible. Others were convinced it was insane, and called him "crazy Judah."

Starting work on the line from Sacramento to Folsom, Judah hailed it as "the grand avenue of approach to the metropolis of the Pacific." His flamboyant language caught the attention of Daniel (Doc) Strong, pharmacist in the foothill mining town of Dutch Flat, Placer County, eager to boost the town's economy. An amateur surveyor, he had mapped a route for a wagon road east from town over the Sierra, a much more benign route than the terrible trail east of Donner Pass. Strong craved the backing of a professional surveyor.

He and Judah hiked along the granite ridge that inclined steadily from a plateau between the American and Yuba Rivers to the crest at the old emigrant pass. From there it bent southeast along feasible slopes to the Truckee River valley, thence east to Great Basin flatlands.

On the new Sacramento Valley Railroad, the maiden train chuffed the 22 miles from Sacramento to Folsom on Feb. 23, 1856. Each day, two dozen stagecoaches met the train at Folsom to take on passengers and freight for the northern mines. This traffic built a bustling town at the railroad's Folsom terminus. Actually the railroad was projected to run east as far as Placerville. But the Panic of 1855 had financially crippled the line, stalling it at Folsom. It finally reached Shingle Springs, 10 miles from Placerville, by June 1865 but would never reach farther. Great expectations collapsed after it arrived in Folsom. After the panic, the nearby gold mines petered out, Folsom's population dropped like a brick and the tracks suddenly became a "Railroad to Nowhere." Folsom's present railroad depot, now a museum and headquarters for Folsom Chamber of Commerce, reposes on the site of the original 1856 depot and roundhouse.

In a Dutch Flat drugstore in 1860, Judah and Doc Strong drafted "articles of association" for the proposed transcontinental railroad, and collected $40,000 in pledges from people of Dutch Flat, Grass Valley, Nevada City, and Illinois Town (Colfax). To comply with state laws, they needed $70,000 more.

In San Francisco, Judah solicited the town's financial barons, but they treated him like a leper and spurned the idea, fearing a railroad with Sacramento as its western terminus would short-stop much of the commerce to San Francisco. The jealous tycoons damned it thereafter, or tried to, by alluding to it as "The Dutch Flat Swindle." All this rodomontade of a transcontinental railroad, they insinuated, was just a smoke-screen for the real scheme, which was to lay track only to Dutch Flat, where they could pirate the lucrative freight carried by stages bound for Nevada's Comstock mines — and drive the stagelines out of business.

More on why they opposed Judah's plan: They really didn't want a transcontinental railroad, least of all one built by uppity merchants from hicktown Sacramento. Panama steamship companies would lose an enormous business from people now coming West via the Isthmus. Wells Fargo feared a big loss to its lucrative stageline commerce with Nevada. Sitka Ice Co. shipped ice to California from Alaskan glaciers, and wanted no truck with competitors in Sierra snowfields. In short the Establishment was afraid the Iron Horse would chomp away at its profits.

But everybody else, it seemed, wanted a railroad to the Pacific. Few could afford the longer ways around: The $300, 30-day voyage that included a crossing of the Panama Isthmus, or the six-month voyage around Cape Horn. Historian Hubert Bancroft summed up the general yearning: "The sunburned immigrant, walking with his wife and little ones beside his gaunt and weary oxen in mid-continent, the sea-sick traveler, the homesick bride whose wedding trip had included a passage of the Isthmus, the merchant whose stock needed replenishing: everyone prayed for a Pacific Railroad."

Judah, rebuffed, and Strong scheduled a meeting with 30 Sacramento businessmen. Judah had worked out a new strategy for these small-town merchants because he figured they would hardly jump at the staggering plan to lay rails across the continent. He figured they probably would go for something cheap that could be built fast and yield fast profits. So he told them that building a railroad through the Sierra would monopolize traffic with

Nevada's silver mines. Now he was talking their language. They knew Nevada was crawling with fortune-seekers, like California in 1849. Every day, immense loads of freight departed Sacramento in wagons bound for the silver mines. Rates were exorbitant, and Judah was offering them a way to get their hands on a fat chunk of that money.

They raised the $70,000 needed to help finance the thorough instrumental survey of the route across the Sierra. Among the contributors was a foursome who would come to be known as the Big Four: Hardware merchants C. P. Huntington and Mark Hopkins, drygoods merchant Charles Crocker, and grocer Leland Stanford.

The Big Four organized Central Pacific Railroad, with Judah as chief engineer. Stanford was president; Huntington, vice president; Hopkins, treasurer, and Charles Crocker.

Charles Crocker — later, after the board's split with Judah — retired from the board to spearhead construction as chief engineer, and was succeeded by his older brother, attorney Edwin Bryant Crocker, who had come to Sacramento in 1852 at age 34 with his new bride, the former Margaret Rhodes.

After Judah completed the survey, CP directors authorized him to go to Washington and wangle appropriations of land and construction bonds. Along with his prospectus, Judah presented his wife Anne's watercolor sketches of scenery near Donner Pass, so the politicos could envision the terrain to be crossed.

In an earlier case, the California Supreme Court had ruled that the Sierra commenced 31 miles east of Sacramento, where a definite gradient begins near Newcastle. But CP president Stanford recalled a geology text that fixed the base of the Rockies at the Mississippi River, because of the continuous slope between. Perchance the Sierra had a similarly long slope. In fact, California's state geologist found, in flatlands seven miles east of Sacramento, soil eroded from the Sierra — "proving" just that.

In Washington, the geologist's data was presented to President Abraham Lincoln, "proving" that the Sierra really began less than seven miles from the State Capitol, or 24 miles west of where it actually did. The intimation was that the California Supreme Court hadn't bothered to get out of its office and eyeball the situation.

Lincoln accordingly "moved" the Sierra 24 miles westward, and probably was partly motivated by a desire to get the railroad issue off dead center. The ruse netted CP a handsome additional subsidy of $700,000 because of the costlier work of laying track through all those additional "mountains" in the flat Sacramento Valley.

On July 1, 1862, when Lincoln signed the Pacific Railroad Act — giving the green light to transcontinental trains — Judah telegraphed his Sacramento associates: "We have drawn the elephant. Now let us see if we can harness him up."

One of the men who had presented the state geologist's data to President Lincoln later boasted: "My pertinacity and Abraham's faith moved mountains."

The Railroad Act stipulated that CP would jump off from the West, and Union Pacific from the East. The bill granted the railroads a free right-of-way 400 feet wide over all government lands on the entire route. The government also agreed to cancel all Indian titles to lands it donated to CP, and one wonders what the Indians might have thought of this giveaway of their lands.

Judah had rough-surveyed several trans-Sierra routes, but thoroughly surveyed only the one traversing the mountains via Dutch Flat. This route, he contended, had three advantages over competing routes: It had the shortest snow-line. It crossed only one Sierra summit, whereas rival routes would cross a double summit. It also was one of the most direct routes between Sacramento and Nevada's silver mines.

By the time Lincoln had signed the 1862 Act, CP was committed to the Dutch Flat route. Yet for months afterward, CP officials pretended to no definite choice, apprehensive of reprisals from communities not benefited by the Dutch Flat route. So they published newspaper ads calling for information on other potential routes. Supposedly, after data on all routes were in, the decision would be made. But the ruse failed. For several years, animosity toward CP officials festered in towns linked to the other routes.

To many, Central Pacific's success in Washington demonstrated that its "greedy, grasping propensities" maneuvered the bill through Congress by dirty tricks, not the route's merits.

Placerville's angry citizens challenged Judah's claim that his route had the shortest snow-line. This was the route, they pointed out, where heavy snows had doomed the Donner Party in 1846. They said Judah lied in declaring he had checked out the Placerville route.

Wielding a silver shovel, Leland Stanford tossed the first spadeful of dirt on Jan. 8, 1863, as Central Pacific formally broke ground on the levee at the foot of K Street for the stupendous project.

Now Judah began to squabble with the Big Four, who wanted to halt construction at Nevada until settlement of new towns along the right-of-way had caught up. Judah was infuriated. In October 1863, he quit arguing. His eight-year campaign had strained his health and finances and left him in no mood for endless bickering. He and Anne packed up and departed for the East; Judah vowed to recruit new backers to buy out the Big Four — Big Four with small minds.

Crossing the Isthmus of Panama, Judah was stricken with yellow fever, contracted after nobly giving his mosquito net to a fellow traveler. He died in New York less than a week after he arrived. He was 37 years old.

Central Pacific, the company he had given birth to, ousted him, wiping out his name from the transcontinental project, but paid him the backhand compliment of using the trans-Sierra route he had surveyed — boldest and most arduous in the cross-country chain.

The Big Four were interesting cases. Personal fortunes of two — hardware merchants Huntington and Hopkins — had been grounded in shovels so to speak, during the Gold Rush. They had cornered all available at $2.50 a dozen and sold them to prospectors at up to $125 each — dirty profits that made them filthy rich. Huntington, on his way to California, got stuck in Panama because of a dearth of California-bound ships, but determined to capitalize on the contretemps. He walked no less than 20 times the tropical trail between Atlantic and Pacific, carrying his wares on his shoulders — buying and selling jerked beef, rice, potatoes and sugar. By the time he sailed for San Francisco, he was 400 percent richer than when he started.

Hopkins, at age 50 in 1863, was the oldest of the Four. He had come west from Michigan via the Oregon Trail. His main joys seemed to be driving a hard bargain and growing vegetables for his meatless diet.

Stanford, at 39 the youngest of the Four, had arrived in California in 1852 from New York to join four of his brothers in the grocery business. Their stores in the gold country mushroomed into a major chain.

Crocker, a brawny blacksmith from Troy, New York, wandered westward with a party, reaching the Missouri just as the last wagon trains of the year on the other side were setting out for California. When a steamboat captain refused to ferry Crocker and friends across the river, Crocker persuaded the reluctant captain to cast off, with an argument he couldn't refuse — a six-shooter brandished in a convincing manner.

Later in 1863, CP purchased the Sacramento Iron Works blacksmith shop — just north of today's Old Sacramento — to build rolling stock in. The company would then go on to build the tremendous shops that one day would become the biggest west of Pennsylvania, serving its vast fleet of rolling stock, fabricating steam locomotives and passenger and freight cars until the 1920s.

It took more than a year for Central Pacific to lay track only 18 miles from Sacramento to the junction with California Central Railroad's tracks at Grider's Ranch, in February 1864. Daily passenger service — first on the CP railroad — started by year's end between Sacramento and "Junction," today's Roseville.

California Central was an extension of Sacramento Valley Railroad to Lincoln, named after railroad founder Charles Lincoln Wilson.

But Sacramento Valley Railroad's tracks were three and a half inches wider than standard gauge — useless to other railroads. Originally envisioned as the first part of the transcontinental railroad, the Sacramento Valley line — which became a "Railroad to Nowhere" — eventually would haul granite from Folsom to Sacramento, a considerable comedown from transcontinental glory.

But the transcontinental job — longest and toughest in railroad history: All of CP's rails, rolling stock, tools and other equipment had to come 15,000 miles around Cape Horn from the East, then be transshipped at San Francisco to riverboats to Sacramento, where they resumed their journey by rail to the end of the line. CP at one time had 30 ships at sea laden with machinery and material. Much of the food for workers also had to come to California by sea also, vast quantities of it from China and other Asian nations. Much of the money to buy goods had to be borrowed. Even so, it was difficult to buy them because of wartime scarcities.

In California, white laborers were scarce, as good wages were paid in the mines and farming was expanding. Furthermore, many men shied away from the mere thought of building a railroad over the mountains with pick and shovel. Crocker once brought 2,000 laborers from San Francisco and set them to work. In a few days, only 100 were still working.

The unusually balmy winters of 1863 and 1864 would have permitted construction in the Sierra. But CP hadn't yet received any federal loans and was in dire financial straits. So the company was denied the chance to build during mild weather. Construction halted at Newcastle, 31 miles from Sacramento. Years later, Leland Stanford rued the lost chance. Without that wasted time, CP could have gotten a start that would have laid its tracks all the way to Cheyenne, Wyoming, rather than merely to Promontory, Stanford claimed. "It would have given to San Francisco complete control of the business of Utah, Wyoming, Montana and Idaho," he said.

But tracklaying of a sort slowly went on. By May 1865, steel rails stretched 36 miles to Auburn. In the following year, as tracks climbed higher into the ranges, construction boss Charles Crocker proposed hiring Chinese workers. Most of the Union Pacific tracklayers driving from the East were Irish. Construction superintendent J. H. Strobridge greeted Crocker's idea with derision: Orientals were too frail to heft ponderous railroad ties. Argued Crocker: Maybe one alone couldn't, but two could.

The first Chinese in California, two men and a woman, had arrived in 1848, lured by stories of the "golden mountain." Thousands followed, many settling along I Street bordering Sutter Slough. Some opened groceries and laundries, while others hired out as domestic servants. In the 1850s, some of the local Chinese were publishing their own newspaper. But life in the Chinese community was not all tea and chow mein. One time 500 Chinese from two rival tongs, or secret societies, fought a pitched battle on I Street, scourging each other with lances and tridents.

Crocker recruited the first 50 Chinese tracklayers in 1865. To anyone skeptical as to whether they could do the job, he said "They built the Great Wall of China, and that's the biggest run of masonry in the world." In California, Chinese workers had dug hundreds of miles of ditches to deliver water to sluice boxes. And they helped reclaim the Sacramento-San Joaquin Delta by building the first levees.

Construction superintendent Strobridge, age 36 in 1865, was a lanky six-foot New Englander who had learned railroad building in Vermont's mountains and didn't regard the Sierra as a bigger challenge. An artist with profanity, he drove his workers as if they were slaves, supervising up to 15,000 at a time. He wore a patch over the socket of one eye — lost one time while he was imprudently investigating a retarded powder blast. To the Chinese, he was "One-eye Bossy Man."

When the first 50 Chinese were hired, the skeptical Strobridge put them to work. In a week, they finished the longest and smoothest stretch of grading on the route. Strobridge begged: "Send up more coolies!" At Sacramento, 50 more were loaded in a freight car and sent to the end-of-track. The Chinese proved willing workers — first on the job in the morning, last to quit. They lived tranquilly in their own camps, eating rice and seafood and drinking tea.

Before railroad employment opened up to thousands of Chinese, some who had had only dismal luck in the mines came to the end of their rope. One February morning in 1864, a Chinese man was found hanging from an oak near 8th Street, Sacramento, in his pocket a note in Chinese: "I came from the mountains to this city, could not find any friend, any house or place to go in, and I hang myself between the sky and the ground and make myself dead." He was 28 years old.

Results of Crocker's decision to hire Chinese were eye-opening. Even skeptics' eyes bugged. The Chinese were paragons of endurance. They moved vast quantities of earth, pushing wheelbarrows and driving one-horse dump cars. Soon agents were hiring thousands more Chinese — from California and from as far as South China.

At the zenith of construction, CP employed 15,000 Chinese, up to 80 and 90 per cent of its crews that carved tunnels through stubborn Sierra granite and laid down the mighty steel rails.

The most formidable obstacle was Cape Horn, a granite cliff three miles east of Colfax, soaring 1,500 feet above the American's North Fork. Surveyors said the rails had to pass along a ledge of the cliff. But there *was* no ledge! That's not our problem, the surveyors said. The ledge had to be carved from the sheer face, with no footholds but empty air from which men could work.

Yet the Chinese solved the dilemma, proving themselves as brave and ingenious as they were dependable. The solution derived from similar labors along the Yangste Gorges.

With reeds and bamboo transported from San Francisco, the Chinese workers wove large waist-high wicker baskets. With block and tackle, men equipped with sledges, hand drills and kegs of black powder were lowered down, swaying against the fearsome precipice. They drilled holes into the rock, tamped them with powder, and set fuses — sometimes cut to various lengths so a whole battery of charges would explode simultaneously. When the workers in the baskets signaled with gestures, the men above hauled them high enough to be out of the way when the charges went off. The exploding charges catapulted avalanches of rock into the canyon. Sometimes, after fuses were lit, the baskets weren't hauled up fast enough, and men died. Sometimes ropes broke, and men died, tumbling into the great gulf.

The savage winter of 1866-67 was another terror, bringing 44 blizzards. One howling storm lasted a solid two weeks, dumping 10 feet of snow. Temperatures dropped to as low as 5 degrees, and many Chinese froze to death. Many others perished in avalanches that swept entire bunkhouses of men to death over precipices. Not until spring could workers recover the broken bodies of their comrades.

For the Orientals, it was such a disastrous winter that it engendered the saying, "Not a Chinaman's chance." There is no casualty list for that winter, but as many as 1,000 Chinese died in the six years of the railroad's construction.

Even in this disastrous winter, the Chinese toiled whenever they could, punctuating the frigid silence with hammers pinging on steel and the *crump* of explosions. They also used explosives to build railroad tunnels and would, all told, bore 15 tunnels through the granite range, and also build nearly 40 miles of heavily-timbered showsheds to shelter the tracks.

Many tunnels progressed less than a foot a day, because of the obdurate granite, and black powder was the only explosive available. Gangs of 30 to 40 Chinese chipped through the granite inch by inch, drilling deep enough to place charges. At the zenith of tunnel construction, more than 500 kegs of powder were expended daily.

Boring of the Summit Tunnel, the longest at 1,653 feet, took two years, delaying the whole project. To catch up on the schedule, crews were leapfrogged ahead some miles to Truckee, to start building the roadbed back toward the summit, while other crews from Truckee started laying track toward Reno in the northeast. To get what they needed to Truckee, teams of up to 20 and 40 oxen dragged it up the awesome slopes on wagons — and on huge sleds built from pine trees. And sometimes gangs of up to 500 Chinese were hitched to the sleds. With infinite labors, they transported three ponderous locomotives, 40 flatcars, 40 miles of rails, plus tools and equipment, from Cisco to Donner Lake, then 28 miles down a dangerous stage road through icy winds and swirling blizzards — to Truckee at last.

To bore the Summit Tunnel, workers sank a shaft from above, so crews could work each way from the center, while other crews chipped away from both entrances. Because the granite was so tough, it took nearly a year just to dig the shaft deep enough to work on the lateral bores.

The little engine that could: Believe it or not, the first locomotive ever to reach the Sierra summit during construction of the transcontinental railroad — incidentally, it was named the *Sacramento* — did it *without wheels*. How it happened: Engineers wanted a steam engine to power the elevator cage in the Summit Tunnel's vertical shaft, to move men and supplies in and out. Every detail was worked out. The locomotive *Sacramento* was dismantled at Sacramento, stripped of cab, tank and stack to lighten it. Then it was pulled up the line to end-of-track at Gold Run, jacked up, and wheels pulled off. Traveling jacks shifted it 14 inches at a time to a huge logging wagon, with wheels 24 inches wide, where it was braced and bolted down.

Teamsters in charge of 10 yoke of oxen drove it eastward. Half a mile east of Dutch Flat, the black apparition terrorized 10 mules in a freight train. Eyes bulging, they broke harnesses and tug chains, kicked loose of the gear and stampeded for the hills. Similar incidents occurred daily until officials passed the word around the countryside that teamsters should blindfold their animals, as otherwise they would run off the road. That worked fine — except in the cases where travelers didn't get the word. The Big Black Thing exerted a powerful rejuvenating effect on every horse and mule that confronted the horror. Remarked John R. Gillis, an engineer working on the Summit Tunnel: "It mattered little whether it was a young team, or an old pair of skates trotting along with their heads down. Just one look, that was enough to brighten their eyes, forgetting they were old, having taken on new life, now ready for the hills." Just one look, was all it took.

When *Sacramento* reached the divide above Emigrant Gap, it faced a steep downgrade skid to Crystal Lake — worst problem of all, for one slip, and there would go the engine into the canyon. Workers buckled logging chains to rugged pine trees, then lowered the engine as far as the chains would reach — repeating the process until they reached the bottom. The steepest grade lay between Crystal Lake and the Yuba River. Several times when no big tree was handy, workers implanted a "Dutchman," or pole, as an anchor — named perhaps in tribute to the Dutchman's legendary tenacity; if he decides to stay put, hell and high water won't budge him. Witness the dikes of Holland.

The last leg to Summit was almost easy. After the six weeks it took getting there, *Sacramento* was at last jacked up on huge timbers over the shaft — and soon repaid all the tribulations of the long haul up the mountain.

By June 1867, the indefatigable Chinese tracklayers had conquered Donner Pass, highest on the route, with steel rails. It was downhill now, mostly, but it took until some time in 1868 before they could put the Sierra behind and really get going. In that year, they put down 364 miles of track, a mile a day.

During the long and arduous conquest of the Sierra, the mountains for miles on each side of the tracks were denuded of forests, as timber was turned into logs for ties and for snowsheds, and fed hungry maws of construction locomotives.

Beyond the Sierra, and now invading the high desert of Nevada, CP crews began to pick up speed. Far to the east, Irish tracklayers of the Union Pacific were going all-out westward. Early on, Congress had calculated that CP and UP would link up near California's eastern boundary, because of the horrendous hurdles of the Sierra. Later, Congress examined the situation again and authorized CP to build 150 miles of railroad into Nevada. Finally, in 1866, Congress took the handcuffs off the dynamic Central Pacific, declaring that the two companies could build until they met each other — and the land between would belong to whichever company could lock it up with steel rails. It was a race for empire.

Central Pacific had few problems with Indians harassing construction gangs, as its track passed through domains mostly of Indians not nearly as bellicose as the Sioux on the plains. And when CP did invade the land of the more belligerent Paiutes and Shoshones, Collis Huntington drafted a treaty that was a neat bit of PR. "We gave the old chiefs a pass each, good on the passenger cars," he said, "and we told our men to let the common Indians ride on the freight cars whenever they saw fit."

Union Pacific, on the other hand, had no end of trouble with Sioux and Cheyenne. Warrior bands attacked railroaders and destroyed equipment. As attacks intensified, more and more soldiers were sent to guard the track, until by 1868 some 5,000 soldiers were patroling the advance.

CP crews, laying rails across the desert, worked also by night, illuminated by the flickering light of sagebrush fires, while UP workers toiled by lantern light.

Construction superintendent James Strobridge kept his mobile "office" close to the advance: He lived at end-of-track in the camp train, containing cozy sleeping quarters, a kitchen, store, and a telegraph office. The camp train housed and fed the officials, clerical force, and white laborers. The Chinese workers evidently handled their own housing and feeding logistics. Strobridge's mobile home was a residence "that would not discredit San Francisco," according to the *San Francisco Alta California* on Nov. 9, 1868. Added the *Vallejo Evening Chronicle* of Jan. 11, 1869: "Mr. Strobridge's residence and office is neatly fitted up and well furnished, and an awning veranda, with a canary bird swinging at the front door, gives it a homelike appearance." Strobridge's wife accompanied him in the camp train all the way from Sacramento to the ceremony at Promontory. She was the only Caucasian woman, and maybe the only woman, on the construction scene from beginning to end. Somebody dubbed her "Heroine of the CP."

Early in 1869 came the disquieting word that UP's Irish tracklayers had laid six miles of track in one day. Strobridge's Chinese workers then laid seven. Whereupon UP construction boss John S. Casement prodded his crews to lay 7.5 miles of track in a day. That irked Crocker, who boasted his men could lay *10 miles* in a day, and backed his boast with a wager of $10,000. UP vice president Thomas C. Durant took the bet.

Crocker told Strobridge: Wait until CP and UP are too close to give Casement a chance to top them. Strobridge mustered everything into position for the supreme challenge: 5,000 men, and five trains loaded with 25,800 ties, 3,520 rails, 55,000 spikes, and 14,080 bolts. Ties were distributed for several miles along the right of way, and the project planned like a military operation.

At 7 a.m. on April 28, the workers leaped into action, witnessed by newspaper reporters, visitors and company officials. All day they labored, save for a lunch break, until at last at 7 p.m. they threw down their tools. They had done it! They had laid 10 miles and 200 feet of track in a single day — a feat unmatched before or since in all railroad history. The 10 miles in one day was half as much as CP had laid down in each entire year of 1863, 1864, and 1865!

As tracklayers closed the few remaining yards of the gap on May 10, 1869, at a windy place called Promontory, Utah, circled by rolling hills of grass and sage — 690 miles from Sacramento — the people in Sacramento, San Francisco and many other cities across the nation were already celebrating, jumping the gun. They knew what was about to happen because the newspapers had told them so. Firebells tolled, cannon boomed, delirium reigned.

CP's Chinese coolies and UP's Irish paddies lowered the last rails onto the ties and spiked them in place. Shortly after noon, construction superintendents from each railroad shoved a special laurel-wood tie into place beneath the rails. Now CP's *Jupiter*

"The Last Spike" hangs in Old Sacramento's Railroad Museum. On a line with visitor's hand, the dark-bearded Theodore Judah is portrayed — though he had died six years before.

engine and UP's *No. 119* slowly chuffed toward each other.

After opening remarks and a prayer, Thomas Durant, for UP, dropped two gold spikes into prepared augur holes in the tie near the east rails. Into two holes near the western rails, Leland Stanford slipped a silver spike and one of an alloy of iron, gold and silver. An iron spike —partly driven into a nearby tie and wired to the telegraph system — was to be hit with a wired sledgehammer. Stanford would wield the sledge, then hand it to Durant. The world instantly would learn of the victory.

Stanford and Durant each hefted the sledge and took a wild swing — both missed. But the nearby telegrapher clicked out the momentous news: "Done." Jack Casement, UP construction chief, grabbed the sledge and swung it time and again, driving the spike in with piercing pings, while rousing cheers rose from his Irish gangs.

Someone smashed a bottle of champagne on the laurel tie, and dignitaries shook hands and slapped backs. *Jupiter* and *No. 119* took turns snorting across the junction onto each other's rails, symbolically touching cowcatchers, then backing up to let the other have the honor. Thus they commemorated the union of the two railroads — and the union of East and West. A famous photo shows bottles being passed around as the engines touched cowcatchers. Some scholars hint that that might explain why Stanford and Durant couldn't hit the target.

Today, each day in this desert scene known as the Golden Spike National Historic Site, the event is re-created for visitors. Glossy replicas of the two historic engines — painted red and black, gleaming with brass — perform again the memorable meeting.

In 1869, something amazing had happened, for the first time ever, and perhaps it was the greatest adventure in railroad history. East and West for the first time, and for all time to come, were connected with steel rails, permitting passengers and freight to ride from sea to sea. No more did cross-country travelers have to put up with the discomforts of jouncing stagecoaches and rotten grub at wayside inns. Now they could dine on steak in the plush comfort of chandelier-illuminated dining cars, and slumber in cozy Pullmans, lulled to sleep by the clickety-clack of the railroad track, and the occasional *whoooee-ta-hooee* of the lonesome whistle, while the tireless engine thundered on. The West would never be the same. A new age had begun.

Theodore Judah — whose dream turned the cross-country railroad into reality, but never lived to see the triumphant link-up — is memorialized in Old Sacramento with a monument at 2nd and L Streets. But his biggest monument is the transcontinental railroad.

During construction of the immense project, scandals had proliferated, tarnishing scores of reputations. Senator George Hoar years later summed up the public's disenchantment: "When the greatest railroad in the world, binding together the continent and uniting two great seas which wash our shores, was finished, I have seen our national triumph and exaltation turned to bitterness and shame by the unanimous reports of three committees of Congress that every step of that mighty enterprise had been taken in fraud."

One of the frauds he may have had in mind was the "moving" of the Sierra 24 miles closer to Sacramento, to gain a fat increase in subsidies.

Although the cross-country railroad lured many interstate passengers, as well as immigrants to California, passenger traffic failed to rise to optimistic predictions. Most cross-country travelers, after the long ride for the adventure of it, opted to make any later coast-to-coast journeys by ship — to Panama, then by train across the Isthmus, and resume their journey by ship. Yet the railroad battened on profits from its near-monopoly on freight transport.

The new railroad helped spur California's economic expansion by giving it an open door to the nation's eastern markets. It also helped spread settlers across the country, and stimulated exploitation of natural resources.

Arrival of a train in Sacramento was a momentous event for locals. Front Street — hub of city commerce — pullulated with travelers, merchants, peddlers, the curious, and rumbling wagons churning up the dust. It was also a momentous event for arriving passengers, if they viewed the scene with the glad eyes of a notable arrival in 1877 — Frank Leslie, publisher of *Leslie's Illustrated Newspaper*, in New York. Leslie, who rode in his private car attached to the overland train, painted a pretty word picture of his stop in River City: "Shall we ever forget that half-hour in Sacramento? Under that blue midsummer sky, in that clear atmosphere and soft, bracing, flower-scented air, it seems to us the very most delectable spot that man might ever call home. It looks so quaint and foreign, with its low, wide buildings and wooden arcades, its great, broad, sunny streets, planked sidewalks. Oh, there never were such homes and such gardens as we see in Sacramento!"

Many rail passengers debarking at Sacramento transferred to posh river steamers for the 120-mile ride to San Francisco. The water trip was shortened by September 1869 when rails were laid from Sacramento through Stockton, Livermore and Pleasanton to the East Bay, where a four-mile, 20-minute ferry ride ended the journey to San Francisco.

By 1879, a new track — a "water-level route" — re-routed transcontinental trains from Sacramento via Davis and Suisun-Fairfield to Benicia, to embark on the train ferry *Solano* and cross Carquinez Strait to Port Costa, where they rumbled on to the ferry at Oakland. Today's trains cross on a trestle.

Even before the historic 1869 juncture, Central Pacific officers were scheming to control a transportation monopoly. To nail down the water route to San Francisco for cross-country travelers, they acquired California Steam Navigation Company's riverboat empire. By 1884, CP was only one component in Southern Pacific's "octopus" empire dominated by the Big Four — now the targets of newspaper editorials. The San Francisco *Examiner* called Huntington "as ruthless as a crocodile." And a local paper came in for one of his excoriations: "The Sacramento Union hurts us very much. If I owned the paper I would control it or burn it."

The Big Four relocated to San Francisco in the 1870s, building their mansions on Nob Hill, today the site of posh hotels including the Mark Hopkins, named after one of the quartet. Hopkins requested that on his death he be buried in the Sacramento City Cemetery, and he rests there today.

But what about "The Other Big Four?" A bronze plaque in Sacramento's Chinese Center, near the Sun Yat-sen Memorial Hall, reads,:

> CENTRAL PACIFIC'S
> OTHER BIG FOUR
>
> When the task of building the CPRR line over the Sierra proved too much for the Irish, Chinese laborers from Kwantung took over. Called Tze Yap or Four Districts men, their hard work and perseverence earned them the nickname of "Cholly Clocker's Pets."

The plaque was placed in 1960 by New Helvetia No. 5, E Clampus Vitus, a society devoted to alcoholic beverages, merrymaking and history, not necessarily in that order.

A remarkable man named Andrew J. Stevens, arriving in Sacramento in 1870, won renown here for innovations in construction and design of locomotives, while working as a CP master mechanic. He devoted his life to designing railroad equipment, rebuilding engines and patenting some of his inventions. One mark of the esteem fellow railroaders held him in is the monument they erected to him in 1889 in Plaza Park, 9th and J Streets. The inscription reads, "Erected to a friend of labor by his coworkers."

Chapter 38
The Railroad Showcase

When I hear the Iron Horse make the hills echo with his snort of thunder . . . it seems to me as if the earth had got a race now worthy to inhabit it.

Henry David Thoreau

As far back as 1937, railroad buffs began to build up steam, as it were, for a California museum of antique rolling stock when members of Pacific Coast Chapter of the Railway and Locomotive Society began acquiring old engines and cars. By 1951, the 20 pieces accumulated were getting ever rustier in their outdoor storage. By 1964, San Francisco's Bethlehem Shipyard took on the task of restoring the deteriorating machinery. With endless labor, workers turned virtual scrap into gleaming museum pieces.

The Society first envisioned a museum in San Francisco, but lack of adequate space sidetracked their efforts. In 1967, they shifted the site to Old Sacramento — which after all had been the birthplace of railroads in California. But a tornado loomed in April 1968 when San Francisco newspapers got wind of the scheme to switch the locus to Sacramento, and denounced the move as "The Great Train Robbery." But Old Sac, argued its proponents, was the appropriate site, being the commencement of the transcontinental railroad, and of California's first railroad, the Sacramento Valley

Railroad. So Old Sacramento edged out San Francisco for the prize. The first engines and cars were rolled in here in 1969 under auspices of California Department of Parks and Recreation.

First phase of the grand project, the restored Central Pacific Railroad passenger station, opened in 1976. For the next five years, work went on to build the California State Railroad Museum, which finally — to plaudits of legions of delighted rail fans — opened its doors in 1981 at a cost of $22 million, occupying the large brick building at the north end of Old Sacramento.

Your visit to this world-class showcase of railroading starts with a short movie focusing on memorable episodes in the age of steam trains. As the film ends, the screen rises. You exit the theater in that direction, walking into a full-scale diorama of a construction scene in the snowy Sierra during the adventure of building the transcontinental railroad. The diorama's centerpiece is an 1862 Governor Stanford locomotive in mint condition.

Moving along, you encounter one stunning display after another. Twenty-one restored locomotives and cars are on view in this 100,000-square-foot building — over two acres — and many more are available for future rotation of displays. Here and there you can pick up an earphone and listen to the story of some classic engine. All are in sparkling condition.

On a wall hangs Thomas Hill's famous painting, "The Last Spike," celebrating the 1869 link-up of East and West. Below the painting, a plaque lists names of dignitaries portrayed, with a silhouette identifying each. Plain to see in the painting — and identified in plaque and silhouette — are the face and figure of Theodore Judah, though he had died six years before the link-up. It's only a painting, so it's not as eerie as if it were a photograph, with Judah's ghostly face haunting it. Some other notables — Crocker, Hopkins and Huntington — are portrayed and identified, though absent at the site that day for reasons other than death. Moreover, there are three persons prominently portrayed, but not identified — the three tracklayers in the foreground, two of them Chinese.

If you want to see what more than one million pounds of iron on the hoof looks like, roll your eyeballs at Southern Pacific No. 4294, a cab-forward steam locomotive all of 126 feet long, over two-fifths of a football gridiron. Awesome. SP bought it in 1944 to drag trains of cars up the mighty Sierra grades. Imagine 6,000 horses, and you have its power equivalent. To non-railroaders, the cab-in-front

Which is the real Dick Denison? Denison the genuine, right, modeled for this conductor manikin in the Railroad Museum.

arrangement may give it something of a backward look. The loaded tender attached adds another 393,300 pounds to the locomotive's million-plus.

Just how a steam locomotive — or any steam engine — works is shown in a large electronic cutaway, or cross-section, model in the roundhouse, and the explanation comes to you via earphone. The steam engine is defined as "the simple machine that transformed the world."

Also in the roundhouse, a sleeper car is rigged so that when you walk through you feel a rocking motion, see passing lights, and hear wheels clicking along the track. But you get off at the same place you boarded —you haven't left Sacramento after all. Nearby stands a mail car, where docents demonstrate mail-sorting and show how the "catcher" came in handy — enabling trainmen to pick up mail bags without stopping, saving time and coal. Over yonder you can stroll through a pit under a 125-ton switch engine to inspect its running gear. In another space, you get a hint of what traveling was like for someone affluent enough to own a private car. The luxurious *Gold Coast*, which belonged to author and railroad aficionado Lucius Beebe, has two staterooms, a formal dining room, kitchen, built-in china cabinets and a stall shower. Not too shabby.

Rolling stock on view represents only a third of the museum's collection. Other engines and cars are pulled out of storage from time to time for variety's sake.

Railroaders in a freeze frame: In another stroll, you come upon a cluster of railroad people, and you might do a double-take before you realize they are not real people, but manikins. Each however, is a life-size replica of a real person. Museum guide Dick Denison, who modeled for a conductor, said each model's face was slathered with salad oil, then a moulage, and then plaster of Paris. "I'd never do it again," he said with a rueful laugh. "It gets very dark and lonely in there. I became numb and claustrophobic from having to hold still in the dark for hours while the plaster set."

Manikin faces and hands were airbrushed, lacquered and antiqued. Eyes are glass. Hair and eyebrows are wigs and barbershop clippings.

Tickets to the Railroad Museum — $2 general and $1 for seniors and children — are good for same-day admission to the nearby restored Central Pacific Passenger Depot, a hundred yards away at Front and J Streets.

But first you may want to go next door to the Railroad Museum to take in the Huntington-Hopkins hardward store, and the Milepost 1 bookshop in the Big Four building, admission free to both. Milepost 1 has an incredible 1,600-plus titles of railroad books, which may be the largest collection in the nation. The shop also exhibits a collection of handsome brass builders' plates — logo-like ornaments attached to locomotives.

The top floor of the Big Four building ensconces a railroad library, open to browsers, and a paradise for researchers. Its collection embraces both history and technology, with hundreds of books, loads of unpublished manuscripts, 50,000 photos including 1,500 glass plates of antique Pullman cars, 40,000 drawings of old steam-engine constructions, and most of Southern Pacific's early financial records — including those of its 400-plus predecessor companies.

The Passenger Depot, reconstructed to circa 1876, served as the first terminal in California for the transcontinental railroad. You can ramble through the waiting rooms, ticket office and baggage room of more than a century ago. Pick up a "wand" that receives recorded messages and learn about old-time railroading as you go on a self-guided tour of seven pieces of rolling stock. Admission tickets — same price as the Railroad Museum — are good for same-day admission to that museum.

Living History Day in Old Sacramento comes several times a year. Many locals and visitors greet these special days by slipping into historical costumes, but they're not mandatory. You can enjoy a hand-car ride, pumping your way along the track. Workers operated these old-style hand-cars along the rails to fix ties, ballast, and signals. Today they use gasoline-powered cars, but decades ago they were human-powered by means of the teeter-totter-like apparatus that you use to propel your way along the steel in Old Sac.

Chances are 50 percent of Old Sacramento visitors have never ridden a steam train. Even those who have are delighted at the chance to renew their acquaintance, by riding in an antique passenger car hauled by a vintage engine, steam boiling from its stack, on a three-mile run south to Miller Park and back.

Future plans are to run the old steam trains farther down along the river to Freeport, 8.5 miles, and Hood, 15.6 miles, utilizing an abandoned Southern Pacific track. The southern terminus of this excursion train one day may connect with a riverboat system, so visitors can ride the train one way and a riverboat the other.

Next up: All about riverboats.

Chapter 39

Steamboats A-comin'!

Oh, where are you going to, all you Big Steamers?
Rudyard Kipling

At Sacramento, transcontinental passengers bound for San Francisco debarked from trains and stepped across the levee to waiting steamers — and were flabbergasted to see "floating palaces" waiting for them at this frontier town. W. F. Rae, an English writer, described the steamer he boarded at Sacramento in 1870: "The upper saloon resembles a large hall in an English country home, furnished in the style and with the taste of a splendid drawing-room . . . . The dining saloon is in the lower part of the vessel. This is a lofty, airy, and well-lit apartment. During the day the light streams through large windows; after nightfall many gas jets make it as brilliant as if the sun shone . . . On the deck there is ample space for the comfortable accommodation of those who delight in walking or sitting in the open air."

The floating palaces had ancestors that were less than palatial. Before 1847, Sutter's schooner *Sacramento* plied between New Helvetia and Yerba Buena, the only regular packet on the river. Sutter bought it from the Russians (in the Fort Ross purchase), who had built it as the *Constantine* for the sea otter trade. It was the fastest boat on the river. William Grimshaw, skipper of the converted longboat *Susanita,* recalled seeing the *Sacramento* loaded with so much wheat it spilled over hatch coamings. The *Sacramento*, with Kanakas as sailors, was skippered by John Yates, not renowned for his sobriety; then by Lewis Keseberg, a Donner party survivor; and later by Heinrich Lienhard, Sutter's assistant. It was last reported in 1858 across from Sacamento at Washington, Yolo County, converted to a habitation for fishermen.

Another Russian-built vessel, first steam-powered ship on the river, signaled the advent of the floating palaces that would dominate the river for nearly 100 years: William A. Leidesdorff's 37-foot sidewheeler *Sitka*, named for its home port. Dissassembled in Alaska after he bought it sight unseen, it was carried to San Francisco Bay on a bark and reassembled for the run to Sacramento. Not only the first steamer on the river, it was also the slowest to ever cruise the Sacramento, crippled by its dinky engine. Casting off from Yerba Buena Nov. 29, 1847, it arrived at Sacramento on December 5 — nearly a week for the 125-mile trip. On the return journey, it was beaten to Benicia by an ox team! The day after it arrived back in San Francisco Bay, it was sunk there by a big wave during a southeaster. It was raised and the engine removed, converting it to the schooner *Rainbow*. It ran as a packet on the river during the Gold Rush, carrying people who hoped to find a pot of gold at *Rainbow's* end.

Early steamboats burned a cord of wood an hour, with bull pine preferred and oak next. They later switched to low-grade coal and, around the turn of the century, converted to oil.

As the Gold Rush quickened, paddlewheelers from the Hudson and Mississippi Rivers steamed around the Horn to San Francisco. Others were dismantled and carried around the Horn aboard sailing ships, and reassembled at San Francisco to carry gold-seekers to Sacramento. By August 1849, no less than 46 steamers were hustling on this route. The brisk commerce brought some of America's best steamboats to this river.

One was the Boston-built sidewheeler *Senator*, 750 tons, which arrived in the fall of 1849 and speedily (pun intended) became the travelers' favorite. For nearly two decades, it left San Francisco at 2 p.m. every other day, making the 125-mile run in less than 10 hours, then cast off at 7 a.m. next day for the run back.

Besides its celerity, *Senator's* passengers were lured by its handsome appointments, including four bridal suites, rosewood staterooms and capacious dining saloon. Affluent passengers at times paid up to $65 for one of its luxurious cabins. In its first years on the river, it hauled in profits of $60,000 a month.

Frank Marryat, the young English writer mentioned in the chapter "In Old Sacramento," recounted his river trip in June 1851: "It is now dusk, and we enter the Sacramento river. Presently we pass a large steamboat going down, who gives us a close shave, and complimentarily strikes three bells, upon which we strike three bells; and in a few minutes we pass a small steamboat also going down, who gives us a closer shave, and shrieks three times out of something connected with her steam-pipe, upon which we groan three times out of something connected with our steam-pipe. These salutes are invariably observed, and the greater the rivalry between the boats, the louder they scream at each other.

"The banks of the river are, for the most part, marshy; but in the fading light we catch glimpses here and there of small cultivated inclosures, with comfortable-looking shanties peeping between the oak trees."

As steamers proliferated, cutthroat competition slashed fares from over $25 per person to less than half that by the end of 1850. One time in the fall of 1850, competing steamers offered passage for only one dollar. Freight rates dropped to equivalent lows. Each company assigned agents to departure scenes, to recruit passengers. While one bragged about his ship's speed, safety and comfort, another a few steps away might be sneering at the same ship as a "scow," "junk," or "the rottenest bottom on the river." He then extolled his own steamboat's speed, safety and comfort.

Every passenger boat raced up and down the river, going all out in a frenetic effort to leave competitors behind. With boilers threatening to burst, the steamboats were floating powderkegs. Tragedy was inevitable.

The steamer *Pearl* blew up north of Sacramento on Jan. 27, 1855. Workers dragged the river for days, recovering 70 bodies —laid out for identification in Sacramento's Water Works building. The *Sacramento Illustrated* journal lamented: "Many a form lay there unknown and unwept, in the habiliments of death, that in another land, far away was the object of a parent's love and care, and had many a warm friend whose heart vibrated with emotion, as this fearful tale of death was told. Very few of those who thus perished by this terrible casualty were claimed or recognized .... All business of the city suspended. Over three thousand people attended the funeral."

The sidewheeler *New World*, launched in New York in 1850, came around the Horn after its skipper Captain Ned Wakeman kidnapped it from a sheriff's sale to escape creditors. It carried enough passengers to California to more than pay off its debt. On Aug. 3, 1850, it entered the Sacramento River run, where it won fame not only for speed but for its cuisine and calliope.

The Rev. Benjamin Akerly recorded a journey on that vessel: "We are aboard the steamer New World bound for Sacramento. The passengers are many; the males, mostly mustached very fiercely and bearded very patriarchically . . . .

"Eight o'clock p.m. — we are entering the Sacramento River which is here, as I judge, half a mile wide. The wind from the ocean is cold and raw . . . . At one o'clock this morning we landed at Sacramento, the capitol and second city of California."

The *New World* in 1851 set a record on the Sacramento-San Francisco run of five hours and 35 minutes, hours under the previous record. The fact it had previously killed some passengers when a steam line burst in Steamboat Slough didn't deter the captain from setting the new mark.

Disastrous competition began to rage in 1854 when various ship owners organized into California Steam Navigation Co., which would dominate river traffic for two decades. Ill-feelings between the company and its competitors led to racing, collisions, explosions, and assorted other mishaps. The company's flagship was the 245-foot sidewheeler *Chrysopolis*, built in San Francisco, and the snazziest of all riverboats. Launched in 1860, it carried 1,000 passengers and specialized in "the conveyance of bridal parties" and as the "carrier of the elite." It boasted a band, fetching murals, stunning chandeliers, and staterooms that were marvels of Victorian elegance, lavish with mahogany and red plush. A promenade circled the upper deck, save for the paddleboxes. The big engines and slim hull made it the fastest ship on the river, proving it New Year's Eve 1861 when — 35-foot sidewheels propelling it at nearly 20 knots — it knocked the time from Sacramento to San Francisco down to five hours and 19 minutes, averaging 19.8 knots or 22.7 miles an hour, a record never equalled or surpassed.

Because of its speed, *Chrysopolis* succeeded the aging *Senator* as the travelers' favorite. In its 15 years on the route, its timetable was so precise people along the river said they could set their watches by its passage.

When *Chrysopolis* became too old for river runs, it was converted to a ferryboat in 1875 and renamed *Oakland*. It shuttled passengers between San Francisco and Oakland until 1940, when it

*Busy Sacramento waterfront is shown in this 1855 lithograph, with the steamer **Young America** on the left, **Queen City** in center and **New World** on right. Note railroad train on right. Courtesy California State Library.*

was burned and scrapped. Few trans-bay passengers in its dotage had any inkling of its glory days as the toast of the river.

Because swift vessels lured the most passengers, captains ran them at reckless speeds, leaving competitors in their wake. Accidental collisions, mostly caused by congested traffic in narrow channels, were not uncommon. But as skippers were a hot-headed breed, some collisions were on purpose. One day the *Antelope*, departing Sacramento 30 minutes behind *Sacramento*, caught up at the entrance to narrow Steamboat Slough and tried to pass. The *Sacramento* crowded it into a mudbank, wedging it in. Minutes later, Captain Enos Fouratt backed *Antelope* off, then steamed off in pursuit, revenge in mind. Some of his irked passengers loaded their pistols, preparing for marine warfare. But Captain Fouratt had a better idea. At Rio Vista, he jammed *Antelope's* bow into the *Sacramento* at the starboard quarter. *Sacramento's* skipper ordered the engines full speed astern. This swung *Sacramento* directly across Antelope's bow. *Antelope* continued at full speed ahead, pushing *Sacramento* sideways down the river for several miles until common sense was regained.

Although California Steam Navigation Company's *Chrysopolis* was the fastest ship on the river, and the company owned most of the other fast vessels, rivals didn't let them rest on their honors. And a promising new challenger entered the tournament in 1861 in the person of Captain Kidd — Captain George Washington Kidd — with his sidewheeler *Nevada*. Kidd's first grief came two years later, in 1863, as his *Nevada* and the *New World* steamed abreast into Steamboat Slough, just upstream from Rio Vista. With sounds of splintering timbers, *Nevada* struck a submerged snag and began to take on water fast, but the pilot maneuvered it to the bank before it sank, enabling passengers to swim ashore. *Nevada* was totaled.

The worst disasters, some with heavy loss of life, were caused by boiler explosions.

Kidd, vowing he would have his day, designed a challenger with larger boilers and named it *Washoe*. Construction, begun Oct. 1, 1863, at Hunter's Point, San Francisco, was completed some months later. Leonard Goss of the Sacramento company of Goss and Leonard built the machinery to Kidd's specs. Kidd swore to set a new record — and California Steam Navigation Co. assigned *Chrysopolis*, pride of its fleet, to run the same schedule as *Washoe*.

With Kidd in command, *Washoe* departed San Francisco on Sept. 4, 1864, a few minutes after *Chrysopolis*. *Washoe* stopped at Rio Vista to embark more passengers, and was told the glittering *Chrysopolis* was 45 minutes ahead, its band playing a victory song. Kidd told the black g ang to pour it on — and Chief Engineer D. M. Anderson complied, pushing boiler pressure up to a perilous 135 pounds per square inch. Kidd was fretting about the boilers because on the steamboat's first trip they had leaked, requiring expensive repairs — a bad omen.

Casting off from Rio Vista, the shuddering *Washoe* steamed at full speed, 12 miles an hour, into Steamboat Slough, smoke boiling from its stack, foam curling from the bow. But *Chrysopolis* was far ahead.

Too much speed and boiler pressure did it. As *Washoe* heeled to negotiate a sharp turn, water in the boilers surged to one side, exposing the overheated flue, the rod that heats the water. The naked flue's fierce heat was more than the boilers could take. *Washoe* went up in a horrible explosion that blew out all the lights and touched off fires. Screams rent the air as scalded people flung themselves into the river, desperate for relief in cool water. Some reached the bank and died, groaning. Others staggered away until they dropped in a moonstruck meadow.

As the stricken ship ran aground, hissing steam, splintering wood and agonized cries merged in an awful discord. Passengers milled in confusion, some trying to help the injured. Kidd and his officers dashed about, doing what they could to succor the injured.

Washoe was alone with its agony nearly three hours, until *Antelope* rounded the bend. Injured and dying were transferred to *Antelope*, which departed for Sacramento, decks covered with victims.

The disaster scene was only seven miles from where the *Nevada*, also piloted by Kidd, had sunk a year earlier while racing with the *New World.*

On the *San Francisco Call*, reporter Mark Twain wrote his disaster story from dispatches published by the evening papers: "The explosion of the boilers of Washoe took place . . . just above the Hog's Back, about ten miles above Rio Vista, on her up-trip on Monday night.

"One of her boilers collapsed a flue, and, it is said, made a clean sweep aft, going overboard through the stern of the boat . . . .

"The upper works of the boat were completely shattered, some portions of them, with the staterooms being blown overboard . . . .

"She was about 20 yards off the left bank at the time, and the whole steering gear being destroyed, she took a sheer and ran ashore, her bow providentially touching a tree, to which those not injured fastened the boat.

"Had she not run ashore, almost everybody on board would have been lost, as they could not steer the wreck, and they had not boats, the steamer sinking gradually at the stern. The boat was set on fire in three places, which added to the horror of the scene. The fire, however, was put out by the few who were uninjured . . . .

"The Antelope being behind, came up and took off the wounded and a large number of the dead, and brought the first news of the sad affair to Sacramento."

Reported *The Sacramento Union* on September 7: "The Washoe tragedy is appalling . . . . the boat is a wreck. The dead, scarcely to be recognized, strew the splintered planks, the maimed and scalded are crying or moaning for help . . . . Then the long agony of waiting for succor, which comes at last as the Antelope's lights shine over the dark waters."

Antelope embarked all the injured it could carry. Decks and cabins were crammed with moaning passengers — and some who had died. Many of *Antelope's* original passengers had stayed on the *Washoe* through the terrible night to do what they could for victims.

As *Antelope* neared Sacramento, Captain Albert Foster tolled the ship's bell to signal the tragedy. *Antelope's* overcrowded condition, plus the morning low tide, grounded it on a sandbar opposite R Street. By the time it was afloat, the levee was teeming with distraught friends and relatives of *Washoe* passengers. As Sacramento's firebells began a lugubrious toll, ten thousand Sacramentans crowded to the river, many knowing they had had friends or relatives on the *Washoe*. The Vernon House on J Street was turned into a makeshift hospital, to which strong hands carried tragic burdens from *Antelope* to waiting doctors. Some were carried to private homes — or coroner facilities.

Washoe's chief engineer D. M. Anderson, borne ashore from *Antelope*, stammered "Rotten iron in the boilers" — then died. Some said he protected his captain with this deathbed utterance.

As doctors tended the suffering, Howard Benevolent Society members appealed to the public for bandages, and collected relief funds for relatives.

Later that day, the steamer *Visalia* cruised to the *Washoe* scene to help officers and passengers who had remained aboard, and found the wreck resting cattywampus on the riverbank. Kidd, a few uninjured crewmen and two or three local residents, were searching for bodies, and had found five thus far. That evening, Kidd boarded the *Chrysopolis* on her downriver trip to San Francisco. On September 9, Kidd sent a gift of $1,000 to Howard Benevolent Society for the injured and their families.

Mark Twain wrote that Kidd was, according to telegraphic reports from Sacramento, accused of ungenerous and unfeeling conduct, in remaining with the wreck, instead of accompanying the maimed and dying to Sacramento. "In defense of himself," Twain added, "he says he was satisfied that the wounded would be as well and kindly cared for on the Antelope as if he were present himself, and that he thought the most humane course for him to pursue would be to stay behind with some of his men and search among the ruins of his boat for helpless victims, and rescue them before they became submerged by the gradually sinking vessel; he believed some of the scalded and frantic victims had wandered into the woods, and he wished to find them also . . . .

"That his impulses are kind and generous all will acknowledge who remember that he kept his boat running night and day, in time of the flood, and brought to this city hundreds of sufferers by that misfortune, without one cent of charge for passage, beds or food."

Kidd is not known to be of any relation to the 17th-century pirate, Captain William Kidd. Here's how to distinguish between the two: Ours was the "good" Captain Kidd. The only violence from him was purely accidental.

Catastrophe also lay in store for *Washoe's* famed sister ship, the proud *Yosemite*, a year later. It was a lovely evening Oct. 12, 1865, when *Yosemite* departed Rio Vista at 6 p.m., bound for Sacramento. The decks were swarming with 300 passengers, and 50 more passengers, Chinese laborers, had been jammed into the hold.

Just as Captain Poole steered away from Rio Vista, the pilothouse, upper cabin and forward deck went up like a volcano, flinging bodies through the air. A hundred passengers died instantly. Fifty more died in the next hour. All the Chinese below decks were among the dead. As the blazing ship listed against the wharf, horrified people on shore rushed to rescue survivors, and *Chrysopolis* transported them to Sacramento. Nearly a ton of gold aboard was recovered. Faulty boiler iron was blamed for the calamity.

The wreck of *Yosemite* was salvaged; the vessel was cut in half and a 35-foot splice inserted, giving it a hull length of 283 feet and overall length of about 300 feet, or gridiron-length, making it the longest river steamer in California history. Maximum length was dictated by sharp bends in the river.

Yosemite continued in river service, then worked the Vallejo-San Francisco run for Central Pacific Railroad. Later it worked on Canada's Fraser River, and finally on Puget Sound until 1909. Loaded with over 1,000 excursionists, it was caught in a turning tide near Bremerton, Washington, and its back broken as it swept full speed onto rocks. All aboard were saved, but *Yosemite* was totaled. Two reasons are given for the wreck. One says it was widely believed it was deliberately wrecked for its insurance. The other says the captain neglected his duty while in his stateroom, distracted by a lady's charms.

In 1869, when Central Pacific Railroad bought out California Steam Navigation Company, the new corporation put on brass knucks: To crush competition, it dropped the fare for the river trip to as little as 10 or 15 cents, and sometimes to nothing at all. When the competition still hung on, CP actually *paid* passengers to ride.

This merciless competition showed itself in ways other than fare wars. One day as the steamer *Defender* approached Sacramento, it found levees barricaded with an unbroken line of vessels, offering no place to tie up, so it moored temporarily to the storeship *Dimon*. Just then the steamer *Pike*, also moored to *Dimon*, cast off and swung out into the current. *Defender* quickly slipped into *Pike's* slot and tied up — only to find that *Pike's* crew had boarded up all gangways on *Dimon*, to prevent *Defender* from unloading passengers and freight. *Defender's* crew had to chop their way through oak timbers with axes to hew a way to the waterfront.

As departure neared, *Defender's* band started playing, and passengers thronged aboard. A stern-wheel steamer churned close and cut loose with a loud whistle blast, drowning out *Defender's* band. When the band stopped playing, the whistle stopped. Again the band played — again the whistle blasted. Irate bandsmen shoved aside their instruments and leaped to their feet, looking around for firearms. The crowd on the levee hollered its fury at the stern-wheeler for spoiling the concert. Meanwhile, men and boys were clashing Chinese gongs to advertise the merits of their company vessels. It was pandemonium. A judge holding court nearby had to adjourn until the bedlam died.

New gold stampedes into the northern mountains accelerated traffic on the upper Sacramento. Riverboats of course became the workhorses of transportation, being the swiftest and most efficient way to carry passengers and freight from San Francisco and Sacramento. And from Sacramento, a fleet of small sternwheelers, many drawing less than two feet of water when loaded, serviced the upper Sacramento and tributaries, chugging ever farther upstream with men and supplies for the northern mines.

The head of navigation kept moving north — changing from Colusa to Benton City, to Tehama, and lastly to Red Bluff. Each rivertown had its heyday, then faded into history as the channel farther north was cleared of obstacles. Red Bluff for many years served as northern terminus of river traffic. The decline set in as hydraulicking in the Sierra began to clog streams with slickens. As early as 1866, steamers started to abridge their trips on both the Sacramento and San Joaquin.

Steamboat whistles — announcing arrivals and departures — also were handy safety devices. They warned other ships of their approach. In darkness and Delta tule fogs, skippers bounced their whistle-blasts off buildings, riverbanks, and echo-boards set up on levees, groping along by listening to the echoes — a primitive form of sonar. One story tells that a captain dutifully sounded his whistle each time he rounded a certain bend, to estimate his distance by bouncing the echo off a barn — not visible in darkness. One night no replying echo resounded, but the captain continued on, confident of his course. At the next stop he learned that the barn had burned down.

If passenger steamers were the royalty on the river, plebeian vessels in much greater numbers were the workhorses. Many were stern-wheelers with flat bottoms that let them cruise in waters much too shallow for larger vessels. Small steamers running up from San Francisco stopped often to land passengers and freight at landing after landing — their light draft permitting them to land almost anywhere.

Families on riverside farms relied on steamers to take their crops to market. Without them, they would have had to haul their produce over bad roads to faraway towns. And in high water seasons, sometimes the land would be drowned for weeks, and whole towns had to look to the riverboats for food for man and beast.

Popular in remote stretches of the river was the "store ship," or "floating variety store," a kind of floating mini-market. Three long blasts on the whistle heralded its coming to isolated towns. Everybody in the neighborhood scurried to the landing to stock up on food, clothes and other needs, paying with lugs of fruit, cans of milk, sacks of potatoes, or sometimes a pig, calf, or crate of chickens. The paddlewheelers not only brought all the things needed by isolated communities, they offered the remote families chances to sell or trade produce and livestock.

River traffic rose even more in the mid-1860s when farmers found the valley's soil and climate superb for growing wheat. So much land was planted to wheat that from 1865 to 1890 the annual harvest rose from less than 6 million bushels to more than 50 million, and the Sacramento Valley became the third largest wheat-producer in the nation. Each autumn, miles of levees were lined with sacks of grain. Enormous loads were heaped high onto barges and steamers for the run to Carquinez Strait, where the wheat was graded and stored, then transferred to sailing vessels bound to many faraway ports. Docks and warehouses lined both sides of Carquinez Strait for miles in the wheat-trade heyday.

The great wheat-growing bubble lasted into the 1890s, when it collapsed because of soil exhaustion and stiff competition from new wheat-growing centers in Argentina, Australia and elsewhere that sent prices plunging. But river traffic remained heavy for years.

Sacramento's Tower Bridge in 1936 rises — to salute the Delta Queen *and let her steam through. Today the* Queen *cruises the Mississippi and Ohio, while her sister ship* Delta King *is docked permanently in Old Sacramento. How can a* King *be a sister to a* Queen? *Photo courtesy Mary Hanel, California Department of Transportation.*

Fast luxurious steamers shuttled daily between San Francisco, Sacramento and Stockton, while the fleet of bantam stern-wheelers bustled passengers and freight on the upper Sacramento and tributaries.

In summer and fall, the Sacramento often ran so low much of it was closed to all but small shallow-draft steamers. Some drew so little water the joke was they could cruise "wherever the ground was a little damp."

Even so, the small steamers were so heavily burdened going upstream they sometimes ran aground, then had to lift themselves by their bootstraps, so to speak. Crewmen leaped overboard with a heavy rope and lashed it to a tree trunk. With the other end wound on the ship's capstan, the captain ordered the engineman to give 'er the gun. Assisted by the churning paddlewheel, the steam-driven capstan rotated, winding up the rope, dragging the steamer over the shallows. If that trick didn't work, people upstream had no recourse but to tough it out until winter rains lifted the river.

In the early 1890s, the manager of a theatrical company had a brainstorm: He chartered a light-draft stern-wheeler, converted lower-deck cargo space into a theater, and turned the ship into a showboat, first in the West. The ship cruised on the Sacramento and Feather, bringing melodramas to small towns, renting a hall and performing several days in each town. If the town lacked a hall, the company performed aboard ship. Intermissions were times for "commercials" — hucksters patrolled the aisles, hawking bottles of cure-alls.

Two of the most magnificent riverboats ran on the Sacramento well into modern times — the *Delta King* and the *Delta Queen,* sister ships built in Stockton and put in service in 1927, biggest and costliest paddlewheelers in California, hauled cargo and passengers.

The *Delta* twins had two predecessors, the *Capital City*, launched in 1910, and the *Fort Sutter*, 1912, both of which boasted staterooms with baths. Would wonders never cease? They also pioneered the splendid four-deck design adopted by the *Deltas.*

The *Deltas* had 250-foot hulls, with sternwheel overhangs giving them overall lengths of 285 feet. Their four roomy decks, air-cooled staterooms and other appointments made them the last word in river travel. During Prohibition, they offered Roaring Twenties kicks fueled by gambling and whoopee juice. When booze was legalized, enthusiasm for the *Deltas* went out with the ebb tide.

The final curtain was drawn on the paddlewheel drama by the Depression and by new highways and bridges that siphoned off much of river traffic. The twins were taken off their routes, but during World War II they were drafted to serve as barracks, as hospital ships, and as shuttles to ferry sick and wounded around San Francisco Bay. The twins were designed to float in only a few feet of river water, but with their 50-foot-high superstructures buffeted by 30-knot winds on the Bay, they offered scary rides. Many a soldier said his most terrifying wartime ordeal was sailing across the Bay on one of the twins. After the war, the King was towed to British Columbia to house workers on Alcoa's Kitimat aluminum mining project for seven years until 1959, when it was towed to Stockton.

Cretins vandalized it, and it continued to rot. In 1969, Sacramento attorney Geoff Wong and cohorts slipped down to Stockton and in darkness pirated the *King*, towing it upriver to Sacramento. With world attention focused on the imminent American moon landing, who would notice a slight case of steamboat piracy? Yet so irresistible was this derring-do that the secret leaked out, and the Huntley-Brinkley Report, right after covering Neil Armstrong's "one small step for man, one giant step for mankind," reported on the Sacramento pirates who took one giant step for steamboat preservation.

Alas, Attorney Melvin Belli and co-owner Max Mortensen took a jaundiced view and won a suit to regain possession. But the Solano County tax collector seized it for nonpayment of taxes. When it was auctioned in 1979, a San Francisco family bought it for $35,000. It was anchored off Richmond, but sank and remained sunk for a year until developers Walter Harvey and Joe Coyne bought it for $500,000. Once more in 1984, it was returned to the Sacramento waterfront. Original engines and boilers were gone, and it was drawing six feet of water because of its burden of nearly 400 tons of debris. With that excess baggage removed, it now draws five feet.

Delta King now is docked permanently in Old Sacramento as a memorial to the floating palaces, of which this monarch was the grandest in California history. In a $10.5 million restoration, the floating palace has been turned into a floating luxury hotel, with two restaurants, 120-seat dinner theater, conference rooms, two bars, offices, and 44 hotel rooms. The most opulent stateroom is the captain's quarters, commodious enough to accommodate receptions for 50 people. Its staircase ushers visitors up to the wheel house for a commanding view of the river.

The *King's* twin, the *Delta Queen*, fought in the 1946 "Battle of Alcatraz" when several of the toughest cons, armed with guns, tried to crash out. They took over a cellblock but didn't get much farther. The *Queen*, serving as a floating gun platform for sharpshooters and grenade launchers, circled the island to prevent escapes, as did Coast Guard vessels. No shots were fired from the *Queen*. All would-be escapees were killed when law officers stormed the prison.

Later the *Queen* traveled to far horizons as it was towed back through the canal to the Mississippi and Ohio, where it carries passengers on cruises into nostalgia. In 1986, it celebrated its 60th birthday by winning a 14-mile race with the *Belle of Louisville* during the Great Steamboat Race of the Kentucky Derby Festival.

Riverboats of Today

River City Queen, which replicates in aspect a 19th-century riverboat, offers cruises in May through September, leaving from the barge in Old Sacramento at the foot of L Street. The two-hour cruises explore stretches of the Sacramento and American Rivers. The two-decker, 65 feet long, actually is powered by two concealed 150-horse outboard motors, but the paddlewheels on the side rotate as the ship moves, creating the illusion they are propelling the ship. Capacity is 100 persons, and it is available for charter. Beverages and snacks are at the ready, together with live music and a commentary on points of interest. Call 371-4288 or 448-7447.

Elizabeth Louise, a 160-foot sternwheeler, is operated by Hal Wilmunder, who named it after his wife. This authentic steamboat is the only commercial steamboat west of the Mississippi, and the first genuine steamboat to sail on the Sacramento since the *Delta* twins in 1940. Wilmunder spent a decade building it, and installed steam engines built in 1884 and used in four previous vessels — still working after more than 100 years. Available for charter by groups up to 400, it boasts the largest full-service bar on the river. Entertainment too. Call 638-7212.

The *Matthew McKinley*, a riverboat styled to represent one from Gold Rush times, offers narrated diner cruises and Sunday Captain's Brunch, embarking passenters from Old Sacramento's waterfront. The vessel also is available for charter. Built in 1984, the 82-foot, two-story riverboat is powered by two diesels, but its big paddlewheel turns as the ship moves, giving the illusion it is propelling the ship. A cocktail lounge and sumptuous main salon round out the nautical ambience. The owner, Channel Star Excursions, in 1991 will replace this 150-passenger vessel with a 400-passenger riverboat. Call 441-6481.

The 500-passenger, red-and-white *Harbor Emperor* offers weekend cruises through the Delta between Sacramento and San Francisco from June through October. Cost of a one-way cruise on the sleek, three-level, 93-foot vessel is $44 per person, which includes a two-hour stopover at Fisherman's Wharf before the return bus trip in the evening. The cruise takes seven to eight hours. Those departing from San Francisco may spend two hours in Old Sacramento before the return bus trip. Another alternative is to go both ways by riverboat, $95 to $118 per person, depending on hotel occupancy. A narrator on the p.a. system recounts stories about the many interesting points along the way. Call Delta Riverboats, 372-3690.

Chapter 40
Breezes of Change

Something in the chemistry and physics of this floodplain where two rivers meet gave it a touch of magic and made it a magnet for history. From the Gold Rush to the turn of the century and beyond, Sacramento grew and prospered. Changing winds were blowing, and they affected the currents in the city's life. Some currents bore Sacramento to the end of an era, and others to the beginning of a new one.

Some innovations had repercussions that never could have been dreamed of by their initiators. Colonel James Lloyd Lafayette Franklin Warren, a Massachusetts seed merchant, had a name as long as your arm, and both of *his* arms had green thumbs. He came to California to look for gold. He didn't find much "color" in the mines, but in 1852 opened a Sacramento business with more colors than a rainbow. He located his New England Seed Store on J Street near the levee, ordered a shipment of camellia plants and seeds from New England, then advertised the debut of this fair flower on the Sacramento stage. He couldn't have found a more propitious climate, for his camellias flourished far better here than any he had seen back home.

The camellia one day would become Sacramento's official bloom, and in time local gardens would grow them in such profusion as to earn Sacramento the sobriquet, "Camellia Capital of the World." Each March, the city celebrates its month-long

Camellia Festival, climaxing the mid-winter blooming of over one million camellia bushes in Sacramento County — more camellia bushes than people!

Stentorian-voiced Ed Combatalade, "Mr. Camellia," originated the Camellia Festival, which burgeoned in 1955 — an annual riot of color that may be the only kind of riot nobody is unhappy about.

He said the idea stemmed from one camellia slip. Or slipped from one stem. "My mother put a slip in a glass of water on a window sill. When the flower fell off, she liked the green leaves so much she kept the slip in water. One day she noticed it had roots, so she put it in a flower pot. It grew too big for her room, so she gave it to my aunt in Berkeley, who put it in a larger container.

"When my aunt sold the house, I told her I wanted the camellia, so I brought it back to Sacramento and planted it in front of our house.

"My wife Barbara and I were talking about camellias — we were members of the Camellia Society — and I said, 'Why not have a festival?' So I put some people on a committee." Being an idea whose time had come, it was welcomed with open arms, instead of being told to take a hike. Everybody takes a hike together — in the annual parade.

The original camellia Combatalade planted in front of his house so many years ago is still thriving, now 12 feet tall, and he claims it bears "a thousand or more" flowers each year. "Blooms like crazy," he said.

Combatalade — who has in jest has been called Whispering Ed — also admits to being called Foghorn. "I developed my voice when I started coaching in 1929 at Sacramento High. Talking loud was the only way to get the attention of some of those kids."

In the Language of Flowers, the white camellia signifies "perfected loveliness," while the red modestly whispers of "unpretending excellence." Camellias also have Whispering Ed, a man with a heroic voice, to express their beauty.

Now back-flash to the seed-merchant colonel:

Warren's destiny didn't end with camellias, for he would become a power in launching the California State Fair. As early as 1852, he showcased many of the city's proud floral and agricultural products in his store, first in Sacramento to do so — creating in effect a State Fair in miniature. In that calamitous year of 1852 —when the city suffered its worst fire and worst flood — the optimistic Warren was urging people to plant seeds. His own store burned down in the fire, but the undaunted nurseryman rebuilt it in only weeks.

The Legislature in 1854 authorized the first State Fair, held in San Francisco, then the year after in Sacramento's old State Capitol, 7th and I Streets, with harness-racing and livestock shows. The next three years saw it successively in San Jose, Stockton and Marysville. Sacramento got hold of it again in 1859 and 1860, and the Legislature gave it to Sacramento permanently in 1862 — thanks to being constantly jump-started here by Warren's high-voltage promotion of agricultural and floral displays in his own store.

After a couple of close-in sites, the extravaganza relocated to the State Fairgrounds on Stockton Boulevard, 1906 to 1967; and to its present Cal Expo site near Arden Way from 1968. Though Warren knew big oaks grow from little acorns, he never could have surmised the big things that would grow from his little camellia seeds.

The passing years were seeing boomtown Sacramento take on aspects of a well-ordered city. A correspondent for the *Boston Cultivator* newspaper, who signed himself only as "Jack," reported in 1855 that Sacramento's schools were "one-handed," explaining: "There are ten schools and ten teachers, scattered all about the city — each school numbering about fifty scholars. Were they united and graded, something might be done. They are old fogies, for they have gone back into the dark ages, and dragged out the barbarous notion that the sexes must be separated in schools. Their schools will never be American schools while they separate the boys from the girls!"

He advocated corporal punishment for members of the Sacramento Board of Education because they, being "determined to meddle with what is none of their business, have passed resolutions forbidding any kind of corporal punishment in schools — for which act of foolish *barbarism* they ought to be fed on goat's milk for six months."

He arrived at "the site of Sutter's Fort," explaining his choice of words: "I say the site — for the Fort is among the things that were, having been levelled, and its walls taken to fill up the road. The destruction of this fort was a piece of vandalism seldom equalled."

Three miles from town, he arrived at "Smith's Gardens," 60 acres under cultivation: "A large steam engine pumps water from the American River into a reservoir, from whence it is conveyed by underground pipes all over the garden, for nothing grows here except by irrigation. It is not a favorable season to visit this place, still, we can see how the desert has been turned into a paradise!

Here are long lines of peach-trees, whose growth exceeds belief. The growth of one year here is greater than that of five in the east. Those trees bore abundantly this year, but the grasshoppers, which devoured every green thing, ate up all the fruit and stripped the trees of their foliage. Their voracity was incredible; they devoured melons, squashes, everything vegetable, and for three weeks hovered like a black cloud over the place! . . .

"The shade trees of Sacramento add much to the beauty of the place; it will be, in a few years, the city of trees. In the great fires which ravaged the place, the large, native sycamores were all burned down, but, so rapidly is the growth that the trees set out along the streets already cast quite a shade; in this respect, Sacramento looks like a New England city. As I walked along, the rustle of the dead leaves on the sidewalks made me think of home again. Oh, how slight a thing turns the current of our thoughts!

"The city has now a population of about fifteen thousand. My visit there was a delightful one; I came back here bringing with me pleasant recollections of the friends and teachers of the city — quite a contrast to my stop there two years ago, when I knew not a soul in the city, and had not a friend in the country."

By 1856 when 500 brick buildings had risen in the city, Sacramento had become a hive of brickyards. Thirty in the local area could disgorge a quarter of a million bricks a day, not only for local needs but for the Bay Area. Two lumber mills spewed nearly 14,000 board feet daily. Other industries were thriving: Six flour mills ground out 585 bags of flour daily; five breweries were able to pour over 1,000 gallons of beer daily, while four soda water plants had a capacity of 17,400 bottles daily; a pottery works turned out irrigation pipe and earthware; two soap factories were working; sounds of an industrial symphony reverberated from two foundries, turning out brass and iron products. And all this was only 1856 — Sacramento hadn't seen anything yet.

Private entrepreneurs supplied water to the populace in Sacramento's first five years, 1849-54, delivering it door-to-door in horse carts. William P. Henry is credited as first.

Construction in 1854 of a three-story building at the foot of I Street — Sacramento's first city hall — phased out the water carts because two tanks on the roof containing 240,000 gallons distributed water throughout the city by gravity. William Henry, the water-cart pioneer, became the city's first waterworks superintendent. The waterworks consisted of a small steam engine that pumped river water up to the rooftop tanks — earliest mechanical water system west of the Rockies. Sacramento was the first city in the west to develop a municipal water system — the disastrous fire of 1852 having demonstrated its urgent need.

Sacramento, though bounded on two sides by rivers of fresh water, had had, almost from the city's birth, a water problem — getting *clean* water to the people.

Jack, the Boston man, mentioned the waterworks and described the product: "The water is of a dirty yellow color, yet a better quality than that obtained from wells, which is highly impregnated with alkali."

Citizens looked askance at the muddy water from local taps, calling it "Sacramento Straight" — meaning it came straight from the river without treatment, except sedimentation. Tanks now and then were drained so three feet of accumulated mud could be shoveled out by the jail's chain gang.

The gravity system's low pressure couldn't send water any big distance, so in 1872 the Holly Waterworks, named after the Holly Pump Manufacturing Company, was installed next door to the old plant, with big steam engines and pumps to boost pressure, forcing water to the town's widening outskirts. Pressure could be further increased to fight fires. But high pressure had a drawback — it sometimes blew out weak spots in the ancient pipes. Electric pumps in 1910 replaced the steam engines.

Voters in 1919 okayed a bond issue to build a plant to filter and treat the muddy water pumped from the Sacramento. Five years later, clean water gurgled through city faucets. "Sacramento Straight" — one of the bad things of the good old days — was now history.

Sacramentans got their water mainly from the Sacramento until 1940 when the city started digging wells to serve areas not easily reached from the river. Because most well water was inferior to that from the American River, the city in the 1960s built a large treatment plant on the American.

The city waterworks building would suffer from structural ailments most of its 60-year life from the tremendous weight of water bearing down on it.

Public executions were held in this city building in its early history. In 1860, Peter Lundberg was hanged for murder from a gallows constructed in the building, and another murderer was hanged there in 1861. By 1880 all city offices had vacated the building save the jail and police court. Captured lawbreakers were brought in on foot until 1895, when the city bought its first patrol wagon, dubbed "Black Maria."

By century's end, it was clear the city jail was doomed. Crooked walls and makeshift alterations contributed to its rundown aspect. Southern Pacific, expanding its waterfront facilities, coveted the property. In 1906 the city sold the jail to SP on condition the city could use it until a new jail could be built.

The new site for the jail and police station — on 6th between H and I — was purchased from the county in 1912, and the city in the following year abandoned the old jail, which had been condemned. Prisoners were moved to a temporary facility. The only portion of the old building that survived was a common wall with the adjoining Holly Waterworks. After nearly 60 years, the end came for Sacramento's first municipal structure. Yet it survives as a reconstructed building that houses the new History Center.

In the same year the first city hall was built, 1854, military adventurer William Walker, 30, following his failed attempt to conquer Mexico's State of Sonora, went to work in Sacramento as editor of the *Democratic State Journal*, which occupied a two-story building at 130 K St. Walker, of Tennessee, a banty rooster of only 100 pounds, had studied medicine and law, fought duels and, in New Orleans, edited a newspaper. In that city he became enamored of a lovely deaf mute. When she died of fever, he decamped to California. After a stint as a lawyer in Marysville, he got his nose bloodied in the Sonora fiasco, then gravitated to Sacramento to edit the *Journal*. He left the paper in February 1855.

Later that year he sailed from San Francisco with only 58 men and conquered a nation — Nicaragua — and got himself elected president. Sutter's youngest son, William Alphonse, joined Walker in Nicaragua. The warrior band gained renown as "The Immortals." With no artillery, they captured a fort in Honduras in 15 minutes. Some of Walker's men were so reckless that, armed with only pistols, they would jump over a wall into the midst of the enemy. For a long time Walker's 2,500-man force held off attacks of 18,000 men from four neighbor countries. But his problems mushroomed faster than he could cope, and he died suddenly in Honduras. Cause of death was a firing squad.

The young Sutter returned to California to settle in Nevada City and died there in 1863, apparently of fever contracted in the tropics.

Sacramento in 1856 witnessed the birth of the Republican Party in California when the GOP held its first mass meeting April 18 at the Orleans Hotel on 2nd Street, with Edwin Bryant Crocker as keynote speaker. Twelve days later, with Crocker as chairman,

Republicans held their first state convention in the Congregational Church on 6th Street between K and L, drawing 125 delegates from 13 counties.

Year 1857 was one of scandal in the state treasurer's office, Sacramento. Henry Bates, who had taken office the previous year, had also taken off with $250,000 from the treasury, to parts unknown. Bates, when first seated as treasurer, had had to post a surety bond. Among bondsmen was Samuel Norris, owner of the immense Rancho del Paso. Norris's middle name could have been Litigation, because he spent so much time suing people in various courts all over the land. He lost many of his suits, and some were so trivial people wondered if he had any common sense.

When the State tried to collect the $100,000 bond for Bates, Norris pleaded inability to pay, owing to the egregious fees he owed attorneys in his lawsuits. The Legislature in early 1859 released Norris and other bondsmen from their obligations.

That apparently didn't sit well with somebody. For on March 3 of that year, *The Sacramento Bee* ran a paid ad in the form of a letter titled "Bates and his Bondsmen," apparently authored by Abraham Keefer, a former Norris employee. The letter blasted the Legislature's action, saying Norris had large land holdings and other assets in the local area and Texas, had resources to raise the $100,000, and furthermore owed Keefer $1,500 for work on his rancho, and had refused to pay.

The following afternoon, as Norris chatted with friends in front of a saloon, Keefer struck Norris several times about the head with a heavy cane, inflicting serious wounds. Keefer was arrested but for some reason never prosecuted. Norris later said the blows left him deaf for several months, blind in one eye for several years, and with permanent nerve damage.

Moving along to 1863, farming in the Lower American region hit its zenith under direction of master agriculturalist Joseph Routier, among the first in California to farm on a large scale. The little town of Brighton — later engulfed by Sacramento, and situated in the vicinity of today's California State University, Sacramento — was the hub of this domain of orchards and vineyards and the state's biggest hop fields, important to beer-drinkers. Routier grew prunes, grapes, walnuts, apricots, peaches, almonds and oranges. Routier Road, running south from Folsom Boulevard, is named after him.

One of the busy Brighton area farmers of the time was Tom C. Perkins, who as a boy had walked all the way to California from

Illinois. Perkins sorted mail as Brighton's postmaster until 1884. Besides tilling the soil, he found time to work as a distiller, storekeeper and justice of the peace. The Perkins community, swallowed by expanding Sacramento, was named after him. It was located east of today's junction of Folsom Boulevard and Jackson Road.

The *San Francisco Chronicle* was born in Sacramento in 1864 when Charles De Young founded it here as the *Dramatic Chronicle,* a small throwaway. Nine months later he relocated it to San Francisco and renamed it the *Daily San Francisco Chronicle.* It was one of only three newspapers that survived of more than 80 founded here in the Gold Rush epoch, when Sacramento gained notoriety as "graveyard of newspapers." The other two are *The Sacramento Union,* "oldest daily west of the Rockies," and *The Sacramento Bee* of the McClatchy empire.

The Sacramento Observer, founded in 1962 by William Lee, is the most honored black newspaper in America, having collected countless awards.

Sacramento's most famous newspaperman — Mark Twain — came here after he had made a bit of a name for himself in the business, and after having been "invited to resign" from the *San Francisco Morning Call.* Earlier, he had covered the Sacramento beat for the Virginia City, Nevada, *Territorial Enterprise.* Twain rhapsodized over the Sacramento climate: "This is the mildest, balmiest, pleasantest climate one can imagine. The evenings are especially delightful — neither too warm nor too cold. I wonder if it is always so?"

Apparently not, for at another time he penned some searing remarks about searing Sacramento weather: "In Sacramento it is fiery summer always, and you can gather roses, and eat strawberries and ice-cream, and wear white linen clothes, and pant and perspire at eight or nine o'clock in the morning."

Sacramento was also very "wet" in one sense of the word, indicated Twain, who called this "the City of Saloons," noting there were "a good many of them" and confessing an acquaintance with a good many: "You can shut your eyes and march into the first door you come to and call for a drink, and the chances are that you will get it."

Calling on *The Sacramento Union* publishers James Anthony and Paul Morrill, Twain laid a proposition on them: He had been invited to sail on the ship *Ajax* to the Sandwich Islands. Would they pay his expenses in exchange for a series of articles? On scenery, native customs, and the booming sugar industry? Engrossing reading for *Union* readers. Impressed by his reputation, the

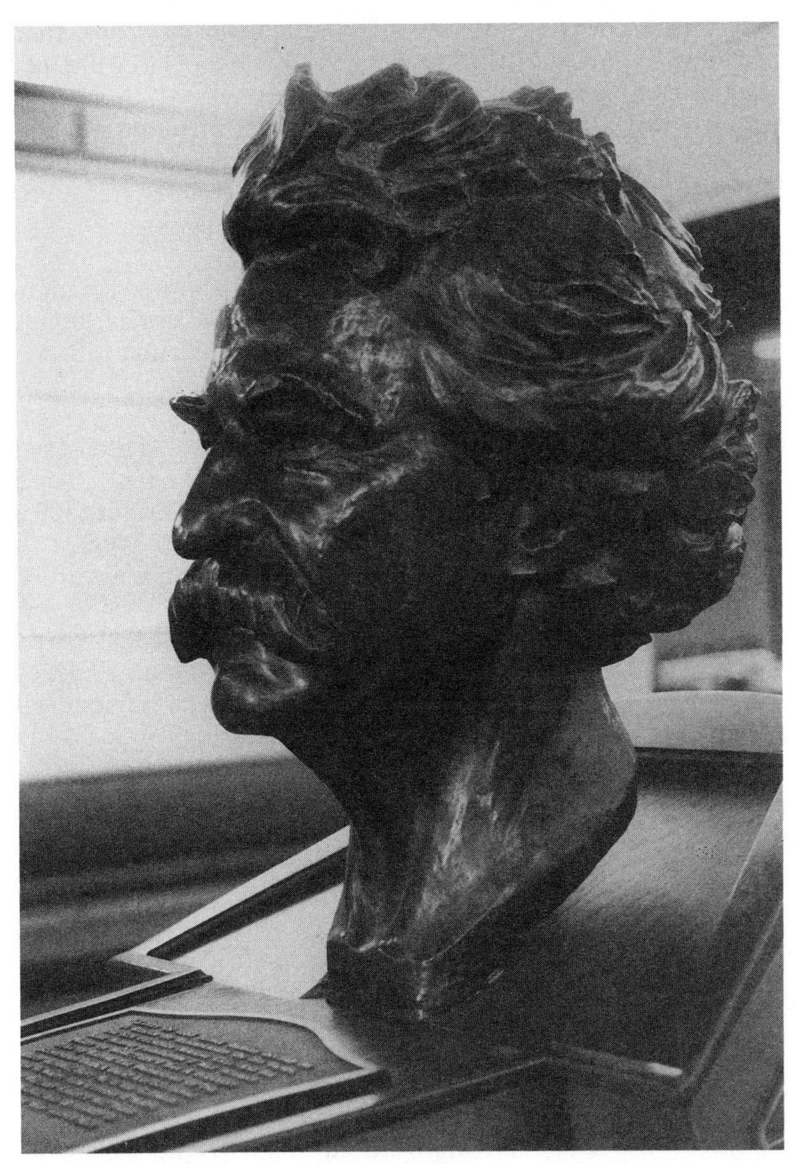

Mark Twain, the newspaper's most famous reporter, interviewed visitors in the lobby of the ***Sacramento Union****. The paper expired in 1994.*

publishers gave him the go-ahead.

Twain sailed March 7, 1866, arrived 11 days later, and sent back 25 features, at $20 each, to the newspaper during his four-month stay. An incorrigible punster, Twain offered this conjecture: "Sandwich Islanders always squat on their hams, and who but they may be the original ham sandwiches?"

But a real news beat would earn him a fat premium when he crawled out of a temporary sickbed and struggled to a Honolulu hospital to interview 11 people who had saved themselves in a tiny lifeboat from the clipper *Hornet* when it burned and sank. No other paper had the story.

Twain embarked for San Francisco July 19 and wended on to Sacramento, to find the last of his Sandwich Island stories running in *The Union*, to reader acclaim. Twain figured it was time to dicker for some extra pay for the *Hornet* scoop.

"How much do you think it ought to be, Mark?" Anthony asked.

Twain had received $20 each for the other features. The disaster story had run three front-page columns. "Oh," he said, "I'm a modest man; I don't want the whole Union office. Call it $100 a column."

Perhaps Twain was just opening negotiations, and was startled when the publishers chuckled and scribbled out a payment order. Twain presented it to the cashier, who stared at it and nearly fainted, or so Twain recalled. "He sent for the proprietors, and they only laughed, in their jolly fashion, and said it was a robbery, but 'no matter; pay it.' " Anthony and Morrill, in Twain's fond memory, were "the best men that ever owned a newspaper."

Acclaim for his Sandwich Island pieces inspired Twain to capitalize on it with a lecture tour, titling his talks, "Our Fellow Savages of the Sandwich Islands." After his first two engagements in San Francisco, he returned to Sacramento for the third. *The Bee* on Nov. 12, 1866, reported that he drew a full house in the Metropolitan Theater, and added: "Mark was in good trim. Instead of having been made a meal of by the cannibals of the islands, he comes back to us in the flesh to revivify those of us who have not been fortunate enough to take his reconstructing trip."

Fuller Paint Company, later famed as "the paint that covers the globe," originated in Sacramento, in the Rivett-Fuller Building on K Street near 2nd. Partners included John Rivett, William P. Fuller, A. A. Waldron and John Heather. From 1856 to 1869, the firm was known as Fuller and Heather; from 1869-79 as Whittier and Fuller. In the early 1870s, they leased the entire first floor of the Orleans Hotel on 2nd Street and made the building their headquarters. The upper floors continued for a time as the Orleans Hotel, which had lost its appeal to affluent travelers, who lodged at more fashionable hotels. For the hotel, an era had ended. For the paint company, an era had begun. Whittier's name was dropped from the firm, and Fuller Paints began to cover the globe with its fame.

Across the river in Yolo County opposite Sacramento's K Street, three Sacramento men in 1864-66 perfected the process that spawned a multi-million-dollar salmon canning industry — not here, but on the Columbia River, 500 miles north. Brothers William and George Hume, from Maine, who sold fresh and salted salmon here in the 1850s, were joined in 1864 by their friend Andrew Hapgood, a fisherman and tinsmith who had canned salmon in New England, and brought along some crude can-making equipment. The three partners lived in a cabin on the Yolo bank, their cannery on a nearby scow. They packed salmon in cans painted a fiery red so customers could identify them sans label. Because Sacramento's salmon run proved hit or miss, the entrepreneurs quested for a better place — and found it on the Columbia, inaugurating that river's immense industry.

At Raley's Landing, West Sacramento, a stone monument with bronze plaque commemorates the "First Pacific Coast Salmon Cannery" — which had to evacuate because hydraulicking slickens devastated our salmon runs.

National fame came overnight to Rancho del Paso in 1886 when Ben Ali won the Kentucky Derby. The horse was named after the middle names of its owner, James Ben Ali Haggin, whose middle names derived from his grandfather, a Turkish physician.

The Kentucky Derby was just the beginning of laurels. In the same year, Ben Ali and other Haggin horses distinguished themselves by winning 37 races. The next year was even better — 71 races. In 1888, Haggin's horses galloped to 67 first places, 60 seconds and 52 thirds, making him the winningest stable owner in America. There didn't seem anything Haggin could do for an encore — but his horse Salvator had something up his sleeve. He set the record for the mile by dashing the distance in only one minute and 35.5 seconds.

Originally the ranch was a 44,000-acre — nearly 70 square-mile — land grant to Eliab Grimes in 1844 from Mexican Governor Manuel Micheltorena. It was named after El Paso de los Americanos, the ford in the American near today's H Street Bridge. The grant's boundary lines ran along the north bank of the American for eight miles, then north eight miles along today's Northgate Boulevard, east along today's U Street, and south along today's Manzanita Avenue.

Hiram Grimes, inheriting the land from his father, sold it to Samuel Norris in 1849. Ten years later, Norris borrowed $65,000 from his attorney Lloyd Tevis, giving him a mortgage on the ranch. Less than a year later Tevis, who had started foreclosure, proposed that Norris settle up by deeding the ranch to Tevis's partner James B. Haggin for $5,000. By 1862, Haggin and Tevis were sole owners. By 1884, they were pasturing 20,000 sheep, cattle and horses and growing hay and hops.

Rancho del Paso made an ideal thoroughbred farm. It was blessed with rich bottomland and plenteous water for growing wild oats, wheat and alfalfa. The climate was excellent for horse-breeding, because eight months of warm weather fostered growth of the young horses, and they could be exercised all year, instead of languishing in snowbound months, as in the East.

But Haggin sneered at Derby purses as not enough to cover expenses, so he moved his horses to Kentucky's Latonia Track. For some reason he also quit Latonia in disgust, swearing this was his last race in Kentucky.

Haggin's racing success was phenomenal. In 1886, as the third largest winner in America, his winnings totalled $87,779. In 1887, his winnings aggregated over $101,000 from 369 races. The next year was his topmost, with winnings totaling over $125,000 — more than any stable in the nation.

What molded Haggin's champions? One force stemmed from 1873 when he hired veteran horse trainer John Mackey as rancho superintendent. Previously, Mackey ran a stable of trotters in Sacramento, winning laurels as trainer-driver. His skill and Haggin's wealthy exchequeur and rancho milieu, the wise boys said, combined to make Rancho del Paso racehorses famed across America, after Ben Ali dashed to vistory in the Kentucky go-round. Save some credit for Ben Ali — he was the only Haggin horse that ever won the Derby.

Rancho del Paso's shipping and sales center, with two dozen big red barns and other buildings, was dubbed The Arcade, for its avenue of overhanging trees. The Arcade became today's Arcade Boulevard, west of today's junction of Marconi Avenue and Auburn Boulevard.

Haggin's name also survives in sundry places, including Haggin Oaks Golf Course. Even his most famous horse, Ben Ali, is remembered in the name of a neighborhood. How many horses can say that?

Two commodious stables housed 50 horses each, and the ranch had 24 other barns, some with 64 stalls. Trainer John Mackey was a stickler for cleanliness, demanding that even the earth around the stables be swept bare as a floor.

The renowned Barbara Worth Stables, for many years until 1963, used some of Haggin's original buildings and racetrack. Barbara Worth, whose firm now occupies a site at Cal Expo, tells how she received her name: When her mother, whose married name was Worth, was pregnant with her, she happened to be reading a best-seller by Harold Bell Wright. Title of that novel: *The Winning of Barbara Worth*. There was magic in the name.

Haggin couldn't have dreamed that horseracing one day would become a jubilee on that parcel of Rancho del Paso that would become today's Cal Expo.

Today the vast lands of the Rancho are also occupied by such populated communities as Del Paso Manor, Arden Park, Town and Country, Country Club Centre, Hagginwood, Del Paso Heights and North Sacramento — and the sprawling McClellan Air Force Base.

The break-up began when the automobile age brought developers across the country to Sacramento to subdivide our suburbs. In 1910, two companies bought up the entire rancho, its nearly 70 square miles being two-thirds of the present area of the City of Sacramento.

The same year that Ben Ali won the Kentucky Derby, a great cathedral began to rise in Sacramento. It began as the dream of one man, Bishop Patrick Manogue, who migrated from Ireland to Chicago in 1842, then journeyed to California during the Gold Rush. Worldly riches financed his journey to spiritual riches. Desiring to become a priest, he prospected by day to raise money for his schooling, and studied on his own in the evenings. Successful as a gold-miner, he traveled to Paris to attend the San Sulpice seminary, where he was ordained. He came west again in 1861, served as pastor in Virginia City, Nevada, for 20 years and became a bishop in 1881. Five years later, he began construction of the cathedral in Sacramento.

Cathedral of the Blessed Sacrament, 11th and K Streets, was completed in 1889, with the top of its dome soaring to 170 feet and the top of the middle tower to 224 feet, nearly as high as the Capitol. An early observer described its neo-Italian Renaissance architecture: "The elegant proportions of the structure . . . its classic arches and arched ceiling set in frames of various frescoes, the harmony of due proportions in dimensions, the storied windows, rare paintings and the statuary it contains, endear both the structure and its venerable building to Sacramento citizens, irrespective of creed or class."

Stained glass windows in sanctuary and transept areas are 15th-century works from Austria. The cathedral contains a reproduction of Raphael's "Sistine Madonna," donated by Mrs. Leland Stanford. The King of Saxony, owner of the original, instructed the court painter to make two reproductions for her. The other hangs at Stanford University.

The four bells, among the finest ever brought to the West, weigh over six tons. But Bishop Manogue would never hear them peal — they arrived in 1895 as he lay dying, and pealed for the first time to announce his death.

It was the year that Sacramentans were blown out of their beds by a cannonade announcing that electric power had arrived from Folsom, ready to light up the whole town.

The story of lighting the streets began 40 years earlier, with the advent of the gas-light era in 1855. By the following year, the gas-works had 113 customers, mainly business owners. Seven years later, with 600 customers, the city contracted for 45 street lamps — and, perhaps for economy reasons, mandated that they were to be lighted only during Legislative sessions. When the Legislature adjourned, Sacramento plunged back into primeval darkness.

Electric street lights arrived in 1885 when Electric Light Company installed four arc lights — at 15th and H, 15th and O, 21st and O, and 21st and J Streets — on 150-foot poles. Each dazzling arc light was 3,000 candlepower, or 1,600 watts — four times the wattage of modern street lights. The lights were high enough to illuminate backyards and alleys as well as streets. To service them, workers climbed steps on the pole to a crow's nest 100 feet aloft. They could lower the lamps to the crow's nest to change the carbon rods. After about a decade, incandescent lamps began to glimmer in city streets.

Some Sacramento industries ran on electricity generated by steam, Southern Pacific shops being the largest. H. Fisher and Company used its own electric plant to manufacture up to 4,000 pounds of candy daily for Sacramento's myriads of sweet tooths. The drawback of steam-generated electricity was the high cost of coal, $5 to $8 per ton.

A solution was proposed in *The Union* as early as 1881 when a visitor, seeing a dam built by Natoma Water and Mining Company

For whom the bells tolled: They tolled for the first time when Bishop Manogue died. His dream became Cathedral of the Blessed Sacrament.

on the American near Folsom, wrote that dynamo-electric machines worked by turbines could produce all the power California would ever need. Just such a project was outlined a few years later by Horatio G. Livermore of Folsom.

The power came to Sacramento on July 13, 1895. On the banks of China Slough across from the newly-built powerhouse substation at Sixth and H Streets — still standing — a detachment of soldiers from Battery B awaited the signal in the dark hours before dawn. They got it, firing endless thunderclaps from two field guns, rousing Sacramento to a new epoch, waking everyone to the reality that the new Folsom Powerhouse was zapping 11,000 volts into Sacramento. Reported the *San Francisco Chronicle:* "It was 4 a.m. in Sacramento when a 100-gun salute shattered the quiet. People not planning on getting up early that morning never forgot it . . . . It was when electric power arrived in Sacramento over 22 miles of line from the new Folsom Powerhouse."

At that time, it was the longest distance electricity had ever been transmitted.

The Folsom Powerhouse, acclaimed as "the greatest operative electrical plant on the American continent," began as the brainchild of Horatio Gates Livermore, who in 1850 came from Maine to California.

To celebrate in proper style, Sacramentans staged a "Grand Electric Carnival" in early September, combining it with State Fair and Admission Day festivities. In the Plaza, a lighted mast represented a maypole. Lighted arches and electric horseshoes spanned the streets. Buildings were festooned in colored lights. Thirty thousand people swarmed Sacramento for the Sunday and Monday gala, September 8-9. Native Sons of the Golden West found housing for outlanders in hotels and private room at $1 per person, with meals for 15 cents and up. Some 2,000 rooms were occupied on Sunday night.

The Sacramento Bee boasted that no other city in California had ever matched Sacramento's enthusiasm for decorating the town: "Hundreds and hundreds of electric lamps were blazing brilliantly." Both sides of J and K Streets were lined with paper lanterns for three miles. Businesses were draped with bunting shaped in stars, crosses and diamonds. Somebody compared the lights on Capitol Park's trees to the fruit "like the ones in the gardens in the fairy tales."

The Capitol dome and facade gleamed with electric lights. Twelve arc lights, each of 2,000 candlepower, dazzled spectators 50 miles away. Across the west entrance, light bulbs blazoned the names of Franklin, Morse and Edison — Franklin, who captured electricity from the clouds; Morse, who taught it to talk on a wire; and Edison, who gave it eyes and ears.

Along streets many-splendored with lights, clanging electric streetcars — drawing current from overhead trolleys — pulled dazzling floats. Sixteen brass bands and 12 floats from the SP railroad shops joined the parade. On the Carnival Committee's float, an 8x10 American Flag was composed of colored lights. Two Bear flags flew over a log fort, while a grizzly invaded the fort's walled enclosure.

The 12 floats from the railroad shops won universal raves. Said *The Union*: "Everyone was utterly amazed by the combination of original design, ingenious mechanism, and dazzling splendor." One, "Hive of Industry," represented a huge beehive made of rope, with bees in the form of electric bulbs. Petite Jessie Barton, as the queen bee, sat under a canopy entwined with roses, wielding a lighted scepter, while behind her a bear was battling a swarm of bees. *The San Francisco Examiner*: "Description gets lost in admiration of the witching delights of this night's brilliant display. The temptation is to pile superlatives as high as . . . the dome of the Capitol."

The streetcars were the most modern models of our original Light Rail: First came horse-drawn cars on dirt roads, in 1861, then horse-drawn streetcars on rails, in 1880, and battery-operated streetcars, in 1889. At times a battery would go dead — with the car at the end of the line, of course — and a horse would have to haul the car back to the barn. In 1890, the first overhead wires were strung and the cars became trolleys. Undependable electricity crackled from two or more local steam-generating plants of Sacramento Electric Power and Light Company. Came 1895: The new Folsom Powerhouse, in electrifying Sacramento, rejuvenated the streetcars.

Sacramento had eight streetcar lines in 1894, all fanning out from the Southern Pacific Depot — the G, H, J, M, P, and 3rd, 10th, and 21st Streets lines.

Sacramento followed the cue of cities across the nation, whose streetcar companies were constructing amusement parks to promote patronage on weekends. In 1889, Central Street Railway began to develop Oak Park as an amusement mecca named Joyland, with pavilion, dance platform and picnic areas. Sacramento Electric Power and Light took over in 1892, adding a merry-go-round, baseball diamond, zoo, and velodrome for bike races. Ingersoll Amusement Company in 1913 leased the property, investing hundreds of thousands of dollars in new rides, including a towering Giant Racer, said to be the biggest roller coaster west of New York's Coney Island.

As summer began in 1920, controlled burning of weeds got out of control, razing much of Joyland, with a good part of the Giant Racer. Joyland's owners made repairs and introduced new concessions, but failed to reverse the decline. Customers were staying away in droves. In 1927 after the owners called it quits, V. S. McClatchy bought it and donated it to the city as a public park.

Alas for those fond of streetcars, in 1947 owing to postwar changes in transportation patterns — expansion of the suburbs and proliferating motorcars — the streetcars rolled into history. Much of this information comes from Bob Blymyer, a streetcar aficionado. Where does he work? Sacramento Regional Transit District, of course.

David Lubin, the remarkable Sacramento merchant who founded Weinstock-Lubin department stores, also became a renowned economic philosopher — and incredibly established an agency of the United Nations, 40 years before the UN's birth! Sacramento historian Willard Thompson has detailed the story in the public prints.

Soon after David's birth in Poland in 1849, the Lubin family fled Czarist tyranny. David grew up in New York's lower East Side, then knocked about, working as a craftsman, cowboy, gold prospector and traveling salesman. A steamer in 1874 brought him to Sacramento, where he rented 120 square feet at the southeast corner of 4th and K Streets — where Macy's stands today — and opened a store, selling overalls, red flannel shirts and sundries, all at fixed cash prices, no bargaining allowed, contrary to prevailing customs. It was a big hit.

Three years later, with younger brother Harris Weinstock as partner, he opened the "Mechanic's Store" — six times bigger than the first, adding many new lines. By 1891, with 300 employees, Weinstock Lubin & Company was "The largest General Retail Establishment on the Coast." It occupied a new building and published a 226-page mail order catalog posted to 250,000 readers in the West.

After a trip to the Holy Land in 1884 with his mother, David brought his fascination with relics of the past, time capsules in effect, back to Sacramento, where he induced Margaret Crocker to donate her art gallery to the city as a memorial to her late husband, Judge E. B. Crocker. He then outlined a proposal that blossomed into the State Indian Museum.

This man of many talents then wrote and published a novel, *Let There Be Light*, that helped him sort out his economic philosophy — which went into a draft of a proposal for an international chamber of agriculture. High freight rates discriminated against farmers. Tariffs that protected manufacturers against low-priced imports dried up foreign markets for American produce.

In Italy, he called on King Victor Emanuel III, age 35, who thereupon wrote to his Council of Ministers on Jan. 24, 1905: "Mr. David Lubin explained to me with that warmth which comes from sincere conviction, an idea which seemed to me practical and valuable." The King called an international meeting to organize a world-scope organization for all farming components. He invited other heads of state to join. To ensure a good turnout, Lubin traveled Europe, persuading government figures to attend. Emissaries from 41 nations thronged into Rome in May 1905 to draft plans for the International Institute of Agriculture.

Lubin spent his last 15 years in Rome, where the UN's immense Food and Agriculture Organization, founded on his idea, today serves worldwide interests. A street and library in Rome bear his name. In Sacramento, a school named after him stands at 37th and M Streets. On the K Street Mall, two blocks east of where he first sold overalls in 1874, stands the headquarters of the Weinstock's department store chain.

Bicycles once thronged the streets of Sacramento — and the 1893 bike race season, perfervidly greeted by local fans, opened with the second annual Stockton-to-Sacramento relay race. Each team rode a 104-mile round trip starting from Stockton and Sacramento. The Stockton Wheelmen won in six hours and eight and a half minutes. The Sacramento team, blockaded by a cattle drive, took 12 minutes longer.

With 2,000 bikes in Sacramento, *The Sacramento Union* in 1895 began a column devoted to bicycle topics, such as the latest innovations: A device called a "dog gun" — a rubber nozzle filled with ammonia; and a homemade bike lamp; for the ladies a description of a riding skirt and knickerbockers.

Capital City Wheelmen reckoned they had a good idea when they voted on March 30, 1896, to construct a cinder path to Folsom. First an experimental path was scraped out from 31st and J Streets to the levee near Brighton Junction, present site of the filtration plant. On April 12, with the opening of the stretch to Brighton, 500 wheelmen sprinted along the course. After completion of the next section to Alder Creek, the club asked Folsom citizens to finish the route to Folsom. Folsom merchants gave generously to the fund. Although county supervisors banned vehicles other than bikes on the path, fining violators $5 or five days in jail, wagons ruined the stretch from Brighton to Perkins. A new link was built and covered with crushed granite. Yet by the end of November, wagons had reduced it to a mass of ruts. At any rate, the bike path proved to be a forerunner of the latter-day path that follows the American from Discovery Park to Folsom Lake.

Smoke billows from the burning Sacramento lake, in this 1906 photo. Southern Pacific Co. filled it in later that year. Photo courtesy California State Library.

The lake that burned: Southern Pacific Railroad in 1906 filled in a lake, ending a migraine of many years duration. From the 1870s onward, Sutter Lake a.k.a. China Slough had been the source of offensive aromas. Chinese laundry houses on I Street along the south shore emptied wastewater and other refuse into it, while railroad shops on the north shore contributed generous heaps of oily debris. The lake became so saturated with oily stuff that a time or two it caught fire and burned. SP's filling it in ended the paradox of a combustible lake.

For many years, the Sacramento area called the West End earned dubious renown as the largest Skid Row in the West. One can only conjecture on how Sacramento won the distinction: During the Gold Rush era, many failed prospectors drifted back to Sacramento, many of them ashamed to return to their faraway homes in the East to confess defeat. Some succeeded in the numerous businesses that mushroomed in boomtown Sacramento. But many others poured whiskey down their throats to deaden the pain of failure — and the proliferation of grog shops Mark Twain observed in 1866 may have been an early stage of the West's biggest Skid Row. But consider other contributors: Sacramento being the hub of an agricultural empire, harvest workers flocked here for jobs, and for places to flop in the off seasons, and wine to keep them warm, and it became a magnet for other down-and-outers.

Whatever, sometimes things get worse before they get better. Such seems to have been the case with the West End. The onetime dominion of dismal bars, grog shops and flophouses has been rehabilitated into one of posh apartments and commercial buildings, and one large section has been cleaned up and restored and set aside as the historic enclave called Old Sacramento — of which more later.

Chapter 41

China's George Washington Slept Here

Dr. Sun Yat-sen visited Sacramento during the first decade of the century as a rebel with a $500,000 price on his head. To China's Manchu Dynasty, he was the most dangerous man in the world — for his occupation was revolution and his goal was no less than to overthrow the Dynasty. He came to Sacramento on world tours to raise funds from local Chinese people to finance his revolution.

From Sacramento, he traveled under cover of darkness to Delta towns and then to Marysville, which had one of the largest Chinatowns in the nation. In the Delta, he was sheltered by Chong Chan, father of Lincoln Chan of Courtland, in a cabin on his Courtland ranch for a week or more in 1910. Lincoln Chan said he tore down the old cabin a few years ago, and now wishes he had preserved it for its historic significance.

Sun, born in 1866 in a mud hut, son of a coolie, studied medicine from 1886 to 1892, graduating from Hong Kong College of Medicine with high honors. After setting up clinics in Macao and Canton, he gave up medicine to devote himself to revolution — convinced that major surgery was needed to cure China of the Manchu cancer.

Traveling the globe, he stopped at almost every little Chinese colony, while Manchu spies and assassins stalked him. In London in 1896, he became the victim in a sensational kidnapping case. For many days, Manchu agents held him prisoner in the Imperial Chinese Legation, planning to ship him to China for execution —by boiling in oil. No more Mr. Nice Guy. Newspapers got wind of his captivity and raised a ruckus that triggered his release. The publicity helped fan his revolution.

The San Francisco Examiner noted his coming on April 6, 1904: "His arrival in this city yesterday caused a flurry of excitement in the local Chinese quarter and many were the harsh denunciations uttered by members of the merchant class." Seven years later, he returned to San Francisco and founded a newspaper, *Young China*, that is still being published in the city's Chinatown.

China endured 10 unsuccessful revolutions before the 11th and final uprising on Oct. 10, 1911, boiled across China like a typhoon and toppled the Manchus, ending 4,000 years of dynastical rule and establishing the first democratic republic — thanks in part to Sacramento area contributions. Sun became China's first president Jan. 1, 1912.

Sacramento attorney Geoff Wong said his great-grandfather, Wong Chong, who owned a restaurant in Sacramento, renamed it the New Chinese Republic Restaurant to honor Dr. Sun's revolution. The restaurant site is now occupied by Vagabond Inn, a motel at 909 3rd St.

Dr. Sun blueprinted his republic on the best of his Chinese cultural heritage and the best of western ideas, notably Lincoln's classic theorem: "Government of the people, by the people, and for the people." He is revered as the George Washington of China because like America's Washington he led his people through revolution to victory, then was inaugurated first president of a new government structured on democratic foundations.

Strangest of all local stories about Dr. Sun tells how his enemies won a victory over his air force — in the Delta. Jack C. Chew of Sacramento says his father, Courtland rancher Chauncey Chew, c. 1920 helped to buy about 10 World War I surplus airplanes. Using Chauncey Chew's alfalfa field as a landing ground, Chinese pilots practiced maneuvers across Delta skies. Came the day the aircraft were crated for shipment to China, and stored in a warehouse at Hood. But a fire destroyed the building and contents. "Sabotage," says Lincoln Chan. Remembers Jack Chew: "That was the first time I ever saw my father cry." Remnants of the warehouse pilings are still visible at water's edge.

Dr. Sun died in 1925 of cancer, after many years of trying to unify vast, seething China.

Dr. Sun Yat-sen, who came to Sacramento in the flesh in the early 1900s, remains in bronze in Sacramento's Chinese Center.

To perpetuate his memory, Sacramento area Chinese people in 1968 organized the Sun Yat-sen Memorial Association. Chinese communities across America contributed funds to pay for the $227,000 Memorial Hall, dedicated in 1971. It stands in the Chinatown Mall, bounded by I and J and 3rd and 5th Streets.

Dr. Sun's seven-foot bronze statue, cast in Taiwan, stands in front of the hall. The hall is two stories high, but has no second story, being entirely open inside, save for the roof. It operates as a free museum and library containing documents of the revolution and books on Chinese history and culture, including Dr. Sun's works. A huge photo of Dr. Sun dominates the east wall. Other walls are hung with Chinese brush paintings. One exhibit shows photos of each of 72 men beheaded in abortive uprisings against the Manchus. Another photo portrays a beautiful Chinese woman, also executed as a rebel. Showcases display carved jade and ivory, Ming Dynasty vases, pottery horses, pottery human figures, and bronze vessels from as far back as the Shang Dynasty of 1800 B.C.

The Mall also has restaurants, a store, and offices of Chinese associations, all occupying buildings of Chinese-style architecture. On I Street, the Confucius Church interior is adorned with two enormous murals offering glimpses of the Chinese presence in California. One shows early Chinese toiling on the railroads and mining gold, while the other depicts Chinese working today as doctors, attorneys, scientists and teachers.

Photo of the amazing Dr. Sun Yat-sen dominates interior of the memorial hall named after him in Sacramento's Chinese Center.

Chapter 42

The Delta: Our Islands In the Sun

Much of this material appeared in the author's article, "Tales From the Delta," ***Sacramento*** *magazine November 1985.*

Seven Delta islands lie within Sacramento County — Sutter, Grand, Tyler, Andrus, Brannan, Twitchell and Sherman, plus a few islets near Sherman.

In early times, the Delta was a primordial marshland where the Sacramento and San Joaquin Rivers mixed in a labyrinth of channels before gliding west to San Francisco Bay — a labyrinth that bedeviled Captain John Sutter for eight days until at last he found the mouth of the Sacramento, gateway to his future empire.

Zillions of ducks and geese, refugees from the tyranny of Jack Frost, wintered here. High tides washed and rinsed half of the Delta. High tides combined with high winds and flood-stage rivers whelmed this entire alluvial basin. Bulrushes known as tules grew and rotted for untold millennia, forming ever deeper beds of peat. This fertile soil was first tilled by failed gold prospectors, who found it as lucrative as a gold mine — and found boomtown Sacramento a ravenous market for produce. Hiring Indians and Chinese, they raised the first levees in 1850 on Grand Island. The entrepreneurs were Armstead Runyon, Reuben Kercheval and James Collins. Sacramento advertising and PR mogul Jean Runyon said Armstead Runyon was the great-grandfather of her late husband. James Collins was the grandfather of Ellis Collins of Sacramento, mentioned later in this chapter.

The fertile ground by 1851 was bursting with potatoes up to 33 inches around and cabbages hefting up to 53 pounds.

Earth to build early levees was first hauled in baskets, then in wheelbarrows, later by "Fresno scrapers" — scoop shovels dragged by mules. The story of Delta levees is a litany of breaks, calamitous floods, and epic struggles to build ever stronger ramparts against the fury of Old Man River.

Meanwhile, the Gold Rush accelerated river traffic. By 1850, 28 steamers cruised Delta channels, linking San Francisco with Sacramento, portal to the mines. Pilots were forever trying to set new records, and sometimes overtaxed boilers just couldn't take it any more. Two disasters in the Delta dimmed the glory of the "floating palaces," and both occurred near Rio Vista. They are recounted in the earlier chapter on steamboats.

No stranger to disaster, Rio Vista (River View) was founded on the Sacramento near Cache Slough. In 1862, residents got a view of more river than they really wanted, as floodwaters swept away the whole town. The new town rose farther south, where the Montezuma Hills lift from the river. It didn't take a genius to figure that high ground is the place to be when the river goes berserk.

The same year Rio Vista washed away, Freeport was founded on the river by Sacramento Valley Railroad people — steaming at Sacramento's new port tax on all goods crossing its wharf. They set up a tax-free port — Freeport — and laid nine miles of track, scheming to bypass Sacramento. But giant Central Pacific bought out the little guys, to get rid of a nuisance.

The first successful dredges in the Delta were the "floating steam shovels" designed by Joel Parker Whitney on Roberts Island in the 1870s. A decade later, steel jaws of ungainly behemoths called clamshell dredges went to work, taking giant bites out of river muck, building levees faster and cheaper. Today the Delta's 1,100 miles of levees bulwark 55 farm islands, or tracts.

Reclamation was the name of the Delta game, and Ed Salisbury of Grand Island, who died in 1986, summed it up. He was the great-grandson of John Sharp, who in 1850 settled in Walnut Grove. Remarked Salisbury: "The Delta was brought from 'inaccessible swamps' to a beautiful reclaimed area, one of the most productive farm areas in the world, and it was all done by private enterprise — no government support whatsoever. In fact, just the opposite, really." He laughed, and said he didn't really mean *that*, but added: "I would call it apathy, more than anything else. But they collected taxes, of course, as soon as there was something taxable."

A dozen men perched on 4.5-cubic-yard bucket of dredge ***Yolo*** *circa 1910. Photo courtesy Dutra Museum of Dredging, Rio Vista.*

Busy dredges built the modern levees. You might call Edward A. Dutra "king of the dredgermen," for he worked at it for half a century, and even designed and built four leviathans — *Alameda, Sacramento, Frances* and *Liberty* — all busy dredging today. When Ed retired, son Bill took the helm, and Ed and his wife Linda opened an astonishing museum, furnishing their entire two-story Rio Vista home with memorabilia. This free dredging museum is open to the public by appointment. Call (209) 334-0284.

Dutra even wrote a big book, *The Tule Breakers: The Story of the California Dredge,* that tells how the colossal dredges evolved — right here in the Delta.

Moving dirt is the name of another game born in the Delta. By chance the world's largest manufacturer of earthmoving equipment grew from a Delta taproot. West of Stockton in 1904, tractor-builder Benjamin Holt tested his invention: a tractor with tracks, not wheels. "Crawls over mud like a caterpillar," he chortled — and Caterpillar Tractor Company was born. Grim footnote: Holt's Caterpillar in 1916 spawned the British army tank, first tank ever used in battle.

Another Delta-bred enterprise: The Bank of Alex Brown. Brown came to Walnut Grove in 1879 at age 30 and plunged into sundry businesses. In 1905, he and son John opened the bank that today has 14 branches. Brown also is credited as the first to plant asparagus here — a momentous event, as one day the Delta would supply 90 percent of world production, and proud little Isleton's claim to fame would be: "Asparagus Capital of the World."

The biggest produce terminal in the West once stood west of Lodi at Terminous, named by somebody who flunked spelling. Up to 10,000 workers processed and loaded produce into rail cars for shipment across the nation. The decline began with the advent of refrigerated trucks hauling crops to market from many smaller packing sheds. Big warehouses now used by Tower Park Marina are all that fires left of buildings that once stretched half a mile along the river.

Since Gold Rush days, Chinese people have toiled in the Delta, and the intriguing town of Locke was once the largest rural Chinatown in America. Tin Sin Chan, its founder, raised the first building in 1912, leasing land from George Locke — with a handshake the only contract. When a 1915 fire leveled Walnut Grove's Chinatown, entrepreneur Lee Bing led the exodus of burned-out residents to nearby Locke. Dozens of houses and businesses arose, including whorehouses owned and staffed by whites, who practiced no racial discrimination. On the bench in front of Dai Loy, biggest of five gambling houses, a "snoozing" lookout could press a buzzer, warning that cops or robbers were on the horizon. Cops padlocked it in 1951. Today, as a museum, it's open weekends.

The unofficial mayor of Locke since 1954 is Ping Lee, operator of the Big Store in Walnut Grove. He said the Dai Loy gambling house was owned by his father, the aforementioned Lee Bing, a remarkable man who, without formal schooling, operated many other enterprises and died c. 1970 at age 97.

Locke in its heyday 50 years ago teemed with as many as 1,500 residents. Today the population has dwindled to less than 50, half of them non-Chinese. Old and tired wooden buildings give Locke the air of a frontier town haunted by the ghosts of yesteryear.

Grand Island's River Mansion, the most extravagant house in the Delta, conjures images of ante-bellum mansions in the Deep South. Back in the 1850s, Henry and Sophia Meyers arrived from Germany to enter the Delta picture. Meyers ignored the Gold Rush, and set about developing lucrative orchards on 143 acres of Grand Island, fronting on Steamboat Slough. In the natural course of events their son Louis took over the operation of the fruit ranches. Half a century ago he began building his future home which would become the most palatial home in the Delta. The finished four-story house with 58 rooms and 28,000 square feet — more than half an acre — cost nearly half a million, an appalling sum at the time. Louis and wife entertained lavishly in their manse like your regular lord and lady.

One flood-besieged winter as Louis toiled in the struggle to save levees, he caught pneumonia and died. In time the grieving family sold the property. As the years passed, the property passed through several owners, and for a time it became a restaurant, and then a private home again. Today the renovated mansion is open to the public for Sunday brunches from 10:30 a.m. to 3 p.m. Call for reservations: 916-775-1705.

From the grand staircase, the visitor can delight in the restored loveliness of the grand entry hall and the enormous ballroom, and be amazed that the mansion also has its own theater and bowling alley.

Also on Grand Island, the flamingo-hued Ryde Hotel, at Ryde, has been restored to its 1920s Prohibition-era ambiance, with basement speakeasy and casino with slot machines. During a political rally there in 1928, Herbert Hoover announced his candidacy for president.

The Delta today is America's No. 1 pear-growing area, mainly because pears thrive in wet soils that tend to kill off other fruit trees. Lincoln Chan of Courtland, asked if he is still "Pear King of California," smiled and replied: "So they say." Asked how he received his first name, he said: "I was born on Lincoln's birthday."

Another man who still has his hand in Delta pears, so to speak, is white-thatched Ellis Collins, though he has lived in Sacramento many years. Collins vividly recalls the years on Grand Island when he helped his parents grow pears. "We had a terrible wind one year — 1921 — and lost all our pears. You could see nothing on the ground but a carpet of green pears."

After that disaster, to help out the family exchequer, he drove a school bus around Sutter Island for two years, 1923 to 1925, for Courtland Joint Union School District. "To get to and from my driving job," he said, "I used to row across Steamboat Slough night and morning." Then he entered banking. In a sense, he was still a "grower" — making money grow in interest accounts. And greenbacks were the same color as growing things.

Collins retired after more than 42 years with Bank of America, mostly in Sacramento. At the time of the interview in July 1985 he was 82 and had been retired 18 years. But never will he forget the halcyon days of his youth on Grand Island. "The Delta was a great place to live when I was a young guy. Gee, that was a paradise I grew up in — not just for me, but for everybody that lived there." How so? "Nobody killed anybody. Nobody robbed anybody. No juvenile delinquency. We didn't realize how wonderful it was at the time."

Today the Delta cornucopia faces peril because levees are in woeful shape. Built mostly of peat — which floats — some are so buoyant they rise and fall several inches with the tide. "It's getting worse, because it's related to the subsidence of the interiors of the islands," says Delta specialist Ray Williams, R.E., Army Corps of Engineers, Sacramento. "The lower the inside gets, the less stable the levees are."

And peat burns. Countless fires over the years -- mostly set to burn away tules to clear land for farming — burned down to the water table, sending rich soil up in smoke. And when peat soil dries out during cultivation, winds blow away up to half an inch a year, creating noxious peat dust storms in Delta towns. So the land surface keeps sinking. Up to 90 percent of Delta farms lie below sea level, with some at least 20 feet below, Williams says.

The late Erle Stanley Gardner, creator of the Perry Mason mysteries, wrote three nonfiction books about the Delta, because he was so fond of it. Even the peat dust storms didn't vex him, because he claimed they created "some of the most beautiful sunsets in the world." To Erle Stanley Gardner, even peat dust clouds had golden linings.

Perhaps the most surprising cause of levee breaks that bring on disasters costing into multiple millions is — beaver tunneling. Item: Pesky beavers were blamed for the June 21, 1972, Andrus-Brannan Islands flood that bashed the Spindrift Marina, sending boats and all through the breach into orchards, flooding Isleton four miles north and soaking growers and townspeople with $28.5 million in damages, according to Ray Williams. Item: Rascally beavers were indicted for the Sept. 26, 1980, levee rupture on Lower Jones Tract that flooded 12 homes and 5,500 acres. As those floodwaters began seeping through the railroad embankment dividing Lower Jones from Upper Jones, President Jimmy Carter declared it a disaster area. Some 250 floodfighters slung sandbags, while rail cars

Delta waterways have been channels since our earliest history for ships voyaging to and from Sacramento including, in 1987, the full-size replica of Sir Francis Drake's ***Golden Hinde****.* Myriads of

dumped 1,400 loads of rock. In vain. Suddenly at 2:35 a.m. October 23 as a train rumbled on top, the embankment caved in, engulfing two engines and a flat car, but the train crew scrambled to safety. Floodwaters submerged 6,000 acres. Property losses and floodfighting costs on both tracts surpassed $12 million.

A levee break from beaver-tunneling means business for the dredges, notes Linda Dutra, adding with a smile: "Sometimes we get accused of feeding the beavers."

Other Delta islands flooded in recent years include Webb Tract, Holland Tract, Dead Horse, Liberty Island, Boulding Island, Staten Island and Tyler Island.

In some tracts, all was lost when growers had to abandon a too-costly struggle. Lower Sherman Island, flooded since 1925, is a state wildlife area. Big Break is the only name for a large farm area south of Jersey Island, inundated since c. 1926. Franks Tract, submerged since 1938, today is a state recreation area — a lake for boaters.

Growers on Mildred Island, flooded since 1983, are seeking

birds took to the air when the ship fired its cannon. No doubt many ducks were in this welcoming party — a fitting tribute to a famous Drake.

federal aid to pump it dry.

Do those underwater tracts offer a prelude to the future? Will the whole Delta someday revert to aboriginal swamps? Or can the future be foretold on the islands where the fight goes on, where there is no surrender?

Meanwhile the Delta remains a world of its own for recreationists — houseboaters, water-skiers and fishermen. Anglers still catch sturgeon in these waters, but not as big as a century ago when they weighed half a ton or more, and had to be dragged out of the water by horses.

The Delta being a waterway wonderland, it's no surprise — but intriguing — to learn that many denizens receive their mail delivered by a letter carrier on a mail-boat. From Herman & Helen's Marina on Little Connection Slough, the carrier casts off in an outboard on a 100-mile roundabout of Delta islands, plunking letters into about 40 water-edge boxes. Add "high tides" to the hindrances that shall not stay this courier from the swift completion of his appointed roundabout.

The Prince of Whales: Humphrey, the crazy mixed-up whale, swam around the Delta for 25 days in 1985, a saga that drew the eyes of the world to this everglades of the West, carried to global audiences via newspapers, magazines and TV. Finally Humphrey got his bearings — if he had lost them — and headed back to sea, having ignored recordings of whale-talk and boats that had been trying to guide him back to salt water. He left without ever explaining what had prompted him to embark on his headline-making exploration of Delta mazes.

Chapter 43
Press Conferences in Winoland

From the author's article in ***The Sacramento Union*** *on April 6, 1958, originally headed: "West End Drifters Stewing Over End Of Their Bailiwick."*

His appearance is one of the many variations on the West End's derelict theme. His clothing is bedraggled and forlorn, his face livid and seamed, his eyes bulging and bloodshot. "I used to own a home out in North Sacramento," he boasted in his rasping voice, and bemoaned the fate which had brought about his descent from that relatively idyllic existence to his present melancholy estate.

He is one of myriads of forgotten men who prowl, stagger, stumble, or limp through the West End, questing for a bottle, a bowl of soup on occasion, and a place to flop when the weather is wet.

And sometimes a job.

"I think it would be a wonderful thing if they clean out this bughouse down here," he said.

He alluded to Sacramento Redevelopment Agency's program for razing 62 blocks of slums in the West End, and replacing them with beautiful new buildings.

"And the sooner they do it, the better," he rasped.

Where the tired old buildings now stand, lush garden apartments will rise, lavish shopping centers will go up, and high apartments will soar. Their magic casements will look out on a wonderland of gardens, sunken courts, futuristic children's playgrounds, and enchanting swimming pools.

"I don't care if I die tomorrow, as long as they clean this bughouse up," he said.

Skid Row will give way to Shangri-La.

"What kind of a statement are you making?" demanded another West Ender, an old-timer with a short white beard fringing his face. He said it with an injured air. It was hard to tell whether he was joking or serious.

"I mean it," the first man said. "From the bottom of my heart. Take this fellow," he said, indicating a pint-size man of crestfallen appearance who, previously unnoticed, was taking in the conversation. "Take this fellow. I know him well. He'd work in a minute if he could get it. We're out of work and down and out. We're down in the dumps and we're lucky to get a bowl of beans."

Occasionally he gestured animatedly. A small crowd was beginning to gather. "Something's got to be done," he insisted, "before it gets any worse."

Another bystander, carrying what appeared to be half a dozen loaves of bread wrapped in newspaper, put in: "You haven't seen anything yet."

"A patrol wagon comes by," the first man said, ignoring the heckler. "They pick us up and throw us in that rotten old drunk tank, and then throw us out — and no work. I don't care if they hang me. I just hope somebody does a job here."

His brow creased as his gaze wandered down the street of dreary bars, fly-specked restaurants, and second-hand stores and pawn shops. "I hope they take a scoop shovel and level 'er down! At least it'll get rid of the lice."

"I'd like to say this," said another man in the crowd, when he noticed that notes were being made of the conversation: "Sacramento is the capital of the state — and has the dirtiest slums in the state!"

"Oh, now, now, now. Don't say that," gently admonished another man, wagging a forefinger at the speaker.

He was tall and wore a navy blue suit that was sadly deteriorated. His face was swollen and red. His hand trembled as he puffed on a cigarette butt.

"You take all these small businesses here," said the man in blue, with a sweep of his arm. "You take all these tramps off the street, and what's going to happen to these small businesses? They'll go out," he said, answering his own question. "There's a lot of money comes through this town through these tramps. I can't talk intelligently," he apologized in an aside, the hand that held the butt trembling, "because I've been on a drunk."

But his viewpoint is reiterated by other West End people.

"They shouldn't make here big stores," commented a gray-haired widow who operates a second-hand store at 1013 Second Street. "They'll gonna kill the town because nobody's gonna come here to shop. They's plenty shopping centers all over. So your wife will come here to shop? I wouldn't come here to shop. Absolutely, why I should come here? At the end of Sacramento? I could shop anywhere. I wouldn't come here.

"Of course, maybe I won't live to see that. God knows I'm not going to be here much longer. But the younger generation, they raising families. Because I don't care what nobody says, they will take away the people, the working class. Where will they go? How they gonna make a living? Why don't they think about it?

"It's just a wild idea," she said, shaking her gray head. "I don't know why they wanna do that."

Willie Nicholas, 1117-A Third St., a warehouse longshoreman, took the affirmative as he sat in a chair leaning against a wall. "Sure, I'd be glad for 'em to tear 'em down and put up new ones," he said.

When a friend of his standing nearby was queried on the subject, and replied a noncommittal "I don't know much about that," Willie retorted:

"You mean to say you wouldn't want to live in a nice place and eat good food and live decent?" he exclaimed, letting his chair come down hard. "You mean you want to keep living in these old places?

"These old buildings will fall down on you! Roaches and everything. You take any of these buildings, they begin to get roaches in them when they start getting old. A decent living — that's the way you should look at it. That's what we should have."

His friend hadn't replied to Willie's oration.

"Each and every man," Willie said, "should look for good living conditions."

He struck a match, lit a cigarette, leaned back in his chair, and continued for a short time longer in that vein.

In the historic Western Hotel at 215 K Street, built more than 100 years ago and onetime Sacramento's leading hostelry, an old, unshaven man leaned on the bar.

"What are they gonna develop?" he asked, his rheumy eyes

blinking. “Just put in there how I can make more money at the State Line,” the old man said, and cackled lengthily at his joke.

The bartender interjected: “I don’t think most of them care whether they redevelop or not.”

“Oh, that’s what you want,” the old man said. “Like they said here a year ago . . . a year and a half ago. I don’t think they’ll tear anything down here for years to come. If they figure on tearing things down, they should figure on building a place that they should have clean rooms, cheap places to eat. They’re working men, and they got to have a place to stay according to the wages they makes.”

He patted the bar to emphasize his point.

“They’s a million big shots who got this figured out a lot better’n me,” he said. “The only one I figure it’s going to help,” he added, “is the big man.

“Sure as hell ain’t gonna help me,” he said, cackling.

Chapter 44

Sacramento Vice: A Cop on Skid Row

*From the author's article in **The Sacramento Union**, April 13, 1958, originally headed "West End's Passing Parade Through Patrolman's Eyes."*

"Here's the hole where that fellow got shot that time," said Officer Alexander J. McCormick ("Just call me Mac," he said), putting the tip of his finger on the edge of a small raw wound in the shellacked wall. "That's just one bullet hole," Mac said to the bartender in the Second Street tavern. "I think you got a couple more around here, haven't you?"

The bartender said he had, which wasn't surprising, since the crazed gunman had fired 11 times inside the bar. He killed one man. It happened about a year ago.

"It seems funny now," mused the bartender, "but I'll never forget that night. Death in a violent form I don't go for. It's a miracle the joint wasn't packed."

Mac, who joined Sacramento Police Department in 1943, is a good tourist guide in the West End, which he has been covering the last 10 years. He knows the characters, history, and settings.

Mac, 49, walks his beat from 8 a.m. to 4 p.m. He says most of the action occurs in the shift that follows his — the one from 4 p.m. to midnight. He covers the area bordered by Front, Sixth and I Streets, and the J and K Streets alley — an area included in

Sacramento Redevelopment Agency's vast 62-block slum clearance program.

Mac is noncommittal about redevelopment. "I'm neutral," he said. "You know how the feeling is about tearing it down."

In the bar where the shooting occurred, there are large cartoon murals that show considerable proficiency, and prove that talent may be found in unlikely places. The artist, Carl Jordan, once worked with Walt Disney, Mac said. Where he is now, Mac didn't know.

The burly bar patrons looked like a rough crowd. "I'd say 50 percent of them are losers," Mac said out in the street. "Ex-convicts — been in and out."

Mac's tour led to another bar. "Hello, Bob," he greeted a lean, aged man who was sitting on a stool and guarding a tall glass of draft beer.

"Back all right now?" Mac asked, and the old man indicated it was.

"He fell from a second-story window across the street," Mac explained. "He was sober at the time — or at least he says he was. There was a fire escape there or something, and he fell through it. I don't know exactly how it happened."

Mac continued the tour to one of the West End's largest flophouses. Men loafed on numerous beds in this unprepossessing building. "The fellow that runs this was in for perversion," was Mac's one-sentence biography of the owner.

It costs a fellow only a nickle to check his "balloon" (bedroll) in Joe's Baggage Room on Second Street, which seems to be an active enterprise in this part of town.

"These balloons can come anywhere from a good blanket to a lot of paper wrapped up," Mac said.

In another large flophouse, Mac walked up to a man who lay on a cot with an army blanket covering him. The man was emaciated, pale, and had a dark shadow of beard.

"This old fellow is paralyzed," Mac explained. "Albert has a crippling curvature of the spine. Do you know me, Albert?"

Albert looked at Mac with dark, weary eyes that seemed to be sunken in their sockets. "Sure, I know you," he said listlessly.

"Is it all quiet in the bullpen, Albert?"

"Oh, yeah."

"I see you got a radio there, Albert."

Outside, Mac explained, "Albert is completely bedridden. He has to get his buddies to carry him to the toilet. Albert doesn't drink

— not that I know of, anyway."

There are, however, a number of other customers of the flophouse who are known to touch the stuff. A West End businessman's comment on the beverage consumption in this flophouse was: "This dump here it takes a truck and a trailer just to haul the empty bottles out of there every two weeks."

For Skid Row habitues who can't muster the price of a flop —the average price is 50 cents — the alternative usually is just not having any place to stay all night, a condition known as "carrying the banner."

"They also might say," Mac reported, " 'I'm going to sleep in the Weed Hotel under a Muscadoodle blanket.' " Mac said this means the fellow will bunk in the open air with only a bellyful of Muscatel wine to keep him warm.

Farther south on Second Street, a half dozen down-and-outers were arguing boisterously. "Right now you might have a beef over there," Mac observed. But nothing developed that made Mac think he ought to summon the wagon.

Mac then stopped in a Mexican restaurant and talked with the proprietors in Spanish. This circumstance led to the disclosure that Mac, who looks like an Irishman, is only half one. Mac was born in the Philippines. His mother was Spanish and his father was a sanitation engineer of Irish descent who was working there .

Chapter 45

Old Sacramento Returns to Those Thrilling Days of Yesteryear

Nostalgia is a thing of the past.
Author Unknown

Much of this material appeared in the author's article, "Old Sacramento: 100 Years Behind the Times," in ***Southwest,*** *the airlines magazine, November 1984.*

Listen hard, here in Old Sacramento, and you can almost hear the hullabaloo of braying mules and caterwauling gold-seekers buckling up to make tracks to the mining camps in the stampede of 1849. Echoes of the past seem to whisper at each cobblestoned street corner and brick wall of this restored Gold Rush-era boomtown, today a functioning commercial center whose merchants boast of being "100 years behind the times."

You can almost hear antique buildings murmur legends of riverboats, Wells Fargo stages, the Pony Express, and steam trains. Sometimes you really do hear them — as steamboats cruise, stagedrivers slap leather, pony mail buffs gallop off on a re-ride, and antique trains whistle-wail and belch clouds of steam.

Old Sacramento is the biggest restoration in the western hemisphere. Some 100 buildings from the 1849-76 epoch have been rebuilt or restored to their Gold Rush-era semblance. And work continues. Its cost aggregates over $100 million so far, and no doubt some taxpayers are graveled by that aggregate. It may mollify them to know that about two-thirds of the cost is private investment. Merchants, civil servants and others are doing their best to keep Time marking time, as it were, if not moving backward when the occasion presents itself to regain some new aspect of olden times.

These treasures of historic buildings — our legacy from the past —might have succumbed irrevocably to decay and the wrecking ball if it hadn't dawned on the locals in the 1950s that Old Sacramento had been the arena of momentous events, and was an irreplaceable heritage that *must* be saved. But saving it was not done without storm and strife.

Suddenly a crisis: State Division of Highways announced preliminary plans to steam-roller the projected Interstate 5 freeway through the West End between Front and 2nd Streets — which would have obliterated almost the entire historic precinct. The announcement stirred up a feeding frenzy of attacks by history buffs, out for blood with a vengeance. The badly-mauled and all-shook-up highway people later presented finished plans for routing it between 2nd and 3rd.

That still didn't sit well with eminent artist-historian Ted Baggelmann. He proposed moving the freeway another 80 feet to the east, to rescue the historic buildings on the east side of 2nd. Suggestion adopted — sending the highway people back to their drawing boards again.

Baggelmann said Frank Durkee, state public works director, told him he was "the most expensive historian in California — because it cost the state another million to re-draw the freeway plans."

Now the city clamped a freeze on any alterations to exterior architecture of historic buildings in the preservation site, and in 1963 Sacramento Redevelopment Agency — with city, state and federal funds — set to work on a $100,000 planning study. Upshot: The National Park Service two years later registered Old Sacramento as a National Historic Landmark. The Legislature in 1966 officially created Old Sacramento State Historic Park. In the next year, federal funds paid for incorporating additional areas into Old Sac. Today, in a Cinderella story of a sort, 28 acres have been metamorphosed from Skid Row to the Gilded Age that once was, Sacramento version.

One local man as early as 1931 had advocated preserving the

historic waterfront, Baggelmann says. He was Harry Claude Peterson, onetime curator of Sutter's Fort."In 1933," Baggelmann said, "he told me that instead of painting flower pots, I should devote my art to Gold Rush buildings — which I've done ever since. Peterson said, 'Today, nobody cares about these old buildings. Some day they'll wake up to find that there's money in preserving them as historic landmarks — because they draw tourists.' "

Actual construction in 1967-70 of a $27.6-million stretch of I-5 freeway and interchanges razed four blocks, but protestors were appeased in some measure when many historic buildings were taken apart and moved piecemeal to vacant lots in Old Sacramento. The freeway effectively confined Old Sac restoration to the area west of the freeway. Of the threatened buildings that were relocated rather than destroyed, most notable was the Huntington-Hopkins Hardware. It was shifted to a site west of the Railroad Museum. In this immortal building the Big Four met to charter the Central Pacific Railroad, which undertook the formidable task of building the western half of the transcontinental railroad. Today the hardware store, open as a free museum, displays a typical 19th-century inventory of tools, household goods, and whatnots of the age.

Asked what he thought was the most interesting thing about Old Sacramento, project manager Ted Leonard replied: "Probably the individual significance of each building — very few people know the names and histories of the individual buildings."

Yonder two-story building at 117 J St. today houses The Union Restaurant, decorated with newspaper memorabilia and named after the onetime occupant, *The Sacramento Union*. Founded in 1851– the onetime oldest daily in the West – occupied a handsome building at 301 Capitol Mall. A larger-than-life head of Mark Twain, its most famous reporter, dominated the lobby.

Twain, not averse to a drop or two, called Sacramento "the city of saloons" and claimed he could shut his eyes and march into the first door he came to, call for a drink, and most likely get it.

Twain's ghost, perchance, celebrated his 150th birthday in front of The Union Restaurant on Nov. 30, 1985, with the help of Sacramento Mayor Anne Rudin and Old Town officials and visitors. Rudin blew out the 150 candles on a large cake decorated with Twain's portrait. The crowd sang "Happy Birthday," then dispatched the cake with as much celerity as Twain would toss

Seeking clues to lifestyles in Gold Rush days, David Abrams, anthropology instructor at Cosumnes River College, and his students dig deep in basement of Enterprise Hotel, Old Sacramento.

down a shot of grog.

For many a year until restoration of the first buildings began in 1968, this now-developed Sacramento region — of which restored Old Sac is but a small fraction — was known as the West End. Flophouses billeted a tired and thirsty population of transients, many of them farmworkers. One 12-block section was awash with 167 bars and wineshops. The West End then bore the dubious laurel of largest Skid Row west of Chicago. Unlike early transients, questing for gold, latter-day transients were questing for red — red wine. Old Sacramento even today is not underprivileged in its number of drinking places, containing 30 alcoholic licenses in its 28 acres, highest density in northern California save for San Francisco's North Beach.

Another newspaperman, more famous as a filibuster — 19th-century term for military adventurers who went looking for trouble in Latin America — William Walker served as editor of the *Democratic State Journal,* housed in that two-story building on the southwest corner of 2nd and K Streets. Walker's story is told in the earlier chapter, "Breezes of Change."

Formerly, guided walking tours of Old Sacramento were offered. One guide was elderly docent Elden Wall, strolling the same cobbles his grandfather did in Gold Rush days.

Today, walking tours are self-guided, with maps offered at the Visitors Center, 1101 Second Street, or at any of the six information kiosks in Old Sacramento. Advantage of a self-guided tour: You can tailor it to suit your fancy.

Those who prefer riding tours of Old Town can hitch a lift in horse-drawn vehicles. Five outfits make the circuit, stopping at sundry stations marked "No Parking, Horses and Wagons Only."

Horses of Top Hand Ranch and Cowboy Carriage and Wagon Co. drag covered wagons -- "prairie schooners." Also clattering on cobbles are horse-drawn rigs of Old Sacramento Carriage Co., Classic Coach and Carriage Service, and Elegant Dreams. Some rigs are surreys with the fringe on top.

Across the street from the CP Depot stands the Old Eagle Theatre at 925 Front St., originally built of canvas sails over a wood frame, and rebuilt in 1975 to resemble the original. Canvas was handy in Gold Rush days because so many sailboats were abandoned here as crews lit out for the mines. Many other canvas-walled houses and tents sprinkled early Sacramento. Old Eagle Theatre today is the scene of many of Sacramento Opera

Association's Brown Bag Opera series in noon-hour programs, with local singers of professional caliber. Patrons may bring their own lunches. Wine and other beverages may be purchased.

Next to the Eagle Theatre at 917 Front, The T. McDowell and Company Building replicates an 1849 wood-and-canvas store. Dedicated in 1983, it houses Golden Era Handicrafts, a retail nonprofit store managed by senior citizens.

At 2nd and I Streets, you get an inkling of how Sacramentans — well over 100 years ago — conquered the floods. At this corner a "sunken" brick courtyard, now bounded on two sides by a restaurant and other businesses, lies 12 feet below the current street level, which bounds the courtyard on the other two sides. Actually the courtyard wasn't sunken — everything else was raised. In a decade-long ordeal, Sacramentans carted in rock and earth fill to raise the streets up to 12 feet above former levels, the full story of which is told in the earlier chapter, "Jacking Up the City."

This sunken courtyard also demonstrates how merchants built one brick wall at the curb and a second in front of their businesses. The two walls supported the raised sidewalk, creating a labyrinth of catacombs that over the years became a home for destitute persons. Some, alas, were not averse to using the underground as staging areas from which to burrow into adjoining businesses for nefarious reasons such as burglary. Eventually city officials locked them out by walling up the catacombs. The story goes that a tunnel once ran from the catacombs to an opening by the river. To dodge encounters with authorities, illegal Chinese immigrants were funneled from riverboats into the city via this tunnel. Many of the surreptitious newcomers may have been among the 15,000 Chinese who went to work on the transcontinental railroad.

At 2nd and J Streets, you confront a dynamic bronze statue of a horse and rider, opus of sculptor Thomas Holland. This was the end of the line for horse and rider in the early stages of the Pony Express. The statue could also symbolize the energy and daring that won the West. The full story of the pony mail is told in an earlier chapter.

Erection of the statue culminated a decade-long effort to raise funds. Meanwhile, site planning went on. Old Sacramento project manager Ted Leonard said it was agreed the city would construct the park, and the state would own it and do all maintenance. What should the park look like? State Parks reps felt it should depict a rugged Sierra scene with the rider galloping through granite and pine. City staff wanted to portray the valley, with grass and oaks. As a compromise, the little park has all four — granite boulders, pines, grass and oaks. Explains Leonard: "Our staff called to their attention that there was a place where the two zones meet — and everybody was happy."

Catty-corner from the pony statue, the Hastings Building housed western headquarters for the Pony Express — and also offices of the telegraph that doomed the pony mail. The Hastings Building was rebuilt after the 1852 fire that destroyed two-thirds of town. The tall iron doors on the exterior were installed during the rebuilding, to guard against flying embers in future fires.

The Hastings Building — today open as a free museum — also contained the Wells Fargo office, the State Supreme Court, and the office of Theodore Judah, the young surveyor who talked of building a railroad across the Sierra. Over those avalanche-plagued mountains? Only a fool would think of it. Small wonder they called him "Crazy Judah." But with a one-track mind, as it were, he refused to give up and at last sold his hare-brained scheme to the tycoons who became known ever after as the Big Four. Sacramento's role in the adventure of linking the two oceans with iron rails is told in an earlier chapter. A monument to Judah, with a bronze portrait, stands at 2nd and L Streets.

On Front between J and K Streets, the two two-story Booth Buildings are surmounted by a roof platform with a pole for signal flags. From that vantage, proprietor Newton Booth aimed his telescope at signal flags of incoming ships far down the river, as they hove into view around the bend. Booth worked out a cozy deal with steamboat captains. Their flags told him the quantities and prices of merchandise that ships carried —giving him an edge on competitors. If signals told him a certain product price would plummet, he would sell fast at cut-rate, capturing the market. Booth carried his commercial astuteness into politics, and one day would become Governor of California. A Sacramento elementary school is named after him.

On I Street opposite the Railroad Museum, the Hawaiian Cotton Co. opened a clothing store, its proprietors having relocated here from Hawaii – the latest Hawaiian link with Sacramento that began with Sutter's Sandwich Islanders. And it proudly flew the Hawaii state flag. Alas, it was aloha and goodbye.

Old Sacramento businesses try to recapture some of the moods and tones, the pleasant ones, of Gold Rush days. In two old-time photo studios — McGee's, 1107 Front St., and O'Grady's, 908 2nd St. —patrons gussy up in period costumes to pose for photos. Hammons Archives & Artifacts, 1115 Front St., stocks a boggling collection of books, pamphlets, manuscripts, maps and ephemera, offering windows on the past. Restaurants abound, occupying such sites as a former hotel of the 1860s, a one-time stagecoach office, a Gold Rush saloon, and an early-day bank. Los Padres restaurant's patio and parasols remind you of California's Spanish and Mexican heritage.

California Fats restaurant used to be China Camp restaurant, its basement quarters and heavy-beam decor evoking a mine shaft. The new restaurant is much more light and airy, and susurrous with a sheet of water coming down a wall — an indoor waterfall — illumined by skylights during the day and by lights at night. Where else in Sacramento can you dine by falling water, unless a pipe is leaking?

The adjoining Fat City restaurant is owned by the same Chinese-American family. Fat City's ornate rosewood-and-mahogany bar and back-bar were carved in France over 115 years ago, shipped around the Horn, then transported to Leadville, Colorado. For decades this fixture helped thirsty miners lubricate their tonsils. The bar is the same that the incomparable Molly Brown tended in Leadville. She was the wife of J. J. (Jonny) Brown, whose talent for finding gold ran their fortune up into the millions. Molly's heroism in a lifeboat during the 1912 sinking of the *Titanic* made her famous. Tammy Grimes portrayed her in the musical, "The Unsinkable Molly Brown." In the early 1970s, Fat City proprietor Tom Fat bought the bar at auction. Loss of the prized antique from their state got Coloradoans in such a swivet that their legislature passed a law clamping down on such exports. Fat City also is adorned by an illuminated window portraying a figure dubbed the "Purple Lady." The window captured first prize for stained glass at the 1893 Chicago World's Fair.

Los Padres, California Fats and Fat City occupy separate but adjoining Brannan Buildings, brick legacies of Mormon leader and storekeeper Sam Brannan, once the richest man in California.

The Firehouse restaurant building was erected in 1853 as a genuine firehouse. Abandoned in 1919, it was restored in 1961 and converted to a beautiful dining spot, brass pole and all — smashing enough for Governor Ronald Reagan's two inaugural banquets. The building has three full bars and six separate dining areas, and some people say you need a map to find your way through the labyrinth of winding corridors and odd staircases. Firehouse president Cathy MacMillan has served as honorary mayor of Old Sacramento.

Best little whorehouse in Old Sac? In an archeological dig, clues to life in a Gold Rush brothel were pieced together in a four-year excavation of the Enterprise Hotel on 2nd Street by more than 60 Cosumnes River College instructors, students and volunteers. They unearthed a trove of wine bottles, shards of china, combs, hairpins, perfume bottles, cold cream jars, toothpaste holders and a $5 gold coin. The garbage-pile detectives also discovered that two other buildings had stood on the site — a tinsmith shop and another brothel. The aptly-named Enterprise is undergoing restoration.

The Lady Adams Building at 119 K St. is the oldest extant building in the Sacramento Valley, save for Sutter's Fort. Built of brick that came around the Horn as ballast in the ship *Lady Adams,* which named it, it's the only structure still standing in Old Sac that survived the 1852 fire-storm. Around the Horn — a horn being a musical instrument, it's no surprise to find that music dominates the building today, with over 1,000 music boxes on sale.

The Orleans Hotel on 2nd between J and K Streets was one of the many buildings that rose again within an incredible 30 days after the 1852 fire. Nowadays, as tour guides note, it would take a deal longer to get the necessary permits. In the early 1920s, the Orleans again was leveled by fire — but it will rise again, as a reconstruction

What strikes you about Old Sac, after you fully come to realize it, is that events of great consequence happened right here. Somebody from the merchants' association put it this way: "Old Sacramento is *real*. Not just a plywood set that somebody put up on a back lot." It's not a plywood set, but a *real* stage. Across this rivertown stage, history marched with giant footfalls. The stage remains, but yesteryear's actors and actresses have all made their exits. Yet — or is this just overheated imagination? — the cobbles and bricks still seem to echo with the voices of the thousands who swaggered or traipsed through Sacramento toward one destiny or another. Or stayed to build the city. By coming to this faraway frontier town of Sacramento near the edge of the western world, they demonstrated the one thing they all possessed, saints and sinners equally: Like Ulysses, all had had the courage to go beyond the sunset and seek a newer world. Those were the brave people who lived the Sacramento story.

Restoration of Old Town is receiving some finishing touches as the waterfront comes alive along a 1,000-foot wharf that will be chockablock with freight depots, ticket offices and shops, celebrating the 1870s heyday of both river and rail traffic. Replicas of old-time riverboats will bob in the water, luring visitors to their floating restaurants. Future plans include creation of a waterfront park. After removal of the concrete seawall, the earth bank will be sloped toward the river and planted with grass. Pathways will wander among oaks, sycamores, cottonwoods and willows.

The replica of the sailing ship *Globe*, now moored on the waterfront, was the first Gold Rush ship to be restored. The original 92-foot *Globe*, 139 tons, built in Maine in 1833, sailed in 1849 around the horn to San Francisco. *Globe* was a packet — that is, it carried both passengers and cargo on a regular schedule, typical of hundreds of vessels of the time. Once it carried missionaries on a spiritual mission to Hawaii. By 1850, it was cruising up the Sacramento with hot-eyed crowds on a material mission. In Sacramento, masts and rigging were stripped away and it was converted to a storeship. The reconstructed *Globe* serves as a floating museum — an exhibition mission.

In Gold Rush days, it might cost $15,000 to hire someone to build a small store. But abandoned ships like *Globe* offered free quarters, and entrepreneurs roofed them with shingles, subdivided them into stores, offices and warehouses, and painted them with signs. *Globe* became floating offices for California Steam Navigation Company's steamships. It was broken up c. 1875.

Since *Globe* was so typical of vessels that debarked gold-seekers in Sacramento, Sacramento Housing and Redevelopment Agency in 1984 decided to construct a replica. Distinguished naval architect Melbourne Smith designed and supervised construction. Several Vietnamese boatbuilders worked on the project, after fabricating some of their own tools. Bleachers were built so visitors could monitor the work, and Smith trained docents to explain it. The *Globe* replica — built with a flat bottom for easier maintenance, and so it could be moved in shallow water — was launched in 1985 and tied up at the L Street dock, first of several historic vessels destined to share that mooring place.

The 6.2-acre Old Sacramento Riverfront also offers a permanent haven, at last, to the long-wandering *Delta King*, a king without a

Old Sacramento is one of the favorite haunts of Stan Lemkuil, Sacramento's resident comic genius. If he spots a violation of fire regulations, his imitation of a fire siren brings everyone running. A man of 100 voices, 300 vocal sound effects, and not a few hilarious costumes, he's like a sewing machine — he keeps everybody in stitches. Numerous network TV programs have showcased his talents.

country, as it were. *The King* has been remodeled so as to have 43 hotel rooms and two restaurants — the Paddlewheel Saloon, for families, and the Pilot House, for gourmet diners. A 120-seat theater will present multi-media shows on riverboat history, with old photos, early newsreels, and player-piano accompaniment.

In the 1850s, a dozen ships at a time tied up on the Sacramento waterfront. Some sank into Davy Jones's Locker — Sacramento River department — and remain there, so the quest for clues to lifestyles in Old Sacramento takes researchers even into river mud. Underwater archeologists in 1984 discovered two old ships in the muck at the base of J Street: A paddlewheel steamer, with timbers charred by fire, lies athwart a 100-foot-long copper-sheathed schooner, typical of those that brought immigrants around the Horn to Sacramento. Of the schooner, National Park Service archeologist Roger Kelly said: "We've never found a vessel like this in a river in the western United States." He said it may contain a treasure of 19th-century artifacts and information. Work has been done to preserve both ships.

Divers explored the dark depths in zero visibility, in jeopardy from barbed wire and scrap metal, clinging to lines to keep from being swept away by the swift current. Said maritime archeologist Jack Hunter, team leader: "It's like climbing a cliff — once you let go, you're gone."

The ships were partly exposed because much of the mud that has blanketed the river-bottom for over a century had drifted downstream past Sacramento, notes Jim Henley, director, Sacramento Museum and History Division. "That leaves the enticing possibility that as more and more mud goes down, it will reveal what was sealed in it for a hundred years." Somebody has compared the Sacramento River mud to a time capsule that is just waiting to be opened to reveal its contents.

Another Gold Rush wreck was found in 1986 in river mud south of Tower Bridge, and city officials are hoping it too might yield a treasure trove of artifacts. The wreck seems well preserved. Comments Henley: "An amazing find." The wreck first was detected by sonar, then by divers working on a redevelopment agency waterfront survey between Tower Bridge and Pioneer Bridge. Recovered artifacts include a whiteware mug, two smoking pipes, an anchor stock key and a rusty lock. Divers found the ship's hull sticking out of the mud, and found two sections of keelson (a strengthening structure attached above the keel), hull strakes, copper sheathing, and rigging components. Copper sheathing helps date the ship, because it means pre-1860 construction. Henley believes it may have been a waterfront storeship like the restored *Globe*. Although its name is unknown, local newspapers of the 1860s reported the sinking of the barks *Dimon* and *Ninus* in that area, each over 80 feet long, similar to the wreck.

The ships already found may be only a sample of what lies buried under river goo. John Foster, underwater archeologist for California Department of Parks and Recreation, is confident the river bottom contains "an amazing collection of artifacts" from Gold Rush days.

Henley sums up the importance of the secrets this river holds: "The Sacramento River is one of the most significant rivers (in research potential) because it was one of the most heavily navigated rivers west of the Mississippi. The volume of traffic coming up here was tremendous.

"The river basically protects what goes to the bottom. Things are intact in the river — lots of broken items, but basically intact. The river is loaded with very nice things." Henley hopes for the day when a survey can be made of the river from the Feather's mouth down to the Sacramento's mouth in the Delta, to find maybe a thousand little pieces of history. And big ones, too, to help piece together the historical jigsaw puzzle.

Meanwhile Old Sacramento merchants and citizens are always piecing togther special events: Pony Express Day in April; Railfair in May, with steam train rides; the Dixieland Jubilee, world's largest jazz festival, on the Memorial Day weekend; Independence Day (July 3, here) fireworks *cum* Formula 1 boat races; Native Sons' Admission Day parade in early September; Gold Rush Days Arts & Crafts Festival later the same month; plus several Living History Days.

On one occasion or another, merchants and others relish appareling themselves in historic garb to leaven the antique drama of Old Sacramento with light-hearted antics. During Gold Rush Days, for instance, for the sake of fun — and promotion, too, perhaps — they hold elections to name officers of Old Sac. Offices include mayor, vice mayor, town marshal, judge, fire marshal, town clerk, sheriff, jailor, coroner-undertaker, schoolmarm, stationmaster, harbormaster, and others, even including a town madam.

The costumed candidates embark on whirlwind campaigns to

literally "sell" themselves to the voting populace, at $1 for each ballot. Candidates pursue such time-hallowed techniques as hand-shaking and soapbox oratory loaded with fanciful promises. There's no limit to the number of votes a voter can purchase. And a candidate can vote for himself, limited only by the amount he's willing to spend. That is, he can buy his election, if his pocketbook can stand it. Not surprisingly, winning candidates regard themselves as "the finest politicians money can buy."

Chapter 46
Here Comes the Blue Canyon Gang!

*From the author's article in **California Highway Patrolman,** July 1983.*

On some days in Old Sacramento, a fulmination of gunshots rattles the windows. Not to worry — it's only a shoot-out by the Blue Canyon Gang. In a typical skit, outlaws stage a robbery and blow a strongbox, but lawmen sprint onto the scene. Guns crash and smoke clouds flare as goodies and baddies meet in a crunch — and take movie-style tumbles as they bite the cobbles in choreographed performances worthy of Hollywood.

The Blue Canyon Gang has been haunting the streets of Old Sac since 1972, when half a dozen gun-slingers banded together, aiming to revive the Old West by re-enacting legendary scenarios of a hundred and more years ago.

Don Woolcott as an outlaw — in widebrim hat, scraggly beard, and long duster, sucking on a kitchen match to improve his air of menace — tells how it began: "A bunch of us were Clampers — members of E Clampus Vitus, the western history group. Many of them were rowdies who seemed more interested in drinking and shooting out street lights. But some of us had a serious interest in the Old West, and in learning about weapons, and in doing skits to show people what life was like in the old days."

Besides Woolcott, this group included Robert Hayes, Ron

Johnson and Nevada Jack, a.k.a. Eldridge Frodge. They named their group after a well-known Sierra canyon because a friend who lived there had a falling-down cabin and gave them the lumber to build a false-front western town for their skits at Cal Expo.

For some reason, Cal Expo Director Kirk Breed took a dislike to the false-front town and said he would have it dismantled so it could be stored between shows. But the town mysteriously ended up demolished, instead of dismantled. So the miffed Gang members relocated their local performances to Old Sacramento.

The Gang's roster today numbers about 25, including seven women, wives of members, who perform with as much elan as the men. Item: Juanita Griffith, as an Indian woman in buckskin, blasts away with a shotgun. Her husband Chris plays a mountain man. Real-life occupations run a wide gamut. Their common bond is a passion for the Old West. They relish putting on costumes of bygone days to impersonate sheriffs, outlaws, fancy dudes, saloon gals, frontier women, ex-soldiers and other early types.

In show biz tradition, they don't let bad weather daunt them. They've done skits in the snow, with snow falling, in Tonopah, Nevada, and in Colfax, and in torrential rains in Old Sacramento. "There was no place to fall without falling in water," Woolcott said. "Those were the days when we used 'blood bags' — containing red food dye. When shot, you slap yourself, breaking the bag, which makes a big red stain. We were shot and laying in the gutter in inches of water, and the water was carrying all the red color down the gutter. Very effective.

"We don't use blood bags any more because it's too hard to clean the dye out of clothing, and it makes the skits a bit too realistic — scares the kids."

One of the Gang's most distinguished members is grizzled Bill Taylor. He wears a widebrim hat, black frock coat, and black eye patch (he lost the sight of an eye in a motorcycle accident). In 1963, he captured the title of world's fast-draw champion. Three years earlier, when he won the national meet, Clint Eastwood — then appearing in TV's "Rawhide" series — confronted him. "Anything you can show me I'm doing wrong?" Eastwood asked. And Taylor taught him some lightning techniques to help him get the drop on TV and motion-picture foes.

Taylor is a distant relative of outlaw John Wesley Hardin —but doesn't know whether to brag or complain about it. His great-grandfather, a Texas Ranger, was a cousin of Hardin. But the two never tangled with each other, unlike many a fictional story of relatives fighting on opposite sides of the law.

Gang members often play different roles at different times. Jerry Rushing straps on a Colt .45 and dons a black sombrero and black frock coat — and he's a gambler or outlaw. Sometimes he pins on a silver star, and he's a marshal or deputy.

He contributes the expertise he gained years ago in gunfights in Calico Ghost Town, near Barstow. "I like to think we give people some idea of what the Old West was really like," he said. "The only way to do that is re-enact it. If we can't re-enact it better than you see on television, we might as well hang up our guns."

Their guns make up an arsenal ranging from derringers to double-barrel shotguns, with a mix of pistols and rifles. Some are black-powder muzzle-loaders dating from the Civil War.

"Nobody holds a loaded gun until right before the show," notes Mike Hiestand, as a townsman in levis and red suspenders. "We preach gun safety."

To start each show — and demonstrate the need for caution —one member plunks a beer or pop can on the ground and fires a blank. The blast shatters the can, bouncing it down the street. Moral: Firearms loaded with blanks aren't all that harmless. Craig Pack adds a case in point. In one skit, somebody grabbed his hat, mischievously flung it to the ground, and stepped on it. As the action continued, many hats littered the ground. Pack spied what he thought was the offender's hat. To get even, he fired at it — and found he had shot a big hole in his own hat.

"Where do we get our costumes?" Jerry Rushing said, repeating the question. "Definitely not out of Hollywood. We don't wear fancy belt buckles. We try to keep everything authentic. We make a lot of our clothes — by looking through old library books."

Some women members enjoy sewing fancy dresses and accouterng themselves in styles of a century and more ago. "Or we find the actual clothes themselves, sometimes, in an antique store," Rushing said. "Some of mine are original turn-of-the-century hand-stitched clothes I bought in an antique store in Old Sacramento. Or, if you're lucky, you can find something in a thrift store, at a reasonable cost."

Members learn to improvise, as the need arises. Bill Taylor: "If someone blows a line, someone near him will usually think of something to say that's even funnier. We have lots of talented people." In one finale, Nevada Jack was supposed to shoot outlaws Woolcott and Johnson. He raised his shotgun — *click,click.* Anticipating shots, Woolcutt flung himself against the building

Smoke flares from Jerry Rushing's pistol as the Blue Canyon Gang hams it up in Old Sacramento. Ken Fontaine advances at center.

and Johnson threw himself into a horse trough. Oops.

Woolcott: "Looks like you forgot to put some shells in your gun, sheriff."

At that, Nevada Jack whipped out a pistol and dispatched the pair.

Mike Samaritano — in Civil War cap, blue pants with yellow stripe, suspenders, sleeve garters, bandana — portrays a Yankee deserter-turned-outlaw. In one skit, he and Woolcott had robbed a bank and just then were confronted by the law. "I'm going to blow you away, sheriff," Woolcott said, leveling his dragoon-style Colt. 44.

At that, the barrel fell off the pistol. "That's what I get for buying a bargain-basement gun," Woolcott said sadly.

Jerry Rushing remembers lying in the street, pretending to be dead. With eyes closed, he couldn't see what was happening. Had the skit ended? He opened his eyes and raised his head.

"The heavies were walking over to me to see if I was dead. I was hoping one of them still had another blank left, so he could shoot me and cover my booboo."

Luckily one gunslinger shouted: "Here's one that ain't dead yet!" He fired, and this time Jerry made sure to stay "dead" until the skit ended.

Sometimes improvisations spring from sheer spontaneity. Mike Casha recalls a skit in the false-front town at Cal Expo, with Johnson and Woolcott as bandits, firing at lawmen. From a second-story hotel window, Woolcott was shooting with one hand and drinking beer with the other. Fifteen feet away, Johnson was shooting from atop the assay office.

Eyeing the beer mug in Woolcott's hand, Johnson had an impulse: "Hey, I want some of that!"

Also on impulse, Woolcott yelled back, "Here you go!" and flung the beer mug. It arched through the air, turning over in mid-flight. Somehow Johnson managed to catch it by the handle — incredibly, without spilling the beer.

The crowd loved it — and of course the Gang added that bit to its repertoire. Unfortunately, try as they might in many a future show, they never could duplicate that first impromptu bit that went off so beautifully — because each time they tried it, the mug slipped through the catcher's fingers and crashed to the ground.

Robert Hayes cuts a comic figure as a grubby-looking country doctor in top hat, stiff collar, pin-stripe pants and black frock coat. "Doc" Hayes prescribes big doses of humor. "We try to put enough comedy in what we do so it doesn't seem so violent," he said. "It kind of rounds everything out."

Blaise Vanderlinden is a laugh-getter as the town drunk, "Mudslide MacBride," so named because he was "orphaned by a mudslide," supposedly. "One day they needed a drunk scene," he said, "and I just happened to have a bottle, and I pushed my hat back and staggered around a bit. It went over real good."

He wears trousers over his red long-handles, and a floppy hat. "I saunter up to the bandits in the middle of a robbery, and usually I'm the first one shot because I stumbled into it. I'm the clown — a kid pleaser. I like to see the kids laugh. Then all of a sudden I'm dead, and they're really booing the bad guys."

Vanderlinden explains his fondness for doing the shows: "You're able to forget who you are, and let loose and act silly. Mudslide MacBride lets me do that."

In one skit, several performers were idling on a curb in Old Sac as Nevada Jack moseyed past with his mule Raindrop, burdened with an enormous load of pots and pans. Somebody must have buckled the cinch strap too tightly, because Raindrop suddenly went into a violent kicking spasm, sending pots and pans flying in every direction, to the crowd's delight.

Once a performer not included in the cast of characters felt compelled to get into the act — and stole the show. It happened as Jerry Rushing's then-wife Sharon was sitting in the audience in Calico with their big brown puppy Coco on a leash. When Coco heard shots and saw his master fall, he got so excited he jerked the leash from Sharon's hands and dashed off.

"I was supposed to be dead," Jerry said, "but Coco was whining and licking me so much I couldn't keep a straight face."

Ken Fontaine remembers the time he, as sheriff, burst out of an outhouse when he heard a shot from the nearby saloon. A woman ran from the saloon.

"What happened?" Fontaine asked.

"I saw the whole thing, sheriff. He shot him in the back — it was self defense."

That tickled the crowd, and the rest of the dialogue was ad lib because the king-size Fontaine was quaking with laughter and blew his lines. "Get back in the saloon where you belong!" he ordered.

"You wanna come along with me?"

"Sure."

"Well, you'll have to take a bath first."

Fontaine cracked up and couldn't utter another line, even if he could have remembered one.

Fontaine reflects on what he derives from the shows: "In costume, you become someone completely different. You kind of escape into a character. It's a way to escape the ordinary doldrums of life." But most members agree that sheer fun is also a main reason they enjoy living in the past, and making old legends come true.

The Gang used to hold mock hangings, with Ron Johnson as "guest of honor." One day they were erecting a huge new scaffold. About 10 members were working on it, struggling to hoist into position the ponderous beam from which the hangman's noose is suspended. Just then the whole structure collapsed.

"After we found out that by some miracle nobody got hurt," Don Woolcott said, "we just lay there, laughing ourselves silly."

Bystanders began clapping. One walked up and said: "Wow, that was a neat show! When's the next one?"

But they never did another hanging. They would have had to re-build the gallows, and some people thought that hangings were carrying things a bit too far. Johnson, Woolcott said, had a great talent for mimicking a man strangling at the end of a rope. "But it was too realistic. He scared a lot of people."

Sometimes the Gang sets up a jail on the cobbles of the old town and holds kangaroo-court trials in which frontier justice is meted out for highly-imaginary violations. One day they collared a celebrity. "Along came Earl Holliman," remembers Jean Melendez, who glitters as a barmaid in a purple satin gown, fishnet nylons and a pink feather in her hair. "Of course we all recognized him from his western roles in TV and movies. We walked up to him and arrested him. Ken Fontaine was the judge. We had a mock trial, and Earl had to give us a dollar to get out of jail."

Like Bill Taylor, Lee Boblet also has a distinguished lawman ancestor — his great-grandfather was Robert A. Anderson, first sheriff of Butte County. Boblet recalls a shoot-out at Old Sacramento's Eagle Theatre, where Chris Melendez flipped over a stairway rail in a trick fall, and split his britches in an embarrassing place. When the performance ended, someone loaned him a raincoat until his wife Jean could fetch another pair.

Boblet — who wears boots with spurs, leather pants with brass rivets, sleeve garters and a plainsman-type hat — also likes to do falls. He flings himself backward, combining this with a roll that makes a dramatic bit.

Blaise Vanderlinden: "Tony Scurro, who has some kind of Hollywood background, has taught us how to take falls and take things in a roll."

But sometimes a fall doesn't go exactly right, and the performer may end up with aches and pains. To remedy that sort of ailment, the Gang has a chiropractor handy in the person of Mark Casha, D.C., who as a Gang member dons a slouch hat and denims and packs a cannon-like .70-caliber muzzle-loading shotgun. Casha explains his interest in the wild-and-woolly: "It gives a taste of the Old West to the tourists and the people of Sacramento. And it's fun."

The Gang has a deep, dark secret: They've done benefit shoot-outs for various local charitable organizations — but they never breathe a word about being do-gooders. They wouldn't want to ruin their reputation.

Chapter 47

Discovery Museum: In Remembrance of Things Past

Over four decades ago, the City Council organized a Landmarks Commission – which as time passed acquired numerous historical artifacts that fairly cried out for space to exhibit them. In due time Sacramento's original history museum debuted above a bar, the TNT Club on Seventh Street, but nobody thought that was a dynamite location. Prospects for a more ambitious history museum at times were bleak, but the founders' dream of such a "real" museum never gave up the ghost, though there were times when it had to go on life support.

Today the collection of artifacts, which has snowballed to enormous dimensions, is housed in the new $5-million History Center, opened in 1985 in Old Sacramento, near the turntable of the Railroad Museum. The center's exterior replicates the exterior of Sacramento's First City Hall and Water Works Building that stood on that very site from 1854 to 1912. The building also housed the city jail. The History Center has been renamed the Discovery Museum.

Today's building exterior is the most accurate reconstruction in Old Sacramento, and Director Jim Henley explains why: "When the original building was constructed, the contractor got in a lawsuit with the city for extras he had put into the building, and as a result, all the specs were made court records. So in reconstructing it, the people got extremely detailed facts to go on."

The History Center dramatizes the panorama of valley history and the saga of Sacramento's growth from marshland to metropolis – by means of state-of-the-art or innovative techniques putting together the exhibits. The drama is re-created in four galleries, each offering a quick focus, like a zoom lens, on one phase of the human presence in our natural dominion of land and water.

On the ground floor, the Agricultural Technology Gallery centers on farming and its mechanization and the fruitful results. Farm inventions and their effects on people are showcased. A cannery "line" donated by California Almond Growers Exchange demonstrates how food packing plants in Sacramento operated for many years. The cannery line originally was loaded with tempting cans of roasted almonds, and they swiftly vanished. Sacramento once had five major canneries, of which only two remain. Historic films of agriculture are shown.

Also on the ground floor, the McClatchy Gallery features the Gold Rush-era history of printing and local newspapers, and theater history in the Sacramento region, a subject fond to Eleanor McClatchy's heart. This gallery tunes in on the need to communicate. Gallery facade and lobby were rebuilt from bricks and sandstones salvaged from the old *Sacramento Bee* building at 7th and I Streets, occupied from 1902 until 1952, the year *The Bee* moved to its present building at 21st and Q Streets. Relics of early printing and publishing were donated by McClatchy Newspapers. Miss McClatchy had one of the nation's finest collections of printing memorabilia. Here you can see specimens of printing development as early as 1285 A.D. A replica of a 19th- century print shop is set up, with an 1854 hand press and an 1888 job press.

On the second floor, the former Topomorphology Gallery has been replaced by two new galleries. But it's worth recalling that that gallery – topomorphology signifies the evolution of man and the land – described the Sacramento region as one of the most man-altered places on earth. Henley explains why: "Man has leveled the land, ripped minerals out of it, channeled the rivers, built levees, drained swamps, and built dams for flood control and for hydroelectric power. The magnitude of these changes in the historically brief scope in which they happened is staggering."

A display, "Old Sacramento Trash," showcases discards ranging back through our history that time has preserved – bones, bottles and broken dishes. A sign here: "One of the richest places to find historical artifacts is in a midden, better known as a trash pit," or garbage dump. When you call it by its scientific name, it doesn't sound as nasty, maybe. Another sign: "Middens are like time capsules." What is garbage to most people may be treasure to historians.

No doubt anthropologists far in the future will be thrilled when they come across our city dump.

The California Gallery hosts rotating displays. And the Gold Gallery exposes a mockup of a miner's cabin, a hands-on mining area where visitors can pan for gold, and the stunning million-dollar collection of gold specimens Bank of America garnered from the Mother Lode. It's said to be the largest in the nation. No, none of these specimens will be found in the spot where visitors pan for gold.

Moving along, you step through a portal that replicates that of Dunlop's Dining Room, an Oak Park restaurant launched in 1929 by a distinguished African American family. Housed in a residence, it was a city landmark for 38 years, hosting politicians, business people and countless others, magnetized by its reputation for fine cooking and old-fashioned hospitality.

The Community Gallery also portrays the changing and developing valley as a place to live and work and play, from the time of the Nisenan Indians as far back as 10,000 years, and up to our own time. Among rare objects is the landau carriage Governor Leland Stanford rode in as he scurried through Sacramento streets. The carriage was restored to its original splendor by an artisan who still makes carriages today – an Amish carriage-maker in Pennsylvania. Also on view: beautiful gowns of Jane Lathrop Stanford, California's First Lady in 1861 and 1862.

Ethnic groups who lived in the valley in the past and today are spotlighted. The story explores why they came, where they came from, how they got here, how they made a living, cultural and religious groups, and discrimination problems. More than two dozen ethnic groups were prominent in our early history, namely: Native Americans, Hawaiians, Russians, Blacks, Japanese, Italians, Portuguese, Finns, Danes, Serbs, Chicanos, Filipinos, Germans, Jews, French, Swedes, Ukrainians, Southerners, Chinese, Koreans, Creeks, Irish, Dutch, Norwegians, Poles, Croatians and Pakistanis.

Credit for designing the Museum exhibits goes to Barry Howard of New York, who also designed those in the nearby Railroad Museum.

Cost of the Museum is shared by the city and county, aided by generous private donations. The city contributed $1.7 million and the county $1.2 million. *The Sacramento Bee* contributed $500,000. Other major contributors: The Natomas Company, Aerojet-General Corporation, and the Sacramento Regional Council of Rotary Clubs. Another sturdy backer is the Sacramento County Historical Society, formed in 1953 to promote "a greater interest and awareness of the history of Sacramento County, of marking historic buildings and sites, and stimulating and supporting the preservation, restoration, and maintenance of historic landmarks."

Will the Museum focus only on the past? Not hardly, strange as it seems. Its people recognize that history is being made every day, and you and your family and business are part of the story. The Museum will continue to acquire memorabilia that mirror today's economic and cultural life, and will update displays to portray changing conditions.

Jim Henley says the Museum is charting new courses; "We're doing things that I think are going to be guiding influences on the way other museums are going to be in the rest of this century."

Chapter 48

State Archives & Museum: The Past Is Prologue

Sometimes things have to get worse before they get better, and such was the case with State Archives at 1020 O Street. The former deficient structure has been replaced by a stunning new building on the same site.

In the same complex, Archives' Golden State Museum opened in 1998, illustrating the saga of California from many perspectives, namely: PLACE, PEOPLE, PROMISE and POLITICS, not to mention many sub-perspectives.

Light, sound, spectacle and historical treasures were amalgamated to make each chapter of the California epic come alive.

In another venue, vintage recordings, photos and rare mementos tell poignant tales of immigrants thronging in from every nation on earth. Yonder stands a re-creation of the herbalist shop of Dr. Herbert Yee, patriarch of five generations, encapsulating the moving story of the Yee dynasty and other Chinese families.

The Gold Rush, described as a defining point in our history, is here defined with golden themes – golden poppies, golden sands, the golden Oscar, "black gold," and fame and fortune's glitter.

Historic political campaigns seem to live again via projected images, newsreels, bright banners and recordings of ringing oratory.

Constitution Wall is the stunner: Soaring 95 feet and stretching 140 feet long, it is blazoned with 36 enduring words from our State Constitution. It backdrops the central courtyard of native trees, shrubs and a waterfall splashing down a boulder.

Six floors of environmentally-controlled stacks and vaults house ever-growing collections of the state's most significant documents, papers and artifacts.

The third floor harbors labs for processing, preservation, and microfilming. Observation windows let visitors eyeball specialists at work.

California governors: Pat Brown and son, Jerry Brown.
Courtesy Sacramento Bee Photo Morgue and Sacramento Archives and Museum Collection Center.

Among records and documents preserved here are California's original Constitutions of 1849 and 1879, scripted on parchment, plus legislative materials, governors' proclamations, and Sen. Robert Kennedy's assassination material, with the murder gun. Individual state agencies have contributed tons of documents.

Got a yen to research your family history?

Genealogical data is on tap here in many record groups, revolving around: Censuses, military service, education, elections, courts, prisons, corporations, trademarks, professional and vocational standards, controllers' records, county records. Many more.

Documents may not be removed from the Archives, but copies may be obtained for nominal fees. Call 653-7715 for information.

Taking a break from research, or whatever, you can dine and relax in the 230-seat Golden Poppy Cafe, on the second floor. From tables under parasols on the terrace, you get a fetching view of the central courtyard and Constitution Wall.

Who knows what evil lurked in the heart of the old Archives? Then chief archivist John F. Burns knew. Declared he: "This is a totally unacceptable archival facility because it lacks almost everything necessary for modern archives." Menaces were poor control of temperature and humidity, insect infestations, and water springing from a leaky roof. Priceless and irreplaceable documents were threatened with ruin.

Inasmuch as "the past is prologue," Archives and Museum tell of promises kept and hint of things to come.

The year-by-year evidence of Henry Ford's genius was illuminated in this car museum.

Chapter 49

Towe Auto Museum: History on Wheels

The slogan of yore, "Watch the Fords go by," took an ironic twist in 1997 when the IRS forced the auction of over 100 cars.

It's been a long and bumpy journey for this museum – from a money bank in Montana to a riverbank in Sacramento, a financial disaster, and a surprising metamorphosis.

Formerly known as the Towe Ford Museum, it recaptured the evolution of Henry Ford's car, an evolution that brought revolution to the car industry, and accelerated America on the road to industrial supremacy.

Ford was the world's largest car-maker, and this was the world's largest collection of Ford cars, numbering more than 170.

You could almost survey the history of America on motorized wheels here in this Sacramento museum.

The museum's history begins with Edward Towe, who at age 14 in Iowa, bought his first car, a Model T. He raced his Tin Lizzy with other Ford drivers, then began rehabbing abandoned Model T's and selling them.

In years to come, his prosperity as a small-town banker in Montana — he came to own more than a dozen banks — gave him the wherewithal to collect Fords like some people collect license plates.

Fords had captured his fancy, and it was no passing fancy. It became a lifetime love affair.

When Towe built a new bank in Circle, Montana, he designed it with a roomy basement to house his collection. Even so, it outgrew the basement, so he rolled his Fords into the State Museum in Helena, the capital. Still later, he hauled the ever-expanding collection into an old territorial prison at Deer Lodge, Montana.

His restless search for the ideal venue in which to show off his Fords ended in 1986 when he dispatched over 89 cars in a miles-long convoy of 13 car carriers — plus several Fords being driven, plus support vehicles — to Sacramento, a thousand miles away.

Crossing Nevada, they weathered a blizzard. "I drove through it in a '36 Roadster — with no windshield wipers, no side curtains and no heater," remembers museum director Ernest Hartley. "I was dressed for skiing, so I was quite comfortable. Every so often I reached out the window to wipe ice off the windshield. I had a great time!"

Towe and his wife Florence rode in a Ranchero, pulling a trailer with a car aboard. Chief restorer Lewis Rector drove his pickup with a trailer and a car on it.

Hartley said the long haul by the car carriers was done free by Hadley Auto Transport Co., and is equivalent to a $100,000 donation to the nonprofit museum.

Arrival in Sacramento of the wandering museum, after all the work and worry, touched off an explosion of happy emotions, with not a few joyous tears.

Towe, in his 80s, still working as a full-time banker, "comes to Sacramento every so often to bring more cars." Hartley said. About 100 remain in the Montana museum.

Docents, many garbed in period costumes, help you trace the evolution of cars from origin to modern times. You might say this collection displays the physical evidence of Henry Ford's mass-production genius, which jump-started America's other car-makers.

From 1912 to 1924, Henry Ford manufactured half of all the cars in the United States.

Ford's Model T debuted in 1908, emphasizing utility, not beauty, but utility has a beauty of its own. The Society of Automobile

Farmer, portrayed by Stan Lemkuil, loads a Tin Lizzy pickup for a drive to market.

Historians honored it as the greatest car ever made, Hartley said, and explained why:

"It transformed America from a horse-powered society to one dominated by the automobile."

Ford's 1926 Model T Roadster was the world's lowest-priced car —sticker-priced at $260.

Edward Towe is the dauntless breed of collector who travels to the uttermost parts of the earth, if need be, to bring home a coveted addition.

Twice, he brought 1930-era Ford V-8 Phaetons — open touring cars with side curtains and four-cylinder engines — home to Montana, driving one from Uruguay and one from Argentina.

The first time, he was on a People-to-People tour in South America with Montana ranchers in 1968 when, at a gas station, a Ford V-8 Phaeton, owner at the wheel, caught his eye. He negotiated to buy it.

He reconditioned the motor, installed new brakes, battled red tape to take it out of the country, then set out, not shrinking from the challenge of driving it on the long, long road to Montana, half a world away.

He and companions fretted with mechanical woes as they tooled it over rotten roads, splashing across countless streams, sputtering over high passes in the Andes, eating dust in endless Chilean deserts. More mountains and jungles had to be put behind, and somehow they did it. However, on the leg between Colombia and Panama, they sent the car by ship because Panama's Darien region of swamps and jungles was impassable.

On the second trip, in 1979, Towe steered clear of flying bullets as a revolution fulminated in Panama.

On each trip, he drove the Fords over 10,500 miles, or 21,000 miles of high adventure — and a bit of lowdown adventure when brazen thieves in Colombia ripped off some valuables.

All told, Towe purchased over 40 Fords in South America, bringing the others home aboard ships.

Hartley, who joined Towe's organization in 1976, began working his way up by restoring woebegone wrecks back to showroom sheen and humdinger running condition.

Today he is director of Sacramento's car museum and his wife Kristin, daughter of Edward Towe, is business manager.

Of all the Fords here, Hartley regards the Model A as his personal favorite: "It's a wonderfully simple machine, easy to operate and repair. Also, it offered Americans a car with styling and high performance at a low price."

Calamity befell the museum in 1997 when the IRS forced the auction of 112 cars to satisfy the indebtedness of founder Edward Towe, who had filed bankruptcy. The auction brought in $4.4 million, business manager Kristin Hartley told an audience of history buffs.

The good news is that 34 of the auctioned cars – cars bought by friends of the museum – will remain at the museum on loan for indefinite periods. More good news is that the museum has undergone a metamorphosis in which it showcases a wider scope of automotive history.

With 130 cars on November 25, 1997 – the day David Springett, president of California Vehicle Foundation, the museum's sponsor, announced the official reopening – he said the museum "will continue as a work in progress, a dynamic museum." He added: "Values of some of the cars here are well in excess of $200,000 each."

Museum director Ernie Hartley: "The remaining vehicles represent the best and most expensive of the Towe collection."

Hundreds of volunteers labored untold hours to create the new "dream" themes, namely:

The Dream of Speed: Includes all types of racing motor sports, illustrating the ancient urge to push it to the max.

The Dream of Independence: Looks at early cars as a source of new freedoms, accelerating travel to work and on vacations.

The Dream of "Cool": Fondly recalls what was *hip* and *in* with car buyers through several decades.

The Dream of Luxury: Shows classic dream machines whereby affluent drivers indulged their yens for gorgeous wheels.

Sunday In the Park: Takes you on an afternoon stroll through a turn-of-the-century village green.

Down Memory Lane: Trips into nostalgia to look at remembrances of things past.

Hall of Technology: Shows changes in mechanical design, with cutaway engines, transmissions and other innards.

The Dream of a Rich Harvest: A Tin Lizzy ate no oats, never got tired, went a lot faster, carried more produce to market, worked around the spread all week, then shuttled folks to town on Saturdays for shopping.

At 2200 Front Street, the museum is open seven days a week, 10 a.m. to 6 p.m., except for Thanksgiving, Christmas and New Year's Day. Call 916-442-6802 for information.

There's a whole lot of dreaming going on around here.

Chapter 50

The Capitol: The Pride and the Passion

Most of this material appeared in the author's article, "A Stately Dream Fulfilled," in ***Westways*** *magazine, March 1983.*

Sacramento almost didn't make it as the state capital. Other cities coveted the honor and economic perks, but Sacramento won out with a combination of luck, planning — and a smidgen of chicanery.

The Legislature's rambling quest for a permanent abode had taken their sessions to Monterey, San Jose, Vallejo, Sacramento, Vallejo again, Benicia, and at last back to Sacramento. Vallejo, twice the seat of state government, became a strong contender for its permanency when General Mariano G. Vallejo, a state legislator, lured legislators to the city named after him by offering 156 choice acres of his own land there for a state capitol. This magnanimous offer made another offer — tendered by a committee on behalf of Sacramento — look chintzy by comparison.

But in the town of Vallejo, lawmakers ran into vexing problems: lack of suitable places to meet, dine or sleep. Sacramento began to look ever better by contrast, for this city had a plenitude of hotel space, saloons, restaurants, theaters, churches, and a 7,500-square-foot courthouse at 7th and I Streets to serve as the Capitol.

After a sojourn in Sacramento, legislators returned to Vallejo because the latter was still the official seat of state government. Yet

The restored Capitol at night is an opus of light and shadow.

Vallejo remained in bad shape. Even into the following year, the town seemed helpless to do the proper honors to the Legislature. No facilities had been constructed, so the Legislature had to find another place — fast. Sacramento — still in the throes of recovery from near obliteration in 1852 by fire and flood — was no longer a candidate. So the desperate lawmakers jammed into the cramped Benicia City Hall, where their bickerings about its accommodations made the stay an unpleasant two years.

Sacramento by 1854 had recovered from its agonies and was ready to do itself proud for the legislators. Local citizens had some tricks up their sleeves to ensure victory. Shortly before the Legislature reconvened in Benicia in January, 300 Sacramentans traveled to Benicia and reserved all the hotel rooms, tying up all lodging space. When the flummoxed legislators arrived, they found no place to bunk save for state offices and saloons, and some were even forced to lay their heads in stables. A fine mess. It was no surprise when the harassed legislators adjourned from Benicia and at last chose Sacramento for their permanent home, ending the long search.

But Sacramento needed a proper building, and construction of the magnificent State Capitol began in 1860.

Construction was starved by lack of funds and swamped by floods. Just before the 1862 inundation, Supervising Architect Reuben Clark had publicly sworn that construction costs would never surpass $500,000. The fact that they shortly did exceed that figure was only one of the blows that finally unhinged him. Construction problems simply drove him around the bend. He took a four-month leave, but it failed to restore his mental health. In February 1866, a month after being relieved of his duties, Clark was committed to Stockton Insane Asylum. Hospital records list the cause of his illness as "monomania — the continued and too-close attention to building the State Capitol." He died the following July at age 51.

Mark Twain seemed to think construction of the Capitol would never end. "The new Capitol is a slow coach," he wrote Nov. 30, 1866, in the *San Francisco Bulletin*. "I would like to be superintendent of it for life, with the privilege of transmitting the office to my heirs and assigns forever."

It would take eight more years to complete. When finished in 1874, costs had soared to a staggering $2.5 million — five times the figure poor Reuben Clark had sworn would never be exceeded.

But that was nothing compared to the cost of the six-year

The restored Capitol — biggest fixer-upper in the western hemisphere — gleams in the emerald setting of Capitol Park.

restoration, completed in 1982 — a whopping $67.8 million, making it the most expensive restoration of any state capitol in America.

You can view the magnificent restoration any day of the week, on your own, or on a free guided tour. Tours start on the hour from 9 a.m. to 4 p.m. daily. Go to the tour office in the basement, or call 324-0333 for information. The basement also houses a museum on Capitol architecture, history, the restoration, and the legislative process, and shows an orientation film.

Two tours are offered — "The Restored Capitol" and "The Historic Capitol." Signed tours for hearing-impaired persons are offered on Mondays.

Your guide will show you the monumental staircases, now restored, and tell how in 1906 the originals were ripped out and replaced by elevators. To meet the needs of expanding government at that time, workmen also added a fourth story and built 12 more rooms.

If an observer could have focused H. G. Wells' fictional Time Machine on the Capitol at the onset of those changeful years and punched the Fast-Forward button, he would have seen wires, pipes and heat and air ducts stitched throughout the building, faster than a weaver's shuttle.

Post World War II years found the building splitting its 19th-century seams and starting to decay. Now the splendid east apse, a three-story semi-circular structure housing the State Supreme Court, fell to the wrecking ball, to make room for a six-story annex, completed in 1952.

Came 1972, and State Architect Fred Hummel published a report saying a moderate earthquake could turn the century-old Capitol into a heap of rubble.

Noting that safety was the prime motive for restoration, State Senator Nicholas C. Petris added: "Nobody could argue with that. I suppose a few of the more radical, anti-governmental conservatives might be willing to let the bureaucrats go, but it's pretty tough to write off all the school children on their civics field trips."

The Legislature in 1974 hired Welton Becket and Associates, Los Angeles architects, to draft plans for reconstruction. Welton Becket hired South Pasadena architect Raymond Girvigian as historical consultant. At the same time, legislators were arguing the feasibility of building a new $300 million Capitol. "We had no assurance that the old Capitol would be preserved," Girvigian said. "I had to come to my own conclusions. I concluded that the Capitol is the most important historic building of its kind in California. It had to be saved."

"I was president pro tem of the Senate at the time," recalled State Senator James R. Mills, whose preservation instincts were honed in his onetime job as curator of San Diego's Junipero Serra Museum. "One day I was asked by the press if I thought we should really go forward with the new project. I said no — I thought we should restore the old building. Ronald Reagan was Governor at the time. He sent his legislative representative up to see me to tell me he very much agreed with what I said, and was prepared to support restoration of the old Capitol. I asked him to make a public statement in favor of it — and he did — and got the ball rolling."

The new Capitol idea was scratched, and a $42-million Legislative appropriation gave the old Capitol a new lease on existence. That was the prelude of six years of wrangling over the specifics of how things should be done — wrangling that sometimes exploded into yelling and shouting. But sound and fury were succeeded by peaceful compromise.

Girvigian found 1900-1910 the period of greatest architectural significance, explaining: "Following that period the building was gutted and lost much of its integrity and was bastardized and changed."

The design team spent a year examining the building, squinting over old photos, stretching measuring tapes, and punching thousands of facts into computers. Photographers took countless pictures of carvings, moldings, murals and other decor. This was the mystery that had to be unraveled in its myriad details: What was the Capitol really like around the turn of the century?

"We knew the building could tell us a lot of things," said John Worsley, restoration project architect and former state architect. "And the workmen were hep to it. It became kind of a game. Under the podium in the Assembly chamber, they found a gold mine of broken pieces of decorative plaster, concrete and iron." The 1906 remodelers, instead of hauling away the debris, had shoveled it under a rug, figuratively.

Workmen discovered hair-raising conditions. Some floors verged on collapse, not just from quakes. Floors never designed to support over 40 pounds per square foot were groaning with up to 150 pounds of filing cabinets per foot. In the brick walls, the mortar had decayed, and little more than gravity held the bricks together — you could pull them apart by hand.

Workers peeled away the inside foot of the 30-inch-thick brick walls. Now they sprayed on a foot thickness of "shotcrete" — similar to gunite, but containing gravel — bonding old and new construction with thousands of anchor bolts. In the basement, they poured a three-foot slab over existing foundations, then poured new floors in sequence back up to the top. In short, they created a monolithic shell inside the fragile old brick shell. Worsley compares the rebuilt Capitol to a concrete ship able to breast the waves of earthquake energy just as a real ship rides the waves — intact.

The Capitol's copper dome had leaked rain for a hundred years. Sheetmetal worker Karl Mindermann fixed it — and won a Craftsman of the Year Award. He designed the machine that stamped out 300 new interlocking copper panels to re-sheathe the dome.

Several dozen giant figures, the work of famed sculptor Pietro Mezzara, studded the Capitol's original roofline. A state senator at that time charged that the bare-breasted women were indecently exposed. Tongue in cheek, he asked a $30,000 appropriation to clothe them. Request denied.

Some of the figures fell off in quakes and others were chopped off in a 1950s renovation. Guided by photos and fragments of the originals, Spero Anargyros of Brisbane, near San Francisco, re-created six of them — two Indians on horseback and four Grecian women. In 1982 they were raised to their former posts. Anargyros is a world-class sculptor whose numerous other stunning works include the re-creations of the eight 23-foot-tall figures that ring the top of the Palace of Fine Arts, San Francisco.

Under the Capitol dome, the rotunda soars a breathtaking 125 feet. Your tour guide probably will mention that laser devices were used to peel off the 23 layers of old paint, readying the surface for restoration. Clues from plaster fragments helped Frank Bouman of A.T. Heinsbergen & Company, Los Angeles, restore its original decor of plaster relief, paint and "Dutch metal," a gold-leaf imitation. Someone has compared the rotunda to a Faberge Easter Egg turned inside out. In the historic Governor's office, Bouman left his playful "signature" — a small Medfly painted on the high ceiling.

Michael Casey, plasterer and sculptor, rediscovered a lost art when he used pastry decorating tubes to squirt plaster designs onto ceilings and friezes. Casey also sculptured the five-inch-high lions' heads that line a pediment off the rotunda's second floor. He says he modeled them after actor Jack Palance's "leonine face," just as ancient sculptors used to anthropomorphize animal subjects.

The tour guide will lead you to the Senate and Assembly chambers, which include the original legislators' desks. They were crafted c. 1869 by John Breuner. Breuner, who came to Sacramento in 1856, founded a furniture business that today numbers 16 retail stores in California, Nevada and Arizona, and some 27 rental furniture stores.

Today the Legislature uses electronic panels to show voting progress on bills. Closed-circuit TV also had to be accommodated in the restoration. Historic ambiance was saved by concealing technology behind drapes and sliding panels.

One Capitol oddity that was *not* restored was the hideaway bar where drinks were dispensed under an Assembly staircase in the late 19th century. Some legislators would invite women friends in for a happy hour, and the sergeant-at-arms would have to ask them to hold the noise down, so the other legislators could hear themselves think.

In what may be the world's largest jigsaw puzzle, 600,000 pieces of marble mosiac tile on second floor corridors were restored under direction of master mosaicist Hanns Scharff, 75. The mosaic was cut into four-foot squares, plywood was glued on top, and the slabs were lifted out. All 35 tons was shipped to a barn in the Tehachapis, southern California, for cleaning and polishing of each piece. Based on photos taken before disassembly, the tiles were re-set on plywood squares in their original floral patterns and returned to Sacramento.

Scharff, now an American citizen, served Germany's Luftwaffe (Air Force) in World War II as a reportedly genial interrogator of captured Allied airmen — a friendly enemy, in short. He maintains contacts with some of his former prisoners. While he worked in Sacramento, one of them dropped by for a visit — Oroville rancher Hub Zemke, captured in 1944 when his Mustang conked out over France.

The return of Columbus: Since 1883, the rotunda had housed a statue of Columbus and Spain's Queen Isabella, carved from Carrara marble by Larkin Mead, an American living in Italy. Banker D. O. Mills, the owner, gave it to the state. As restoration began, the six-ton statue was shifted to a nearby state office building. Controversy long swirled over whether to return it to the rotunda. Architect John Worsley was opposed: "It disrupts traffic flow across the rotunda and turns it into a round corridor."

Senator James Mills, a staunch preservationist, demurred: "I don't see how we can call this a historical restoration if we left it out."

Senator Petris added: "As far as historical significance is concerned, it is the very statue before which Ronald Reagan took his first oath of public office in the dead of night in 1967." Reagan was sworn in as Governor of California in the rotunda.

Columbus and Isabella, after repairs and polishing by sculptor Spero Anargyros, were moved back to the rotunda and unveiled on Columbus Day, Oct. 12, 1982.

To some people, in these times of state budget austerities, the $67.8-million restoration pricetag may seem a bit much. But others note that the project was launched well before passage of tax-revolt Proposition 13, when state government was wallowing in tons of money, a treasury surplus of $5 billion. Contractor Mike Heller, board chairman of Continental-Heller which, with the firm of Swinerton & Walberg, formed the consortium of general contractors for the restoration, said: "If you take the original appropriation of $42 million and just add the escalation (inflation) factor each year, it comes to more than was actually spent."

Compared to an estimated $300 million for building a new Capitol, architect Worsley deems it a bargain, adding: "How do you estimate what it's going to cost when you've never done anything like this before? And down the road, they said we'll have to have furnishings and a museum room."

The Capitol's original furnishings had disappeared — sold as surplus, or junked. Teams ransacked antique shops, auctions and state offices, acquiring what Senate representative Daniel Visnich said "may be the nation's best collection of American Renaissance."

Completion of the six-year restoration was celebrated by a week-long $600,000 gala paid by private donations. In a $250-per-person black-tie dinner, 850 persons jammed into the rotunda to dine on foods of early California — quail eggs, smoked salmon, pinon nut soup, stuffed trout, wines. *San Francisco Chronicle* columnist Herb Caen called it "a strange meal that replicated one served at the Capitol a century ago, using the original ingredients." On the crowded mall, cheers rang out as skyrockets burst overhead in what was billed as the largest fireworks show ever in northern California. Sirens wailed as fire engines converged on a temporary building to douse a fire on its roof, ignited by fireworks.

In the ensuing week, a plague of mice invaded Capitol offices. One jumped into somebody's cup. Others frightened staffers with arrogant stares. They put out trays of rodent poison, but the mice "went through that stuff like it's candy," someone said. By degrees the mice became less conspicuous. Either the poison was working, or their sergeant-at-arms told them to hold it down.

A few days after the mice problem, vandals carved initials in an ornate railing, and someone stole crystal pendants from legislative chambers. "We were naive enough to have thought the beauty of the building would be enough to overcome the jungle instinct," said Richard Reese, chief executive officer, Assembly Rules Committee.

To scare away pigeons, who were soiling the walls, artificial inflatable snakes were placed on the roof.

All told, 1,300 persons labored on the restoration, believed the largest of its kind in the western hemisphere. Continental-Heller received a Contractor of the Year award from Sacramento chapter, American Public Works Association. And American Institute of Architects gave the Capitol its highest accolade, the Honor Award — the only restoration project in the country to get this award in 1982. Girvigian, for his contribution, received California Historical Society's 1982 Historic Preservation Award.

Energy incarnate, an Indian on horseback battles a grizzly on the Capitol roofline. This re-creation is the work of renowned sculptor Spero Anargyros, whose latest Sacramento opus is a statue of Captain Sutter, unveiled in October 1987 at Sutter General Hospital.

In Girvigian's opinion, some work remains: "At the very least, the wrought iron fences and granite posts that rimmed the block in the 1870s should have been restored. I'm hopeful that in some future phase the Legislature can find funds to do a proper job."

Yet one might hope that if the ghost of the troubled Reuben Clark is haunting Capitol corridors, he may find serenity in gloating on the restoration of the splendid edifice he pushed forward at its origin, at such personal sacrifice.

Chapter 51

A Capital Park

Would you believe a tree in Sacramento sprouted from a seed that traveled through outer space? The tree today stands 25 feet tall in Capitol Park. More later on the arboreal astronaut.

Capitol Park, its 40 acres encompassing the Capitol, is planted with nearly 100 species of trees and unnumbered varieties of other plants from all over the United States and from many foreign lands.

Free one-hour walking tours of the park are offered every day at 10:30 a.m., starting from Room B-27 in the Capitol basement.

The Trout Pond contains rainbow trout, but no golden trout, though the latter is the state fish. Charlene Jacobs, a tour leader, explains why the state fish were omitted: Golden trout can't abide the water temperatures that prevail in Sacramento's torrid summers.

All around the park, everything seemed to be some shade of green. Even the hangings in the windows of the Governor's office on the Capitol's southeast corner reprised the vernal color. "See those green drapes?" Jacobs asked. "They're not really green — they're white. They look green because you're looking at 'em through bullet-proof glass."

As the tour proceeded, Jacobs, a master gardener from UC-Davis, identified notable trees, adding pithy facts. A few items:

- The lovely dawn redwood looming yonder is a "living fossil."

Civil War buffs re-enact a famous battle in Capitol Park — which contains a Memorial Grove of trees transplanted as saplings from Civil War battlefields.

That is, it was known only in fossil form until 1944, when living specimens were discovered in China. The dawn redwood is also unique in that it is the only species of redwood that is deciduous; its leaf tufts open in March.

- The Canary Island date palm is easy to distinguish from other palms because its trunk texture reminds you of pineapples.
- Don't pick the oranges on the sour-orange tree. There's a $50 fine for molesting it.
- That small sugar maple was brought here several years ago by Canada's prime minister Pierre Trudeau.
- That Italian stone pine was planted by then-Governor Ronald Reagan.
- A huge Guadalupe cypress appears to be dying. Perhaps it is, as this tree's average lifespan is 85 years, but this rugged individual has survived the heat and cold and winds of all the seasons since 1872.

The tour ends at a grove in which each tree was transplanted from a different Civil War battlefield. Jacobs explained that the group had taken only one of the three tours here, as the park is too big to conveniently cover in one tour. She notes that a special tree in one of the other tours is a sago palm, or dinosaur palm, so named because it thrived in dinosaur days and is believed to have composed a good part of the diet of those colossal vegetarians.

Tree tours are fun for everyone who wants to check out his or her ability to identify, and add new trees to one's vocabulary of recognition. For the novice, there are too many here to learn in one tour, but one has to start somewhere. The tours also are great for sheer casual enjoyment of the green canopy in Capitol Park. The tour leader will give you a pamphlet identifying each tree in this downtown oasis.

The tree whose seed traveled through outer space? Dubbed the "orbit tree," it's a redwood standing on the north side of the Capitol, just east of the L Street entrance to the East Wing. Its seed was one of scads of seeds that in 1970 circled the moon aboard the Apollo 13 space vehicle. The seeds were sprouted at Harvard and sent as seedlings to various places, Sacramento included. So far this sapling has shown no untoward effects from its lunar adventure, but who can say what tomorrow may bring?

Chapter 52
The Old Mansion: The Governors Slept Here

Like a proud dowager, a Victorian mansion stands at the busy corner of 16th and H Streets, seemingly a bit out of context in this commercial district. It was built in 1877 by Albert Gallatin, gold miner manque who became rich by selling hardware to miners. The three-story mansion with tower is enhanced with bay windows, gables and mansard roofs.

Gallatin is a classic American success story. In 1861 at age 25, he arrived in Sacramento, penniless, but found a job as a humble porter with Huntington and Hopkins hardware store. But he didn't intend to stay humble — and soon rose to salesman. Gallatin stayed with the firm 27 years, becoming the managing partner in 1868 and president in 1888 of what had become the largest hardware on the West Coast. It reaped enormous profits by selling tools and supplies not only to miners, but of greater consequence to the builders of the transcontinental railroad. The two hardware owners constituted exactly half of the Big Four.

Gallatin spared no expense in construction. He imported Italian marble for the mansion's seven fireplaces. Three are brecciated or variegated marble, while four are of pure white Carrara marble with carved designs. He also imported French mirrors, and mahogany from South America for stairways, doors and archways. Door knobs and hinges are works of art crafted from bronze.

You can rent the Governor's Mansion for weddings and parties.

Rooms are decorated with furnishings from the 13 governors' families who lived here. The ameliorations include Persian rugs, marble statues, a 1903 Steinway piano, handcrafted silverware, and gold-trimmed china. Visitors can view 16 rooms, including the kitchen, the formal parlors and dining room on the first floor; the second-floor bedrooms and one of the first indoor bathrooms in California, a point of pride to Gallatin.

Gallatin and his wife Malvina, one of Sacramento's most beautiful ladies, once staged a masked ball that was — because of the bizarre costumes — the talk of the entire state of California for years.

Before moving to San Francisco, where the hardware company had expanded, Gallatin in 1887 sold the mansion to his friend, drygoods merchant Joseph Steffens. Steffens's son Lincoln, who spent his boyhood years there, would become a famous muckraking journalist and author of *The Shame of the Cities,* exposing municipal corruption. His autobiography, another bestseller, told of his work in the American radical movement. How many radicals come out of a governor's mansion?

The State bought the property in 1903 for $32,000, and it became the official residence for California governors, who had been bunking in hotels and private residences. The first governor, George Pardee, moved in the same year, after a small wing had been added and the building refurbished and furnished.

In olden days, familiar sounds in the neighborhood were the clangs of streetcars, clatter of hooves, faraway steamboat whistles, snorting trains, and even the lowing of cattle. It was that kind of a time. Today, the uproar and screech of traffic envelop the mansion. Many trees and shrubs planted here in 1877 have reached giant size. Camellias, normally of shrub size, shade the walkway, grown as large as trees.

Neighbors of Governor Pardee and his family included the prominent Weinstock and Breuner families. Their children played with the Pardee kids.

On that terrible April 18, 1906, when earthquake and fire scourged San Francisco, Governor Pardee immediately wired San Francisco officials a pledge of state aid — and by noon of the same day he had ordered 3,400 National Guardsmen to San Francisco and other Bay points to maintain order. Before sunset, Pardee himself was aboard a train bound for the disaster scene, to spearhead relief efforts. Not for another three months would he return to Sacramento — visibly aged. But in that interval, help had been distributed to 350,000 victims of the fire that destroyed 28,000 buildings, with losses aggregating up to $500 million. The number of lives lost would never be determined.

Happy days at the mansion were interrupted again when a dynamite charge rocked the building on Dec. 17, 1917, during the 1917-23 tenure of Governor William Dennison Stephens and wife Flora. The blast damaged the kitchen and laundry, but no one was injured. But Sacramentans were shocked by the apparent assassination attempt. Newspapers blamed terrorists, "almost certainly agents of the German government with I.W.W. affiliations." The mansion's carriage house contains wall displays, including a copy of the Dec. 18, 1917, *Sacramento Bee* with a banner headline: POLICE SEEKING DYNAMITERS.

A week later, police nabbed two leaders of the Industrial Workers of the World, who were driving a delivery wagon with nine sticks of dynamite hidden in a box of soap; they later arrested 28 more IWW members. The case never was formally solved, although *The Bee* denounced the blast as an IWW job.

Grief: In 1918, the Stephens' son-in-law, Major Randolph T. Zane, was killed in action in France. His widow Barbara returned home to her parents at the mansion, bringing her small daughter Marjorie. On April 25, 1921, Barbara and Dr. John N. Osborn were married in the mansion.

Lightning struck the mansion cupola Feb. 8, 1922, while Mrs. Osborn was back home again, visiting her parents. It touched off a small fire that was speedily doused.

Governor Friend Richardson, a 1923-27 tenant, never shook hands with anyone. "Unsanitary!" he said, with an air of repugnance. On moving in, the Richardsons gave the manse a vigorous cleaning —whereupon their daughter Ruth, 23, lit a fire in her west bedroom fireplace. *Whump!* A quarter of a century of accumulated soot and ash in the chimney cascaded into the fireplace below, spilling out into the room. Henceforth, fires were prohibited in mansion fireplaces.

During World War II, Governor Culbert L. Olson was planning a contribution to the war effort when on Oct. 2, 1942, he made his way to the roof with a crowbar. From roof edges, he pried loose two tons of ornamental iron grillwork. Private junk dealers were handling the scrap iron drive, but then somebody determined that the state was not allowed to give away state property — namely, the grillwork — to private persons. The iron is said to be in storage somewhere, but nobody seems to know where.

Governor and Mrs. Goodwin J. Knight, tenants in 1953-59, used to hold annual open houses for the public, beaming and greeting everybody with a handshake as they entered. Guests totaled 7,004 at the fifth annual open house, Jan. 5, 1958, up from 6,202 the previous year. This author covered the 1958 event as a reporter for *The Sacramento Union*:

> Knight was jovial, always ready with a quip, and he refused to admit his own hand was tired because of having to pump the hands of the 7,000-plus friends who came to say hello.
>
> Mrs. Knight was radiant in a pink brocade gown with gold thread and trimmed with pink satin. She wore a pink camellia corsage.
>
> One woman reported that it took her 35 minutes to get from the end of the line to the entrance.
>
> At one point Knight, concerned over the many waiting in the chill air outside, urged his wife to go outside with him for a moment.
>
> "We've got all day!" Knight shouted to the long line. "In fact, we've got a whole year ahead of us!"
>
> Mrs. Knight: "And there's no hurry when you come in. I want you to stay a long time."
>
> Knight got laughs when he cracked: "But we don't mean a week."

Governor Ronald Reagan and Nancy and their son Skipper, 8, moved into the mansion Jan. 1, 1967, knowing the building had been labeled a fire hazard. One day a false fire alarm propelled Nancy and Skipper into a hasty exit. That did it for the Reagans. On April 1, they packed their bags and moved to a rented house in East Sacramento. They were the last family to live in the mansion.

With the building vacant, California Department of Parks and Recreation started guided tours. They began on Admission Day, Sept. 9, 1967, when Nancy Reagan snipped the ribbon across the front steps. The following year, the mansion was designated a state historical landmark.

It is now open daily — except Thanksgiving, Christmas and New Year's Day — from 10 a.m. to 5 p.m. Living History Day is generally scheduled twice a year, with activities focused on a specific date. You meet the Governor and family, portrayed by docents, and relive a day in their lives — for example, that of the Pardee family in 1906, the Youngs in 1927, and the Warrens in 1944.

Pardee docents reflected the way things were on Aug. 6, 1906, four months after the San Francisco disaster. Docents in costumes of the day led visitors from one room to another. In one chamber, Governor Pardee rehearsed aloud a speech he would soon deliver.

One costumed docent, as one of Pardee's daughters, remarked that when her father had left for San Francisco in April, "his beard was as brown as a hazel nut. Now, three months later, it's as gray as a San Francisco fog."

The carriage house, converted to a visitor center, offers more information on the great house and its occupants. Souvenir hunters and collectors may be intrigued that for a small donation they can obtain a handmade shingle from the carriage house's original roof.

A much more startling fact is that anybody can rent the mansion — as a setting for a wedding or a party.

For more information on the mansion, call 323-3047.

If you want to add horses and carriages to an old-fashioned mansion party, call Rick Stevenson, Fashion Stables, 447-1086.

Another many-splendored dwelling — built for California governors but never yet occupied by a governor — reposes on 12 acres near the American River in Carmichael.

That story unfolds in the next chapter.

Chapter 53

The *Other* Mansion: La Casa de los Gobernadores

"For the Governor to live in an ordinary house just doesn't make sense to me." — Matt Franich

The new Governor's Mansion at 2300 California Ave., Carmichael, came into being after friends of then-Gov. Ronald Reagan paid some $200,000 for the parcel in Carmichael, then donated it to the State.

Hundreds of people chipped in small contributions, each paying for a small piece of soil. Agreements with contributors stipulated that if for any reason the land was not used for its intended purpose, all monies would be refunded.

Ground was broken in 1974, but construction ceased in the following year after the State spent $1.3 million on the building. Meanwhile, Reagan was out as Governor and Jerry Brown was the new chief of state. But Brown decided to lower his expectations —and elected to move into an apartment (placing a mattress on the floor) more fitting to his "small is better" lifestyle, rather than into what he called a "Taj Mahal."

After a time the State elected to put the great house on the auction block.

In Palos Verdes, southern California developer Matt Franich was startled to see an auction notice in the *Wall Street Journal.* Recalls he: "I said to my wife, 'Can you believe they're selling the Governor's Mansion?'"

This was actually the second auction. In the first auction, which he hadn't known about, none of the bids proved high enough to please the State, so all were rejected.

In the second auction, Franich said, his own bid was the highest but the State said his bid didn't arrive in time. Franich insisted it did. Finally his "lost" bid was found. State attorneys, fearing a lawsuit, rejected all bids and held a third auction. This time Franich won, with a bid of $1,550,000.

Of a sudden, Franich received a subpoena from an attorney representing the donors, saying his bid was invalid. "They claimed the State had no right to sell it to me," he said.

Franich said he later learned that the State worked out some settlement with the donors, but won't tell him the details.

"The title policy," he said, "showed the problem of the individual donors, but the State finally let us have clear title, because it didn't want to go to court."

It took nearly a year to close escrow — which by chance befell on his birthday, Sept. 18, 1984.

The mansion's original architect, chosen in a statewide contest, was the Pasadena firm of Conrad Buff and Don Hensman, who were awarded $150,000.

"Nancy Reagan probably spearheaded the design," Franich said. "She would say, 'I don't like it. I want to change this, or I want to change that.' After the Reagans visited the Presidential Palace in Mexico City, Nancy wanted to change everything. She wanted a Spanish hacienda.

"When we first looked at the property, the grounds were nice and green. Before close of escrow, we suggested to the State that we put our own people in, to take care of it. The State refused.

"After close of escrow, the mansion and grounds were in bad shape. Trees were dying and the grass was dead.

"When they gave us the keys, we couldn't get in! None of the keys worked.

"The State hadn't even finished the construction job. The house was basically a shell — little or no lighting, for example. Floors weren't in. They were basically concrete, with some tile.

"The grounds had no walls, no gates, no landscaping. The fence was chain-link, with a chicken-coop gate.

"At the first rain, the Governor's office and library and formal dining room were inundated. The 'state of the art' solar system was leaking like a sieve, and never did work. Expanding ice in the first freeze broke all the parts. The State architect said it would cost $35,000 to replace.

"The roof was leaking badly. There were two inches of water in the living room on the first rain.

"The caretaker was manufacturing furniture here. And his wife was canning and processing food for sale. Two catering companies worked out of here. And about 15 people had this address listed as their residence.

"We moved 350 cubic yards of garbage and trash that had been dumped here.

"The State shouldn't have let people live here — which it did, during the Jerry Brown administration. They were letting homeless people live here. They were abusing the place.

"But I wanted it so badly I felt we could overcome anything."

He wanted it so badly because he had fallen in love with it, not only its lovely setting, but its awesome dimensions. Item: The main roof beam, a whopper 220 feet long and almost six feet deep, cost $148,000 in 1974, more than most houses cost today. "One stick cost that much," Franich marvels.

Franich launched improvements galore. He installed 11,000 floor tiles, and laid down 40 Persian rugs. He planted over 200 trees, erected an adobe-type wall fence with wrought-iron gates that open and shut electrically. He installed 607 outdoor security lights and closed-circuit TV monitors. He also put in a 50x30 swimming pool, with fountains, a spa with lion's-head fountains flanking a waterfall, an opulent bathhouse and sauna, and much more. The mansion accommodates 10 bedrooms, 11 bathrooms, two kitchens, three dining rooms, and has a total of 31 rooms.

"I spent more money to restore it than it cost to build.

"We installed the heliport — the large lawn in front of the building. We planted 400 to 600 trees — peaches, nectarines, cherries, avocados, persimmons, etc."

They bought antiques and furniture from all over the world, including three chandeliers from Italy for the formal dining room, and a huge 60-inch diameter chandelier with hand-cut crystals from Austria — identical to those in Louis XIV's Palais de Versailles —for the ballroom.

The mansion has 80 exterior French double-doors, with German locks. The front doors are 20 feet high, and each weighs 850 pounds. "I personally installed 800 rolls of wallpaper," Franich says. And they installed 5,000 square feet of mirrors.

Ken Stringfellow, the present caretaker, remembers: "The first night I stayed here, it was a dark and stormy night" — the kind where you hear strange noises. As he stepped into the dining room he was startled by what he took for an intruder — his own reflection. "It's a good thing I didn't have a gun," he says, "or I would've shot myself."

The mansion's Old Sacramento Room has a beautiful bar where Black Bart slaked his thirst in Jackson. The bar was salvaged from the razing of the Jackson Hotel c. 1980.

Fifty-seven carpets, half from Persia and half from China, decorate the floors of the mansion, whose floor plan is 26,400 square feet, three-fifths of an acre.

But Deukmejian balked at the notion the State should pay the $18,000-a-month rent Franich was asking, for a building the State had just sold. So he turned thumbs down on Franich's offer and moved into a $400,000 home purchased with contributed money.

The Franiches have hosted as many as 1,100 people here at one time for social functions, and raised $1 million for charities.

But Franich still has a bone to pick: He is suing the State for $800,000 on these grounds: The mansion was not in the condition represented, and there was no mention of a flood plain being part of the property, nor of the existence of an Indian burial ground.

Franich says the State brochure advertising the auction said the flood plain was only 0.4 acres, but in reality it covers 4.3 acres —"and you can't build on a flood plain."

When the land was purchased in 1910 by the Deterding Ranch, the original deed showed it stretching to the center of the American River. Since then, Franich said, the river has shifted 600 feet farther south, adding 4.3 acres, making total gross acreage 16, instead of 12.

He plans to give that unexpected bonus of 4.3 acres to County Parks and Recreation "to square up the parkway corridor," contingent on his getting approval for four more lots — on which he plans to build luxury homes.

Franich tells of another jolt: "In 1984 before close of escrow we became aware of the existence of the Indian burial ground. In 1978, the U.S. Department of the Interior had certified there was an Indian burial ground on the property.

"If the prospective purchasers had known that, nobody would have shown up for the auction. An Indian burial ground — that's dynamite!"

Franich said he was told, "Take it or leave it."

From the burial ground in 1937, 117 bodies were unearthed and stored in a quonset hut. "But somebody had a party, and the place caught fire, and all the bodies were lost."

As far back as 1,000 BC, Nisenan Indians lived and died in Carmichael and were buried where Matt Franich's Governor's Mansion now stands. Archeologist Melinda Peak and Franich were among scores of people on hand for dedication of the burial ground.

In 1972, the State spent $110,000 on an archeological dig to see if the burial ground would hamper plans for the Governor's Mansion, Franich said. "They discovered 11 more bodies, which were left *in situ*. The bodies were from the Middle Horizon Period, 1,000 BC to 500 AD. We have arranged with the Nisenan Indians that we will not disturb the bodies, and they agreed to let us go ahead with the project."

"There could be several hundred bodies left," says archeologist Melinda Peak, who studied the burial grounds.

"The best thing we can do is leave them capped off by soil — banking them for the future — so that, with technological advances in carbon-dating and other dating methods, we can learn a lot more."

In ceremonies on April 7, 1990, the burial ground was commemorated with a bronze plaque affixed to a two-ton boulder outside the mansion gate. William Franklin, a Nisenan, was a speaker.

Franich has received county approval for construction of a subdivision of eight houses on his land, each one on an acre.

Franich is confident the great house one day will be the home for the official it was designed for: "There'll be a Governor here someday. It's a terrible disgrace to sell something like this, after all the hard work.

"This house was designed to demonstrate the power and stature of a California Governor, and be a place where he could bring in dignitaries to discuss things, in a proper place to entertain..."

Franich was shocked when Governor Deukmejian moved into a $400,000 house: "For the Governor to live in an ordinary house just doesn't make sense to me.

"So we paid off the house and decided to live in it."

Franich says that in five years he has spent over $5 million on the mansion, including purchase price. He adds; "Biggest refurbishment job I've done. Now that I look back at it, I'm very proud of it. It's more magnificent now than ever."

Franich and his wife Patricia remain in the building they call "La Casa de los Gobernadores." Franich says the mansion "will remain as a private residence until a future governor decides to live here, and we will continue to preserve this 'one of a kind' jewel to fulfill its expressed design and purpose as part of California's history."

Only time will tell if a future governor chooses to dwell in the House of the Governors. Speaking of time, a time capsule on July 4, 1976, was embedded in cement near a fountain by the state architect. Franich says, though he is the owner, he will leave it untouched until its scheduled opening date, July 4, 2076. The capsule contains Reagan memorabilia, photos, newspapers, and documents. By the time its contents are opened, no doubt the fate of the mansion also will have been revealed.

Chapter 54
The Magnificent Crocker

Art is long and Time is fleeting.
Longfellow

The story of Sacramento's Crocker Art Museum, 216 O St. — one of the nation's finest examples of museum architecture, and the oldest art gallery in the West — really begins 3,000 miles away, in New York State, with brothers Edwin and Charles Crocker. And in Indiana, with Margaret Rhodes, who botched a sewing job.

The brothers are said to have shown an early passion for trains. But what boys *aren't* fascinated by trains? Yet how many boys grow up to help build a transcontinental railroad? Edwin became a lawyer and at age 24 was admitted to the bar in Indiana, where the family had moved, and swiftly rose in the profession. One day he would combine this profession with his early mania for trains, when he became legal counsel to the Central Pacific Railroad.

Edwin's first wife Mary became ill and died, leaving him with their young daughter, Mary. A quirk brought him his future wife, Margaret Rhodes. Margaret, working in a tailor shop in South Bend, Indiana, inadvertently sewed a pocket wrong on a customer's coat — the customer being Edwin Crocker. Edwin for some reason was not so much annoyed as amused, and asked to meet the seamstress. As often happens, one thing led to another.

Judge E.B. Crocker took his family to Europe on a shopping spree that made history.

Meanwhile, Edwin's younger brothers — Charles, Clark and Henry — had gone to California and were thriving as Sacramento merchants. Their enthusiastic letters persuaded Edwin to join them. Only a few days after their marriage, Edwin and Margaret Crocker boarded a steamship at New York, and arrived in San Francisco on Aug. 26, 1852.

In Sacramento, they established their first home in the Crocker brothers' store at 246 J St. In the next few months they endured, with other Sacramentans, the perils and woes of a typhoid epidemic, the city's largest fire ever, and a flood. While they lived in the renovated J Street store, Edwin worked in his brothers' mercantile business. One day he quit to resume practicing law. In 1853, he was admitted to practice before the State Supreme Court. In the next year, he founded the law firm of Crocker, McKune and Robinson, which prospered. Also in 1854, he and Margaret relocated to their own home, an undistinguished wooden building at 83 7th St. between F and G Streets.

Edwin's wide interests included music, art and horticulture. He grew a variety of produce and exhibited it in State Fairs, displaying potatoes, corn, raisins, peanuts, tobacco, sugar cane, cotton, vinegar plant and mangoes. He named a hamlet a few miles south of Sacramento — Florin — because of its extravagance of flowers.

Edwin and Margaret in 1854 also became parents of their first child, Kate Eugenie. Three more were born in the next several years: Edwin Clark in 1856, who died 16 days later of whooping cough; Nellie Margaret, in 1860; and Amy Isabelle, in 1863.

Edwin joined other anti-slavery advocates in founding the California Republican Party in 1856, and delivered the keynote speech at the first meeting, April 18, at the Orleans Hotel. He chaired the first state convention on April 30.

Edwin Crocker bought the former B. F. Hastings house standing in a fashionable neighborhood at 3rd and O Streets and hired architect Seth Babson to expand and transform it into a splendiferous Italianate villa. Their lavish new home boasted a large conservatory and an indoor swimming pool. Babson also is renowned for designing the Stanford Home.

Edwin contracted with Babson to build an art gallery just west of the new home. Babson designed the gallery to epitomize the Italianate mode, with ornately carved wood, twin curving staircases, elaborately inlaid and tiled floors, and exquisitely-painted plaster decor. It embodied an enormous ballroom, an elaborate library, a rollerskating rink, a bowling alley and a billiards room. The ballroom is said to have been constructed as a showcase for the Crocker daughters, to display their charms to best advantage to eligible suitors. Non-eligible suitors need not apply. The gallery became a gathering place for Sacramento's high society, and Mrs. Crocker hosted many parties, from grand balls to dinners and games of whist.

Governor Leland Stanford in 1863 appointed Edwin Crocker an associate justice on the State Supreme Court. In seven months on the bench, he handed down a record 237 opinions. To save time, he took a lunch pail to work.

Back in private life, he accepted an appointment as legal counsel for the Central Pacific Railroad, and poured his energies into the transcontinental effort. A month after the golden spike ceremony in 1869, he suffered a stroke in San Francisco. He would never fully recover, but in the next several years he kept working on his art gallery, amassing a collection that one day would become the largest private art collection of the era.

To buy art works, he and Margaret and their daughters in 1870 embarked on a two-year Grand Tour of Europe — and came home with more than 700 paintings and 1,000 drawings. The entire collection was hung, covering nearly every inch of wall space. Their gallery now housed the largest art collection in America. Besides European works, mostly bought in Germany, Crocker was a major force in commissioning works of California artists — including Charles Nahl, whose most famous painting is "Sunday Morning In the Mines," and Thomas Hill, famed for "Great Canyon of the Sierra, Yosemite," and "The Last Spike," the latter now hanging in the Railroad Museum.

Edwin, who died in 1875 at age 57, appears to have intended the art collection and gallery to be enjoyed not just by family and friends, but by the general public. Margaret hosted many friends and dignitaries, including deposed Queen Liliuokulani of the Sandwich Islands, President and Mrs. Ulysses S. Grant, and playwright-poet Oscar Wilde.

Margaret was hoping to sell the gallery to the city, but the city lacked enough money to buy it. Sacramento's merchant-philosopher David Lubin, founder of the Weinstock-Lubin department stores, suggested she *give* it to the city. She asked for a couple of days to think it over. And decided.

Margaret Crocker made a noble gift to Sacramento. Photo courtesy California State Library.

Came the day in 1885 — Sacramentans threw the biggest bash ever seen in the West, to celebrate her gift to Sacramento of the finest art museum west of the Mississippi. The floral extravaganza was put on fittingly in the largest building in California — the State Agricultural Pavilion near 16th and M Streets, a building with nearly three acres of floor space.

Rehearsals were held each afternoon for nearly a month. From the *Daily Record-Union*, May 5, 1885: "FLORAL FESTIVAL NOTICE. It is desired by the committee that every man, woman and child who attend the Floral Festival will carry in their hands a few flowers, or a small hand bouquet to present to MRS. CROCKER."

All Sacramento closed down for the great day — banks, schools, shops, even Central Pacific Railroad. Up to 20,000 people thronged to the festival, amazing considering the city's population then numbered only 30,000. Being photographed was no casual thing, so the program contained this advisory to alert everyone: "As it is desirable to perpetuate the scene by photography, at this point a drum will call the roll and immediately afterwards a gong will strike *Ten* strokes. During the striking of the gong the cameras will be pointed at the audience from different portions of the building, and in order to obtain perfect pictures it is necessary that all should remain motionless for the ten seconds, particulary avoiding the waving of FANS."

The largest of all the floral displays represented Sutter's Fort, 24 by 20 feet, the work of Sacramento Association of California Pioneers. "Some 3,000 school children entered the pavilion in double file, each with a bouquet, and . . . passing in front of Mrs. Crocker, where each deposited his or her floral offering," someone wrote. *Everybody* brought flowers for her.

Margaret Crocker, as she formally granted the property to Sacramento, told the crowd: "The only wish I breathe as I bestow it is that good may come to Sacramento by its possession."

In a 1985 Centennial Festival, Maypole dancing and other entertainments reminiscent of the one a hundred years ago were relished by a large crowd.

Margaret Crocker didn't have to donate the gallery, but did it of her own free will. If she hadn't been generous, she could have kept it in the family, or disposed of the collection piece by piece for profit. Big destinies sometimes turn on trifles — like the war that was lost for lack of a horseshoe nail. Margaret Rhodes bungled the pocket of a customer's coat — and thereby met her future husband, traveled to faraway California, and one day donated the greatest art collection in the west, and its magnificent showcase, to the City of Sacramento. Save for that muffed pocket, Edwin no doubt would have married some other woman — a woman who might not have been half as generous as Margaret.

The splendid gallery still stands, better than ever, having been improved by a $2-million reconstruction completed in 1980. It is listed on the National Register of Historic Places. To recognize its artistic significance, American Institute of Architects gave it a national honor award.

Two of the Crocker's strong suits are 19th-century German and American art. The museum also harbors some of the finest examples of northern California art that captures life in the early days. Many esteemed American paintings have augmented the collection since the Judge's day. Famous works include Peter Breughel's "Peasant Wedding Dance" and Wayne Thiebaud's "Boston Cremes." And the museum is noted for its galaxies of European art, Old Master prints and drawings, and drawings by Rembrandt, Durer, and Jacques-Louis David.

Among its diverse collections is Oriental art, of which Japanese armor forms another strong suit, any way you look at it. Exhibitions from cultures around the world are calendared each year.

As the Crocker's popularity ratcheted upward, demand for more exhibit space escalated. The new $400,000 R.A. Herold Wing was annexed to the back of the original gallery in 1969.

The Crocker Mansion, "reborn" in 1989 as a wing of the existing mansion, added three floors of new gallery space. The wing's exterior replicates the Italianate decor of the original mansion, on whose site the wing was built. Besides offering more exhibit space, the interior encompasses a re-creation of the original family parlor. The parlor is a window back in time, helping visitors to conjure up a vision of what life was like for this affluent family of over 100 years ago.

In the Crockers' time, the house often was full of merry visitors enjoying ditties from tinkling pianos. Today's re-created parlor contains a Weber square piano, one of the mansion's three original pianos. You can almost hear echos of music and laughter.

At opposite ends of the parlor, matching marble fireplaces face each other. Above each hangs an eight-foot tall mirror with gilded frame. Walls are hung with paintings the Crockers acquired in their Germany excursion, and with portraits of Edwin and Margaret, whose eyes seem to follow you.

A five-foot Carrara marble portrays the lovely figure of "Rebecca At the Well." An Italian table bears enchanting mosaics of ancient Rome. Underneath, among the legs of this masterwork, are sculptured Rome's infant founders Romulus and Remus and the she-wolf that in legend suckled them.

The thing about this parlor is that all these marvels did not just emerge in a minute from a production line, but were individually created over a long period of time by the loving hands of masters.

Linking the new wing with the existing Crocker, a modern three-story pavilion shows contemporary ceramics, northern California art and Asian art, plus exhibitions from the museum's collections of photography, German art, Victorian costumes, and Indian and Persian miniature paintings, all rotating in the galleries throughout the year.

The Crocker's Art Ark – a long, long trailer – cruises an 11-county district, dropping anchor at 20 schools, delighting 20,000 students a year with art happenings. The first Ark was launched in 1980 with generous donations from Raleys, Inc. In 1997, the museum received a substantial donation from Pacific Bell Foundation to fund a brand new state-of-the-art Art Ark equipped with interactive art booths and a computer station. Staffers in November 1997 launched the new ark on its maiden voyage. Noah would have been proud.

Docent-led tours of the museum throughout the week include signed tours for hearing impaired and "touching" tours for visually handicapped. The museum is closed on Mondays and some holidays. Call 264-5423 for information.

Chapter 55
Once in Love With Amy

From the author's feature in ***The Sacramento Union,*** *c. 1957, originally headed, "Aimee Crocker: She Was Stakes In $10,000,000 Poker Game."*

The beautiful, auburn-haired woman dealt playing cards to two fashionably-dressed young men seated at the table — Richard Porter Ashe, nephew of Admiral Farragut and a member of the family for which Asheville, N.C., was named, and Henry F. Gillig, past commodore of the plush Larchmont, N.Y., Yacht Club.

This was a poker game, but there were no chips on the table. The beautiful woman — heiress of a $10 million fortune — was the stakes.

She was Amy, or Aimee, Crocker, headstrong belle of early Sacramento and daughter of Judge and Mrs. E. B. Crocker, whose mansion was to become the city's Crocker Art Museum. She changed her name to Aimee after leaving Sacramento.

She had announced to her two suitors on that day in 1882 that she would marry whichever bested the other at a hand of poker.

Amy, born in 1863, was about 19 then, and destined to live a long life, scandalizing the nation with her zany capers.

The story goes that Ashe had the winning hand — four aces.

Amy is supposed to have told the crestfallen Gillig: "Better luck next time."

She and Ashe were married, but it didn't last long. Amy had begun thinking about her other swain, and soon she obtained a divorce from Ashe, marrying Gillig not long after.

Aimee Crocker lived an endless melodrama.

A second version of the fantastic game of chance that determined Amy's first husband (she was to marry five times) was reported in the *San Francisco Chronicle* of Dec. 25, 1921, as the result of a story told by J. J. Livingston, onetime Sacramento printer who said he witnessed Amy's wedding.

"According to Livingston," the *Chronicle* said, "Porter Ashe and Billy Wallace shook dice for the heiress. Wallace won.

"The party left Sacramento by train for San Francisco, where the ceremony was performed. Wallace left the coach in which his prospective bride was riding and went into the smoking car. Ashe, vanquished at dice, seized upon the groom-to-be's absence to press his suit.

"He won. Ashe and Miss Crocker left the train, boarded another one bound for Martinez and were married in the latter city while Wallace pursued his way to San Francisco.

"Livingston, then a youth, and his sister were visiting at the home of the rector of the Episcopal Church, Rev. Abercrombie, and Ashe and Miss Crocker called and asked to be married. The rector invited the young folks into the church to witness the ceremony." The date was Dec. 16, 1882.

The *San Francisco Call* of Jan. 16, 1883, "exposed" the wedding and revealed that the couple traveled to Sacramento afterward. According to the *Call*, Margaret Crocker held a reception in her home the following week.

A Sacramento woman, Mrs. Beryl Reynolds, 1500 - 22nd St., said her brother, the late Fred Patrick, worked as a coachman for Amy and Porter Ashe when they moved to San Francisco. Amy apparently was a demanding employer. "She worked him so hard driving his team to meet ferries and so forth, he had to give it up,"

Mrs. Reynolds said. "Have you ever seen horses when they've run and become all foamy? She ran him ragged. She was a wild Indian."

The "wild Indian" commentary was echoed by Mrs. Arthur McNeil of 2625 P St., whose father was a first cousin to Amy. Mrs. McNeil remembers Amy's "making eyes at the opera stars in San Francisco. Amy turned night into day," Mrs. McNeil said. "She would sleep all day and go gallivanting at night."

Amy shocked friends and relatives when, as a young woman, she embarked on a sailing vessel bound for Hawaii. She was the only woman aboard. But a bigger jolt was in store for the folks back home: Souvenirs Amy brought back as a result of her passage on this ship included tattoos on her upper arms.

She arrived in Hawaii during the grass-hut era when the islands were still largely in their unspoiled splendor. She looked up King Kalakaua, with whom she had made friends when she met him in England, which she visited as a young girl about 1879.

The king was so taken with her he presented her with a small island and the title of Princess Palaikalani (Bliss of Heaven).

But ever-restless Amy soon was on her way again. She traveled to the Far East, where followed amazing adventures with a Japanese baron, a Chinese nobleman six-and-a-half feet tall, a "wild man" of Borneo, and an Indian maharajah, in whose harem she lived — but only as an observer, she said.

On the Borneo incident, American newspapers related that Amy had been "kidnapped" by the "wild man," but the truth, Amy later said, was that she went along willingly with the prince on a tour of his domain.

When the native ruler insisted that Amy rule permanently in Borneo as his queen, that was a bit much. She stole a canoe and paddled down a jungle river a night and a day to freedom.

She also visited King Thebaw in Burma. Ruturning to Burma years later, she found his son ruling, after the death of his father.

Amy had become almost a legend in the interval, it seems. The young king said something like this to her: "I do not know when you will be with us again, in person. In spirit you must remain. There should be a monument, a shrine, erected in your honor and your memory." A Russian architect drew up plans for Amy's shrine, and she supervised an army of natives in its construction. It was said to have included an altar, temple bells, and a mural depicting Amy's first visit to Burma.

But the end of the shrine was ignominious. In 1942, a cruising

Japanese aviator spotted it and dropped a bomb, scoring a direct hit.

Amy's travels in the Far East induced her to become a great collector of Oriental art objects (she once had 200 Buddhas in her apartment), a student of the mysticism of the East, and a lover of snakes. Of snakes, Amy said: "They have more sympathy and understanding than humans — especially women."

She died Feb. 7, 1941, shortly before her 75th birthday, in a lavish suite of the fashionable Savoy-Plaza Hotel in New York City. Her obit appeared next day in *The Sacramento Bee*, with a comment by her cousin Bessie Crouch of Sacramento: "Aimee . . . was always giving. She was a fine, sweet girl." The hotel register listed her as "Princess Galitzine," a title she adopted after her marriage into a European royal family.

Her madcap adventures would fill a book — and they really did. A few years before her death, Amy set down her life story, *And I'd Do It Again*, available today in Sacramento's main library. In the preface, she declares: "And if I could live it again, this very long life of mine . . . the only difference would be that I would try to crowd in still more . . . places, more things, more women, more men, more love, more excitement.

"Let the Mrs. Grundys arch their eyebrows and reach for their smelling salts."

Chapter 56

The Stanford Mansion: Triumph and Tragedy

"Mrs. Stanford said his pleading was so pitiful she could not endure it." — Bertha Berner, secretary to and biographer of Jane Stanford, whose son lay dying.

Leland Stanford Jr. was born in this mansion, the Stanford House at 8th and N Streets. Might one even say that one of the world's greatest universities had its origin here with him? But what a heart-rending story is the tragedy that created it. More on that in a minute.

Today the beautiful brick house with decorative plaster exterior is dwarfed by neighboring high-rises, whereas in olden days it was "surrounded by a sea of wood-frame houses," notes Patricia A. Turse, lead guide with State Parks and Recreation. The property is both a state historic landmark and a national historic landmark.

Originally the mansion rose as a two-story house, designed in 1856 by Seth Babson and built for merchant Shelton Fogus. Another Sacramento merchant, Leland Stanford, bought it in 1861. Later that year, he was elected Governor of California.

A bit to the east, a separate small building was constructed to serve as Stanford's office.

On Inauguration Day, Jan. 10, 1862, streets were flooded by storms, and Stanford was forced to leave his front porch by rowboat. After being sworn in, the new Governor returned by boat to find the water even higher, and had to effect an entrance by scrambling through a parlor window.

The next Governor, Frederick Low, lived here during the four years of his incumbency, starting in December 1863. And Gov. Henry Haight used the office here in the first few months after his inauguration on Dec. 5, 1867, even though the Stanfords had moved back into the house.

Leland Jr. was born here May 14, 1868. When he was only weeks old, the Governor invited some friends to a dinner party. The waiter carried in a large covered silver platter and placed it on the table. "My friends," Stanford said, "I wish now to introduce my son to you." He lifted the cover — to reveal the baby lying on flowers in the platter. The smiling infant was carried around the table and exhibited to each guest.

Mrs. Stanford was said to be as surprised as everyone else to see young Stanford make his novel debut.

Unfortunately, Leland Jr. was not destined to a long life.

The copious flow of wealth into the Stanfords' exchequer accelerated following the 1869 completion of the transcontinental railroad. Since 1863, Stanford had served as president of Central Pacific Railroad, builder of the transcontinental's western half.

Now was the time to enlarge the house: In an 1871-2 expansion, workers jacked up the two buildings one story, and sandwiched them between a new ground floor and a new fourth floor topped with mansard roof. They demolished a small service wing of the Fogus building, replacing it with a new three-story service wing at the rear of a newly-built four-story crosswing. The crosswing joined with and incorporated the Governor's office.

New additions brought total floor space to over 19,000 square feet, nearly half an acre.

The building was warmed by no less than 13 marble fireplaces, plus stove heaters in the Governor's office, all burning coal. A fireplace in a parlor next to the dining room sports a "petticoat mirror" near the floor, covering the firebox, keeping out drafts, and perhaps allowing ladies to check if their petticoats were showing.

In the capacious kitchen, seven speaking tubes are mounted on the dumbwaiter. You can turn a lever on each to open its aperture, to communicate with any of various stations in the house.

Eyecatching features on the exterior include bas-reliefs of mustachioed faces on window frames, and decorative frieze panels and moldings under the eaves.

Rutherford B. Hayes, first American president to visit California, lodged here on his 1880 sojourn.

The Stanfords set forth on European travels. On Jan. 1, 1884, they left Vienna in brutally cold weather. Half-frozen, they crossed the Danube in an open boat at dawn.

From Constantinople, they cruised on a steam launch to the Black Sea, and Leland, 15, was permitted to steer. All day he stood at the wheel with a chill wind in his face and spray flying, reveling in the adventure.

That evening Jane Stanford noticed that her son seemed pale and weak. Leland Stanford dismissed it as probably due to his day-long excitement, but Jane remained worried.

They arrived at Athens in mid-January during this bitterly cold winter. Young Leland waded through knee-deep snow as he took in the sights. He also relished a visit with archeologist Heinrich Schliemann, examining his magnificent collection of antique treasures. Schliemann was the onetime Sacramento banker who discovered the lost city of Troy. His incredible story is told in "The Moneymen" chapter of this book.

After Leland Jr. toured some temple ruins, Mrs. Stanford once more discerned unusual fatigue.

The family arrived in Italy in mid-February, touring Naples, Rome and Florence. By this time the youngster was running an alarming temperature, and doctors were called in. They used drastic methods, then in vogue, to try to reduce it. They wrapped him in "ice-cold, wet sheets," wrote Bertha Berner in her biography of Jane Stanford.

"He always pleaded to be spared," Berner added. "Mrs. Stanford said his pleading was so pitiful she could not endure it, and only when Mr. Stanford told him he would willingly take the treatment for him did Leland keep quiet."

All efforts were in vain. Leland Stanford Jr. died of typhoid fever March 13, 1884, two months short of his 16th birthday.

The parents were devastated. Stanford, who had stayed at his son's bedside night and day through the terrible ordeal, as doctors fought the fever, sank in such a deep despair they feared for his life too.

At last he emerged from his coma, remembering a vivid dream: As he mourned that he no longer had any reason to go on living,

Leland Stanford's dead son appeared to him in a dream — and caused him to found one of the world's greatest universities. Courtesy Department of Parks and Recreation.

his son appeared and pleaded: "Papa, do not say that. You have a great deal to live for. Live for humanity!

"Don't spend your life in a vain sorrow. Do something for humanity. Build a university for the education of poor young men."

Build a university!

He told his dream to Jane, and said, "The children of California shall be our children."

Stanford said Leland Jr. had said so much in the dream he couldn't remember it all. Years later, he would often rue: "How I wish I could remember all he said to me in that dream.

"I know I resolved from that moment to build the university, and we both from that night resolved on this."

Ever since Stanford had started piling up his share of the enormous riches pouring in from the railroad, his thoughts had inclined toward philanthropy. Leland's death brought his nebulous notions to a sharp focus.

In Paris, only six weeks after his son's death, Stanford told an American minister:

"I have been successful in the accumulation of property, and all of my thoughts of the future were associated with my dear son. I was living for him and his future. This is what brought us abroad for his education. Now, I was thinking in the night, since Leland is gone what my wealth could do. I was thinking that since I could do no more for my boy I might do something for other people's boys in Leland's name."

One biographer wrote that the minister was "the first of a long line of people" who claimed to have given Stanford the idea of founding a university, or of expanding on the idea.

Even before leaving Paris, the Stanfords drafted a new will to provide for the university.

Before returning to California, they visited eastern universities to pick the brains of educators. Harvard President Charles W. Eliot warned it would cost at least $5 million to establish a university. Stanford just smiled and said he could handle it.

The institution — at a cost of $30 million — opened in 1891 on the Stanfords' Palo Alto farm of 8,800 acres, over 13 square miles, and was named the Leland Stanford Jr. University, still its legal name.

A museum of art and archeology, today known as the Stanford Museum of Art, was based on collections made by Leland Jr., including some small objects from Troy that Schliemann had given him.

Students from the university's class of 1907, touched by the story of the family tragedy, affixed a bronze memorial marker under the windows of the hotel room in Florence where Leland died.

Stanford, president of Central Pacific until his death in 1893, also had been president of Southern Pacific Co. in 1885-90, and from 1885 to his death served as a U.S. Senator.

Strangely enough, Stanford almost received an "Oscar" from the motion picture industry.

The story begins when Stanford's trotting horses held every training record in the world, related Bill Conlin, dean of Sacramento sportswriters. Somehow the argument arose as to whether a trotter ever had all four hooves off the ground simultaneously. Stanford swore it did, but somebody wagered $50 it didn't.

Stanford hired the foremost daguerreotyper of the day, Eadweard Muybridge, who stationed a battery of cameras 20 yards apart along the old race course on 21st Street. As a trotter hoofed the circuit, Muybridge snapped the historic photos that won Stanford's $50 bet – which was but a small fraction of the expenses he ran up.

Conlin said the Academy of Motion Picture Arts and Sciences posthumously honored Stanford for his contribution to the evolution of movies. While Muybridge was the photographer, Stanford of course was the "producer."

After Stanford's death, Jane continued to support the university until her death in 1905 — by poisoning.

Historian Richard E. Brown, in a letter to the author, said she died in Waikiki's Moana Hotel: "Apparently some servant of hers had a mad-on at her and poisoned her. She detected strange tastes in the water at her San Francisco home, so left for Honolulu to get away. However, she took the wrong servant with her! She woke up at night in the Moana with excruciating pain, saying she had been poisoned, and soon succumbed."

Jane had deeded their Sacramento mansion in 1900 to the Roman Catholic Diocese of Sacramento, for use as a children's home, in memory of her parents, the Lathrops, and her deceased husband's parents. The Diocese placed it under supervision of the Sisters of Mercy.

In its early history, it was known as the Stanford-Lathrop Memorial Home for Friendless Children.

In 1936, the Sisters of Mercy moved with the children to a new orphanage on Franklin Boulevard, and the Stanford Home became a residence for troubled teenagers under direction of the Sisters of Social Service.

The mansion in 1978 was sold to the State for $1.3 million for preservation as a historic building, though it continued to house teenagers until 1987, when the Stanford Home operation relocated.

To examine the historic structure, California Department of Parks and Recreation asked a team of its archeologists and architects to probe the structure, using archeological techniques. The team came up with findings so interesting it was decided to show them to visitors during pre-restoration tours, begun in 1988.

Item: In a front parlor, Patricia Turse shows a spot on the wall where archeologists had scraped paint away, down to the plaster. Ordinary light discloses the contours of several layers of paint. When Turse shines an ultra-violet inspection light onto the site, no less than 22 layers are revealed — testimony to at least 22 maintenance jobs in all the years.

Item: In another room, archeologists chipped away plaster to explore inner-wall construction — and found vestiges of mud believed deposited by the flood that had forced Governor Stanford to make his awkward exit and entrance via rowboat on Inauguration Day.

On completion of restoration some time in the 1990s, the mansion will debut as a house museum offering daily tours, living history programs and other special events not unlike those at the

Old Governor's Mansion. Meanwhile, tours will continue during restoration, within the limits of public safety. Call 324-0575 for information.

Troubled teenagers have lost a refuge — but only temporarily. Some of the $1.3 million received from the mansion's sale went to purchase 9.5 acres at 4144 Winding Way, where the Sisters of Social Service are building a $2.9 million facility.

It will be a brand-new building in every respect except for the name: Stanford Home.

The Stanford Home served as a temporary Capitol while the Capitol was under construction. It had 13 fireplaces.

Chapter 57

The Proud Breed: More Stately Mansions

Ordinarily, pinpointing the location of a house is no problem: The address is all you need. But in the case of Mory's Victorian, reposing at 917 H St. at this writing, you may discover it at another address in days to come.

Owner Mory Holmes sold the mansion in 1989 to developer Joe Benvenuti. At first there were fears he might tear down the historic edifice to make room for a high-rise on its prime real estate soil. Then word came out that he planned to *move* the mansion.

This grand mansion on H Street, constructed in 1885 at a cost of $16,000 — regarded as a prime example of 19th-century "stick-style" architecture because of its profusion of intricate bracketing and other oddities — incorporates two floors plus an attic and a full basement. Commanding the interior decor are a fine-looking hallway and hand-carved staircase.

Architects James Seadler and Seth Babson — the latter wearing laurels for his designs of the Crocker Mansion and Stanford House — schemed it for Llewellyn Williams, an affluent pioneer who knew how to relish the good life. Proof of that: J.J. Woolridge, in his *History of the Sacramento Valley*, wrote of the mansion: "There was little opportunity at any time for a dull moment to be found there, and entertaining on a lavish scale was the order of the day."

But those were the happy days before it became the address and haunts of the longest-continuing funeral business in California.

The mansion sold in 1907 to H. Edward Yardley, owner of Clark and Booth funeral company, a firm descended from one founded in Sacramento by undertaker John W. Wick in 1848.

In the ensuing years, various partners came and went. A.M. Hólmes, father of Mory Holmes, entered the business in 1946 as a partner with Charles Monro, and on Monro's death two years later became sole owner. Mory joined the firm in 1956.

For many years it had been known as Clark, Booth and Yardley, "California's oldest operating funeral home." In 1967, it was renamed Holmes Funeral Home, and operated there until 1971.

For about two years, it was leased to the University Club, a men's organization. In 1973, Holmes named it Mory's Place, offering its 19th-century atmosphere for luncheons and private parties.

But that's all history. As to when and where it may be moved, perhaps only Joe Benvenuti knows for sure.

Early announcements said it would be transported a few blocks to a lot on F Street directly opposite Dorothea Puente's famous boarding house, to serve as lodgings for American Youth Hostels.

If so, one might wonder if any ghosts that may be haunting the Victorian — remember, it served as a funeral parlor for many years — will find congenial spirits among those perhaps-uneasy spirits hovering about the boarding house where seven corpses, possible murder victims, have been unearthed from the yard.

Skeptical about ghosts? Consider: If you *were* to go questing for ghosts in Sacramento, would you be more likely to encounter one on a sunny day in the park? Or on a dark and stormy night near the eerie old mansion that harbored the longest-continuing funeral business in California? Or maybe in the shadows of the macabre boarding house where somebody hastily buried seven corpses in the dark of the moon?

Secret of Heilbron House

Since 1974, the Heilbron House at 704 O St., another superb example of Victorian architecture, has housed the Sacramento office of San Diego Federal Savings and Loan Association, which recently changed its name to Great American Bank — and in June 1991 is scheduled to merge with the Wells Fargo empire.

For some years until 1971, Heilbron House had been the home of the elegant Antonina's Restaurant.

This mansion is the tangible evidence of an intriguing history, and harbors a secret of a sort, of which more in a minute.

Heilbron House has a high mansard roof and a facade embellished by a portico supported by Corinthian columns. Like most Sacramento houses at the time, it was built eight feet above the ground to safeguard it from floods.

Next time you look, Mory's Victorian may have vanished from this scene at 917 H St. Photo courtesy of Mory Holmes.

Heilbron brothers August and Adolph arrived on the Sacramento scene in 1856. One of the brothers escaped being drafted into the Prussian Army when he stole some women's clothes from a clothesline and fled in drag to sanctuary in Holland.

As partners here, August and Adolph opened a grocery store, Heilbron A. & Bros., at 177 3rd St. Four years later, they acquired the Washington Market, a meat-packing firm at 147 J St. In time they added to their enterprise a slaughterhouse at 29th and P Streets, then a store at 217-19 J St., selling farm hardware and supplies.

By 1874, to raise their own beef, they established a breeding farm for Hereford and Durham cattle. They leased 54,000 acres bordering the Kings River. They purchased that land in 1880, plus 15,000 more acres. Now they owned 69,000 acres, or 107 square miles, in two counties — Fresno and Tulare.

On a visit to Germany, August married Louisa Scluer. The couple raised eight children. By 1880, August and his family found the house they were living in growing smaller as the size of the family increased. To build a larger home, they hired architect

Heilbron House, built by Cattle Kings, once housed Antonina's Restaurant, where you could dine on cattle — or beefsteak, if you will.

Nathaniel Goodell, who was relishing his laurels as designer of the prestigious Gallatin residence, future home of California governors. The Heilbron mansion at 704 O St. was completed in 1881.

Goodell had come to California from Massachusetts, where he had designed three factories and several hundred homes. He failed in the goldfields, but re-established himself as an architect in Sacramento. He waved his magic wand — or drafting pencil, if you will — and hundreds of other Sacramento houses and commercial buildings sprang into existence.

August Heilbron died in 1893 at age 58. Family members dwelt in the home until 1953, when they sold it.

Adolph served as president of Buffalo Brewery for nearly a quarter of a century, and both brothers had investments not only in his brewery, but in Sacramento Brewery.

The "secret" of the mansion? This marvelous urban mansion was

Once the center of the capital's social life, the restored Senator Hotel today is an office building.

owned, not by city boys, but by Cattle Kings, who lorded it over vast ranches on the Kings River in two counties — and who bred cattle that became famous and sought after not only on the West Coast, but in Mexico and as far as South America, Hawaii and Japan.

Save for the Governor's Mansion, the most photographed house in Sacramento is claimed by its owners to be the gingerbread manse with turret and "witch's hat" at 1931 - 21st St., corner of T Street. It has appeared on covers of city directories, tourist guides and real estate publications. Classes of art students zero in on it with sketch pads. Two movies have featured it as a backdrop, according to owners Bill and Alice Smith.

The newly-finished house in 1900 greeted its first owners, Fred and Caroline Mason. He owned Mason's Haberdashery, 628 K St., and Mason's Steam Laundry, which Caroline had started to do the ruffled shirts marketed in the haberdashery.

Some mansions have been converted to restaurants or bed-and-breakfast inns. One is the capacious Driver Mansion at 2019 - 21st St., with 6,500 square feet. It was built in 1899 by prominent Sacramento attorney Philip S. Driver. The mansion has a corner tower, columned entrance porch, clinker-brick chimney, and curved terrace. Driver and his wife Elisabeth and their family lived there until he died in 1923. Five of their six children were born in the master bedroom, distinguished by its curved glass window. During Driver's lifetime, funerals were held in the home. And when he died, all the State Supreme Court justices gathered there to pay respects. The property stayed in the family until Driver's son Robert died in 1977. In 1984, Sandra and Richard Kann bought the house and turned it into a bed-and-breakfast.

In Orangevale, the Victorian mansion at 8999 Greenback Lane is now a restaurant, L. W. Calder's, named for its original owner. It was built in 1907 as a retirement home for Scottish actor-producer Lord William Calder. He had fought for the South in our Civil War, then moved to Chicago, where he produced plays. This was Calder's second house in Orangevale, the first being the Calder Mansion erected a decade earlier across Greenback from the present restaurant, but razed some years ago. It is not known why a man who fought for the South ended up in Sacramento's North Area.

Some restored houses of distinctive architecture have been revamped into offices. One is the late Beaux Arts version of a French country home at 2015 - 21st St., built in 1910 by Dr. Wallace and Ella Briggs. Briggs, a physician and surgeon, lived in the house until 1920. Another is the Diepenbrock mansion at 2315 Capitol Ave., built in 1906 and owned by the early-day Diepenbrock family. Sacramento has numerous other early-day houses of felicitous architecture.

Reigning supreme among restored commercial structures is Hotel Senator, 1121 L St., opened in 1924 after being built for the locally unprecedented cost of $2 million. It was designed by Kenneth McDonald Jr. and Maurice Couchot after the Farnese Palace in Florence, Italy, and built by Cahill Brothers, San Francisco.

The Senator hosted big conventions and other major wing-dings. For Sacramento's high society, this was the place to be seen on glittering Saturday nights in the Empire Ballroom — and be reported on in *Bee* and *Union* society pages, making readers who weren't there sick with envy.

In its 1930s to 1950s heyday, it was dubbed the "Second Capitol" because legislators and lobbyists got together here to engineer power plays while relishing the good life, slurping highballs in the long bar and performing a feeding frenzy on steak and lobster in the Duncan Hines-extolled restaurant.

The Senator was the hotel presidents and presidential aspirants stopped at while in town. In 1975, President Gerald Ford, while walking from the hotel across the street toward the Capitol, was ambushed by Lynette "Squeaky" Fromme, who aimed a pistol at him, but it misfired.

The Senator's scintillating career seemed to have come to an inglorious end in 1979 when inspectors closed its doors after finding 78 violations of fire and other safety regulations. But it got a new lease on the good life later that year when Sacramento tycoon Buzz Oates bought the hotel for $2.5 million, after discovering he could save millions in taxes by restoring its exterior, portico and lobby to their 1924 appearance, and listing it with the National Registry of Historic Places. The rest of the hotel has 10 floors converted to 150,000 square feet, or nearly three and a half acres, of office rental space. Oates completed the restoration in 1983, after two years and $7 million invested, then began to spend $4 million more to build a dazzling restaurant and bar. In 1987, Oates and associates sold the Senator for $30 million to Equitable Real Estate Investment Management Inc.

Another renovated commercial edifice is the Ruhstaller Building, 900 J St., with 19,000 square feet of office space. Built in 1898 by Frank J. Ruhstaller, manager of Buffalo Brewery, it housed the brewery's executive offices. Not missing a bet, brewery people installed a tap room on the ground floor. A copper dome surmounts the corner cupola. The building originally was cooled by water pumped from the Sacramento River and shunted through a cooling apparatus. Paula Boghosian was the restoration consultant, Dan Mallicoat the builder-developer, and Deming Chew the architect.

Chapter 58
Life in the Forest

Except possibly for Paris, the City of Sacramento has more trees per capita than any city in the world. Fact is, Sacramento is populated with three times as many trees as people — at least one million trees versus 340,000 residents.

The city maintains 150,000 trees on streets, parks and other city property, says Martin Fitch, parks superintendent for tree services. He estimates that trees on private property escalate the total within city limits to at least one million.

Fitch says the county, outside the city, probably has at least as many trees as the city. Sacramento Tree Foundation confirms that estimate, bringing the city and county total to two million.

As to the old notion of the superiority of Paris with regard to trees per capita, it may not be true. The author's recollection is that the percentage of tree-lined streets in Paris is not as great as in Sacramento.

Sacramento has many times won the annual Tree City USA award from National Arbor Day Foundation. Sacramento is cited "for having implemented a sound management program for its urban tree resources" and for "creating a more beautiful, healthier, and happier environment for its citizens." Sacramento was the only city in California to win the award when National Arbor Day Foundation inaugurated the program in 1976.

The three most common trees maintained by the city are the elm, sycamore and ash. Biggest disease problem? The elm leaf beetle. City tree workers combat the varmint by hammering nails in elm trees, then popping an insecticide-loaded capsule over each nail.

Formerly, when workers planted trees, they planted the same species for block after block. Today, they mix and match — so if a new disease crops up it will damage only one of every three or four trees, instead of maybe several blocks.

If you don't have a city street tree within 12 feet of your sidewalk and would like one — free — call Tree Services at 449-5304. Tree Services reserves the right to determine if enough space exists for a new tree. Of course, your property must also lie within the city limits.

Sacramento Tree Foundation is a private non-profit foundation devoted to planting and preserving trees anywhere in the county. The Foundation offers a grant program in which interested persons may submit proposals for free planting of trees in public areas or in front of their houses. The minimum is 10 trees. For instance, 10 neighbors could join in a request for a free tree on each front lot. Anyone interested may write to P.O. Box 15824-A, Sacramento, CA 95852, or phone 924-8733.

Chapter 59
Animal House

Animals are such agreeable friends.
George Eliot

Lake Victoria, named after the African Lake, has to be the gem of the Sacramento Zoo. Its denizens include African and South American waterfowl such as flamingos and black-crested screamers, a large bird with a blood-curdling voice. They cruise the acre-and-a-half blue serenity that is margined by tropical flora.

Only the fact that their wings are clipped prevents the birds from taking to the air in a great escape. Yet their life in captivity seems to be envied by other birds, because sometimes company calls. "Free-flying birds drop in (for dinner) and hang out for awhile," says Zoo director Maria Baker. "We serve very good food here."

Brutus the giraffe is no longer with us. Suffering from severe foot problems, he had to be euthanized. At 19 feet – two stories high – he was the tallest animal in the zoo. Brutus was *born* tall – six feet tall and a hefty 150 pounds.

Two female giraffes remain to represent their kindred: Tasha, age 24, and 16 feet tall, and Vallynntine, age 3. (All ages mentioned in this chapter are as of 1998.)

Fastest of our zoo animals was Chakula the cheetah. A cheetah can do 80 miles an hour, if given half a chance and room to floor his accelerator. Chakula died in 1995 at age 13, which is "very old for a cheetah," said staffer Leslie Addiego.

The zoo now has three cheetahs to represent the local speed record: Tuli and Chelsea, both 7, females, and Kali, 8, male.

The zoo's deadliest tenant was an 11-foot black mamba, until it died. That kind of snake can jump with such lightning quickness it can capture a bird in flight. Since his passing, the zoo's deadliest title is being held by two red spitting cobras.

Winkie, the elephant, left alone by the death of her elephant friend Sue, was sent to the Detroit Zoo so she could spend her golden years with another elephant, instead of pining away from loneliness caused by the absence of any kindred.

With the elephants gone, our zoo's heavyweight title is held by

Olaf doesn't look like an intellectual, but appearances may be deceiving.

Jewel, age 32, a hippo at a whopping 3,000 pounds.

Rarest of the zoo's animals are Asian lions John, male, 13, and Nadi, female, 16. There may be only 150 Asian lions left in the world. They dwell in a forest reserve in India.

With only 340 tenants, down from 650 a few years ago, the zoo is making a transition to larger and more commodious dwelling places.

One of the most unusual things about the Sacramento Zoo is that it is one of the nicest – being ensconced in a park setting, Baker said. The zoo reposes on 15 acres of 161-acre William Land Park. More precisely, it lies north of Sutterville Road, between Freeport and Riverside Boulevards.

The zoo has become a major propagation headquarters for two highly-endangered primates – chimps and Sumatran orangutans. The zoo has three orangs. One is Urban Orange, male, born in our zoo and named in a contest c. 1979. The females are Ginger, about 43, ("very old for an orang." said staffer Leslie Addiego) and Sayang, 15.

The orangs dwell in a $500,000 digs, largest in the zoo's history, whose amenities include grass, a pool, waterfall, and trees and ropes for climbing and swinging on.

Space in the orangs' old grotto area was used to create the new $300,000 Chimp Arena, which replaces the old concrete and chainlink cage of only 200 square feet. The bamboo-beautified new area of 3,500 square feet has ropes and trees to swing on, and is separated from visitors by glass walls. Three chimps live here: Sammy, 50, Joey, 35, and a female, Josie, 33.

"Sammy and Josie have lived together in the zoo for 33 years," Addiego said. "It's a real strong bond."

These primates are endangered because their forest habitats are falling to the angry chainsaws.

Zoo people in 1998 were making ready to open a new $500,000 home for two snow leopards acquired from the San Francisco zoo. The two are a breeding pair – Shanti, 4, a female, and Ling Shan, 5 – so staffers are holding their breaths, anticipating. Snow leopards' natural habitat is the Himalayas, where they prowl snowy precincts on the roof of the world.

Just as with humans, zoo animals have to adjust their ways of life to extremes of seasonal heat and cold. During these stressful periods, keepers keep a close eye on their charges.

Birds are more sensitive to winter cold than many other animals. Tropical birds get heat lamps in their cages, aimed at their shelters.

Bears hibernate, but Baker says it is a kind of "false hibernation," because, though they linger in their dens for long periods, they exit every day, maybe just long enough for keepers to clean their abodes and serve their rations.

All animals have dens that are heated, and the option of staying inside or taking the air.

Cold doesn't affect the reptiles, because they live all the time, summer and winter, in a building where temperature is constant.

Many animals grow thicker fur coats to adapt to chilly air. Animals – particularly hoofed stock – are given more food in winter. But you have to be careful not to overfeed the animals, Baker said. "They don't expend the energy they would in the wild. If the animals get too fat, it's very unhealthy. It causes heart problems. They get very listless. It cuts down on the breeding activity. They're not willing to do much of anything. I'm pleased to say we don't have any cases like that."

In summer, even Adak the polar bear acclimates to torrid temperatures. His den remains relatively cool, and he can jump into his pool to beat the heat.

In a heat wave, keepers keep a close eye on the birds and hose down their enclosures, keeping the ground wet, keeping the tenants as cool as possible. "They may even sprinkle them to let them get their feathers wet," Baker said. "And they have a little pond they

From beak to belly, a flamingo's food does not travel the shortest distance between two points.

can wade in and splash around." Bears and cats and primates all have dens they can enter to retreat from the heat.

"California zoos are lucky because we don't have the extreme cold of the East, or the long periods of heat — 100 degrees and over, such as in Arizona and New Mexico." Baker said.

Food for the local denizens remains pretty much the same all year. "But in summer we may add more different kinds of fruit that are available — melons or grapes — for monkeys, birds, and hoofed stock."

The Noisy Neighbor

The grotto or enclosure housing two orangutans, Baldy, a male, and Josephine, in 1970 adjoined the one containing two gorillas, Chris, a male, and Suzie.

One day Josephine, apparently out of simian curiosity, climbed atop Baldy's shoulders and leaped onto the dividing wall that offered a vista into the enclosure where Chris and Suzie dwelled. The sudden apparition atop the wall apparently violated Chris's sense of privacy and startled him out of his usual composure. For he let out a jungle scream that could be described as bloodcurdling, then pounded his chest like a bass drum.

The scream apparently traumatized Josephine, for she jumped back down into her own cage, and never dared to look over the wall again. But just to make sure it wouldn't happen again, workers built a concrete lip atop the wall, overhanging the orangs' cage.

The Cheatin' Cheetah

Sometimes a wild creature proves the rule book is wrong. Baker says cheetahs are the only cats who aren't tree-climbers. "Theoretically, they don't climb trees. Their legs aren't constructed for it. They're runners. We received a young male, Chakula." A fairly young cat, he was yellowish-orange with spots. "He was very rambunctious. Everybody was keeping a close eye on him because he was a new and unusual cat."

Chakula's enclosure had trees, but no roof, because everyone knew cheetahs don't climb trees. "One day the keepers were walking past, looked up, and saw Chakula way up in the tree, 12 feet up, looking over the edge of his exhibit area. The keeper was carrying a pail, so he beat on it and scared Chakula, and chased him down the tree." Workmen then trimmed the trees so nothing of the sort would happen again. Moral: Never assume a cheetah can't climb trees — unless he has read the rule book and knows his limits.

Did Olaf Have a Plan?

Olaf, the polar bear, was a full-grown male weighing nearly half a ton. Recalls Baker: "One morning very early some years ago when the gardeners were doing their rounds, they saw Olaf sitting calmly in front of one of the cat exhibits." Somehow he had escaped from his enclosure, and was staring at the leopard, apparently with great curiosity. But how had he gotten loose?

Adds Baker: "Somebody had thrown something into the moat — possibly an apple or orange — and it had plugged up the drain, causing the moat to fill up, so Olaf could swim or float across, and thus reach the edge and climb out. We called vets from UC-Davis — we have an emergency number for them. They came in 15 to 18 minutes from Davis, doing full speed. They used a tranquilizer gun and shot him — and the keepers were able to get him back where he belonged. Now we have signs requesting that people not throw food into the exhibit."

Baker says it is possible Olaf purposely stuffed the drain to get out of jail. But that would take more intelligence that a bear possesses. Or would it? It's too late to give him an IQ test, because he "died of old age," at age 27, Baker said.

The Elephant Who Forgot

This is a tale of an elephant with a bad memory — which everyone knows an elephant hasn't. When Sue, the big elephant in the zoo, first glimpsed Winkie in 1955, she was, in the words of Superintendent Hank Spencer, "scared to death," though Winkie was a mere infant of 425 pounds, less than a quarter ton.

Sue may have been frightened because she didn't realize Winkie was an elephant like herself, Spencer theorized. How could Sue know what another elephant looked like? Elephant lodgings don't contain mirrors.

Yet if Sue had searched back through her elephantine memory, she surely would have recalled a brief encounter five years earlier with a circus elephant brought to the zoo so Sue could get acquainted with another pachyderm.

Sue was the zoo's first elephant ever, and this was her first meeting with another elephant since arriving from Thailand in 1948 at such a tender age even an elephant's memory might be less than perfect. Of course, the meeting of Sue and the circus elephant made local elephant history — duly recorded in the newspapers with stories and photos.

Sad to say, when little Winkie arrived five years later to make her home in the zoo, Sue's memory apparently failed to recall her encounter with the circus elephant. For if she *had* recalled it, wouldn't she have known that no harm could be expected from another elephant? Least of all from puny Winkie.

In time, Sue lost her fear of Winkie, and by 1958 attendants were permitting the two to hobnob. For years they had kept them apart, fearing big, lumbering Sue might injure Winkie — and not the opposite, as Sue seemed to think. The good news is that Sue's memory seems to be okay now.

Sue, who weighed 1,440 pounds when the zoo acquired her through a *Sacramento Union* fund campaign, now is a strapping 9,300 pounds. And Winkie isn't so wee either. From her original 425 pounds on arrival, she has aggrandized to a whopping 9,400 pounds — 100 pounds heavier than Sue, and 22 times her original weight! Each is nearly five tons. They were weighed in 1986 by California Highway Patrol officials using computerized portable scales — designed for trucks, of course. Sue and Winkie have gourmet palates: It was their fondness for French bread that enabled officials to lure them onto the scales for the monumental weigh-in.

Alas, since the foregoing appeared in this book's first printing, Sue's arthritis kept getting worse. Seeking relief from painful joints, she would lean on a rail, then took to lying down and couldn't get up again. Zoo vet Dr. Murray Fowler put her to sleep April 21, 1989, and she presumably was spirited to that great elephant graveyard in the sky.

Since Winkie couldn't get over her depression at being alone, she was shipped to the Detroit Zoo, where she could enjoy the company of another elephant.

Tony Peters, who worked as a zookeeper here from 1964 until he retired in 1978, tells anecdotes about elephants, a bobcat on the loose, a rambunctious bear, an exceptionally ornery billy goat, and a runaway antelope that wasn't recaptured until it reached Capitol Avenue three miles away. And would you believe an aging movie star retired to our zoo? He was Butch, a chimp who played the stellar role of Cheetah in Tarzan movies but, because of old age, had to turn in his script and bow out.

Peters remembers when the zoo had 500 chickens and 80 sheep, among other animals. "Hank Spencer did a great job of starting the zoo, and building it. He fought like hell to have a zoo. That's why we had so many domestic animals at first." Better domestic animals than no animals at all.

"Bill Meeker, the next superintendent, introduced the docent program. And the zoological society came in and promoted fund drives to get things we otherwise couldn't get through our budget. Steve Taylor, the present superintendent, put the finesse on the operation. It took all three of them. Each superintendent was as important as the other."

Peters remembers when Sugar the giraffe was giving birth to a calf. "Giraffes give birth standing up," he said. "That's a long way to drop a calf." The father giraffe, Peters believes, was perhaps the tallest giraffe in the nation, at 17 feet. "He could lick the frost off the shingles on the roof of the barn." His name of course was Shorty.

Shorty was kept out of the corral while Sugar was giving birth, so he wouldn't interfere with the delivery — or interfere with *Sacramento Bee* photographer Bob Handsaker's efforts to record the birth on film. Said Peters: "All I could hear him say was, 'I hope I don't run out of film — I hope I don't run out of film — I hope I don't run out of . . ."

There are 340 stories in this naked city of animals, and the foregoing have been only a few of them.

Chapter 60
Green Mansions: Our Patrimony of Parks

A park is a green island in the asphalt jungle. The "Green Mansions" in this chapter title was stolen from the title of W. H. Hudson's classic novel, a fantasy set in South American green jungles.

The City of Sacramento administers more than 120 oases, or parks if you will, covering more than 2,000 acres, while the County of Sacramento oversees another 32 parks, whose acres total 9,000. Over half of that acreage lies along the American River. Besides city and county parks, 14 local park districts offer neighborhood swimming pools, tennis courts and other amenities.

William Land, who made his pile as owner-operator of Sacramento hotels, bequeathed $250,000 to the city to develop a park. The resulting 161-acre William Land Park lies between Freeport and Riverside Boulevards, and from 13th Avenue south to Sutterville Road. It embraces a nine-hole golf course, amphitheater, arboretum, baseball diamonds, three fishing lakes, an amusement center, archery range, basketball court, wading pool, playground and tot lot, nature area, Fairy Tale Town, a fantasy land for kids, and the Sacramento Zoo, described in the previous chapter.

Six-acre Fairy Tale Town's miniature sets are based on stories that have fascinated children young and old. Children can visit King Arthur's Castle and Robin Hood's Sherwood Forest, both of which can be rented for birthday parties and such. Call 449-5233. Puppet shows, skits and dancing are presented here on weekend afternoons. The town is open daily except Mondays, and closed in December and January.

The amusement center's nine concession rides range from the merry-go-round to a bantam roller-coaster. Nearby, live ponies are ready to hit the tiny trail.

McKinley Park: The city purchased this 36-acre site at Alhambra Boulevard and H Street in 1902 for $12,500. Florence Turton Clunie donated $150,000 for improvements, and the clubhouse was named after her. A double row of Mexican fan palms still brackets the old streetcar right-of-way, the tracks long gone, into this park, running northeasterly from the corner of H Street and Alhambra. McKinley's facilities include the Shepard Garden and Arts Center, and a rose garden containing 190 species. At its peak in June, it's a favorite place for weddings, if you pledged him or her a rose garden.

Del Paso, at Auburn Boulevard and Fulton Avenue, is the city's largest park, with 718 acres. It has one 18-hole golf course and two nine-holers; a lighted baseball diamond (Harry Renfree Field), nature areas, riding/hiking trails, picnic facilities and play equipment. It's the home of Sacramento Trapshooting Club, the only one of its kind in the area open to the public.

Mangan Park, 2230 - 34th Ave., 22 acres next to Executive Airport, has an indoor rifle and pistol range. Operated by the city's Department of Community Services, it was built in 1960 for private gun club members. Members of the public also may shoot there, for $2. The range is one of only a few city services that are self-supporting. Local rifle and pistol clubs use it for target practice, competitive shoots, and gun safety classes. Private security organizations sometimes rent the range for marksmanship training, and Sacramento Police Department uses it.

Miller: The 57-acre park at Broadway and the Sacramento River is home of the 572-slip Sacramento Boat Harbor, offering free launching facilities.

Mexican revolutionary heroes are commemorated in two city parks. One is General Emiliano Zapata, with a statue in a park named after him — Zapata Park, 8th and D Streets. He rallied peasants with the cry, "Land and Liberty!" and became a legend in his own lifetime. Marlon Brando portrayed him in the movie, "Viva Zapata!" The other is Father Miguel Hidalgo y Costilla, who has a bust in Southside Park, bounded by T, W, 6th and 8th

Gibson Ranch has an idyllic lake for fishing and swimming.

Streets. He was the father of Mexico's Independence and has been called the George Washington of Mexico. Hidalgo, unlike China's George Washington, never slept here, not even a siesta.

Of county parks, the most novel may be Gibson Ranch, a 325-acre green haven on the north side of Elverta Road, west of Watt Avenue. It offers youngsters hands-on experience as ranch hands. It was named after the former owner, R. H. Gibson, who raised quarter horses and ornamental birds. The park has a blacksmith and carriage shop, old farm equipment displays, domestic farm animals including cows, horses, sheep, goats, chickens and rabbits. Visitors may feed the animals. An eight-acre swimming pool is rimmed with sandy beaches, the sand imported from Monterey; the water is filtered, for swimming, and stocked with bass, sunfish and catfish, many of them eager to rise to glory on the hooks of young anglers.

Prairie City Off-Highway Vehicle Park: The county also operates this 850-acre park — more than one square mile of ups and downs and roundabouts — that is the venue of motorcycles and muscle cars, and even non-muscular cars. Located at 1330 White Rock Road near Prairie City Road, it has a mud drag-racing strip, two motocross courses, miles of trails for the casual driver, a one-quarter midget track, bicycle motocross track, and a mini-bike area. Each March, this arena hosts the Hangtown Motocross, a pro-am race that beckons more than 30,000 spectators. Admission is $1 for a motorcycle under 100 cc, and $2 for larger vehicles. Or, you can load up your pickup with motorcycles and pay only one $2 entry fee. Hours depend on the season. Call 351-0271.

Elk Grove Park: Outside of the American River Parkway, this is the county's most-used facility. Nearly 800,000 people annually swarm through this 125-acre park off Highway 99 in Elk Grove. Most come to play or watch softball at the county's largest softball complex, with 12 diamonds, half of them lighted. The three-acre lake presents swimming and fishing. Pedal boats can be rented. In the middle of the lake, "Pirates' Island" is rigged with playground equipment. The park has a restored one-room schoolhouse, in which:

Every pupil was a Rhoads scholar. Sloughhouse area children from 1872 to 1946 attended the one-room school, then sitting on land owned by Ralph and Myrtle Murphy. When Murphy heirs donated the building to the county, it was shifted in 1976 to a new foundation in Elk Grove Park. Volunteers toiled countless hours restoring the building and refinishing antique desks, re-creating the school's 19th-century atmosphere, complete with McGuffey Readers and writing slates. The school was named after a Sloughhouse man who helped rescue Donner Party survivors, carrying little Naomi Pike on his back from the mountains to Sutter's Fort. His name: John P. Rhoads.

Rancho Seco Park: Over 400 acres of shaded picnic areas, beach, youth campground and three miles of shoreline encompass the 160-acre lake, a vista dominated by the mammoth cooling towers of the nuclear facility. Add boat launch ramps, docks, fish cleaning facilities, sandy beach for swimmers, concessions, sailing, horseback riding, and fishing. You can't use a boat with an electric or gas motor.

Several county park acquisitions are not yet developed, including land along the Cosumnes River, Indian Stone Corral in Orangevale, and Stone Lake, in the southern county. The county's largest park is so superb it deserves a separate chapter, next up.

Nature walkers set out on safari through luxuriant woods of American River Parkway.

Chapter 61

Wild Kingdom: The American River Parkway

In wildness is the preservation of the world.
Henry David Thoreau

The American River Parkway winds for 23 miles along both sides of the river between Discovery Park, where the blue-green river merges with the cafe-au-lait Sacramento, to Nimbus Dam in the east. Its 5,000 acres makes it more than double the size of San Francisco's Golden Gate Park. Four million people use the parkway each year. If they all came at once, the crowd would be bigger than the population of Los Angeles.

The idea of preserving the greenbelt along the river harks as far back as 1915, but nothing was done to save the virgin green strip until Folsom Dam was built in 1956 for flood control — accelerating encroachment of urban development along the river. The County Board of Supervisors in 1959 charged the new county Department of Parks and Recreation with developing the parkway. Local groups including Save the American River Association helped draft the master plan. Said SARA's Jim Jones: "It sold itself — all you had to do was show people the river." For most people, one look was all it took.

A forest of magnificent trees flanks the river along the parkway, yet this is only 5 percent of the riparian forest that once stretched half a mile to five miles from each bank, as in the days when John Muir tramped through here on his way to the Sierra. Woodcutters long ago felled many great trees to feed ravenous steamboats, and farmers axed many more to make room for crops and pastures. Today's trees are but a forlorn remnant of yesteryear's majestic stands.

Yet venerable oaks still tower in the floodplain, in some cases 300 years old and more. Through an epoch of revolutionary changes, the oaks have been spectators, as it were, to the human drama passing along the river — from the halcyon age of the Indians to the feverish rush of gold miners; from fur trappers and hunters and fishermen to today's recreational anglers and rafters, joggers, hikers and equestrians. For centuries through summer heat and winter cold, these giant oaks, survivors, faithfully stood their assigned sentry duty.

The 23-mile parkway is festooned with several other large county parks, like emerald pendants on a necklace.

At the juncture of the American with the Sacramento lies 275-acre Discovery Park, offering boaters a six-lane launching ramp and floating docks. The confluence waters, where the blue-green American and coffee-with-cream Sacramento merge at a distinctive color line, are a choice spot for fishermen when salmon, striped bass and steelhead are making their runs.

Discovery Park harbors a little-known curiosity that might be called The Bay Bridge That Came to Sacramento, for it arrived here from San Francisco Bay. The concrete and iron bridge on the south side of the park used to shuttle cars between Oakland and Alameda. In the 1920s, the Posey Tube was tunneled under the estuary to carry the traffic. Sacramento County put in a bid for the bridge, and won. The span was cut into sections and barged to Sacramento, then reassembled to bridge the American. In 1968, its job of carrying through traffic was taken over by the new I-5 Bridge, but the old bridge still ushers cars in and out of Discovery Park.

Discovery has one of the finest public archery ranges in the nation, with 30 target bales in a stationary range — meaning the archer remains stationary — and a roving range, containing 28 target sites at distances from 10 to 40 yards. You move around as on a golf course, with safety factors built into the landscape to minimize chances of getting perforated by a wayward arrow. You may shoot the complete course, or exit along a safety path if you want to cut out early. Targets are free, and use of the range is free, except for the regular $2 county fee per car to enter the park. Groups can make rental arrangements by calling 366-2061.

Discovery Park includes 45-acre Bannon Island on the park's northwesterly margin. Bannon's outer edge is dense riparian, while a grass savannah dominates the interior. Bannon contains what is said to be the last remnant of valley oak savannah in the central valley. Bannon's south edge overlooks the junction of Bannon Slough and the Sacramento River. Oaks and cottonwoods fringe almost the entire perimeter. Bannon is an island only when floodwaters cut it off from Garden Highway. You can enter by parking on Garden Highway west of the overhead I-5 freeway, and following a trail into the interior.

At its heart lies the savannah, studded with scattered trees and plants such as goldenrod, prickly lettuce, blackberry, curly dock, Indian hemp and poison oak. Numerous small oaks stand here, but dominating the grassy plain towers the king of the island's trees — a mighty oak 75 feet high and an estimated 350 years old — born not long after the Pilgrims landed at Plymouth Rock.

Bannon also nurtures several rare plants and grasses, and is home to a small colony of the California Valley longhorn beetle, an endangered species. Among other tenants are gray foxes, soaring hawks and tapping woodpeckers. Great blue herons nest in what is called an established rookery — evidently not just one of your fly-by-night rookeries.

The Jedediah Smith Bicycle Trail runs from Discovery Park 31 miles to Beal's Point on Folsom Lake. At Discovery, an offshoot of the bike trail links up to the Sacramento River bikeway jaunting south to Old Sacramento. Each year, 400,000 cyclists hit the paved trail, named after the man who camped on the American River in 1827 and named it "Wild River." Smith was the first white man to cross the Sierra into California.

From Discovery, the bike trail wends along the north side of the river to Arden Bar, then crosses the river on a foot/bicycle bridge. The trail continues on the south side of the river and crosses again on the Hazel Avenue Bridge, then rambles on to Folsom Lake. But before crossing that bridge, cyclists have the option of going off on a tangent along the 14-mile Folsom South Canal bikeway that romps south to Sloughhouse.

Hikers, joggers and fishermen also use the path in vigorous numbers. In 1987, because of increasing traffic, a four-foot-wide path was laid down next to the paved trail, to reduce rush-hour collisions between joggers and cyclists.

Equestrian trails run along both sides of the parkway, with some exceptions, and other trails lace Mississippi Bar, Sailor Bar, and Hoffman Park. Discovery Park also offers a developed staging area for equestrians, with hitching posts, water troughs and horse-trailer parking. Hoffman Park has a small horse arena and hitching posts. Horses can be rented at Shadow Glen Riding Stables, 4854 Main Ave., Orangevale, phone 989-1826.

Recycling a bike path: The Jed Smith bike trail is not a new idea. A similar trail coursed along the river many years ago. Back in 1896, Capital City Wheelmen, a local bike club, built a cinder bike path along the river from Sacramento to Folsom. Later that year, 500 cyclists sprinted along the first section. In time the trail was elongated to Folsom. But over the years it fell into ruin — just as sizeable segments of the modern trail did in the floods of February 1986. All damage has been repaired.

The scheme for the modern bike path was resurrected in 1967. History repeated itself in 1985 when the final leg to Folsom was finished, lengthening the trail to 31 miles.

Bushy Lake, a 300-acre nature preserve, adjoins the parkway south of Cal Expo, and may be deemed part of it from the point of view of wildlife, which thumb their snouts at governmental jurisdictions. Geographically right in the middle of Sacramento's urbanized area, Bushy Lake, and other parkway stretches, teem with birds, including great blue herons. The great blue, often four feet high with six-foot wingspan, wades in shallows and spears fish with its sharp bill. But it doesn't turn down a chance to munch on a side dish of frog, snake or mouse. Its cousin, the green-backed heron, relatively short-legged, has a greater yen for seclusion and prefers thickly wooded places.

Farther eastward, the parkway's C. M. Goethe Park, with 444 acres, is accessed from Rod Beaudry Drive in Rancho Cordova, and named in honor of Charles Mathias Goethe, local conservationist who died in 1968 at age 91. The park offers picnicking areas and access to the parkway's bike, hiking and horse trails. A bicycle bridge joins Goethe with the north bank.

Still farther east, busiest of parkway parks is Ancil Hoffman, 386 acres. Enter at 6700 Tarshes Dr., Carmichael. It has an 18-hole golf course and the Effie Yeaw Interpretive Center (see chapter "Legacy of Effie Yeaw"). The park was named for former county supervisor (1950-65) Ancil Hoffman, also renowned as manager of world heavyweight boxing champ Max Baer. Hoffman died in 1976 at age 91.

One might regard the valley oak as the king of our local trees. The world's largest oak, it reaches as high as 100 feet, even when not standing on tippy-toe. Valley oaks once lorded it over much of the valley, but farming and urban growth cramped their regal style. Curiously, some oaks lose their leaves in winter, and some are evergreen. The valley oak is one of the former, and the interior live oak of the latter.

Also rife in the parkway is the cottonwood, which early explorers mentioned more than any other plant, as a flag signaling the presence of water in arid lands. Its sweet inner bark offered food for horses. Botanists named it the Fremont cottonwood because the explorer admired it, finding it always at good camping places near water. It stretches up to 90 feet high and its leaves flutter like aspen leaves.

The parkway's redbud is called the Judas Tree because a Palestinian legend says Judas hanged himself from it — whereupon the tree, formerly trimmed with white blossoms, blushed a deep pink in shame.

The abundant buckeye got its name because Indians thought its leaves matched the color of a buck's eye.

Tree of Heaven *(Ailanthus)* is one of the parkway's most prolific. In Gold Rush days, Chinese miners brought it to California because it reminded them of home. Another story is that the Chinese valued it because they believed it absorbed malarial toxins from the air. Though it grows only 60 feet high, its name derives from the fact it was deemed related to a very tall tree in Indonesia called heaven tree because of its height. From Chinese camps in the mines, the tree spread everywhere. It is festooned with reddish-brown winged seeds carried by the wind, sometimes long distances. This is the tree that "starred" in Betty Smith's novel, *A Tree Grows in Brooklyn*. How it got to Brooklyn is anybody's guess.

Mistletoe, a parasite, hangs from oaks, cottonwoods and other trees. Europeans used it in rituals to woo good fortune. Druid priests, wielding golden blades, slashed it from their sacred oaks and gave it to people to fend off evil spirits.

Wild grape festoons some parkway trees, its thick stems sometimes 60 feet long, climbing high in oaks and cottonwoods.

Galaxies of wildflowers embroider the parkway, not a few with intriguing names: Ithuriel's spear, from a character in Milton's *Paradise Lost*; fiddleneck, from its shape; miner's lettuce, used in salad greens; bush monkey flower, with its tiny monkey face;

shepherd's purse, from its seedpod shape; butter and eggs, a.k.a. Johnny Tuck.

To Spanish explorers, the poppy was Copa de Oro, or cup of gold. Lupine adds blue splashes to spring-green meadows. The Romans called it Lupus, or wolf, because they saw it growing in poor soil and thought it robbed the earth. In truth, it enriches the soil by giving it a fix of nitrogen.

The animal world is represented by a handsome delegation. The mule deer, named for its big ears, is proud of its distinction of being the largest native animal on the Lower American, and of its pedigree as the only survivor of the hoofed beasts such as the many elk and antelope that roamed here in the great days of old. Mule deer bed down in hideaways during the day and sortie in early morning and late evening to feed.

Coyotes thrive in the parkway. Meg Smart of Fair Oaks says she has seen them play with domestic dogs. Another woman said her dachshund suffered a bad bite from a coyote, whether in sport or not she didn't know.

Our black-tailed hare, or jackrabbit, is an Olympic-caliber athlete, being able to leap astonishing distances. The cottontail rabbit, another parkway citizen, is smaller. The seldom-seen opossum feeds at night, leaving tracks that look like tiny human handprints. Or might they have been left by leprechauns? The raccoon also hunts at night, and sleeps during the day in a hollow tree. A skunk will warn you, if threatened, by stamping its feet and raising its tail, before launching a nasty barrage.

Trappers nearly wiped out the beaver in the early days, because its thick brown fur was so highly prized for headgear, but it has made a comeback. As everyone knows, beavers gnaw down trees to build dams, then collect bark and twigs for food. But in our area, beavers often burrow into riverbanks, instead of building an underwater lodge. Why? Because the rivers here run all year. Only if they dried up in summer would they need to construct a pond.

Yet on occasion they can't seem to forget old habits, and their engineering eagerness gets the better of them. Several years ago, beavers started building a dam in Ancil Hoffman Park, and it began flooding the golf course. Not to worry in winter — but they were gnawing down golf course trees to build with, and that would never do. Bulldozers destroyed their unfinished dam. "There are usually some beavers from the river working here all the time," said golf course superintendent Leonard Theis. "One time they plugged up the eight culverts in the park — and flooded parts of the park."

When Theis calls for help, U. S. Fish and Wildlife people trap the too-eager beavers, then release them at such a distance from Hoffman few are eager to return.

Moving along to birds, the parkway's most common duck is the mallard, cruising in pairs, male and female, often trailed by a flotilla of fledglings. Males sport a bright green-and-rust breast and white collar, while females are garbed more demurely in a mottled brown ensemble.

The yellow-billed magpie — kin to the black-billed magpie in other areas — is found nowhere in the world but in the central valley and some of the state's coastal valleys, and is one of the most intelligent birds. A candidate for avian Mensa, no doubt.

Two owl species inhabit this area. One is the barn owl, about the size of a chicken. It flies silently through the night, hunting mice and other rodents. A small brown owl, the burrowing owl, is often seen in the daytime on a fence post or near a hole in the ground. He turns his head halfway in one direction, then — quicker than your eyes can see — spins it halfway in the opposite direction, so it appears as if he twists his head in a circle. Are some owls hard of hearing? Even when you tell them your name loud and clear, they keep asking "Who?"

The swallows come back to Sacramento each year around March 10, compared to March 19 at Capistrano. Perhaps they arrive earlier here because the air warms up faster in the valley.

Cliff, bank and tree swallows wing in from Central America, while barn swallows fly all the way from Argentina — Argentina! — pumping their pinions for 7,000 miles across land and sea. Some swallows continue north as far as Alaska, while others sojourn in Sacramento, residing in subdivisions of mud nests crowded together under bridges, overpasses and building eaves.

As autumn chills the north, it's time for the great southern journey. Those from northern points stop in Sacramento again in September and October on their way to summer in the south.

Monarch butterflies are other phenomenal winged commuters that pass through Sacramento. On red and black wings, millions flutter down from the north, pausing to refresh themselves on local nectar. Then off they go again, some to congregate for the winter in trees of Santa Cruz County, and Pacific Grove, Monterey County, and in Mexico. Others fly as far as South America — echelons of miniature flying machines winging across a thousand leagues of land and sea.

Pacific Grove fines people $500 for molesting butterflies, and stages an annual festival to celebrate their arrival. John Steinbeck wrote an amusing story telling how the whole town was ready to celebrate — but the tiny winged tourists were woefully off schedule for some reason and didn't arrive for an inordinate time, throwing the festival out of joint.

Like the Monarch, the painted lady is a migrant that visits Sacramento and is said to be the world's most widely distributed butterfly. It's a small orange-and-black creature with four eyespots on the under side of its wings to frighten birds of prey.

Among local reptiles, the garter snake, probably the most common snake in the parkway, is easy to recognize by its yellow dorsal stripe on a dark sooty background. The racer is a fast, sleek snake that forages, head high, in grassy areas for insects, amphibians, lizards and small animals. The gopher snake, or bullsnake, our largest common snake, often vibrates its tail when it feels threatened, rustling leaves. This sometimes causes this harmless snake to be mistaken for a rattlesnake. The parkway is home for a number of rattlesnakes, but no census is available. Rangers point out they are not aggressive — unless you're a mouse. They like to sun themselves on the hot paved bike path in summer, but beat a fast retreat when they feel vibrations of approaching humans. When exercising in the parkway, one should also exercise caution, is the word from rangers.

The non-venomous king snake catches and eats rodents, birds and lizards, and other snakes, including rattlers.

The fence or bluebelly lizard is a well-known representative of the local reptile constituency. When courting, the macho males actually do "push-ups," exposing their blue throats and belly patches to impress females. The alligator lizard — big head and small legs — does look like a tiny alligator. It easily sheds its tail when a hostile creature grabs it.

The horned lizard, incorrectly called a "horned toad," when put on the defensive puffs up and incredibly can shoot blood out of its eyes. It's said to be harmless, save for insects, which it has a fondness for.

Our only local turtle is the western pond turtle, or box turtle, named for its boxy shape. In warm weather, you may spy them basking in a group on a log or rock, until startled, when they plunge into the water.

The tree frog's call, often in chorus (a capella), is a sonorous *kreck-eck*. This frog reverses an adage about children, for it is more often heard than seen.

The bullfrog, up to eight inches long, is our largest local amphibian and resides in quiet waters. It often startles the passerby with a loud *burp*, and a leap into the security of deep water. The breeding call is a deep *ba-room*. At California State University-Sacramento, linguistics professor Kermit Gooch, Ph. D., has taped bullfrog mating calls and fed them into a language-translating computer, which he said printed out the following: "Hey, lovely ladies, the moon is shining on the river, and this good-lookin' guy is in the mood for romance."

No, it didn't really happen, but maybe some day computers will make it possible.

Chapter 62
The Deadly Annual Homecoming

I love any discourse of rivers, and fish and fishing.
Izaak Walton

Would that Izaak Walton were alive at this hour, to read this chapter!

Each year, in one of the amazing phenomena of the natural world, the American River becomes a crowded freeway as tens of thousands of king salmon (chinook) swim upstream to spawn. Some people have estimated the number at about 50,000, but hatchery manager II Terry West at Nimbus Fish Hatchery, on the south bank of the American River near the Hazel Avenue Bridge, discounts this. Yet he declines to offer his own estimate. Says he: "There's no way to count the fish in the river." But he does report that some 10,000 spawn each year at this hatchery. All salmon die after spawning. Many that die in the river become banquets for turkey vultures. Others might host a dinner party of crayfish. Salmon meat from the hatchery ends up on the tables of county and state institutions.

King salmon are anadromous, meaning they spend most of their lives in the ocean, ascending streams only to spawn.

Darlene McGriff, zoologist with State Fish and Game, led a group from Effie Yeaw Center to the cobbled banks of the river to catch the action. Salmon were breaking the surface in shallow water at the interface of a riffle, water with a broken surface, and a glide, rapid but unbroken water. In sand and pebbles on the bottom, the female digs a depression with her tail, then releases her eggs. The male releases milt, fertilizing them. The female churns farther upstream to dig a new pocket, sending sand and pebbles washing down to cover the first batch of eggs, repeating this process several times. The American offers the cool, well-oxygenated water females need for their eggs.

At one time the American offered 100 miles of stream gravels as spawning beds for salmon and steelhead. But completion of Folsom and Nimbus Dams in 1956 blockaded most of the beds, so the Nimbus Hatchery was built to compensate for loss of beds farther upstream.

To protect the spawners, rangers each year from November 1 through December 31 close the American to fishing from Nimbus Hatchery west to Hoffman Park.

The salmon run begins in late September, peaks in mid-November, then tapers off, usually ending in February. But some salmon may dally until spring before charging upstream.

You can see salmon spawning in riffles between Watt Avenue and Nimbus Dam. Three or four years old, they average 20 pounds. Those that don't spawn by the time they reach Nimbus are detoured by a rack blocking the river, forcing them to thrash up the fish ladder — a stairway of resting ponds — until they reach the holding ponds 30 feet above the river. Spectators are welcome to watch this long-running show, and up to 200,000 catch it in a season.

Eggs hatch in 50 to 60 days. From each emerges a larva-like creature with large yolk attached like a backpack — its temporary food supply. When they exit the gravel, they are *fry*, and *fingerlings* when grown to two inches long. By the time they are *smolts*, three or four inches long, they are "imprinted" on the chemistry of their natal stream, and launch themselves on the great down-river adventure to the sea.

Three or four years later, the urge comes on them to go back home. Every stream has its unique chemistry, McGriff said, and the spawners find their way by following the particular smell that tells each "That's my stream."

Yet sometimes things go awry, even in the awesome realm of natural instinct. Sometimes migrating fish travel up the "wrong river," McGriff said. At times a logjam or a new dam blocks the native stream, and the spawners have to find a "foster home," as it were. For some reason, other rivers receive strays from the American. Perhaps their memory of that unique chemistry of their natal waters is not infallible. Could *you* find your way back to your

Nimbus Dam is a favorite rendezvous of anglers during the annual homecomings.

birthplace, using only your sense of smell, with your head under water? Yet sometimes there is a clear reason, and Fish and Game biologist Fred Meyer explained. Each year the American receives about 10,000 strays from the Mokelumne — because that river each fall dwindles to a mere trickle. The American for some reason also receives strays from the Feather. How do Fish and Game people know which fish come from which rivers? They do tagging studies.

More than ever, good salmon and steelhead runs hinge on fish raised in hatcheries because dams, pollution and unscreened irrigation have destroyed spawning streams. Baby fish are raised in holding ponds until grown to planting size, then released, mostly in the Delta. Without Nimbus Hatchery, salmon and steelhead would provide only a pale shadow of the sport these fish now offer California's two million fishermen.

On the American, the annual fishermen's catch from Nimbus to the Sacramento River averages 15,000 salmon, 5,000 steelhead, 20,000 shad, and 2,000 striped bass, according to river buff and writer Tom Evans, who reports that the amount fishermen spend on the sport here is estimated at $15 million a year — or $357 for each fish caught!

Saltwater fishermen also profit from the rivers: Two of every three king salmon caught off the California coast were spawned in the Sacramento River basin, many at Nimbus.

Some people can't wait for fish to be released from the hatchery. One time game wardens, tipped that thieves were stealing from the hatchery, staked it out. At 1:30 a.m. they spotted three men climbing the eight-foot chain-link fence bounding the ponds. Then four more men joined them. Armed with gaffs, snagging gear and landing nets, the poachers started bringing in big steelhead. As the wardens charged out from ambush, the poachers scattered, but the wardens scrambled through brush and rock-piles, rounding up six culprits. One escaped. The poachers later confessed to previous raids, boasting that their stolen steelheads had won prizes in a Sacramento fish derby.

Besides salmon and steelhead, the American's other anadromous fish include striped bass, shad, white sturgeon, and lamprey. The steelhead is really a rainbow trout that spends part of its life in the ocean. The rainbow trout for some reason doesn't migrate — yet both are of the same species. The steelhead is, one might say, a rainbow that decided to go down to the sea, or has a yen to travel. When the steelhead returns to fresh water, it proves its kinship by donning the rainbow's long red racing stripe.

Despite the king salmon's title, the uncrowned king of game fish in this river system may be the striped bass. From April to mid-June, stripers spawn in the American, and in the Sacramento between Courtland and Colusa. Each year, they lure 200,000 fisher folk. Then it's turnabout as the fisher folk lure the stripers.

The American shad is another spring voyager. Generally in May, prodigious numbers churn up the Sacramento and American to their spawning beds. For its size, the shad puts up such a terrific struggle that fishermen dub it the freshwater tarpon. Armed with light spinning gear and fly outfits, some fishermen station themselves shoulder-to-shoulder on the Sacramento at the "minnow hole" south of town and north of Freeport. Others park their boats in fleets at the confluence of the Sacramento and American. Still others stand in waders hip-deep near riffles in the icy American from its mouth to Nimbus Dam.

Migrants in the American also include the eel-like lamprey, most primitive fish-like denizen in local waters.

Biggest and ugliest fish in local waters is the white sturgeon, another migrant. Locally the biggest caught was a 405-pounder at the junction of the Feather and Sacramento, but elsewhere in

North America it grows to 20 feet long and half a ton. With a pedigree 70 million years old, the sturgeon is a throwback to the dinosaur age. It has bony plates instead of scales, and a cartilege skeleton instead of bone. Catching them takes heavy equipment. Best locales are downstream from Sacramento in winter, and upstream in early summer. Sturgeon is tasty, and its eggs are often turned into caviar, by a salting process. Green sturgeon also swim in local green depths.

Alone among local gamefish, the white catfish stays home. No gadabout, he. In torrid summer twilights, catfishermen head for deep holes along the Sacramento, tip-toeing to keep from spooking their quarry, which boasts the most acute hearing of any local fish.

Carp teem in lakes and slow streams hereabouts. Prized when introduced into California in 1872, they have worn out their welcome — because they ruin the aquatic plants relished by waterfowl. And they stir up mud, which injures silt-sensitive fish. Gourmet note: Carp are bony but edible. One tongue-in-cheek recipe: Broil the carp on a plank over a fire. Throw away the carp — eat the plank.

Goldfish, originating in Asia, are domesticated kins of the carp. Once confined to fishbowls, so many were turned loose that they now are not uncommon in local waters, where their raiment reverts to the gray hue of their wilder brothers and sisters.

Mosquito fish, two inches long or less, are small but distinguished members of the local finny tribe, having proven their worth as a no-pesticide way to help impose zero-population growth on pesky mosquito multitudes.

Chapter 63
Walks on the Wilder Side

When we try to pick out anything by itself, we find it hitched to everything else in the universe.

John Muir

Alan Fiers, a volunteer naturalist who leads groups on nature walks from the Effie Yeaw Interpretive Center, Hoffman Park, Carmichael, tells about the bird that wanted to be a movie star. One time as he was trying to film some flycatchers, most were too shy to capture on film. "But one was a real ham. He kept getting so close to the camera that all I could get was a head shot." In other words, birds of a feather may not always flock together.

Birds of a feather also may show curious differences in behavior depending on the region they inhabit, Fiers said. In California, it's rare to hear robins sing. But in his former home state of Minnesota, they present a melodious concert every evening in spring: *Chirralee, chirralee, chirralee*. Birds sing in spring to establish their territories, Fiers said, and speculated: "Maybe they aren't singing in California because they don't have that many other robins to chase away."

Fiers led a group along the American River bike trail to Bushy Lake, south of Cal Expo, and identified each species sighted or heard, for example: finches, western kingbirds, kildeer, mallards, and a flock of Brewers blackbirds, which he said sometimes mill around in the air in thousands. Numbers of cliff swallows flew about. Fiers compared their mud colonies under bridges to hornets' nests, in appearance. Everything swallows eat is caught in mid-air, he said. That is, they eat on the fly, rather than on the run, as some people do. The swallows skim low over land or water, scarfing insects, their favorite entree.

Approaching Bushy Lake from the south, the party startled a deer, which fled into brushy seclusion — a rare vision for a locale a mere quarter mile from busy Cal Expo. "You see their tracks more often then you see the deer," Fiers said. "They hide in the day and feed at night."

Chuck Woodbury, a transplant from Los Angeles, commented: "I couldn't believe all the wildlife I've seen here. Last week, though, I got my biggest surprise. I was walking along the river about 8 o'clock when a deer walked right in front of me. For a guy who grew up in a big city, it's really strange to see wild animals close to home."

Bushy Lake, man-made, was excavated to serve as a water-based recreation area for Cal Expo. At the time of Fiers' tour, water in the irregularly-shaped lake was shockingly low. Usually Bushy is fed by overflow from the American, but in dry years Cal Expo pumped water in to maintain it, with its wildlife. When Cal Expo's negligence shut off the line in 1986, the lake almost dried up. Several hundred fish died and other wildlife suffered. Later that year, County of Sacramento took over maintenance responsibility from Cal Expo.

Great blue herons and other birds skimmed above. On a south bank, beavers had gnawed down dozens of trees and stripped them of their tasty bark. None of the big-toothed vandals was to be seen. Fiers said Bushy also is the home of river otter and muskrat, but none was sighted at this time. Muskrats have an annoying habit of burrowing into levees.

On backtracking, the group perceived a kestrel — a small hawk formerly called sparrow hawk — perched on a dead cottonwood branch. Fiers said a kestrel will hover in one place, wings fluttering to keep it stationary — its stationary position enabling it to discern any small movement on the ground, such as that of an unwary mouse.

Cowbirds are plentiful in the Sacramento area, Fiers said, but the group sighted not a one. Cowbirds have no respect for property rights: They lay their eggs in other birds' nests, sometimes ejecting the other birds' eggs. The young cowbirds are as arrogant as their

Toddler finds "colors" in the American River during a nature walk, aided by ranger Mark Hooten of Effie Yeaw Nature Center.

parents, hogging the food delivered by the witless parents of the other birds. The ingrate cowbird youngsters sometimes go so far as to shove the other small birds out of the nest, without giving them an eviction notice.

Hummingbirds have a very high metabolism rate, Fiers said. When they perch for the night, their temperature plummets, sending them into an energy-conserving torpor, just as bears hibernate.

Another intriguing bird habit: Fiers said mallards sometimes domesticate themselves — attaching themselves to a farmer's flock of domestic ducks and geese, to do a bit of freeloading. Sometimes these stepchildren remain as permanent boarders. But they can take to the airways whenever they feel a longing to get away from it all.

Fiers called attention to a black-shouldered kite, a type of hawk, hovering high, ready to launch into a *stoop*, like a dive-bomber, to catch a mouse. Once Fiers saw one swoop upon a mouse, then fly back and meet a female kite and "hand" the prey to her in mid-air, whereupon she carried it back to her nest of youngsters. The male flew off in the opposite direction, perhaps to catch another.

Legend has it that grebes, or helldivers, who frequent the same wetlands as ducks do, can dive so fast they can duck a bullet. Not so, says Fiers. When they spot the flash from a gun, it frightens them, and they dive instanter.

A flight of starlings reminded Fiers of a lesson humans learned from nature. English sparrows were introduced into the eastern United States, where caterpillars were ravaging trees. When the sparrow population exploded, someone imported their natural enemy, the starling. Now the starling has become a pest. The lesson: "Don't mess with Mother Nature."

Bird watchers often find it difficult to identify birds because of the nature of the creature — it's often hard to get a good look. And the world has 8,500 bird species. Birders identify them not only by appearance, but behavior. Fiers cites examples: "Sparrows hop, robins run, blackbirds walk, and the kildeer scoots along as if rolling on casters."

And by voices, of course: Crows *caw-caw-caw*, whereas the similar but larger ravens, often confused with crows, *squawk*. Some bird calls evoke bizarre comparisons. The rufous-sided towhee has a voice that Fiers says sounds like an alarm clock being wound up — perhaps to let the world know it's one of the early birds, and won't be caught napping.

Two mourning doves were on the wing. Fiers said their sobbing, woebegone call gave them their names.

Fiers identified a melodious call as that of a meadowlark, common locally, but it remained out of sight. It has a yellow breast with black V, long beak, tan back and white tail feathers. Burl Ives celebrated it with a haunting ballad, "In the Land of the Meadowlark."

On a nature walk at Negro Bar State Park, naturalist Rodi Fregien identified a bird-call as that of a wrentic: "Its call sounds like a bouncing ball." The sounds become closer and closer, like those from a dropped ball making ever shorter bounces. Fregien identified another call as that of a bittern: "Two dots and a dash, like Morse code." The mottled brown bittern stands up to two feet tall, likes marshy areas and is kin to the great blue heron.

Another bird was heard, and Fregien offered a thumb-nail character sketch: "Black-headed grosbeak, a songster — rusty orange belly and black-and-white wings," she recited. "It gets in the feeder at my house and just sits there and acts like he owns it. He's worse than a jay."

To calculate bird population trends, Sacramento Audubon Society joins 1,400 bird groups across the country in the national Christmas bird count, conducted since c. 1900. Although the society uses experienced birders in their counts, it schedules many free or low-cost outings for those less experienced. Call 481-0118.

Down a shadowy trail and into brush, Fregien led a group to an Indian grinding rock, a huge slab of moss-tufted granite with four mortar holes. One could imagine Indian women grinding acorns here by the river in the halcyon ages before the world changed forever.

Fregien pointed out some rush-like plants — horsetails only three feet high, a.k.a. scouring rush because its silica content makes it an effective agent for rubbing and cleansing. Today's horsetails are diminutive compared to the horsetails that once flourished here, soaring 100 feet in the dinosaur age 200 million years ago.

A red-tailed hawk soared against the blue. Fregien told how to differentiate between a hawk and a turkey vulture in flight: Hawks show a pronounced bend in their wings, while the vultures turn up their feathers at the end.

The trail led through shaded glens and up and down little hills. Sun glittered in breeze-rustled leaves. Near a patch of poison oak, Fregien found mugwort, a gray-green plant three or four feet high. You can steep its fresh-crushed leaves in water, like tea, and make a poultice to relieve poison oak itch.

A squawking bird with blue wings and white breast fluttered by. "Scrubjay," said Fregien. "Not as big as the bluejay, but more aggressive. It chases other birds off bird feeders."

The group stopped at a wooden footbridge spanning a creek. A tapping noise wafted from a tall pine. Woodpecker, of course. Nobody had trouble with that one.

A red-and-black butterfly wafted past. Fregien named it a Viceroy, which mimics the Monarch's markings but is smaller. Birds spurn Monarchs because of their taste. Monarch caterpillars feed on milkweed, ingesting a bad-tasting substance that remains in the adult butterfly. Birds also spurn Viceroys, though they don't have the same bad taste, because they take them for Monarchs.

Hard by a cluster of oaks, Fregien told how to differentiate three kinds: Live oaks have small leaves with barbs and a leathery feel; valley oaks have indented leaves; blue oaks' leaves are not indented and have a blue tinge.

Oak trees are remarkable water engineers, according to naturalist Mark Hooten on a walk out of the Effie Yeaw Center. "Trees like the valley oaks are among the most powerful water pumps in existence," he said. "They send roots down as far as 100 feet deep, and pump water up to 100 feet in the air."

Near the river, Hooten's group paused near a sizeable valley oak — its main trunk bent over so it stretched horizontally. Several trunks rose vertically from the main. Hooten reasoned that a flood had bent the tree when it was yet a sapling, and heavy sediments pinned its young branches to earth, forcing it to grow disabled, or die. Hooten estimated the oak was half a century old or more, born well before Folsom Dam was built to short-stop high water rushing toward this floodplain. Hooten suggests the prostrate oak offers a lesson in overcoming handicaps: "In the tremendous struggle for life, this tree had its back broken, practically, but it never gave up."

Some oaks are festooned with vines, as is one near the Effie Yeaw Center, draped by a California wild grape as thick as your arm. Hooten said this wild species provided root stock for most of the foreign vines imported into California because its roots are resistant to soil fungi here.

Hooten pointed out a vine climbing a poplar and said it is a manroot, of the cucumber family, though inedible. It was named from its root shaped like a man. Indians and Spaniards painted or carved dots on the large seeds, to play dice.

John Muir made this point, Hooten said: "Don't be turned off because you can't identify many species of wildlife: The beauty is visible, and that we can enjoy."

Some local nature walks explore wild patches outside the parkway, such as the oak woodland in Orangevale Park. Naturalist Nancy Wymer was brimming with intriguing facts, including an explanation as to how coyotes, which can run only 40 miles an hour, can catch jackrabbits, which cruise at 45. They chase them in relays until they wear them down, thus inventing the relay race, maybe. Even a loner coyote can sometimes catch his big-eared prey – by leaping on it from ambush.

Wymer called attention to a peculiar oak and identified it as a hybrid. Peculiar — because it sported two different kinds of oak leaves, that of the blue oak and the live oak. "Oaks are shamelessly promiscuous," she explained. "They fool around a lot." Some people — you never know when they're pulling your leg.

You learn a rule for avoiding poison oak leaves, which bear a striking resemblance to some oak leaves: "Leaves of three? Let it be."

Fair Oaks' Phoenix Park, on the south side of Sunset Avenue east of Hazel Avenue, contains some rare vernal pools. Naturalist Harvest McCampbell said the pools are natural basins that fill with rainwater in winter and are paved, so to speak, with impervious hardpan that lets water exit only by evaporation. Vernal pools are rareties today. Only 5 percent remain of those that once dappled the valley, so prevalent in olden days they were scorned as mere "hog-wallows."

Today naturalists regard them as treasure troves of rare plants and animals, and as spectacles of beauty. In spring their margins become an ever-changing tapestry as the water evaporates and the receding shoreline leaves concentric "bathtub rings" of blooming plants or "fairy rings," if you will. The rings keep moving from the outside to the center, reversing the movement of the rings produced when a pebble is thrown into a pool, notes naturalist Bob Holland.

The vernal pools here are the remnant of a much larger area called the Fair Oaks' "bald spot," reaching to the American River. The bald area was almost bare of trees because the shallow topsoil was underlain by hardpan, and thus never suitable for the citrus and olive orchards that were planted around it in early days after the clearing of the great oak groves.

As a vernal pool's color bands shift by degrees toward the center from March to June, they present a changing spectacle of blossoms: Tiny blue-and-white flowers called downingia; the blue-lavender or pinkish blue of checker mallow; goldfields, which look like buttercups; cat's ears, resembling dandelions; and coyote thistle, which looks like star thistle but is not kindred. Most of the plants here are annuals, which wither and die in the dry season. Seeds germinate in fall and winter, when rain fills the pools, and bloom in spring as the pools shrink until they disappear entirely. As to their animal life, Holland says: "There's a whole arkful of creepie-crawlies adapted to these vernal pools." Among them are small frogs half an inch long, called spring peepers. And clamshell shrimps.

In these miniature seas with their kaleidoscopic shorelines, the shrimps, three-fourths of an inch long, are unique to vernal pools, McCampbell said. The shells of these denizens are so clear you can see their interior movements, like the works of a Swiss watch. The shrimps navigate their miniature seas as boldly as any Columbus, and they really do have a watch — but it is called a biological clock. It tells them when the time is nigh to lay their eggs.

Death comes to all the adult shrimps in the holocaust of summer suns that dry up the pools. But their eggs — nature's time capsules — lie dormant through the fall and winter, harboring their secret life. When spring rains water the land, the eggs hatch. Life begins for a new generation of shrimps — destined to live out their entire lifespans in one brief season, just as do most of the brillant plants that illuminate the shorelines of these tiny, transitory seas.

Perhaps the strangest of all the life cycles in the vernal pools is that of the tiny blue bees called *Andrenids*, who browse on the blue downingia. These bees are not the social animals like the more familiar bees, but are solitary creatures. The female gathers downingia pollen, amassing it into a ball about the size of a pea, three times as large as she is. She digs a burrow some 18 inches into the earth — deep enough to survive the solar holocaust — and leaves the pollen ball by the egg. In similar fashion, she buries two dozen eggs. When an egg hatches, the larva feeds on the pollen until the downingia is in flower. Don't ask how it knows. It's one of the mysteries yet to be solved.

From solitary confinement in their underground dungeons, the bees, having metamorphosed from larvae, escape to freedom in the skies over the vernal pools. But for a male, freedom in the skies means a kamikaze-style death. The bees mate in mid-air. "The male literally blows himself apart to inject the female," Holland said.

As this is a dignified book, the author will refrain from any what-a-way-to-go jocosities.

Chapter 64
Legacy of Effie Yeaw

I once had a sparrow alight upon my shoulder for a moment while I was hoeing in a village garden, and I felt that I was more distinguished by that circumstance than I should have been by any epaulet I could have worn.

Thoreau

"She started as a classroom teacher in Sacramento, then went to Hawaii. She loved the fauna and flora there. But one day a man by the name of Bill Yeaw arrived by boat and wanted to marry her. So she finally said yes, and they moved back to Sacramento."

That's Mike Weber, of the county schools office, remembering how Effie Cummings changed her name to Effie Yeaw. Weber recalls that he and Effie Yeaw worked together on the first edition of the natural history book, *The Outdoor World of the Sacramento Region*, sold today at the Effie Yeaw Nature Center in Ancil Hoffman Park, Carmichael. But the center named after her didn't come into existence until seven years after she died – of cancer.

"She was a great admirer of Dr. Tracy Storer, one of her first professors at UC-Berkeley, because he would take the class on nature walks, and open up a whole new world to them.

"She was a wonderful teacher," Weber said. "She never liked just sitting in a classroom — the world is the classroom, if you recognize and appreciate it.

"Once I went to see her, and she was just full of mud. They were excavating for a school next door, and she found some clay, and got the kids to mix dry clay and water, and they were making a high-quality fire-clay out of just ordinary dirt. Whereas other teachers would have bought the clay, Effie would make her own. She was always doing things like that.

"She had a great affinity for animals. Once she was driving to school and noticed that someone had run over a possum. She stopped her car and found the carcass with live baby possums — I think 12 or 13 baby possums she salvaged from the dead carcass. Then she had to feed them, and they eat day and night. She stayed up all night long and fed them milk with an eye-dropper.

"Her house was like a menagerie. Anyone in Sacramento who found an injured bird would take it to Effie. She took care of them and rehabilitated them, and if they were well enough would let them go. If not, she would keep them in cages. If you went into her home, birds would be flying all over, sometimes. Her husband Bill always complained about the birds. But after she died in 1969, he continued to take care of them just like she did. He would complain, 'All these birds flying around — what a nuisance!' But he gave them just as good care."

She suffered a long time with cancer, but kept up with her self-appointed task of fairy godmother to distressed animals and ambassador-without-portfolio to all living things. American Motors gave her a national conservation award c. 1960.

"She saved the deodara ('timber of the gods') cedar in front of the Carmichael Post Office," Weber said, "when the contractors erecting the building wanted to cut down all the trees and level everything — that's their philosophy."

After the post office was built and the tree no longer in danger of being cut down, Effie received a letter from some government bureaucrat saying the tree could not be saved!

Greenback Lane once was flanked by two lines of magnificent oaks for five to eight miles, Weber remembers. "Effie tried in vain to save them, when the county widened Greenback." The amazing thing about those two straight lines of trees, he said, is that they were planted by birds – scrubjays. "They stored their acorns at the base of fence posts because there is more grass and moisture there, and farmers didn't plow close to the posts. After the county cut down the oaks, for years I didn't drive Greenback because it was

Effie Yeaw is portrayed in a painting that hangs in the Nature Center named after her. The painter is Stuart Billington.

such a bad experience for me."

Carmichael teacher Yeaw (rhymes with "jaw," she'd say) often led her students — and adults too, on occasion — on nature hikes through the magnificent Deterding Woods, named after the family that owned the land. The family left the woods in its pristine condition because it served as a natural buffer against floods that otherwise, before construction of Folsom Dam, would have ravaged adjoining farmlands.

Yeaw took all of nature for her classroom — and its wonders for her textbooks. Living specimens, stories, drawings and crafts helped her pupils spell out the lessons written in the rocks and trees and streams by Mother Nature. Her house bercame a refuge for lost and wounded and orphaned animals. Friends say she was always giving people acorns and coaxing them to plant them, and that it's anyone's guess how many oaks in Sacramento County are living monuments to her. Retirement only widened her horizons, for she then founded the Carmichael Conservation Center, a museum in Carmichael Park. Said Weber: "Hundreds of children came, night and day. She would give lectures in the evenings to youth groups, PTAs and churches."

Her work lives on in the Effie Yeaw Interpretive Center, a 3,000-square-foot building erected in 1976. Today, Deterding Woods still lives in its original beauty as the 70-acre nature area bordering the center. The Deterdings sold the land to the county to become part of Hoffman Park. The building is chock full of exhibits to offer background information for explorations of the nature area. Visitors to the center are greeted by a sign: "Leave only footprints, take only memories." But it's okay to take photos, too.

Pamphlets about local plants and animals are available here, published by American River Natural History Association, based at the center. Three pamphlets lead you on self-guided tours over three different trails:

Discovery Trail follows a path marked by 17 posts identified by a footprint emblem. You stop often to look, hear, touch and smell. You learn that the oak tree aids in the survival of more kinds of animals than any other plant in California. Animals use its acorns, leaves, twigs, bark and roots for food, and its spreading branches, exposed roots and hollowed trunks for homes and hiding places. An open field brims with wild oats, star thistle, vetch, foxtail, fiddleneck, ripgut, filaree and scads of other grasses offering habitat for jackrabbits, moles, mice, shrews, starlings, finches, sparrows, meadowlarks, snakes and insects.

The Observation Trail is marked with 11 posts with an emblem of an oak leaf. You tramp through many different habitats. The 80-foot-high hillside looming close in the northwest is really an ancient riverbank of the American River, from the time this plain was flooded each year, until Folsom Dam's construction. Here's an old log — probably dragged down many years ago by the burden of wild grape vines. To Effie Yeaw, this was a "Listening Log," because it was a strategic site to give ear to sounds of nature, such as the gabble of birds and murmur of bees. Near the river, the rocks you stand on were gouged out thousands of years ago by streams in the Sierra — which you can descry in the far distance. The white ones are quartz, which alerted the Forty-Niners to the potential of gold; salt-and-pepper ones are granite; the darker basalt rocks came from lava eruptions during Sierra mountain-building; reddish rocks are metamorphic, likely rich in iron.

Riverview History Trail, marked by posts bearing a river symbol, takes you through the story of human occupation here and its effects on the wild world. At the first station, you look up at the bluff that may have been a village site of Nisenan Indians. Other stations remind you of the immense riparian forests that in times gone by housed a diversity of wildlife unmatched in California; and that beavers still swim in the river, and in tree-lined Carmichael Creek in Hoffman Park.

Admission to the center is free, but $4 per car is charged for entry into Hoffman Park. For dates and times of ranger-led nature walks and other special events, call 489-4918.

Chapter 65

Challenger Learning Center: Legacy Of the Old State Fair

What a legacy it has been! Sponsors of the Junior Múseum at the old State Fair on Stockton Boulevard never could have dreamed it. It led to the Science Center, and that led to the Challenger Learning Center, with its simulated Mission Control, portal for excursions into the cosmos, and its Challenger spacecraft, the vehicle for those far-out excursions.

At the old State Fair, the Junior Museum was one of the most popular attractions, drawing crowds during a few weeks each summer from 1951 to 1975. It reopened in 1976 as a year-round enterprise in expanded headquarters at 3615 Auburn Blvd., hard by the east end of Del Paso Park, where it became known as the Sacramento Science Center.

The 1986 disaster of the real Challenger is history, and threads of its history are now woven into the fabric of Sacramento history.

After the seven crew members died, grieving parents pondered on what would be a proper memorial, and at last envisioned a nationwide series of hands-on learning centers to fire up young imaginations with the adventure of space travel while honing their skills in math, science and technology. Thirty Challenger centers dot the U.S. and Canada.

Here at Sacramento's Challenger Center, staffers "launch" a spacecraft, blasting off to the moon – or to Mars – or to Halley's Comet. Meanwhile, Mission Control coordinates with astronauts in the spacecraft to solve tough problems. To heighten the adventure, there's always a tough problem.

In one scenario, flight director Reed Steele steers for Halley's Comet in year 2061. The astronauts send a probe into its tail, where it scoops up samples of gases and returns them to the spacecraft for spectrum analysis.

Suddenly a raucous Klaxon horn and a flashing red light give the alarm.

"Mission Control – we have a problem!"

A hazardous chemical is leaking from its container, threatening the crew's safety. Coordinating with Mission Control, crew members manipulate robot arms that reach into an adjoining compartment where the chemical is stored. They replace the lid on the container, then vacuum the spilled toxic out into space.

Back on earth, a visitor who rode in the spacecraft asks a staffer how far they traveled to Halley's Comet. "Forty million miles round trip," she says, "but you can't accumulate frequent-flyer miles!"

Though designed mainly for school kids, adults are welcome in the "community flights" on the third Wednesday of each month. Anyone 11 or older may blast off on an hour-long mission. Or, if one suffers from claustrophobia or fear of heights, he or she may work in Mission Control, and not leave the ground. Cost is $25 per person. To reserve a spot, call 485-8836.

How was Sacramento lucky enough to capture the first Challenger Learning Center in northern California? In 1992, John Menkler and friends at Sacramento Executive Airport perceived the need for one – and picked the Science Center as the site.

The project got a big boost when First Lady Gayle Wilson joined the founders. Many other organizations were thrilled to boost the space adventure. One big boost came from Aerojet, which turned on its booster rockets.

In another step onto the threshold of space, the planetarium darkens every day at 3 p.m. for shows on: Exploring our place in space; from the sun to Halley's Comet; our solar system's planets and moons; and robot discoveries that have changed how scientists look at the universe.

Back down on terra firma, you can learn about the Nisenan Indians, who were the landlords of the Sacramento Valley for over 10,000 years, until the tenants evicted the landlords.

Animal Hall billets its lodgers in terrariums, aquariums and dioramas. Daily animal presentations spotlight such show-biz personalities as Samantha and Bump, box turtles; Oscar and Daisy, hedgehogs; Annabelle, a rabbit; Leo, a turkey vulture; Rusty, a red-tailed hawk, and Haley, the raccoon.

Police captured Haley from malefactors during a drug bust, and donated her to the Center. A month later, she gave birth to four pups, which were assigned to duties in other museums.

Visitors learn how every animal is unique, and how the peculiar

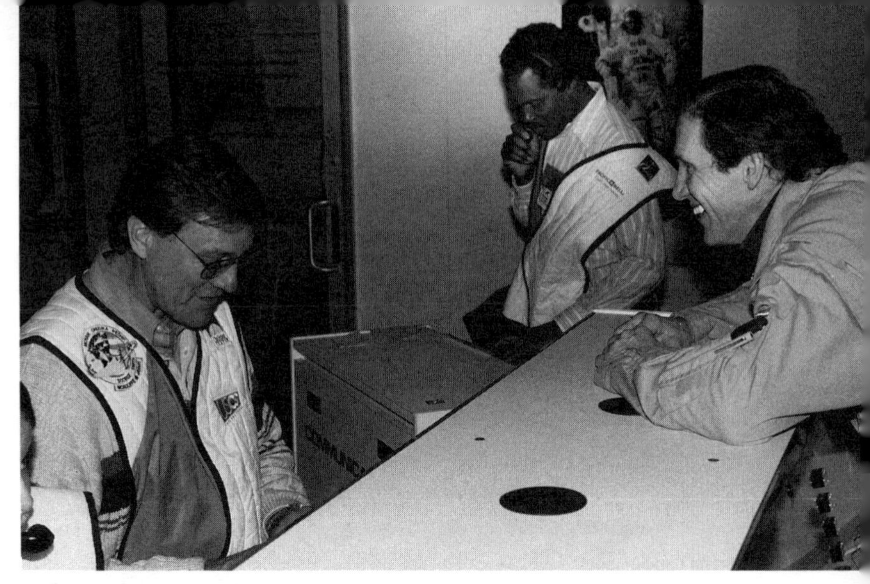

Flight director Reed Steele, right, runs the show aboard the spacecraft.

traits of each help them compete for survival in the remorseless wilderness, which, save for random luck, offers no pity to babes in the woods.

But random luck may include being found, if in distress, by a human who takes pity. The center receives many sick or injured wildlife. Veterinarians doctor them and then turn them back to the wilds, if they can fend for themselves. If they cannot, they don't release them. Example of a critter that wouldn't be released: One that has become so tame it no longer retains a healthy fear of humans or predatory dogs and cats.

Anyone who knows of a wild creature in distress may call the Center's support organization, Wildlife Care, 383-7922.

Outside, a quarter-mile trail winds through the adjoining 12-acre nature area. It's a world in miniature, because the trail crosses or borders different natural communities – grassy uplands, redwood forest, chapparal, streamside woodland, marsh, and a pond. Each is a mini-environment with its own cycles of birth, death and renewal. Arcade Creek wanders through, offering a congenial home to muskrats, kingfishers, bullfrogs and water-striders. The tranquil pond, bedecked with cattails, tules and free-floating plants, offers oxygen and hideaways for perch, frogs and other denizens. A mere pond can hold a treasure of lore. Henry David Thoreau proved that when he lived for two years in a cabin beside Walden Pond, then wrote a book that became a world classic.

For information on the Center, call 575-3941.

Admission to the Center is $2 for adults and $1 for children.

Chapter 66

World's Busiest Rafting River

Originally titled "The Joy of Rafting," this appeared in ***California Highway Patrolman.***

Suddenly you hear a faint roar. By degrees it grows louder. Up ahead, the hustling current crowds against a bluff as the river curves to the right.

Your raft is approaching Suicide Bend.

You spy a dozen dark figures roosting on the bluff. Through your mind flashes the story of Henry Morton Stanley's expedition down the Congo, running a gauntlet of cannibals and shooting cataracts. But this is the Lower American near Sacramento, and the "cannibals" here are only sun-blackened teenagers in swim trunks, watching the rafts go by. And the "cataract"whose muted roar you heard from upstream is only a cross between a riffle and a small rapid.

As the current sweeps you near the bluff, a prankster jumps into the river from 10 feet above. The watery *boom!* sends up a great geyser that comes down on you like heavy rain. But it's a scorching day, and the cold shower is exhilarating. It's cold because the river is fed by Sierra snowmelt.

Where is that strange piping voice coming from? Then you get the direction, and crane to look. In a lofty tree overhanging the river, a slim figure is poised maybe 30 feet above the water. No, it's

Traffic at times is bumper-to-bumper in San Juan Rapids on the American.

not a monkey, it's just a young guy yelling: "For a beer, you can watch me jump! Hey, I'll jump for a beer!"

Alas, by the time you make up your mind to part with a beer, the current swings you past. Too bad. The jump would have added pizzazz to the river adventure. Next time you'll be ready.

Now, just as Stanley escaped the cannibals by shooting a cataract, you escape the natives of Rancho Cordova by scooting into the fast water of Suicide Bend. But you wanted adventure, didn't you?

With suspense at fever-pitch, this is a perfect time to break for a

"commercial" and a flashback, recollecting how you got yourself into this predicament.

You rented your raft from American River Raft Rentals in Rancho Cordova, on the south side of the river just east of Sunrise Boulevard Bridge. Or perhaps you rented it from River Rat & Co., north of the river at 4053 Pennsylvania Ave., Fair Oaks. There are other rentals in the Yellow Pages, and it wouldn't hurt to check out their prices next time. Maybe you even brought your own raft.

Near the Sunrise Bridge, the most popular launching site, you and your fellow river-runners toted the raft, lifejackets, paddles, and ice chest down to the water. You donned your lifejackets, loaded the cargo, climbed in and shoved off, relishing that the current would do most of the work of carrying you to journey's end in Goethe Park, six miles and three hours downstream. You start drifting and paddling, but at first a contrary eddy hampers you. It keeps trying to float you backward. Paddling hard, you stroke far enough out to catch the downstream current — and you're on your way.

Adventure, ahoy!

You glide under the Fair Oaks footbridge, paddles a-chunking to steer clear of the pilings.

Two mallard ducks with an inquisitive air paddle toward you. You might think they'd be terrified of a raft, but not so. No doubt they've grown fond of rafters because of their generosity with picnic goodies.

As you drift in midstream, the shore is far enough so you almost seem to be standing still. Then you catch a glimpse of a shallow bottom cobbled with water-rounded stones sliding under the raft, and realize you're going faster than you knew. Both banks of the river are thick with trees — oaks and poplars, willows, a few skeletonized dead trees, and occasional Trees of Heaven, brought to California by Chinese miners in Gold Rush days.

Even though this is a weekday, rafts galore ride the river. On weekends, the river is a crowded highway. Sometimes it seems as if all Sacramento has gone berserk and taken to the rafts.

An aerial photographer snapped photos of the Lower American on July 6, 1985, a Saturday, and counted 803 rafts — which of course didn't include rafts that had already completed their trips, or those yet to start. "I think there were probably a thousand rafts down the river that day, easily," says Dave Hill, owner of American River Raft Rentals.

A thousand rafts in one day! Topping that, Ranger Gary Kukkola of State Parks and Rec says he understands that spot checks on some summer days have given rise to estimates as high as 1,500 in one day. Nobody can think of any other river that equals it.

Somebody has estimated that each year some 250,000 rafters — we're talking people now — launch on the Lower American. That's equal to three-fourths of the population of the City of Sacramento.

Just then a muted roar sounds as you approach your first riffle, a bit of white water, nothing to get nervous about. The river divides here. One branch flows along the north side of a long, gravelly, willow-tufted island, while the other rambles along the south side.

Choose either course. Decisions, decisions.

This little island harbors a legend of buried treasure. In the early 1900s farther upstream, according to writer and river buff Tom Evans, high water sank a dredge rumored to be carrying up to $1 million in gold. The dredging company salvaged as much of the dredge as it could.

More high water later swept the dredge down to this little island, where it created an obstruction, causing rafts to capsize. In 1974, engineers — unaware of the gold — perceived what they thought was "fool's gold" pouring from the wreck as they dragged it out. Surely the dredging company that stripped the dredge wouldn't have overlooked the gold — if it was accessible. But history is silent on whether they recovered any, so the legend endures.

Tranquil water again — and you put the paddles to work. A mile downstream from Sunrise Bridge, the river begins a sharp bend to the right, and you hear another low roar — announcing your already-mentioned approach to Suicide Bend.

Maps issued by the rafting companies don't identify the bend, which is understandable. They're not eager to frighten away customers. But it *is* identified on the "River Running Map of the American River Parkway," published by California Department of Boating and Waterways. Nobody seems to know the name's origin.

The brisk current here seizes your raft and whips it along as the river hangs a right and surges north to a tranquil stretch. Congratulations! You have just survived Suicide Bend — and now realize that its name is the only scary thing about it. But don't tell anybody that.

Now you just drift again, unless you want to accelerate your pace with paddles.

A nearby raft holds two young women and a large black dog. You ask if the dog is enjoying the trip. The women smile and reply in the affirmative. The dog, for some reason, declines to comment.

"Guy took a parrot down the river one time, sitting on his shoulder," recalls Dave Hill of American River Raft Rentals. But Hill never learned whether the feathered passenger raved about it, or was rendered speechless.

Another riffle whisks you along to another tranquil passage — followed by yet another riffle. Soon the river begins a sweeping bend to the west. You are about to enter San Juan Rapids — so named because Fair Oaks' San Juan Avenue, if extended south, would intersect the river here. Spectators on shore are watching the rafts go through the turbulence.

If you've been perching on your raft's edge, it's advisable to move your buns to the raft bottom before entering San Juan Rapids. Otherwise you risk falling overboard and capsizing your raft. Even if you're a good swimmer and are wearing your lifejacket, wouldn't you rue the loss of your belongings? Capsized rafters have lost cameras, wallets, keys, etc., notes Janet Houston, manager of River Rat & Co. "Anything that's loose," adds Dave Hill. On one jaunt, the author was sitting on the edge with a camera looped around his neck. When the raft lurched in the rapids, he lost his balance and tumbled overboard. The camera was saved, but cost $70 to rid it of water.

Spray splashes your face as you dipsy-doodle through the rapids. This is the roughest water you will encounter on the run to Goethe Park, so enjoy.

Having survived San Juan Rapids, you have four miles to go to Goethe. High bluffs on the right are cloaked with trees sporting summer's dark-green foliage. The water gleams an opaque green, borrowing its color from the trees.

For most of your journey, there is little or nothing to remind you you're navigating past the Sacramento suburbs of Rancho Cordova, Fair Oaks, Carmichael — and Sacramento itself, if you keep going. That's because you're following the American River Parkway's lovely setting, of which the river is the crown jewel. Some scenes are so green and lush you can fancy yourself exploring a jungle river.

No, that's not Tarzan swinging on a vine. It's only a teenager on a long rope lashed to an overhanging tree limb — doing a fair imitation, however — then plunging in.

Another riffle: The last one, perhaps? Time and again, just as you think you've run the last, and resign yourself to just paddling and drifting the rest of the way, another riffle sings a song of the river and hurries you along. This could have been any day when the mercury in Sacramento went over 100, yet here on the snowmelt-born river it seems a mere 85.

Now and then a little fleet of mallards paddles toward you, sometimes eight to 10 in a flock, giving you the eye and appraising you as either good for a mooch, or forget that turkey.

You also might see the Sheriff's $25,000 jet-boat zipping along, checking if everybody's okay.

As you round a great bend, the foot/bicycle bridge spanning the river at Goethe Park heaves into view. This is your signal to paddle toward the gravel beach on the left, journey's end. You portage the raft over the levee to the parking lot, where you can wait for a shuttlebus ($2 per ticket) to carry you back to the raft company. Or, if one in your party had arranged to leave a car here in the park, forget the bus.

An alternative to beaching at Goethe is to ride the river another 45 minutes to a gravel beach on the right, the Harrington Way access, where a shuttlebus stops. Or, you could drift another two hours to the Watt Avenue Bridge, and another shuttlebus access. Either way, you'll ride the Arden Rapids, similar to those of San Juan.

Rafting lures people of all ages, even into the 80s. Minimum age? River Rat discourages parents from bringing children under 5, and American River Raft Rentals sets 4 as the minimum.

Many rafters don't get enough the first time. "We see the same people weekend after weekend," says Dave Hill of American. Adds Janet Houston of River Rat: "Some of our customers go rafting three times a month, and sometimes twice in one day."

This is self-guided rafting, which proffers you the opportunity to stop and picnic on and explore any beach or small island that strikes your fancy. It's not the spectacular whitewater rafting of the American's upper forks, but this Lower American can be deadly to the incautious, so take care. But you probably will never raft it when it rampaged like it did when Dave Hill rafted it in early 1986 as 80,000 cubic feet per second was released from Folsom Dam: "You could hear rocks tumbling on the bottom."

Chapter 67

Folsom In Two Worlds

Jedediah Strong Smith in 1825 became the first American trapper to reach the Sacramento when he crossed the Sierra into the great valley. Smith promptly established headquarters of the Rocky Mountain Fur Company on the American River near present-day Folsom, and engaged in business with beavers.

Folsom also has black roots: William Leidesdorff lived a remarkable life, until cut down by pneumonia at age 38. One wonders what, given a normal lifespan, he might have achieved. Born in the West Indies in 1810, son of a black mother and white father, he arrived in California in 1841, sailing his 106-ton schooner into San Francisco Bay. For four years, he skippered trading voyages between the Bay and Hawaii. As an agent for the Russian American Fur Company, he furnished it with supplies — and collected wheat payments from Captain Sutter for his purchase of Fort Ross. Mexican Governor Manuel Micheltorena in 1844 granted Leidesdorff the 35,000-acre Rancho de los Americanos, east of Sutter's New Helvetia in the area of today's Routier Road and Folsom Boulevard — an area larger than San Francisco. Leidesdorff built an adobe house on the land. Today's City of Folsom reposes on part of that immense land grant.

Leidesdorff in 1845 was named American vice-consul at Yerba Buena (San Francisco). He built the city's first hotel; he piloted the first steamboat into the bay, having bought it from the Russians at Sitka; he served as San Francisco's first treasurer and as a town councilman. When he died May 18, 1848, the city closed down. Flags flew at half-mast and guns were fired. He was buried in the

Mission Dolores chapel.

In Folsom, Leidesdorff is memorialized with a street named after him, and a monument.

The first of the other blacks who figure in Folsom's origin appeared in 1849, working a mining claim on a big sandbar on the south bank of the American. It proved out as a rich strike. By 1851, the town of Negro Bar, ramping nearly a mile along the river, was populated by 700 people, mostly runaway slaves. When a flood washed out Negro Bar, the town was rebuilt and renamed Granite City.

William Leidesdorff lived a glorious life until pneumonia killed him at age 38. This painting by Tony Mastry hangs in Folsom History Museum.

Theodore Judah in 1855 mapped out the streets of Granite City, and construction of the Sacramento Valley Railroad from Sacramento to Folsom began. In one day, all the lots were auctioned in Sacramento. The town was renamed again that year — for Captain Joseph Folsom, recently died. He had served in the war with Mexico and had purchased 22,000 acres of the Leidesdorff estate, making him one of California's richest men.

The original Negro Bar site — today flooded by Lake Natoma — is memorialized by Negro Bar State Park, across the river from where the gold town pullulated.

Negro Bar-Granite City-Folsom is the only survivor of two dozen mining camps in the area. One was Texas Hill, born in 1849 on the south bank near Negro Bar. By the early 1850s it had petered out as a gold camp, but possessed a resource San Franciscans craved to surface their sandy streets with — cobblestones. Goldminers became stone-quarriers, loading cobbles on scows, floating them down to Sacramento to be trans-shipped on barges bound for San Francisco. When the railroad reached Folsom in 1856, cobbles rode the train to Sacramento, before shipment to San Francisco. Countless other tons paved Sacramento streets, and are still visible in Old Sacramento. In the early 1860s, the railroad bought the cobblestone pits and built a branch line to tap them. By

Dolly Giffin shows her painting of black miners prospecting for gold at Negro Bar, forerunner of the City of Folsom. Her painting, chosen from 25 entries, won the $1,500 commission.

the mid-1860s, demand for cobbles dropped like a rock, and the once-lucrative enterprise ended up on the rocks.

Prairie City, another once-auspicious town, vanished without a trace. Mining in hills near Alder Creek began in 1853 when Natomas Water and Mining Co. dug a ditch to the scene. Other miners, getting wind of the venture, swarmed in from all directions. Flourishing Prairie City became the business entrepot for such satellite camps as Rhodes Diggings, Willow Springs Hill Diggings, and Alder Creek. By July 1853, the town could brag of 100 buildings, including 15 stores and 10 hotels and boarding houses. The mushrooming population topped 1,000 the following year. By 1860 the bloom was off the mushroom, and signs of approaching mortality were setting in. Today the only trace of this onetime boomtown is a historical marker off Highway 50 at the Prairie City Road off-ramp.

Mormon Island was another gold rush town that disappeared —but not until it was drowned in the early 1950s by rising waters backing up behind the new Folsom Dam, after having survived for more than a century. Its origin was determined by the pure chance that caused countless other mining towns to spring up--the glint of new-found gold. Two Mormons on horseback stopped to camp for the night near the river. They shot a deer and cooked supper.

"They're taking out gold above us on the river," one man mused. "Let's see if we can find some right here."

Their cooking pan turned up some colors. Next day they confided the breathtaking news to merchant and Mormon leader Sam Brannan at Sutter's Fort. Brannan's shrewd ears recognized opportunity when he heard the first knock. He hustled out to the gravel bar and set up a pre-emption claim, then demanded a tithe from all gold extracted, purportedly for the church. Later he declined to surrender it.

Meanwhile, miners excavated a canal across the bar, forming an isle — Mormon Island — which became an astonishingly rich strike. Miners took out as much as $1,000 worth of gold a day. By 1849, some 400 miners were scrabbling for treasure here.

On December 25 of that epic year, Mormon Island miners put on a Christmas Ball, an event that echoed down the corridors of time with such fond memory that it struck a responsive chord in modern Folsom's yearning for nostalgia, and is remembered each year with a contemporary version. The annual Mormon Island Christmas Ball in the Community Clubhouse commemorates that first gala that brightened what otherwise surely would have been a dreary Christmas in a dreary mining town.

The germ for the 1849 ball came from some nameless patron of the Blue Drilling Hotel in Mormon Island when he suggested it would not be a bad idea if the owner installed a new canvas roof to keep rainstorms from soaking the customers. The hotelman pleaded lack of funds. The customer persisted: Why not throw a Christmas Ball to raise the money? Good idea, concurred the

Captain Joseph Folsom once owned 34 square miles of the Folsom area. This painting is by Tony Mastry of Orangevale.

hotelman. The idea kept growing. Large posters of wrapping paper lettered with blue pencil went up, advertising the ball: Tickets at $20 each included a midnight supper.

The Blue Drilling Hotel never looked better, for it was decked with evergreens and small flags, and illuminated by candles stuck in beer bottles. In the middle of the hall, planks were laid on boxes to form a makeshift table, and an old canvas served as a tablecloth. More planks on boxes did duty as benches. A three-legged stool was set in a corner for the grizzled fiddler.

Miners' hearts no doubt skipped a beat or two when a bevy of ladies, powdered and gussied up in their best, arrived from Sacramento. "It was a delight to witness those hale and buxom maidens with short dresses, gray woolen stockings and brogans with half-inch soles," recalled one observer. "How they did laugh and sing."

The crowd surrounded the table, munching out of tin plates with knives and forks. After hungers and thirsts were sated, the old maestro's singing fiddle signaled the commencement of dancing, playing a polka. A man asked a 14-year-old girl, who weighed nearly 200 pounds, if she'd like to take the floor.

"You bet!" she replied. No coyness there.

In the first whirl, the man lost his balance and fell flat on the dirt floor. Sheepishly he scrambled to his feet and asked for a clothes brush. Nobody had one, but the hefty maiden grabbed a broom and gave him a brushing-off — then gave him another brush-off as she shouted to a friend: "Here, Jim, finish this dance with me. This fellow can't swing under my weight."

Just then the fiddler's string broke. Without four strings, he complained, he couldn't play any more polkas or other fancy dances. But someone persuaded him that less-than-fancy dances would be better than no dances at all, so the ball ran on until 4 a.m. By that time only his bass string remained intact.

Booming Mormon Island by 1853 swarmed with 2,500 people and several proud hotels, an express office, a scatter of bars, and hundreds of less-than-proud miners' shacks. But ill fortune loomed: In 1856, fire leveled the town. The spirit of the town must have died too, for it never rose again.

Some houses, however, untouched by fire, remained there many years. The last occupants were Mrs. Addie Hoxsie and daughter, who lived there until the government bought their property before the new Folsom Dam drowned the valley. The valley had been the scene of two dozen mining towns, some with cemeteries. Mormon

Island, with about 100 buried there, had the area's largest cemetery. The earliest buried there was Dr. D. M. McCall, native of Alabama, who died in 1850 at age 26. The last was Kate G. Edmonds, who died June 12, 1950, a full century later.

In the 1950s before the towns were inundated, graves were relocated to the new Mormon Island Cemetery, with original markers when feasible. Besides the old Mormon Island graves, the new cemetery contains relocated graves of early residents in Salmon Falls, Negro Hill and Condemned Bar. The new cemetery can be reached by driving north on Natoma Street in Folsom past the turnoff to Folsom Prison. Continue on Green Valley Road to the cemetery just across the county line in El Dorado County.

Another Folsom cemetery, established in 1855, not lying in the path of the future lake, didn't have to be moved: Masonic Cemetery, whose graceful Cedars of Lebanon were brought in by early settlers. Cook Cemetery, probably the first graveyard in this complex in southwestern Folsom, lies alongside. Odd Fellows Cemetery, established here in 1860, is embraced by date palms. The nearby Old Chinese Cemetery contains over 500 urns, with the remains in fetal positions. All these graveyards are incorporated in today's Lakeside Memorial Lawn Cemetery.

Folsom originally had three Chinese cemeteries. About 400 are buried on terrain now occupied by Folsom Post, Veterans of Foreign Wars. About 300 other Chinese graves in a cemetery closer to the river were obliterated by small "doodlebug" dredges.

June Chan led a tour of the third Chinese cemetery with mixed feelings about revealing its site because vandals, falsely reckoning valuables were buried with the dead, have dug up graves and scattered human remains all about.

About 500 are buried here. The cemetery's vegetation has been allowed to grow wild because manicuring it would disclose the graves' presence. A large concrete slab bears a bronze plaque with the name of her grandfather, Oak Chan. Teenage vandals smashed the concrete (later repaired), but were arrested after one brought a skull to school to show to his friends — June Chan's grandfather's skull!

Standing in this small cemetery, you think of all those who sailed from far across the Pacific to seek their fortunes at the "Golden Mountain," and now rest here. And you gaze at the great slab with the plaque bearing the name of Chan, and almost think you hear the echoes of a Chinese gong — *Chan*!

In Big Gulch, a mining camp across the river from Folsom, a

wheeler-dealer named Colonel Russ arrived in 1857. He persuaded San Francisco tycoons to organize a company to mine hard rock here for gold. Elated Big Gulch citizens renamed their town Russville to honor their bold entrepreneur. Many tons of quartz were crushed, with frustrating yields. Russ then invented a machine to plane granite, to extract gold from it — another failure. After the company turned up its toes, Russ took up another profession: He was elected justice of the peace.

His peculiar notions of judicial proceedings recall the eccentric Judge Roy Bean of Texas. "Law statutes were of no use to him," said one observer of Russ. "He dispenses his own brand of justice. Any person asking for an appeal was immediately fined for contempt. He soon became unpopular, went broke, and departed."

With the name Russville tarnished, citizens renamed the town Bowlesville. In 1860, they again renamed it, to Ashland. Today it is part of Folsom.

Folsom's early years were plagued by bandits. The worst was Tom Bell — real name Thomas Hodges — who had served as a non-com in the Mexican War, then came west. The sturdily-built Bell, born c. 1826, had sandy hair, a goatee and a mashed nose. First he tried his luck in the goldfields, but found none to brag about. He matriculated into gambling and graduated into highway robbery.

Convicted of grand larceny in 1855, he was committed to State Prison on Angel Island in San Francisco Bay for five years. Later that year he and half a dozen prisoners escaped. Three stayed with him to form the core of the Bell gang. Bell recruited a wild bunch numbering about 50 that ranged the country on robbing forays. In spring and summer 1856, almost every night some wayfarer looked at a pistol muzzle while being lightened of valuables.

Favorite hangouts included Western Exchange House near Auburn, operated by Mrs. Elizabeth Hood and her three daughters. The friendly women tipped the gang off whenever a customer seemed burdened by a heavy bankroll or poke. Later along some solitary road, the customer would be relieved of his excess weight.

In summer 1856, the gang decided to become upwardly mobile — by robbing the Camptonville-Marysville stage, whose strongbox contained $100,000. Six mounted men with guns leveled ordered the driver to halt. But Dobson, an express messenger, pulled a gun and fired, touching off gunplay between passengers and robbers. Some 40 shots were fired, riddling the stage, killing a woman passenger and wounding three other passengers. The gang retreated without the booty, fleeing in every direction, touching off the greatest manhunt in California.

One branch of the gang, led by George Walker, though headquartered in Folsom, launched at least one "business" trip into Shasta County, robbing a Wells Fargo stage of $26,000 in gold. They buried the loot there somewhere, and it has never been found. In a surprise raid at Folsom, lawmen killed Walker and captured some of his men. Other Bell gang members were captured or killed elsewhere, including Franklin House near Auburn, where they fought a raging battle with the Placer County sheriff's posse.

Bell didn't need a thermometer to realize that things were getting too hot here. He persuaded Mrs. Hood to relocate her business to a spot near the Merced River, and he shortly followed. Lawmen there got wind he was in the neighborhood. On a sunny Monday, Oct. 6, 1856, a mounted posse scoured the country for Bell, and luck rode with them, for they sighted him near the Merced River as he sat on his horse, chatting with a henchman. When Bell heard shouted demands to surrender, and saw the daunting spectacle of nine rifle muzzles pointed at him, he knew his luck had run out.

Grudgingly the posse let him spend four hours writing farewell letters, including one to his mother. At sundown they threw a rope over a tree branch, and ended the sordid career of Thomas Hodges alias Tom Bell.

Other bandits who frequented the Folsom area included Rattlesnake Dick Barter and Sheetiron Jack, both robbers and murderers, and Black Bart, who stuck up 28 stages but never fired a shot, and perhaps deserves a good conduct medal for that; and Joaquin Murietta, said to be in cahoots with Bell cohorts.

Mining in Sonora, Murietta had had his claim jumped once, without doing anything. When it happened a second time, he refused to take it lying down, and was badly wounded. The embittered prospector turned outlaw — raiding through northern California in November 1851, leaving a bloody trail. Bodies of 23 murdered men were found. Most had been lassoed from ambush, dragged into bushes, and stabbed.

Some historians speculate that Murietta may have been a composite of several hell-raising Mexicans. At any rate, a pickled head purportedly of Murietta was exhibited in San Francisco, then taken on a world tour. Back home again, it was on view in a San Francisco saloon when it vanished in the 1906 quake and fire.

Ten miles north of Folsom, miners in 1860 discovered the spectacular Alabaster Cave, in present-day El Dorado County, opposite Rattlesnake Bar on today's Folsom Lake.

During the first two years, an average of 40 persons a day explored the cavern. An entrepreneur built a hotel and served food and drink. Sacramento Valley Railroad ran Sunday excursion trains from Sacramento to Folsom, where passengers transferred to stages for the final ride to the cave. Visitors were awestruck by huge stalagmites and stalactites, and the 100-by-200 foot cathedral-like room with limestone formations resembling a giant pulpit. Well-known minister Thomas Starr King preached a sermon there, and at least one wedding ceremony was performed in the subterranean cathedral. By the 1880s, yokels had vandalized the cave's splendors that had been ages in creation. Workmen dynamited the entrance to seal it permanently.

Folsom is distinguished in both transportation and communication history — as eastern terminus of the first railroad in the west, and as western terminus (for a spell) of the Pony Express. The railroad on opening day, Feb. 22, 1856, brought 1,000 people on free excursions to Folsom, where they scarfed up free champagne and other delectables.

The railroad and Pony Express joined forces in July 1860 when trains began to carry the pony mail on the 22 miles between Folsom and Sacramento. A plaque on the wall of the Wells Fargo assay office, 823 Sutter St., Folsom, commemorates the building as the onetime Pony Express terminus.

This building is a reconstruction, completed in 1976. It was 99 years old in 1959 when torn down to make way for a gas station. Luckily, history buffs saved doors, bricks, ceiling joists, the granite facade, steps and historic plaques. Ironically, the gas station went out of business in less time than the 18-month duration of the Pony Express.

Today, Folsom Historical Society manages it as a history museum. The society chose artist Dolly Giffin of Fair Oaks to portray in oil two black men discovering gold in 1849 at Negro Bar. Her 4x7 painting hangs in the museum. And the society has built a new museum, nearly 6 times as big as the old one, incorporating the old one.

A. P. Catlin was a man with vision. Arriving in Folsom in 1851, he founded Natoma Water Co. and within a year was operating a ditch from a diversion dam at Salmon Falls on the American River. His 16-mile complex of canals, reservoirs and pipes funneled water to placer miners at Negro Hill, McDowell Hill, Texas Hill, Red Bank, Mormon Island, Richmond Hill, Willow Springs Hill,

Prairie City, Rhodes Diggings, Alder Creek, Mississippi Bar, and Pennsylvania Flats. Catlin charged each miner $6 a day, and his profits were said to be enormous.

Another man arrived in 1853 and dreamed a bigger dream. As Horatio Gates Livermore stared at the river raging through Stony Bar Gorge, near today's Folsom Prison, a vision shaped in his mind — an industrial city energized by hydropower.

By 1862, Livermore and his sons Horatio Putnam and Charles Edward Livermore had purchased control of Natoma Water Co. — which had immense assets. The water company five years earlier had bought 9,000 acres of Rancho Rio de los Americanos from Charles W. Nystrom, who had acquired it from Captain Folsom's estate.

To create a holding pond for logs and store water for factories and farms, the Livermores needed a big dam. Work began in 1867 to cork up Stony Bar Gorge. In exchange for convict labor to complete the dam, the Livermores in 1868 gave the state 350 acres of land for a proposed new prison, needed to relieve overcrowded San Quentin. Locating the new prison in Folsom was the senior Livermore's idea. He deemed it better for convicts to toil in the granite quarries, rather than let idleness lead them into mischief. The convicts no doubt appreciated his concern.

When Livermore died in 1879, his son Horatio Putnam took over. One day in the late 1880s it dawned on him that instead of using water to directly spin mill and factory wheels, it could spin electric generators — and send the current to Sacramento! In 1892, he incorporated Sacramento Electric and Power Co. to build the powerhouse.

Partners in the venture were his brother Charles, and Albert Gallatin, president and general manager of Huntington Hopkins Hardware, and the builder (in 1877) of that posh residence for himself that one day would become the Governor's Mansion.

The new dam needed for the powerhouse wasn't finished until 1893 because no convict labor was on hand until the prison was completed. The granite dam rose 86 feet high, spanned 450 feet, and backed water up four miles.

Though the nation now languished in a depression following the Panic of 1893, Gallatin asked General Electric Co. to invest $20,000 worth of machinery and equipment in the powerhouse. GE agreed to put the chips on the table. When the contract with GE was signed Sept. 28, 1893, *The Sacramento Union* called it "the most important event that has transpired in the last 20 years." GE dispatched four 29-ton turbine-generators — largest of their type ever built — around the Horn to Sacramento, thence by rail to Folsom. Workmen strung transmission lines the 22 miles to Sacramento.

The diversion canal shunted water from the reservoir into the turbine-generators at both Folsom Prison powerhouse and the Folsom City powerhouse. Now electricity lighted up the prison — first prison ever electrified — and powered 12 hoisting engines in the stone quarry.

From the city powerhouse, transmission lines followed the county road from Folsom to M and 31st Streets in Sacramento, then north to the alley between D and E Streets, west to 6th Street, then to the new substation at 6th and H, built at a cost of $10,500.

Other California cities were eyeballing the "costly works" on the American River. *The Stockton Record* reported that many "embryo companies and hundreds of capitalists" were waiting for its successful completion before starting similar projects of their own.

Construction of the powerhouse began in October 1894 and ended less than a year later. At 4 a.m. July 13, 1895, a GE official threw the switch that sent the juice zapping along 22 miles of copper wires into Sacramento to the substation, still standing at 6th and H Streets. Simultaneously, Sacramentans were blown out of their beds as soldiers triggered a 100-round cannonade to celebrate the marvel. At that time, this was the longest distance electricity had ever been transmitted.

Reported *The Sacramento Bee*: "Not only is this the longest transmission in the world, but it is also the largest electric power plant . . . with a capacity of 4,000 horse power actually delivered for use in this city." A Carnival of Lights, turning night into day, helped Sacramento celebrate the wonder on Admission Day, Sept. 9, 1895. Thirty thousand people converged from many valley points to ogle the spectacle of 25,000 electric bulbs illuminating Sacramento's streets. For more on the festival, see the earlier chapter, "Breezes of Change."

The triumph of the new Folsom powerhouse left many Folsom people with mixed emotions — pride that their facility was lighting up the big city of Sacramento, and a smidgen of natural resentment that their own little burg still lay shrouded in darkness, save for gas lights.

The Livermores' related companies in 1896 were consolidated under the newly-incorporated Sacramento Electric, Gas and

Railway Co. In 1903, the firm sold out to California Gas and Electric Corp., forerunner of Pacific Gas and Electric Co. PG&E shut down the Folsom plant in 1952 when the new Folsom Dam powerhouse began crackling with kilowatts, though the dam itself wouldn't be completed until 1956.

PG&E donated the old powerhouse to the state in 1958, for preservation as a historic building. Open to the public, it stands west of Greenback Lane at the intersection with Scott Street. You can see the giant turbine-generators, transformers, and other electrical equipment, just as they looked in the old days. In Stony Bar Gorge, downstream from the new Folsom Dam, remains of the original dam are visible today. Portions of the old stone-lined canal also remain today, east of Greenback Lane and opposite the old powerhouse.

That was the canal that delivered water from the dam — to spin the turbine-generators — which electrified Sacramento — for 57 years.

Night and day, the four great dynamos hummed with invisible power — but today the mighty engines are silent, supplanted by even mightier engines. The silence here in the old powerhouse may enable you to hear twitterings in the rafters — from bats, their presence also attested by numerous droppings.

Because of overcrowding at San Quentin, the Legislature in 1874 authorized construction of Folsom Prison. The site was chosen because the granite quarries promised to pay its costs with convict labor. Folsom Prison opened for business in 1878 when the first cell block was dedicated.

The prison's four-foot-thick walls were built of hand-cut granite. Its gothic architecture reminded some of a turreted castle from the Middle Ages. The building loomed "massive, chilling, uninviting and prison-like," according to Thompson & West's *History of Sacramento County*, published in 1880. Uninviting and prison-like? A strange criticism. Better it should have been country club-like?

Prisoners apparently shuddered when Folsom's steel gates clanged shut behind them, for they referred to being sent to this prison as "going to the end of the world."

The rock-crusher installed in 1896 — said to be the nation's largest at the time — was intended to supply cities and counties with crushed rock for 30 cents a cubic yard, to drive down exorbitant prices of road-surfacing in Sacramento, Stockton and other towns. Governor James Herbert Budd invited dignitaries to the prison to help him celebrate.

Folsom Prison has been the stage of sensational break-outs and attempts. Eleven convicts escaped in 1883, but eight were captured within days as local farmers became bounty hunters, being paid $50 for each captured.

A railroad spur once ran into the prison, to pick up production from the first commercial electric ice plant in California, and from the first California plant to produce gravel for macadamizing roads. In 1920, three convicts crashed out by driving a locomotive through the locked railroad gates — and into a nearby quarry, where they set fire to brush, hoping to escape under cover of a smoke screen. But the smoke thinned out — to reveal a phalanx of guards armed with rifles, convincing them their train ride had reached the end of the line.

Another prisoner rigged up a small trolley to ride along cables stretching across the river from the prison powerhouse. His imaginative flight died a-borning when a searchlight turned its glare on him before he could hook up his trolley to freedom.

One prisoner in 1932 tried to escape underwater. Carl Reese fabricated a diving helmet out of a football bladder, connected to a snorkel-like intake attached to a float. His pockets weighted with scrap metal, he clumped along the bottom of the canal that delivered river water to the Folsom powerhouse, which would have led him to freedom. But he stepped off into a 10-foot drainage-gate drop he was unaware of, dragging his snorkel below the surface, and drowned. The diving helmet, with eyepiece and snorkel, is on view in the prison museum.

The National Guard was called out in 1928 to put down the Thanksgiving Day riot that left 13 dead — 11 convicts and two guards.

In a break 10 years later, Warden Clarence Larkin and three other people were killed. Larkin had given standing orders to his staff that if he were ever taken hostage they were not to hold their fire to avoid endangering him. Seven convicts charged into Larkin's office, armed with two dummy pistols, seven knives, an ice pick and a bludgeon, and held him hostage. As guards fired, the prisoners stabbed Larkin fatally, but the break failed. Two prisoners and one guard died. Five of the convicts were convicted of first-degree murder, and executed in the new San Quentin gas chamber that had replaced the hangman's noose.

Charles Hall, in charge of the Folsom city powerhouse, one night got a phone call from the prison saying all prison lights were out.

Dashing over, Hall found that some convicts had short-circuited the system. Pending its repair, he switched current from his powerhouse to the prison. As prison lights flickered on, guards spotted two convicts all set to climb a ladder leaning against a wall. With their cover of darkness suddenly gone, the prisoners could only surrender.

Thinking that was the end of a busy evening, Hall fell asleep — only to be roused at midnight as the warden pounded on his door. He wanted Hall to go back with him to the prison — as guest of honor for a staff party celebrating Hall's work in thwarting a prison break.

Two inmates in 1968 started building a bizarre apparatus in the machine shop. They wouldn't say what it was, and no one could guess — until Sgt. Max Price, a supervisor, rummaged through their cells and found a book on aviation containing drawings on construction of a helicopter. It looked suspiciously like the infernal machine the inmates were fabricating. The two denied they were building a flying windmill, intending to wing over prison walls, but officials couldn't swallow their denial, and grounded them permanently.

In the most recent incident, Glen S. Godwin, 28, a convicted murderer, escaped in June 1987 through a storm drain, apparently having received help from accomplices on the outside, who cut security bars in the pipe. Search dogs picked up Godwin's scent on the west side of the American River, downstream, where an abandoned inflatable raft was found, but then lost it. The river runs through prison property.

He was arrested six months later in Puerto Vallarta, Mexico, on weapons and drug charges and sentenced to seven years in a Guadalajara calabozo.

Prisoners in olden days wore clothes sporting the horizontal stripes one sees today only in cartoons. Trusties then wore garments sewn with vertical stripes. Prisoners who tried to escape had to wear red shirts — red flags that helped guards keep tabs on them. In later years, the only prisoners who wore stripes were those who had escaped and been recaptured, or were known troublemakers. Today's uniform is blue denims.

Few women were sent to Folsom. The first arrived in 1885. After the 1920s, women prisoners no longer were sent here.

Folsom Prison has an art and gift shop at the entrance, open daily to visitors. It offers for sale paintings and other works of art and a miscellany of handcraft products. Bigger showings of inmate art and crafts are seen in spring and fall exhibitions open to the public.

In the nearby museum, the centerpiece is a Gatling gun, forerunner of the machine gun. Before completion of the 30-foot-high granite walls, the Gatling was mounted on the prison tower to guard the perimeter. No records indicate if it was ever fired, or if more than one Gatling was on guard. For any prisoners contemplating escape, apparently the Gatling presented an argument they couldn't refute.

An anteroom of the museum houses a mockup of a prison cell, complete with a manikin lying on a cot under a blanket. There were times when these small cells housed three or four inmates.

A new prison, opened in 1987 at a cost of $152 million, has been added to the old one, nearly doubling the capacity of Folsom Prison. The new one — "state of the art" in prison construction — has 1,772 cells housing 3,400.

Special tours of Folsom Prison for organizations, especially those related to law enforcement, can be arranged by calling 988-1707.

The Folsom area might have become a famous wine-growing region if the valley hadn't been dammed. Benjamin Norton Bugbey ran a prosperous winery, published booklets on wine, and may have been the first in California to produce raisins. Harry Mette, arriving with only 50 cents in his britches, prospected for gold at Prairie City, then planted grapes. In 1872, he founded Redbank Winery that each year turned out up to 40,000 gallons of wine and 7,000 gallons of brandy. The Natomas Company until c. 1906 boasted that its vineyards were the world's largest, encompassing up to 40,000 acres, covering all the land it had worked with dredges, according to Folsom historian John Morgan. Because of land needed for the new reservoir, these winegrowers and other owners had to surrender huge parcels.

The American River gorge near Folsom has channeled phenomenal floods. November 1950 witnessed the maximum recorded flood through this gorge when the river crested at 210,000 cubic feet per second. Before records were kept, however, the river crested in 1862 at 280,000 c.f.s. — estimated from high-water marks.

To build the new Folsom Dam (1948-56), costing $90 million, dynamite crews blew up the old dam. The new dam is flanked by an earthfill auxiliary dam at Mormon Island, and eight earthfill dikes curving through the foothills. Folsom Lake drains 1,875 square miles and can impound over one million acre feet of water, enough to cover the state of Rhode Island with a foot and a half of water.

On the dam's completion, officials estimated it would take three years of normal rainfall to fill the lake. Incredibly, it filled in one week — during the staggering tropical storms of Dec. 16-24, 1955, which melted snow in the mountains and accelerated the inflow to 219,000 c.f.s. Without the dam, Sacramento would have flooded with 10 feet of water, with damage in the hundreds of millions. And who knows how many lives would have been lost?

The spillway gates have a capacity to loose an incredible 576,000 c.f.s. — double the all-time historic peak. But if such a flow ever issued, could people downstream ride it out?

Another problem: A severe earthquake — maybe only once in 400 years, but *which* year? — could rupture the Mormon Island earthfill dam, warns US Army Corps of Engineers.

The earthen dam, east of the main dam, holds back water whenever the lake is more than half full. Part of the dam rests on dredger tailings, making it vulnerable to collapse from "liquefaction" — acting more like a liquid than a solid.

If the lake were full at the time, an engineer said, it would cause "great downstream consequences." He means hell would go on a rampage.

Folsom Dam's three giant generators can eject an impressive load of nearly 200,000 kilowatts. Besides its tasks of power generation and flood control, the dam stores water for irrigation and controls downstream flow to benefit fish, wildlife and recreation. For free guided tours of dam and power plant, call 988-1707.

Seven miles downstream, 1,093-foot-long Nimbus Dam, afterbay of Folsom Dam, spans the river. Nimbus's two generators hum with 13,500 kilowatts. Its reservoir, Lake Natoma, has 14 miles of shoreline encompassing 500 acres of water. Nimbus Dam's role is mainly to re-regulate Folsom's outflow, and divert irrigation water. Folsom South Canal, switching away from Lake Natoma, used to send water to cool the hot stuff at Rancho Seco Nuclear Power Plant. Paralleling the canal, a 14-mile paved trail leads walkers and bicyclists to Sloughhouse Road.

The City of Folsom calls itself the place "Where the West came and stayed," and the annual rodeo gives the town booster shots of western vigor. The roping and riding of this five-day championship rodeo goes on in Dan Russell Arena in Folsom City Park. As one of the best rodeos in the nation, it draws many top cowboys.

For other events, downtown Sutter Street is mostly where it's at.

The Gaslight Theater is one of California's best melodrama companies. Candy Store Gallery is said to be a world-class contemporary art gallery. A two-day fair in June combines a music festival with hundreds of the West's best artists offering their works for sale. Other annual events are the Flea Market, Peddlars Fair, Great Snail Race, and the aforementioned Mormon Island Christmas Ball. "Folsom Junction," adjoining Sutter Street, is a congregation of 20 railroad cars converted to shops and restaurants amid shade trees and boardwalks.

Sutter Street also is the venue of a wildlife happening — the exodus each evening of several hundred bats flapping out of roof tiles and eaves on nocturnal adventures. They roost mainly in older buildings on the street's east side, where in the daytime you can hear fluttering and squeaking. Merchants believe the bats are descendants of "early settlers" dating from original construction of the historic buildings. They've tried vainly to get rid of them, and now have resigned themselves to living with them.

Other Folsom wildlife is billeted in what was originally the "Misfit Zoo," named because it gave sanctuary to an eagle with broken wings, a cross-eyed tiger, and animals wounded by hunters or by fires, including Smokey the Bear, who became an international celebrity. Smokey arrived in 1963 as a cub, badly burned in a forest fire that killed his mother. Doctored at UC-Davis School of Veterinary Medicine, he was adopted in the Folsom home of Gordon and Elsie Brong. Brong fixed up some cages for Smokey and other animals, not realizing he was founding the Folsom Zoo. Smokey bore the fire scars all his life, but grew up robust — seven feet tall and over 600 pounds. He and his mate Alice became parents of 14 cubs.

One day came stunning news: The U.S. Forest Service suggested renaming Smokey to avoid confusion with the National Zoo's own Smokey the Bear, symbol of fire prevention. Then came a letter from the Smithsonian Institution saying the National Zoo's Smokey had been named by an Act of Congress, and no other bear could use the name. That touched off a firestorm: "We'll fight this all the way to the Supreme Court if necessary," vowed Brong. Mayor Jack Kipp strapped on his six-shooter: "There's no way we can back off." Newspapers around the world regaled readers with the dilemma of the two Smokeys. But nothing ever came of the threatened confrontation with Washington. Apparently the Feds realized they had stepped into deep stuff.

Smokey died in 1984 at age 21 of abdominal tumors, an ailment common to elderly bears.

In Gold Rush days, legions of prospectors combed every niche and cranny and pocket of the Sierra, supposedly, in their mad quest for riches. It's difficult to believe they missed any significant area — yet they may have, strangely enough. Item: In 1950 when bulldozers excavated the basement for a new building on Sutter Street, Folsom, a grizzled oldtimer discerned opportunity. He rigged up a sluicebox and recovered promising "colors," some as big as watermelon seeds. One can but wonder: How much more gold is hidden under Folsom's old streets?

Even though Folsom is "Where the West came and stayed," the community has plenty of room left over for the new wave of high-tech businesses invading the city. Intel Corp. has built on a 235-acre tract for an eventual 10,000 employees here, dwarfing its Santa Clara headquarters, and turning out microchips. On Blue Ravine Road, Soundstream Technologies looks at the whole world as its market

Apple Hill Gang performs peachy-keen melodrama on Folsom's Sutter Street.

for the high-end automotive and home audio-visual components it designs and manufactures.

Folsom is a city in two worlds – the world of the past and the world of tomorrow. The city's aim is to blend its storied heritage with the promise of the future. It already has plenty of heritage, and doesn't need any more. Now its desire is to lasso more high-tech businesses and help 'em find a home on the range and seldom let 'em hear a discouraging word. To lure them, the city has established the chic Willow Creek and Lake Forest technical centers. You should see this place. The old home on the range was never like this.

The billion-dollar Aerojet General Corporation in 1989 moved its headquarters to Folsom from La Jolla near San Diego. The new headquarters site is 2.3 miles from Aerojet's complex at Rancho Cordova.

The future is full of promise, but Folsom citizens are trying to make sure it won't be just empty promises.

Chapter 68
The Great Gold Machine

"To turn this site into a commercial development would be a great, irretrievable loss." — Robert Docken

Chinese prospectors in Folsom once labored for gold on a five-acre hillside sliced by an immense herringbone-pattern of ditches that delved as deep as 30 feet.

Ditch bottoms were studded with riffles, said Folsom engineer William Pasztor. Water flowed into the complex from a trench stretching along hillside contours for 12 miles from above Salmon Falls on the South Fork of the American.

A tunnel, now collapsed, drained the herringbone-network into the river half a mile away. Pasztor said the Chinese would shut off the water once a week or so, then climb down into the ditches to fetch up the "fines," for further purifying in long toms. "Hard work and lean pickings," he sums it up.

Pasztor likens the pattern of ditches to a colossal machine. "This is the mine — this is the machine," he says in admiration. "The ditches were hydraulic conveyor belts. Everything worked together smoothly."

A machine! In other words, Chinese ingenuity literally turned the entire five-acre hillside into a gigantic machine for extracting gold.

Known as the Chinese Diggings, the site — bordered by Folsom Boulevard, Blue Ravine Road and Highway 50 — is incorporated into a 435-acre Natomas Station residential and commercial development by Sacramento investors Angelo Tsakopoulos and Marvin "Buzz" Oates, and threatens to be engulfed by that development.

The Natomas Co., the original owner, at one time agreed to save the Diggings as a "preservation site." But a 1988 rezoning application by River West Development, the Tsakopoulos-Oates company, asked for elimination of the Diggings.

That touched off a firestorm of protests from history buffs. "Folsom Jim" Phillips called the Diggings the only remaining example of ground-sluice mining, adding: "I don't think there's anything like them anywhere in California."

Robert Docken of Sacramento wrote March 22, 1988, to H.Y. Wong & Associates, Berkeley: "The Chinese Diggins are a monument to all who have mined gold in California — and even more important to those who are lesser known, definitely harder working, trying to make a living, not necessarily to strike it rich...

"The Diggins' value as an interpretive site far exceeds the value of gold removed. The deep bedrock cuts can lend a drama to a spoken description of mining during California's Gold Rush that cannot be duplicated by photographs, videotapes, or the like. To turn this site into a commercial development would be a great, irretrievable loss."

History aficionados hope to persuade the developers to relinquish 10.3 acres for the Diggings site, to allow room for interpretive displays and visitor facilities.

The hillside ditches lie half a mile east of the riverbed where white prospectors worked rich placers — and chased away the Chinese.

Says Dorene (Askin) Clement, in a booklet on the Diggings: Throughout the goldfields, Chinese were cheated, robbed and sometimes murdered:

"Experience quickly taught Chinese miners that any rich new claim they developed would be stolen...but that once others had skimmed the easiest gold...they could work the remainder unmolested. The pattern, then...was for Chinese to occupy ground already worked, carefully washing the dirt for the remaining gold. These diggings, usually of diminished productivity, required painstaking procedures and intensive labor to earn a living from them. As a result, Chinese miners acquired a reputation as patient, diligent workers, content with relatively meager returns."

A few skeptics doubt the ditches were dug by Chinese. Pasztor said he personally knows the site has been called the Chinese Diggings since he arrived in 1957. "They *always* called it the

Squeeze play: Herringbone pattern of Chinese Diggings is framed on the north by Folsom Boulevard and on the south by Highway 50, and jeopardized in the east by commercial development. Photographer unknown.

Chinese Diggings.

"Don't take my word for it. Take Bill Rumsey's word for it. He was here before 1900."

Rumsey, born in Folsom in 1896, is dead, but Pasztor has a tape of his voice — a voice from the dead — in which his words live on:

"When I was a little boy...there were a lot of old men alive that had mined here in the Gold Rush time in 1849...a lot of those old-timers in front of the livery stable chewing tobacco and whittling on a stick, and me, big ears, I listened to all those old fellows."

During the taping of Rumsey's reminiscences on a wide range of topics, someone asked: "Who cut the channel that's so wide and about 30 feet deep?" — which Pasztor says is a reference to the Chinese Diggings.

Replied Rumsey: "The old Chinamen used to do that. They would use that as a race, and they would hydraulic it down through those cuts and they had riffles, see, and every so often they would cut the water off...They would go down and take the riffles up and take out the gold."

The old Chinese men did it, said Rumsey. So engineer William Pasztor insists there's no doubt about their Chinese origin, and he adds:

"The only time when the Chinese Diggings became 'non-Chinese' was when a contractor wanted to build something on it."

Chapter 69
Super Lake

I hear lake water lapping with low sounds by the shore.
W. B. Yeats

Folsom Lake each year hosts 10,000 Canada geese, converging here for their winter convention. In late February or early March, after clearance from their air traffic controllers, they spread their wings for the long flight back home in big-sky country to the north. Magnificent aviators, they fly as fast as 60 miles an hour and as high as 20,000 feet — over a mile higher than Mt. Shasta — and without oxygen.

Later in March, hundreds of white-winged sailboats fly over the lake — given a spanking breeze — during the Camellia Festival's two-day Camellia Cup Regatta, largest inland sailing race in California.

Besides the 10,000 feathered bipeds from Canada during the winter, the lake also entertains up to 50,000 featherless bipeds on summer weekends. Annually, more than 4 million people sample the outdoor pleasures of Folsom Lake State Recreation Area — many more than visit Yosemite.

The lake nestles in terrain ranging from rolling foothills to steep rocky canyons and, when full, covers nearly 12,000 acres (18 square miles), rimmed by 75 miles of shoreline.

The Federal government owns nearly all the property in the State Recreation Area, but contracts with the state to operate it.

Land, water and air media were combined in a recreation festival at Folsom Lake.

The recreation area also includes Lake Natoma, impounded by Nimbus Dam, six miles downstream from Folsom Dam. A five-miles-per-hour speed limit prevails on Natoma, making it a sailboat haven.

Paved boat launch ramps are handy at Folsom Lake Marina on Brown's Ravine, and at Dike 8, Granite Bay and Beal's Point. If you don't own a boat, you can rent either a sailboat or motorboat at Brown's Ravine. Campsites reserved through Ticketron are available at Beal's Point and Peninsula Campground, and also at Negro Bar on Lake Natoma. For information call 988-0205.

Folsom Lake's northern reach harbors a mysterious island — subject of the next chapter.

Chapter 70
Island of the Great Blue Heron

*The author's articles on Anderson Island have appeared in **California Highway Patrolman** magazine and **The Sacramento Bee.***

One spring morning, six Sacramento area people set out from Granite Bay on Folsom Lake in a powerboat skippered by Sal Gianna. Varooming over the water, the boat slammed across rough wakes of other craft with teeth-rattling bumps. But Gianna traces his ancestors to the homeland of Columbus, so the others knew they were in good hands.

Four miles north of Granite Bay, they spied the island they were seeking — Anderson Island, 10 acres of wildness, a state-designated natural preserve floating in the north end of the lake. The author had cruised here the summer before with Bud Fey and Boyce Salley, two friends, in his sailboat and brought back a tale of a rookery of enormous birds that wing among the treetops, casting giant shadows. Now the others were here to see if that far-fetched yarn was true. It was a bright sunny day — but was that a chill in the air? Or just the slightly-chilling thought of birds that cast giant shadows?

After circling the island, Gianna beached his craft on the pebbles of a small cove. The party debarked, binoculars and camera at the ready. In front loomed the trees and thickets of the wilderness island. Behind, across the sheen of blue water, the woodsy eastern banks of the lake climbed abruptly.

The party trekked some yards inland, invading a leafy, sun-dappled loveliness, pleasantly mysterious — mysterious because it seems that few people, even among habitual boaters on the lake, know of the island's existence.

One might almost think that no one had ever set foot here before, and that this gallant little band was pushing forward into unexplored territory. Sad to note, that fancy was dispelled with the finding of a beer can and an old whiskey flask.

The party wandered about in the interior, struck by how big the island seems when you plunge into its green mazes. Shaggy oaks grow in rife numbers. Digger pines reach high. In many spots, one could gaze about and see nothing but trees, with no glimpse of surrounding water.

"If you didn't *know*," one said, "you'd never dream you were on a little island in Folsom Lake."

Here and there, granite outcroppings lift boldly, tufted with moss and stained with lichens. Elsewhere the curtain of trees parts to reveal sunny glades, where wildflowers flicker in the grass. The blue flames of lupine abound. A brilliant purple flower was perhaps a wild iris. A curious vine with fluted seed-pod caught someone's attention. No one knew its name. It was later ID'd as perhaps Dutchman's pipe.

Some shrubs displayed drifts of white flowers. Others flaunted gold blossoms. Again, none of the party knew their names. A fine bunch of explorers!

Days later, another plant was identified by its legacy of rash and itch — poison oak.

Suddenly a huge shadow flew across the ground.

Again, a great shadow swept by. Weird.

Did those wing-shadows really span eight or 10 feet, as it seemed? One could almost imagine some colossal bird of prey soaring above, like the Roc that carried away Sindbad. The sun was climbing close to its zenith, so it seemed unlikely it was causing any distortion of shadow size, as it does early or late in the day, when it throws long shadows.

The average wingspan of the great blue heron — for that is the bird of the enormous shadow — is six feet, according to Ron Schlorff, wildlife biologist with California Department of Fish and Game, Sacramento. Maybe those shadows the Anderson Island explorers saw were those of bigger-than-average great blues.

Maybe they just *seemed* bigger.

Great blues flapped and glided, arriving and leaving their three-foot-diameter nests cradled in the topmost branches of some Digger pines, 60 to 70 feet above the earth. No doubt they were feeding their young, as this was nesting time.

Great Blue Heron on the wing tucks head in, one trait that helps identify it in flight. Photo courtesy California Department of Fish and Game.

The herons' main entree is usually fish, such as the minnows and small bass in Folsom Lake. But they also feed in marshes and meadows, dining on fat frogs and dainty mice, with hors d'oeuvres of grasshoppers and dragonflies. Returning to feed the youngsters, a parent regurgitates the partly-digested vittles. Everyone to his own taste: Yucky to us may be yummy to herons.

From the treetop nests, sounds like ducks quacking wafted downward. Those probably were the cries of the young, Truman Holtzclaw of Sacramento Audubon Society later explained.

The fledglings would be ready for their maiden flights in June and July.

Now and then a red-tailed hawk circled above. Hawks pose no threat to the nestlings, Holtzclaw said, so long as one heron remains on guard while the other does the shopping.

These herons are wading birds, dusty blue in color and of a whopping size. They stand four to five feet tall. Some *people* don't stand that tall. Their perky carriage obviously reflects awareness of and pride in their status as the largest herons in North America.

At the south end of the island, the visitors scrambled up an outcrop to admire the view — a long corridor of green hills flanking the glitter of blue water. Folsom Dam lay seven miles to the south.

Many boaters, zipping along the main channel in the north end of the lake, are unaware they are passing this enchanting island.

"I've gone by here a hundred times in my boat," Gianna said, "and never knew anything like this was here."

Anderson Island was named after a family that once owned property in the area, according to Folsom Lake Ranger Bob Anderson, no kin to the family. It was not an island, of course, until after the lake began to fill in 1955, after completion of Folsom

On Anderson Island, a small safari peeps at the birds that cast giant shadows.

Dam. Nor is it an island at low water, when it is connected to the shore on the east by a small isthmus, usually from October until winter run-offs raise the lake.

California Department of Parks and Recreation designated the island a natural preserve in 1974, mainly because of the heron rookery.

Advisory to boaters: From October 1 to April 15, Ranger Anderson said, buoys are anchored from Dotons Point to just below Rattlesnake Bar. They warn boaters to heed a 5 mph limit because this reach of the lake, encompassing Anderson Island, is a popular rest area for migratory waterfowl. The feathered commuters, dropping in from as far as the Arctic, include Canada geese, mallards, cormorants, whistling swans, loons, grebes and assorted others. Some may stay the winter. For others, Folsom Lake is only a pit stop and fast-food restaurant. After a day or two, they take off again. Rising on strong pinions gilded by the dawn, they enter the traffic on the great Pacific Flyway — the birds' freeway — bound for such winter resorts as the Salton Sea and Baja California.

"Generally, herons also are a migratory species," said Schlorff of

Fish and Game. "But the great blue herons probably stay pretty much in this area."

Fish and Game people have surveyed Anderson Island's heron rookery occasionally since 1969, when they counted six active nests. Figuring two adults to a nest, Schlorff says there were only 12 adults on the island that year. In 1982, the most recent census disclosed 19 active nests, with an estimated 38 adults, according to Gordon Gould of Fish and Game.

The island's heron population is part of more than 6,200 great blues in California, nesting mainly along rivers and estuaries.

Now it was time for the visitors to head back to Granite Bay, leaving the scene to the great blues. Soaring over the treetops, lording it over the beautiful island, they seem fitting rulers of its aerial dominion.

But theirs is a fragile dominion, vulnerable to caprices of nature. Item: In the 1971 count, only two active nests were found. Only three adult birds were seen. Storm winds that savaged the pine-tops, wrecking the nests, had brought on the disaster.

Visitors should be extremely careful not to disturb the herons, especially at nesting time, from March into July. One can only hope the herons will never be troubled by human mischief, because coping with rampaging elements is enough. They don't need any more problems.

The author was tempted to omit writing about Anderson Island and its fragile population, for fear of giving wrong ideas to wrong-headed people. Then he realized only high-class people will read this book.

Chapter 71

Plymouth Rock Of the West: Buried By the City Dump

A similar article by the author, titled "In the Wake Of Sutter," appeared in ***The Sacramento Union*** *on May 26, 1987.*

No sound of trumpet celebrated the launching of our mini-expedition bound for the Plymouth Rock of the West.

The scheme of the little expedition — embarked at Sacramento Yacht Club, West Sacramento — was to retrace the final leg of the 1839 arrival of Captain John Sutter, one of the most astonishing adventurers of all time.

Nor did any trumpet celebrate Sutter's jump-off in Switzerland — for he hit the ground running as a fugitive from the law, fleeing in darkness when his creditors got out a warrant for his arrest.

His five-year, 20,000-mile odyssey took him to the ends of the earth — to the grass shacks of Honolulu in the Sandwich Islands, and to the frozen mountains of New Archangel (the Russian fur colony at Sitka, Alaska), and finally up the unexplored Rio de Sacramento into the heart of the western wilderness.

Our expedition scampered up the Sacramento in a chartered 16-foot Starcraft with 85-horse Evinrude, pilot John Hardin at the helm.

Sutter's motley expedition struggled upstream in two schooners and a pinnace, with Hawaiians on the oars.

The contemporary party included Sacramento playwright-director-actor Victor Larson, in costume as Sutter. Larson has done a couple of one-man shows as Sutter at the Fort, so you might call this caper a moveable Living History Day, albeit an unofficial one. Also aboard was a man who prefers anonymity, but call him A.J.

Hardin issued a travelers' advisory: "I believe there's a sandbar blocking the mouth of the Feather."

North of the I Street Bridge, Hardin opened the throttle and the craft charged up the silt-laden Sacramento, passing houses, docks and marinas roosting on levees. On one bank a derelict minesweeper lay cattywampus. Along miles of the river, big oaks and cottonwoods leaned over the water.

At Alamar Marina, Hardin stopped to gas up. Expedition members seized the opportunity to fortify themselves in the bar. A. J. stood the drinks.

Seventeen miles upstream from Sacramento, the boat approached a fork. Straight ahead lay the broad Feather, while the Sacramento angled in from the west. Here and there a snag poked out of the cafe-au-lait water. As Hardin jockeyed the boat around on one course after another, probing for a clear channel, his propellor kept churning up gobs of mud — sandbar — deposited by the February 1986 floods. Two hundred yards ahead, a man and a child waded shin-deep nearly halfway across the Feather, a vivid demonstration of the humungous deposits glutting the river.

In 1839, Sutter in the pinnace ascended the Feather 10 or 15 miles, mistaking it for a continuation of the Sacramento. Sensing he was going up the wrong river, he told his Hawaiian oarsmen to turn back.

Back at the Feather's mouth, where the two schooners lay at anchor, Sutter found the white men steaming: "All the white Men came to me and asked me how much longer I intended to travell (sic) with them in such a Wilderness," he recalled. "I saw plain that it was a Mutiny."

Grudgingly he gave the order to turn back. They sailed down-river, then up the American two miles, as far as they could navigate in the dry season, and landed. The date: Aug. 12, 1839.

Because of the sandbar in the Feather, our latter-day expedition also had to back-track. At Discovery Park, Hardin steered up the blue-green American. As the boat cruised under five bridges, it was a bit difficult to imagine the pristine river that had enchanted Sutter.

Two miles upstream, as Hardin nudged the craft onto a small beach, Larson stood up: "Watch this — I'm going to re-enact Sutter's landing." He climbed onto the bow, saw that he would have to wade ashore, so he pulled off his costume boots, then stood up. For a second he teetered precariously and it seemed he might fall flat in the water at the crucial moment. But he recovered neatly, vaulted off, and splashed to shore.

"That's how you make a historic landing," he said. "You get out of the boat and wade to shore, one step at a time. Then you sit down and put your boots back on."

Now his brass spyglass scoped the horizon. "You also have to keep your eyes peeled for Indians."

None appeared. But in 1839 when this country was an immense, unbroken wilderness, and the 36-year-old adventurer had had the supreme audacity to land his puny expedition here in the heart of it, several hundred painted Indians — armed with bows and arrows and paddling tule canoes — greeted them.

The contemporary expedition got an unpleasant jolt as we gazed at the high ground looming over riverbank trees and saw two big trucks rolling along the skyline of — the city dump.

Larson slipped into his Sutter persona and threw up his hands: "*Himmel*, my historic landing site! From this landing sprouted my New Helvetia colony, which became Sacramento, capital of the greatest state of the greatest nation. The Plymouth Rock of the West — buried by garbage?"

He focused his spyglass. "From here, it really doesn't *look* like a dump. You can't see any garbage."

That's because it's a sanitary landfill, we later learned, where earth-movers daily cover the new garbage with clean dirt.

This was not precisely Sutter's historic landing site, because this stretch of today's American River courses 500 yards north of its 1839 channel.

Larson continued as Sutter: "On Aug. 12, 1989 — hey, that's getting close! — Sacramentans will celebrate the 150th anniversary of my landing, the birth of Sacramento. But what a laughingstock the city will be when this scandal leaks out. Suppose somebody turned the *other* Plymouth Rock into a garbage dump? Let's go see whoever's in charge."

In the office of the city's solid waste division, manager John F. Boss was unable to identify the rapscallions who first dumped garbage on the historic site. "That disposal site has been there since probably 1940," he said. "It used to be an open burning site, in the

In costume as Captain Sutter, actor Victor Larson wades ashore at the historic site.

1920s and 1930s."

"Let's go see Boss's boss, the mayor, and ask her to move the dump," Larson said, adding with a wink: "I'll ask her to move the river also, to make the site historically authentic."

Mayor Anne Rudin was delighted to meet Sacramento's famous colonizer, even if he was only an actor in the role. Larson reminded her that in 1989 the city will celebrate the Sesquicentennial of Sutter's landing. Rudin, surprised to learn the historic site is buried by garbage, said: "Let me take it up with our city manager and the public works department."

"Could the site be fixed up by 1989?" Larson asked.

Rudin didn't think so: "The dump will be abandoned in three to five years, and we know we have to let the land rest for a few years, so the gases generated by decompositon of wastes can escape." She outlined problems of finding a new site, and developing alternate disposal methods.

As Larson exited city hall, he chuckled. "I forgot to ask her to move the river back where it belongs."

"And she forgot to give Captain Sutter a key to the city."

Larson got into a car. "Let's see if we can pinpoint Sutter's actual landing site, on the opposite side of the dump from the river."

At 29th and B Streets, we spied the bronze marker mounted on a huge gristmill grinding stone, with its beleaguerment of weeds and commercial clutter. The inscription fixes Sutter's landing site at approximately 200 feet north of the marker. To reach the actual site, we had to detour, because private property and a chain-link fence block a direct approach. We drove west one block to 28th and B, then north through the entrance of the city dump, then walked east along the railroad tracks — to the dismal ambiance of the epic site.

I asked Larson to don his Sutter persona again and assess the importance of the landing. Said he: "I think it was the most important thing that ever happened to the United States."

"Jeepers. How do you figure?"

"I *made* California — I closed the gap between Missouri and California. If it hadn't been for me, prospectors and settlers wouldn't have come out — *when* they did. If I hadn't closed the gap, who knows what other nation might have jumped in to fill the power vacuum?" He waved toward the Sacramento skyline. "How soon would all of this have come about, if I hadn't sent Jim Marshall up to Coloma to get some lumber?"

The incredible Sutter: A city boy who beat the country boys at

Victor Larson as Captain Sutter lands at Discovery Park in a rehearsal for celebrating the 150th anniversary of Sutter's arrival. Carl DiStefano (white shirt) provided the antique-style boat. Three Sacramento Hawaiians — Albert Palapala, Darcy Haleamau and David Hanakeawe — represented the eight Sandwich Islanders who arrived with Sutter.

their own game. Who could have imagined this Swiss dude would have lasted more than a week on America's frontier? Among men born and bred in the wilderness, who cut their teeth on rifles and learned to ride horses while still in diapers?

Sutter not only lasted, he triumphed. While Americans were slowly pushing the frontier westward, he sneaked in the backdoor, as it were, and grabbed an immense empire in the wilds of Mexico's Alta California.

The incredible Captain: From a flight in darkness to an empire in the sun — and only a tidal wave called the Gold Rush could sweep it away from him. But he knew how to choose prime real estate. From the wreckage of New Helvetia emerged the lusty rivertown that would become the capital of the Golden Empire that Sutter in the wilderness had dared to dream of.

Did Sutter indirectly save Europe from bankruptcy? In Baggelmann's view, he did, and explains: About 70 percent of the gold mined in California went to Europe, stimulating the economies that had been gravely depressed because of almost continuous wars.

Postscript from city hall: Did Larson's interview with the mayor jog the city a bit? Apparently so, for the city council not long afterward voted to shut down the dump and turn the 150-acre site into Sutter's Landing Park.

As this second edition of *Sacramento* goes to press, the Sesquicentennial is now history. Victor Larson portrayed Sutter on Aug. 13, 1989, re-enacting Sutter's landing — in Discovery Park at the junction of the Sacramento and American, because the actual site, two miles upstream on the American, was still ingloriously buried by the city dump.

Unfortunately, plans to convert part of the dump site into Sutter's landing Park didn't take shape in time for our Sesquicentennial. The good news: Maybe they'll shape up in time for our Bicentennial.

Chapter 72

The *Rest* Of the Story

(Apologies to Paul Harvey.)

Ever since Captain Sutter built his famous Fort, Sacramento has been a-building, with scarcely a let-up.

As Sacramento's physical growth and population increase, the city and area also become ever a stronger magnet for visitors. Sacramento Convention and Visitors Bureau reports that 12.2 million "day and overnight" visitors arrived in 1986, and projects 12.6 million for 1987 and 13.1 million for 1988. No doubt many of those are commuters and other repeat visitors, but if all came at once, Sacramento would instantly become one of the world's very largest cities.

But lately the Bureau has had to undergo an agonizing reappraisal. "Those figures have since been thrown in the garbage," says the Bureau's Ken Mompellier, adding that the true figures are about half those. "Better to say we think we screwed up rather than mislead people."

The latest available figure is a 1993-94 projection of 6,084,000 "day and overnight" visitors, according to Shellie Cook, senior tourism manager.

That would *still* make Sacramento one of the world's largest cities, if all descended here at once.

The rest of the Sacramento story is that there *is* no rest of the story — not yet, because no one can prophesy the end of it.

References

Books

Beebe, Lucius and Charles Clegg. *The Age of Steam; a Classic Album of American Railroading*. New York: Reinhart, 1957.

Blenkle, Joe. *Gold, Blood, Water: Folsom-Auburn and the Mother Lode*. Sacramento: Western Wonder Publications, 1976.

Calhoon, F.D. *California Gold and the Highgraders.* Sacramento: Cal-Con Press, 1988.

Crocker, Aimee. *And I'd Do It Again*. New York: Coward-McCann, 1936.

Dana, Julian. *The Sacramento, River of Gold*. New York: Farrar & Reinhart, 1939.

Davis, William Heath. *Seventy-five years in California*. San Francisco: John Howell, 1929.

Dillon, Richard. *Fool's Gold: A Biography of John Sutter*. New York: Coward-McCann, 1967. Reprinted as *Captain John Sutter: Sacramento Valley's Sainted Sinner*. Santa Cruz: Western Tanager, 1981.

Duffus, R.L. *The Santa Fe Trail*. New York: David McKay, 1975.

Eels, Myra, and Mary Walker. Diaries in *First White Women Over the Rockies, Vol. II*. Glendale: Arthur H. Clark, 1963.

Eide, Ingvard Henry. *Oregon Trail*. New York: Rand McNally, 1972.

Gardner, Erle Stanley. *Drifting Down the Delta*. New York: William Morrow, 1969.

Garvey, Stan, *King & Queen Of the River*; the legendary paddlewheel steamboats *Delta King* and *Delta Queen*. Menlo Park, CA 94026: River Heritage Press, 1995.

Holliday, J.S. *The World Rushed In*. New York: Simon and Schuster, 1981.

Ide, Simeon. *Conquest of California By the Bear Flag Party*. Glorietta, N.M.: Rio Grande Press, 1967.

Lee, W. Storrs. *California, a Literary Chronicle*. New York: Funk & Wagnalls, 1968.

Lewis, Brian, and Burl Waits. *A Car Collection For the Common Man, A Brief History of the Towe Ford Museums*. Carmichael, Calif.: A/A Publishing, 1987.

Lewis, Oscar. *Lola Montez*. San Francisco: Colt Press, 1938.

______ *Sutter's Fort, Gateway To the Gold Fields*. Englewood Cliffs, N.J.: Prentice-Hall, 1966.

Lord, Myrtle Shaw. *A Sacramento Saga*. Sacramento Chamber of Commerce, 1946.

Ludwig, Emil. *Schliemann, the Story of a Gold-Seeker*. Boston: Little, Brown & Co., 1931.

McGowan, Joseph, and Terry Willis. *Sacramento: Heart Of the Golden State*. Windsor Publishers, 1983.

Miller, Robert. *Guide To Old Sacramento*. Sacramento: River City Press, 1976.

Mims, Julie Elizabeth and Kevin Michael Mims. *Sacramento: A Pictorial History*. Virginia Beach, VA: Donning Co., 1981.

Muro, Diane P. *A Complete Guide to Sacramento and Surrounding Areas*. Sacramento: Camellia Press, 1981.

Nagel, Gunther W. *Jane Stanford, Her Life and Letters*. Stanford Alumni Association, c. 1975.

Reinfeld, Fred. *Pony Express*. Collier Books, 1959.

Settle, Raymond. *The Pony Express*. 1959.

Smith, Jesse M., ed. *Sketches of Old Sacramento*. Sacramento County Historical Society, 1976.

Severson, Thor. *Sacramento: An Illustrated History 1839 to 1874*. The Sacramento Bee, 1973.

Steed, Jack, and Richard Steed. *The Donner Party Rescue Site,* subtitled *Johnson's Ranch on Bear River*. Fresno, Calif.: Pioneer Publishing Co., 1988.

Stone, Irving. *Men to Match My Mountains*. Garden City, N.Y.: Doubleday, 1956.

Sutter, John A. *The Diary of Johann Augustus Sutter*. San Francisco: Grabhorn Press, 1932.

Thompson, John, and Edward Dutra. *The Tule Breakers; the Story of the California Dredge*. Stockton: Stockton Corral of Westerners, University of the Pacific, 1983.

Thompson, T., & West. *Illustrated History Of Sacramento*. 1880.

Tutorow, Norman E. *Leland Stanford: Man of Many Careers*. Menlo Park, Calif.: Pacific Coast Publishers, c. 1970.

Walters, Bob E. *Delta*. Fullerton, Ca.: Cordrey and Walters, 1983.

Zollinger, James Peter. *Sutter, the Man and His Empire*. New York, London and Toronto: Oxford University Press, 1939. Reprinted, Gloucester, Mass.: Peter Smith, 1967.

Author not listed. *The Outdoor World of the Sacramento Region*. American River Natural History Association in cooperation with Sacramento County Office of Education.

Booklets

Oliver, Raymond. *Rancho Del Paso, a History Of the Land Surrounding McClellan Air Force Base.* Sacramento: McClellan AFB Office of History, 1983.

Towe, Edward. *Our South American Trips.* Deer Lodge, Montana: Towe Ford Foundation, 1987.

Zauner, Phyllis. *Sacramento, a Mini-History.* Tahoe Paradise: Zanel Publications, 1979.

No author listed. *Historic Landmarks Of the City & County Of Sacramento.* Sacramento: Friends of the Sacramento City and County Museum and Pipper Parrish Printery, 1975.

No author listed. *Sutter's Fort State Historical Monument.* Sacramento: California Division of Beaches and Parks, 1959.

The following are *Golden Notes,* booklets published by Sacramento County Historical Society:

Eaton, James. *From the Memoirs of James Eaton.* Printed in Summer 1986.

Gallucci, Mary McLennon and Lt. Col. Alfred D. Gallucci. *James E. Birch.* 1958.

Helmich, Stephen G. *Sacramento's 1854 City Hall & Waterworks.* Also contains *An Introduction to the Sacramento History Center,* by Connie Miottel. Winter 1985.

Kurutz, KD. *Sacramento's Pioneer Patrons of Art, the Edwin Bryant Crocker Family.* Summer 1985.

Livingston, Robert, Willard Thompson and John Wilhelm. *Gold Rush Bankers.* Winter 1984.

Marryat, Frank. *An Excerpt From Mountains and Molehills, Or Recollections Of a Burnt Journal.* Spring 1985.

McGowan, J.A. *The Ill-Starred Washoe.* March 1974.

Thompson, Willard. *David Lubin, Sacramento's Pioneer Merchant-Philosopher.* Spring 1986.